Surpassing Realism

Surpassing Realism

The Politics of European Integration since 1945

Mark Gilbert

ROWMAN & LITTLEFIELD PUBLISHERS, INC.
Lanham • Boulder • New York • Oxford

ROWMAN & LITTLEFIELD PUBLISHERS, INC.

Published in the United States of America
by Rowman & Littlefield Publishers, Inc.
A Member of the Rowman & Littlefield Publishing Group
4501 Forbes Boulevard, Suite 200, Lanham, Maryland 20706
www.rowmanlittlefield.com

PO Box 317, Oxford OX2 9RU, United Kingdom

British Library Cataloguing in Publication Information Available

Library of Congress Cataloging-in-Publication Data
Gilbert, Mark, 1961–
  Surpassing realism : the politics of European integration since 1945 /
Mark Gilbert.
      p. cm. — (Governance in Europe)
This book evolved from a course of lectures given at the University of
Trento, Italy in the academic year 1999–2000.
Includes bibliographical references and index.
  ISBN 0-7425-1913-9 (cloth : alk. paper)—ISBN 0-7425-1914-7 (pbk. :
alk. paper)
  1. European Union. 2. European Union countries—Politics and
government. 3. European Union—Economic integration. I. Title. II.
Series.
  JN30 .G55 2003
  341.242'2—dc21
                                                          2002153818

Printed in the United States of America

♾™ The paper used in this publication meets the minimum requirements of
American National Standard for Information Sciences—Permanence of Paper
for Printed Library Materials, ANSI/NISO Z39.48-1992.

Contents

Acknowledgments   vii

Abbreviations and Acronyms   ix

Chronology 1945–2002   xi

1   Introduction: An Unusual New Polity   1
       Structure and Content   4
       Themes   8
       Terminology   11

2   Enemies to Partners: The Politics of Cooperation in
    Western Europe 1945–1950   15
       The American Vision for Europe: The Marshall Plan and
          the OEEC   19
       A "Harmonious Society": The Vision of the
          European Movement   25
       Cooperation between Governments: The British Vision   31
       The German Question and the Schuman Plan   36

3   Spillovers and Setbacks: From the Schuman Plan to the
    Common Market 1950–1958   49
       The Coal and Steel Community   51
       The Defense Community   56
       From Messina to Rome   62
       The Treaties of Rome: 25 March 1957   69
       The Uniting of Europe   75

4   In The Shadow of the General: De Gaulle and the
    EEC 1958–1969   85
        The EEC's First Four Years   86
        The "Union of States"   90
        The First British Negotiation for Entry   96
        The "Empty Chair" Crisis and the Luxembourg Compromise   104
        Positive and Negative Integration   111

5   Weathering the Storm: The EC during the Economic Crises
    of the 1970s   119
        Thinking Positive 1969–1972   120
        Monetary Turmoil 1971–1974   128
        Foreign Policy Failures and the Tindemans Report   133
        The European Monetary System   138
        Beyond the Common Market   145

6   The 1992 Initiative and the Single European Act   155
        France Sees the Light   157
        The British Budgetary Question   160
        Mediterranean Enlargement   164
        The 1992 Initiative and the Dooge Committee   169
        The Single European Act   174
        Evaluating the Single European Act   180

7   The Maastricht Compromise   187
        The "Paquet Delors" and the Delors Report   188
        The Bruges Speech   193
        German Unification and Its Consequences   198
        The "Hour of Europe"   203
        The Maastricht Treaty   212
        Making Sense of Maastricht   219

8   Europe since Maastricht   225
        Adopting the Euro   227
        Enlargement to Central and Eastern Europe   237
        The Institutional Question   241
        The EU's Growing World Role   249
        A Constitutional Convention   252

Bibliographical Essay   259

Index   265

About the Author   277

Acknowledgments

This book evolved from a course of lectures that I gave at the University of Trento (Italy) in the academic year 1999–2000. I was very grateful to the faculty of sociology at Trento for inviting me as a visiting professor at a time when I had pressing family reasons for living in Italy. Since that time, I have given several papers at the university in which I developed many of the ideas that are expressed in this book. In March 2002, I was asked to join the faculty as associate professor of contemporary history.

I would particularly like to thank Professor Sergio Fabbrini. I hope this book will repay the generosity and friendship he has shown towards me. I have learned an enormous amount from him and lately have even begun to work (nearly) as hard. It was Sergio who originally suggested that I should turn my lectures into a book, and I have had many conversations on the subject matter of this book with him. Since I am notoriously more lucid on paper than in conversation, he will now discover what I've been talking about all along.

This book was largely written in the academic years 2000–2001 and 2001–2002, when I was lecturer in Italian history and politics in the department of European Studies at the University of Bath. I made too many friends at Bath to list them here, but I enjoyed the hardworking, dynamic atmosphere of the department. Professor Anna Bull was head of department when I had my year in Trento: I am very grateful for the friendship she showed to me on that occasion and throughout the five years I was at Bath. Gianfranco Pasquino of the Bologna Center of the Johns Hopkins School for Advanced International Studies also helped me greatly in academic year 1999–2000.

The manuscript has been read by several friends and colleagues. I would especially like to thank Philip Bell, Gustavo Corni, Alberta Sbragia, Julian Swann and my editor, Susan McEachern.

I have a particular debt to my brother, Martyn. He is an ardent (but very thoughtful) Euroskeptic and I have passed many hours arguing with him about the menace that European unification allegedly presents to British liberties. He has not convinced me (nor I him), but the experience has been a salutary one for both of us, I hope.

Most of all I would like to thank my wife, Luciana, and son, Francisco. They have seen too little of me in the last two years, but I hope now to make amends. This book is dedicated to them.

Abbreviations and Acronyms

ACP	African, Caribbean and Pacific countries
BIS	Bank of International Settlements
CAP	Common Agricultural Policy
CDU-CSU	Christian Democrats (Germany-Bavaria)
CEEC	Committee on European Economic Cooperation (1940s)
	Central and Eastern European countries (1990s)
CFM	Council of Foreign Ministers
COREPER	Committee of Permanent Representatives
DM	Deutsche Mark
EBRD	European Bank of Reconstruction and Development
EC	European Community
ECA	European Cooperation Agency
ECB	European Central Bank
ECJ	European Court of Justice
ECSC	European Coal and Steel Community
Ecu	European currency unit
EDC	European Defense Community
EDF	European Development Fund
EEC	European Economic Community
EFTA	European Free Trade Agreement
EMI	European Monetary Institute
EMS	European Monetary System
EMU	Economic and Monetary Union
EP	European Parliament
EPC	European Political Community (1950s)
	European Political Cooperation (1970s–1990s)

EPU	European Payments Union
ERDF	European Regional Development Fund
ERM	Exchange rate mechanism
ERP	European Recovery Program
ERRF	European Rapid Reaction Force
ESCB	European System of Central Banks
EU	European Union
EUA	European unit of account
Euratom	European Atomic Energy Community
DC	Christian Democrats (Italy)
FPÖ	Austrian Freedom Party
GATT	General Agreement on Trade and Tariffs
IGC	Intergovernmental Conference
IISS	International Institute for Strategic Studies
MCAs	Monetary compensatory amounts
MEPs	Members of the European Parliament
MFE	Movimento federalista europeo
MPs	Members of Parliament (Britain)
NATO	North Atlantic Treaty Organization
OECD	Organization for Economic Cooperation and Development
OEEC	Organization for European Economic Cooperation
OPEC	Organization of Petroleum Exporting Countries
PC	Political Commission (Fouchet plan)
PPP	Purchasing power parity
PSF	Socialist Party (France)
PSI	Socialist Party (Italy)
PSOE	Socialist Party (Spain)
QMV	Qualified majority voting
SEA	Single European Act
SPD	Social Democrats (Germany)
UEF	Union Européenne des Fédéralistes
UEM	United Europe Movement
USSR	Union of Soviet Socialist Republics
VAT	Value-added tax
WEU	Western European Union
WTO	World Trade Organization

Chronology 1945–2002

1940s

4–11 February 1945: Yalta Conference.

17 July–12 August 1945: Potsdam Conference.

19 September 1946: Churchill's Zurich speech on "a kind of United States of Europe."

12 March 1947: Truman Doctrine.

5 June 1947: George C. Marshall's Harvard address. Beginning of European Recovery Program.

17 March 1948: Treaty on Western Union (Brussels Pact) signed. Belgium, Britain, France, Luxembourg, and Netherlands form an alliance for mutual defense and economic cooperation.

7–11 May 1948: Congress of Europe at the Hague.

24 June 1948: Berlin blockade begins (ends 12 May 1949).

5 May 1949: Treaty of St. James establishing the Council of Europe.

15 September 1949: Konrad Adenauer becomes first chancellor of West Germany following elections on 14 August.

1950s

9 May 1950: Schuman Plan announced.

24 October 1950: Announcement of Pleven Plan.

4 November 1950: Convention for the Protection of Human Rights and Fundamental Freedoms signed in Rome by thirteen European countries. Greece and Sweden sign on 28 November.

18 April 1951: ECSC treaty signed in Paris by Belgium, France, Italy, Luxembourg, Netherlands and West Germany.

27 May 1952: EDC treaty signed in Paris by the same countries.

10 March 1953: EPC proposals presented to the government of the Six by the ECSC Assembly.

30 August 1954: French Parliament rejects the EDC treaty.

23 October 1954: WEU treaty signed in Paris.

1–2 June 1955: Messina conference of the Six delegates to an intergovernmental committee headed by Paul-Henri Spaak the task of drawing up plans for an economic community and a community to govern atomic energy.

13 October 1955: Jean Monnet forms his Action Committee for a United Europe.

29 May 1956: Spaak committee presents its report to foreign ministers of the Six in Venice.

30 October–6 November 1956: Suez Crisis.

25 March 1957: Treaties of Rome instituting Euratom and the EEC signed by the Six. They become law, after ratification by the national parliaments, on 1 January 1958.

7 January 1958: Walter Hallstein (Germany) becomes first president of the EEC Commission.

14 November 1958: French government blocks the British idea of a free trade area encompassing all OEEC countries.

1960s

3 May 1960: EFTA formed by Austria, Denmark, Great Britain, Norway, Portugal, Sweden, and Switzerland.

July–August 1961: Britain, Denmark and Ireland apply for EEC membership.

2 November 1961: Fouchet's plan for an "indissoluble Union of States" presented by French government.

14 January 1962: Agreement on CAP reached. Second stage of EEC begins.

14 January 1963: De Gaulle's press conference opposing British membership.

22 January 1963. Franco-German pact of friendship signed in Paris.

28 January 1963: France definitively blocks British membership.

20 July 1963: Association agreement signed with eighteen African states at Yaoundé (Cameroon).

31 March 1965: The Commission presents its proposals regarding the EEC's "own resources" and the budget question.

8 April 1965: Merger treaty signed. ECSC, EEC and Euratom are fused into the EC.

6 July 1965: Empty Chair crisis begins. France boycotts the Community.

9 September 1965: De Gaulle casts doubt on future of EC if national veto not preserved.

28–29 January 1966: Luxembourg compromise agreed. France retakes her place at the table.

1 May 1967: Wilson government formally applies for British membership.

30 June 1967: The Commission signs the Kennedy Round trade deal on behalf of the Six.

6 July 1967: Jean Rey (Belgium) becomes second president of the EC Commission.

27 November 1967: De Gaulle blocks British membership.

1 July 1968: Customs union begins, eighteen months ahead of the schedule anticipated in the EEC treaty.

1–2 December 1969: Hague summit of EC leaders.

1970s

2 July 1970: Franco Maria Malfatti (Italy) becomes third president of the EC Commission.

7–8 October 1970: Werner report on monetary union adopted.

27 October 1970: Luxembourg report on political cooperation adopted.

15 August 1971: United States ends dollar convertibility with gold.

22 January 1972: Britain, Denmark, Ireland and Norway sign accession treaties. Norway rejects membership in a referendum on 25 September.

22 March 1972: Sicco Mansholt (Netherlands) becomes fourth president of the EC Commission following Malfatti's resignation.

19–21 October 1972: Paris summit of EC Nine. They commit themselves to creating a European Union by 1980.

1 January 1973: Britain, Denmark and Ireland join the EC.

6 January 1973: François-Xavier Ortoli (France) becomes fifth president of EC Commission.

23 April 1973: Kissinger announces the "Year of Europe."

9–10 December 1974: Paris summit of EC leaders establishes European Council. The Nine will hold regular summit meetings.

7 January 1976: Publication of Tindemans report on European union.

20 September 1976: Treaty authorizing direct elections to the European Assembly.

6 January 1977: Roy Jenkins (Britain) becomes sixth president of the EC Commission.

27 October 1977: Jenkins appeals for monetary union in a speech at the European University Institute.

4–5 December 1978: Brussels European Council decides to introduce the EMS.

13 March 1979: EMS enters into operation.

16 March 1979: Death of Jean Monnet.

7–10 June 1979: First direct elections to the European Parliament.

29–30 November 1979: British budgetary question explodes at Dublin European Council. Will be a perennial problem for the next five years.

1980s

1 January 1981: Greece becomes tenth member state of the EC.

6 January 1981: Gaston Thorn (Luxembourg) becomes seventh president of the EC Commission.

10 May 1981: François Mitterrand becomes president of France.

4 October 1981: French franc devalued within the EMS. Further adjustments follow in February and June 1982 and March 1983.

19 November 1981: Italian foreign minister Emilio Colombo and his German counterpart, Hans-Dietrich Genscher, explain their proposals for a European Act to the European Parliament.

17–19 June 1983: Stuttgart European Council ends the Genscher–Colombo process by signing the "Solemn Declaration" on European Union.

14 February 1984: The European Parliament adopts a proposal for a treaty on European union.

14–17 June 1984: Second elections to the European Parliament.

25–26 June 1984: Fontainebleau European Council. British budgetary problem resolved amid euphoria. Dooge committee on institutional reform launched.

7 January 1985: Jacques Delors (France) becomes eighth president of the EC Commission.

12 June 1985: Portugal and Spain sign their accession treaties. They enter the Community on 1 January 1986.

14 June 1985: The Commission submits its white paper, "Completing the Internal Market."

28–29 June 1985: Milan European Council calls an intergovernmental conference to decide amendments to the EEC treaty.

17 and 28 February 1986: Single European Act (SEA) signed in Brussels.

23 May 1986: Death of Altiero Spinelli.

29 May 1986: The flag of the European Community (twelve gold stars arranged in a circle on a light blue background) is flown for the first time.

18 February 1987: Paquet Delors proposing big increases in regional development funding presented to European Parliament.

1 July 1987: SEA becomes law after all twelve member states complete ratification.

27–28 June 1988: Hanover European Council renews Delors's presidency of the Commission.

20 September 1988: Margaret Thatcher's Bruges speech. Warns of the danger of a European "super-state."

24 October 1988: Court of First Instance instituted.

12 April 1989: Presentation of the Delors report.

15–18 June 1989: Third elections to the European Parliament.

10 November 1989: Fall of the Berlin Wall.

8–9 December 1989: Strasbourg European Council launches IGC on monetary union and decides to set up a European Bank of Reconstruction and Development (EBRD) to provide loans for the countries of Eastern Europe.

1990s

28 April 1990: Dublin European Council welcomes German reunification. A second Dublin summit on 25–26 June decides to call a parallel IGC on political union and fixes the date that the two IGCs will begin.

19 June 1990: Schengen treaty signed.

3 October 1990: Reunification of Germany.

27–28 October 1990: Rome I European Council reveals a deep breach between Britain and the rest of EU. Prelude to the fall of Margaret Thatcher.

14–15 December 1990: Rome II summit launches the two IGCs.

14 April 1991: The EBRD starts work.

7 September 1991: Hague peace conference on Yugoslavia begins.

9–10 December 1991: Maastricht European Council negotiates the Treaty on European Union. Treaty is signed on 7 February 1992.

2 June 1992: Danes vote against the Maastricht treaty.

20 September 1992: French vote for Maastricht by a hairsbreadth. The vote is preceded by chaos on the financial markets and the elimination of the pound sterling and the lira from the EMS.

11–12 December 1992: Edinburgh European Council allows Denmark various opt-outs from the EU treaty and gives her a second chance to hold a referendum. "Delors II" regional development package approved.

18 May 1993: Danes vote "yes" to Maastricht.

21–22 June 1993: Copenhagen European Council lays down general principles of entry for would-be members of the EU.

28–29 July 1993: Final collapse of EMS after huge speculative attacks on the French franc.

1 November 1993: Treaty on European Union becomes law.

15 December 1993: Uruguay Round trade talks conclude with major accord on liberalization of trade and agreement to establish the World Trade Organization (WTO).

30 March 1994: Austria, Finland, Norway and Sweden conclude negotiations for membership. Norway rejects the treaty of accession on 28 November;

the others ratify and join the EU on 1 January 1995. Membership is now fifteen.

9–12 June 1994: Fourth elections to the European Parliament.

24–25 June 1994: Corfu European Council dominated by wrangling over the successor to Jacques Delors. On 15 July, Jacques Santer (Luxembourg) is chosen at a special European Council meeting in Brussels.

18 January 1995: Santer is approved as ninth president of the European Commission by the European Parliament.

26 March 1995: Passport-free zone between Germany, France, Belgium, Luxembourg, Netherlands, Spain, and Portugal.

26 July 1995: Europol Convention signed. Begins work in October 1998.

15–16 December 1995: Madrid European Council decides the name of the single currency: the Euro will enter into operation on 1 January 1999 and will be available in note form from 1 January 2002.

29 March 1996: IGC on institutional reform begins.

13–14 December 1996: Stability and Growth Pact agreed by Dublin European Council.

16–17 June 1997: Amsterdam European Council concludes IGC on institutional reform with a set of amendments, but no great structural alterations, to the Treaty on European Union.

16 July 1997: The Commission presents *Agenda 2000*, its opinion on the accession of the ten new democracies of central and eastern Europe.

2 October 1997: Treaty of Amsterdam signed.

25 March 1998: The Commission gives a passing grade to eleven states for membership of the Euro. Britain and Denmark opt out. European Council confirms decision on 3 May.

30–31 March 1998: Accession negotiations with Cyprus, Czech Republic, Estonia, Hungary, Poland, and Slovenia begin.

1 June 1998: European Central Bank instituted.

27 September 1998: Helmut Kohl's sixteen-year leadership of Germany is ended when Gerhard Schroeder's SPD win control of the Bundestag.

1 January 1999: Participant currencies in the Euro fix their exchange rates.

15 March 1999: European Commission resigns following the publication of a report on fraud, wasteful management and cronyism. Several commissioners, including Edith Cresson, a former prime minister of France, are criticized by name.

24–25 March 1999: Extraordinary European Council in Berlin names Romano Prodi (Italy) as its choice to be the tenth president of the Commission. He is approved by the EP on 5 May.

1 May 1999: The Amsterdam treaty comes into force.

3–5 June 1999: Javier Solana (Spain) nominated as first EU high representative for foreign policy.

10–13 June 1999: Fifth elections to the European Parliament. Turnout, at 49 percent, is a record low.

15–16 October 1999: Tampere European Council in Finland is the first to give most of its time to justice and home affairs.

2000s

15 January 2000: Accession negotiations begin with Bulgaria, Latvia, Lithuania, Malta, Romania, and Slovakia. IGC on institutional amendments to EU treaty begin in February.

12 May 2000: Joschka Fischer, German foreign minister, argues in Berlin for a federal European state or else the possibility of a group of states pressing ahead to more advanced forms of integration.

28 September 2000: Danes vote against joining Euro.

7–10 December 2000: Nice European Council makes further cosmetic changes to the EU's institutional structures and welcomes a Charter of Fundamental Human Rights without incorporating it into the treaty.

26 February 2001: Treaty of Nice signed in Brussels.

7 June 2001: Irish voters reject the Treaty of Nice. They later approve it in a second referendum on 19 October 2002.

3 July 2001: EU blocks merger of two U.S. companies, General Electric and Honeywell.

11 September 2001: Destruction of World Trade Center. EU begins work on a raft of antiterrorism measures and proposes the introduction of a "European arrest warrant" to eliminate lengthy extradition procedures.

14–15 December 2001: Laeken European Council declares Europe to be "at a crossroads" and decides to institute a "Convention," chaired by the former French president, Valéry Giscard d'Estaing, on the EU's institutional and political future.

1 January 2002: Euro notes and coins begin to circulate throughout most of the Union. Remarkably few technical problems are registered.

28 February 2002: The Convention begins work.

28 October 2002: Giscard d'Estaing presents draft constitution to the Convention.

12–13 December 2002: Copenhagen European Council recommends entry of Estonia, Latvia, Lithuania, Poland, Czech Republic, Slovakia, Hungary, Slovenia, Malta and Cyprus in 2004.

EU member states
Candidate states negotiating accession
Candidate state, not negotiating

Possible Dates of Accession

2003–2007   Cyprus
Czech Republic
Estonia
Hungary
Latvia
Lithuania
Malta
Poland
Slovakia
Slovenia

2008–2010   Bulgaria
Romania

2010–?   Turkey

1

Introduction:
An Unusual New Polity

Since 1945, the nation-states of Western and Southern Europe have engaged
in a historically unprecedented experiment in economic integration and
supranational cooperation. In stark contrast to the narrow economic protectionism that divided Europe before World War Two, the European Union's
(EU) fifteen member states, and their 375 million people, have successfully
created a single market in goods, services, capital and people. Twelve out of
the fifteen states began using a single currency—the Euro (€)—on 1 January
2002 and control of the politically sensitive area of monetary policy has been
handed over to a European Central Bank, which is endowed with the power
to raise or lower interest rates across the Euro-zone. Citizens of the EU are
free to travel throughout the Union carrying only an identity card, and
throughout *most* of the Union without encountering customs formalities of
any kind. Traveling from Bologna to Brussels, or Lisbon to Luxembourg is
as straightforward as traveling from Boston to Buffalo; and although differences of language, culture and bureaucracy (for example, pensions, which are
not portable from one country to another) make moving from one member
state to another to work a relatively difficult experience, more and more people, especially the young and the professional, are taking advantage of their
right to reside wherever they choose. Moreover, with the accession of the
new democracies of Central and Eastern Europe assured by the middle of
this decade, the prospect is now near of Europe's borders extending from the
Atlantic to the Russian border.

The EU should be seen as an institutional mechanism that has been gradually assembled by its member states to manage, extend and further economic cooperation between Europe's states. In 2002, the Union had a
€99,000 million budget (a Euro was worth exactly one dollar when this

1

book went to press), which is raised from a variety of indirect taxes and levies administered by the national governments. The Union's citizens do not pay a tax directly to Brussels (the Belgian city where the EU's main institutions are located) to pay for the services rendered by the EU, although some of the EU's more enthusiastic supporters think that they should. The EU's budget, while a considerable sum of money, is just 1.1 percent of the output of the fifteen member states, which at just under €9 U.S. trillion is second in size only to the United States. The EU is not a federal state on the American or Canadian model, and cannot boast a centralized government that spends a quarter or more of GDP on pensions, welfare, defense and health care (although, once again, its more enthusiastic supporters would like it to become such a state). Most of the EU's money is spent on agriculture subsidies (€44,500 million: 45.2 percent) and regional development (€34,000 million: 34.5 percent), but it also finances considerable programs in science and technology, education, culture, the environment, and in the "candidate" states in Central and Eastern Europe. It provides loans and grants for major infrastructure projects and is coordinating and partially financing its member states' efforts to build a huge network of expensive high-speed rail links.[1]

The EU's broad policy priorities are decided by the European Council, a regular (three or four times a year) summit meeting of the heads of state and government of the member states. The European Council shares the executive role within the Union with the European Commission, a permanent bureaucracy based in Brussels whose chief officials are nominated by the governments of the member states. It is the Commission's task to propose new legislative initiatives in the policy areas within the sphere of its competence. It also represents the member states in international trade talks and monitors compliance by the member states of Community law.

The Union's law in most fields within its remit (all areas of regulatory policy concerning the single market, competition policy, environmental standards, health and safety, social security and working conditions, agriculture, many areas connected with justice and home affairs) is decided in the Council of Ministers. This body is in fact a collection of specialist subcommittees attended by the appropriate ministers of the member states. Its proceedings, despite their importance, take place behind closed doors. The presidency of the Council of Ministers rotates among the member states every semester. The nation holding the presidency also has the opportunity to organize meetings of the European Council: a system that gives tiny Luxembourg, with its population of less than one million, a chance to set the Union's agenda and direct the Union's business every seven years or so.

The Council of Ministers' legislative role is shared with a European Parliament democratically elected every five years by the citizens of the fifteen states. The Parliament, long a Cinderella institution without substantive powers, had by 2002 been granted the right of veto ("co-decision," in the unlovely jargon of the Union) over many of the decisions agreed by the national governments in the Council of Ministers and had gained greater powers to supervise the appointment of the top Commission officials and to decide the Union's budget. The full diversity of Europe's political parties is reflected in the Parliament: the largest "groups" within the Parliament are the Christian Democrats (Center-Right) and the Socialists, but Neo-Fascists, Greens, Liberals, Independents and Nationalists are also represented. These "groups," it should be emphasized, are not supranational political parties but coalitions of ideologically like-minded national parties. Elections to the European Parliament, while they do stimulate debate over the principal issues raised by European integration, have remained stubbornly "national" in many of the member states. Many people treat them as a giant opinion poll on national politics, and latterly many people have failed to vote in them at all. Participation rates, which in most European democracies tend in national elections to be very high by American standards, slumped to 50 percent in the most recent (1999) EU-wide vote.

The most extraordinary thing about "Euro-legislation," for the average citizen with even a smattering of historical knowledge, is that the overwhelming majority of it is passed in the Council of Ministers by a procedure known as qualified majority voting (QMV). In this procedure each state has an agreed number of votes (weighted in such a way that the less populous states are favored) and a specified number of votes (about 70 percent) has to be in favor of a given measure for it to pass. The voting weights are such, however, that the combined opposition of three big countries (Britain, France, Germany, Italy, Spain are currently the most populous member states) suffices to block any regulation or directive proposed by the Commission, no matter how much support the measure may have among the other member states or among the deputies of the European Parliament.[2] Nevertheless, it is theoretically possible, though very unusual, for a member state to have to implement law that its government has fervently opposed in the Council of Ministers. Such European law, moreover, is binding throughout the Union and takes precedence over the laws passed by national parliaments. The European Court of Justice (ECJ) is on hand to ensure that violations of European law by the member states are subject to judicial review. Since the early 1960s, this institution has been very active in ensuring the supremacy of Community law over national law and in ensuring that the member states honor their treaty commitments. The European Union does not (yet) possess a written Constitution and so the final authority upon which the ECJ bases its decisions is the texts of the various treaties signed by the member states since the 1950s.

National sovereignty, which in practical terms means the power of states to decide *unilaterally* what will and will not be the law and policy of the land within the confines of their national boundaries, has thus appreciably retreated

in Western Europe. While it would be an exaggeration to say that France or
Britain or Germany have no more sovereign power independent of the EU
than California or Michigan or Texas have within the American federation, it
would be true to say that these strong nations have opted to pool or delegate
a great part of their autonomous decision-making capability and have thus voluntarily and considerably curbed their freedom of action in a way that has no
parallel since the nation-state became the norm for political organization in the
eighteenth and nineteenth centuries.

For Americans, such a degree of political integration is nothing to marvel
at and may seem unnecessarily convoluted. An instinctive reaction might be:
"what took Europe so long?" But that is to equate the "States of the Union"
with the *nation-states* of Europe. Can we imagine the United States of America voluntarily ceding some part of her sovereignty to a transatlantic or hemi-
spheric federation whose institutions and laws took precedence over law
made by Congress? Probably we cannot, not least because any such proposal
would certainly be deemed unconstitutional. But that is precisely what the
countries of Western (and now Central and Eastern) Europe have at any rate
partially done. They have not done it overnight. Almost fifty years elapsed
between the Congress of Europe in May 1948, when hundreds of statesmen
and intellectuals from all over non-Communist Europe met in the Dutch
capital, the Hague, to propose the rapid economic and political integration
of western Europe, and the concluding negotiation of the treaty on European Union in another Dutch city—Maastricht—in December 1991. Nevertheless, they have made a series of collective jumps towards an advanced and
unique form of broadly confederal organization. Moreover, while giving up
national sovereignty has been for some of the member states of the EU, notably Great Britain and Denmark, similar to permitting a dentist to extract a
series of deep-rooted molars, most of the other nation-states have, at any rate
rhetorically, made a virtue out of this renunciation of sovereignty and have
consistently pressed, in the words of the preamble to the 1957 treaty establishing the European Economic Community (EEC), for "an ever closer
union" between the states of Europe.[3]

STRUCTURE AND CONTENT

The aim of this book is to provide a narrative account of how this unique
form of confederalism emerged. The book begins after World War Two,
when Western Europe was both morally and economically prostrate. The war
against Nazi Germany had led to the destruction of much of the infrastructure of the western half of the continent and the occupation by Soviet Russia of the eastern part. The second chapter, "Enemies to Partners," deals
with how the countries of Western Europe began the work of reconstruction

under the guidance of the United States. The first postwar organization of European states, the Organization for European Economic Cooperation (OEEC), was created to disburse Marshall Plan aid in 1948, and the United States played a major role in placing on the agenda of Europe's nations some of the themes—notably trade liberalization—that would dominate the early stages of the process of integration.

The United States also pressed for Western Europe to adopt a federal form of government like her own. Many Europeans required no encouragement in this direction; enough, however, did. Great Britain, in particular, set its face against the construction of a U.S.-style federation in Western Europe. Since Britain at that time was America's most important ally, Britain was in a position to get her own way. Britain blocked all attempts to move beyond purely intergovernmental cooperation in the late 1940s and early 1950s. But in so doing, she arguably made a serious strategic error. By 1950, Britain was no longer strong enough to compete with the United States and the USSR. Whether she knew it or not, her future lay in Western Europe. When, in May 1950, the French government proposed that France, Germany and any other Western European state that cared to join should entrust their coal and steel industries to the management of a supranational "High Authority" (the so-called Schuman Plan), the British, fearful of losing national sovereignty, stayed out. The result of this decision was that Franco-German cooperation became the mainspring of economic integration in Western Europe. History should never be written in terms of might-have-beens, but there seems little doubt that the postwar history of Europe would have been very different had Britain been prepared to contemplate the cession of sovereignty inherent in the Schuman Plan. Britain's much larger economy and international prestige would have enabled her to shape the nascent European Coal and Steel Community (ECSC) to her own advantage.

The Schuman Plan represented a new approach to the integration of Europe: so-called functional integration. This approach is linked indelibly with the figure of Jean Monnet, the French administrator who is widely regarded as the "Father of Europe." Monnet's insight was that Europe's nation-states could gradually be persuaded to abandon their sovereign prerogatives if they were drawn into cooperation in sectors crucial to their economy. Monnet became the first president of the High Authority of the ECSC, but from 1955 he particularly worked for the creation of an ECSC-like structure to promote atomic energy. Euratom, as this structure became known, was set up by one of two treaties signed in Rome in March 1957. Chapter 3 deals with both the ECSC and with the failed attempt to construct a European Defense Community (EDC) in parallel to the ECSC. It also deals with the negotiations that led to the other (and ultimately far more important) Treaty of Rome: the treaty establishing a European Economic Community (EEC). The EEC treaty created a Customs Union between the six Western European states who had also joined the ECSC: Belgium, France, Italy, Luxembourg, the Netherlands, West Germany. These states, in other words, established a common external tariff upon imports and pledged to abolish all barriers to trade in manufactures and agriculture between themselves over a twelve-year transition period.

Chapter 4 is about the challenge of French President Charles de Gaulle to the incremental supranationalism implicit in the EEC treaty. De Gaulle was not the narrow nationalist of legend. He wanted Europe to punch its weight in world affairs. But he believed that the Six, let alone other European countries with proud histories like Britain, would only adhere to a joint foreign and defense policy if the policy were made by national governments acting in concert. The plan for a "Union of States" (November 1961), proposed by the French diplomat Christian Fouchet in November 1961, was de Gaulle's answer. He envisaged an intergovernmental council of heads of state or government deciding Europe's policy on defense, foreign policy and, eventually, economics, too. The Dutch and the Belgians resisted this dilution of the supranational dimension of the EEC treaty. They also had no desire to strike out independently of the United States in foreign policy, and the Kennedy administration, to put it mildly, encouraged them in this position. De Gaulle proved unable to browbeat the "small countries" into accepting his plan. His failure to do so set the stage for the two tense clashes between France and most of the rest of the Community in 1963 and 1965–1966. In 1963, France, against the wishes of the other member states, but with the crucial support of West German Chancellor Konrad Adenauer (though not the German government as a whole), vetoed British entry into the EEC. In 1965–1966, France obtained a de facto guarantee that she could continue to veto proposals in the Council of Ministers that she did not like (the so-called Luxembourg compromise) and the EEC was confirmed as a forum for co-operation between national governments on certain closely defined economic topics.

Nevertheless, the impulse towards supranationalism remained strong among many of Europe's leaders. After de Gaulle's death, the Six (the Nine from 1 January 1973, when Britain, Ireland and Denmark joined) attempted a relaunch of the European Community (as it was by now commonly known). At the October 1972 Paris summit of the Nine's heads of state or government, the member states asserted that they would move to full economic and monetary union (EMU) by 1980. They would also, they implied, set up some form of Community-level political organization to govern the economic union thus created. This aspiration was soon dashed by the international economic and financial crises of the 1970s. Chapter 5, "Weathering the Storm," describes the immense challenges facing the EC in the 1970s. In retrospect, it is something of a miracle and a powerful testament to the sense of cohesion achieved by the EC that the Community did not revert to economic nationalism in the 1970s. Wildly swinging exchange rates, rampant inflation, low economic growth and soaring oil prices were a recipe for protectionism.

Instead, cooperation intensified. From 1972, the EC's heads of state and government began to meet on a regular basis in what became known as the European Council. This quintessentially intergovernmental body, as de Gaulle had in a way envisaged, swiftly became the EC's "center of decision."[4] The EC also strove to control the damaging effects of fluctuating exchange rates by instituting the European Monetary System (EMS) in 1979, and the member states agreed that the EC Assembly should be directly elected. Thereafter, its pretensions to be a parliament were a little less risible. Part of the reason why the EC could not revert to protectionism was judicial. The sentences of the ECJ had, by the end of the 1970s, clearly established that the Treaty of Rome conferred rights directly on the citizens of the member states and that the regulations and directives made by Community institutions enjoyed supremacy over conflicting national laws. It would not have been possible for a member state to throw up the trade barriers without, in effect, seceding from the Community. This was a risk that nobody, ultimately, was prepared to run.

The turning point in the history of European integration undoubtedly comes in the early and mid-1980s. A European transported forward in time from 1957 would have found the EC of, say, 1983 essentially like the soon-to-be-born EEC of nearly thirty years before. There was much freer trade, of course, but even trade in merchandise was still obstructed by a range of non-tariff barriers. Moreover, there were still physical barriers blocking the movement of citizens of EC member states from one country to another. The EC was still primarily preoccupied with agricultural policy. As late as the early 1980s agriculture took up 80 percent of the Community's budget and the rows provoked by the costs of agricultural policy absorbed (it sometimes seemed) 99 percent of its energies.

Yet just ten years later, the time traveler would have been astonished by the extent to which the Single European Act (SEA, 1986) and the Treaty of Maastricht (1992) had enabled people to move, buy and sell across the member states of what was now called the European Union. He would, moreover, been equally astonished at the substantial number of policy responsibilities that had been transferred to the Community level and at the central role played by the Community's supranational institutions. Chapters 6 and 7 describe how this transfer of responsibilities was decided, and how and why the EC decided to move forward so far, so fast to "complete the single market" and, in the teeth of frantic British opposition, to complement the single market at Maastricht in December 1991 with a plan for a single European currency, an autonomous central bank and enhanced powers for the directly elected European Parliament.

The last chapter discusses the tense decade since Maastricht. The process of integration has pressed ahead since 1992, with the Commission and the most influential member states launching ambitious plans to both "widen" (expand its membership) and "deepen" (add to its legislative responsibilities) the Union. These plans, however, have presented the Union with a number of grave problems. The Union's institutional structure is widely regarded as both too cumbersome and inadequately democratic for a wider and deeper Europe. But what might replace it? Finding an answer to this question will not be easy and may lead to the coming decade in European politics being even more turbulent than the last one. The Maastricht treaty itself was only ratified with bad grace by the electorates of several European countries, notably France and Denmark, and profoundly transformed British domestic politics by turning the ruling Conservative Party into an unelectable assemblage of warring tribes. Euro-pessimists, of whom there are an increasing number, worry that a dangerous gap is emerging between the continent's intellectuals and political élites and its peoples, who are distant from the Community institutions that increasingly decide their fate. The paltry turnout of voters in the elections to the European Parliament in June 1999 confirmed this fear. Since 1999, the European Union's wiser leaders have been looking for ways to rejuvenate the European project, but they face the major problem that their own solutions of choice—democratizing and empowering the Union's existing institutions—are seen as anathema in some member states and are not regarded with enthusiasm in even the member states most traditionally friendly to the cause of European unification.

THEMES

This summary of this book's contents has already given away one point of narrative technique: the book is *not* what the British historian Herbert Butterfield critically called "Whig history" in an influential series of lectures at the beginning of the 1930s.[5] The study of European integration has in some ways been the last redoubt of history of this kind. In much the same way that historians once depicted English constitutional history as a see-saw battle between reformist "Whigs" (Liberals) and reactionary "Tories," in which British parliamentary democracy was at length perfected by Whig statesmen despite the low politics and the self-interested opportunism of the Tories, so many scholars of European integration have portrayed European integration as a historical process whose forward march has been hampered by states and national leaders (de Gaulle and Margaret Thatcher have a starring role as villains) irrationally attached to the principles of national sovereignty: what the Italian historian Bino Olivi has called "difficult Europe."[6]

The problem with seeing any history in terms of reactionaries versus progressives is that it "abridges"—to use Butterfield's own term—the historical process. According to Butterfield, the historian's job is rather the "analysis of all the mediations by which the past was turned into our present." It is to "recapture the richness of the moments, the humanity of the men, the setting of the external circumstances, and the implications of events." When writing general history, which is of necessity a compressed summary of the whole, we have the right to expect that the historian has not, by the selection and organization of his facts, "interpolated a theory . . . particularly one that would never be feasible if all the story were told in all its detail."[7]

I do not know if I have lived up to these injunctions in this book, but I have tried. Rather than starting with an explanatory theory of European integration that I could test against the historical record, I decided to immerse myself in the record, reconstruct the events as well as I could and then see if I could arrive at any conclusions about what has occurred. From a purely empirical point of view, this has led me to diverge in the narrative from both "realist" and the "institutionalist" or "neofunctionalist" interpretations of the development of the European Union. Unlike, say, Andrew Moravcsik, I do not believe that "federal ideology" has been important only "at the margin" for the creation of European institutions (or certainly that de Gaulle was more concerned with the "price of wheat" than geopolitics in his European policy); yet I broadly agree with his central theme that European unification has been driven by the efforts of European leaders to cope with the gigantic changes that have taken place in the world economy since the early 1970s in particular.[8] There is a great deal about monetary policy and exchange rates in this book: but there should, in retrospect, probably have been even more. There is a very strong argument indeed for suggesting that the EC was ultimately the offspring of the postwar system of fixed exchange rates, that the EU was the child of the fluctuating dollar, and that whatever new institutional form the EU takes in the coming decade will be vastly influenced by the impact of the Euro on transatlantic relations. For all the many books and articles that argue that Europe's supranational institutions are themselves the chief motors of European integration, the actions of Europe's institutional actors seem to me, by comparison with the efforts of Europe's governments to deliver prosperity in the face of wildly fluctuating currencies (or to resolve the German question in the early 1950s and 1990s), to have influenced the pace and the character of integration somewhat less. But this does not mean—I hope—that this book is insensible to the effect that supranational policy entrepreneurs (they used to be known as idealists) such as Jean Monnet played in launching the European project, or ignores how the rulings of the European Court of Justice constitutionalized the Community in the 1960s and 1970s, or neglects the role played by the Commission in the mid-1980s in putting the single market, regional aid and social policy on the

Community's agenda. These events were all extremely significant developments in the Community's history and have been given a prominent position
in this narrative.

Despite the centrality of monetary policy and geopolitics in this narrative,
I nevertheless think "realist" interpretations of European integration, with
their emphasis on what J. H. H. Weiler calls "cold calculations of cost and
benefit to its participating member states," risk missing the forest for the
trees.[9] "Realists" concentrate on the facts that they find in the archive documents and dismiss the *thousands* of books, pamphlets, articles and speeches
by postwar statesmen in favor of European unity as windy rhetoric, or even
propaganda designed to disguise the economic consequences of the decisions they have taken.[10]

Like Weiler, I think this approach belittles the extent that "the very idea of
the Community was associated with a set of values which . . . could captivate
the imagination, mobilize broadly based political forces, counteract the . . .
pull of nationalism."[11] By striving to reach compromise agreements on matters of mutual concern through supranational institutions, rather than acting
unilaterally in their own immediate interests, irrespective of the knock-on effects of their actions on their neighbors, the member states of the ECSC-
EEC-EC-EU turned the theory and practice of nation-state behavior on its
head—and their leaders were well aware that they were doing so, as even a
glance at the memoir literature illustrates.[12] In so doing, they achieved greater
levels of economic welfare and geopolitical stability than European states had
ever attained previously.

This is why a perceptible shiver of apprehension still passes through Europe's political class (and public opinion) whenever an individual member
state rejects the discipline of Community institutions and acts unilaterally. De
Gaulle's refusal to bend to the supranational implications of the EEC treaty
in 1965–1966, Britain's bloody-minded intransigence over its budget contribution between 1979 and 1984, Germany's impetuous and arrogant
recognition of Croatian and Slovenian independence in December 1991
were intensely controversial moments in the Community's history precisely
because they were instances of major member states acting with traditional
disregard for the interests and the susceptibilities of their neighbors. But
from the historian's perspective, the single most important fact in postwar
European history is that such episodes have been the rare exception rather
than the rule—and that even these episodes ended in compromise.

This book has been titled "surpassing realism"—surpassing in the sense of
"going beyond" or "superseding"—for this reason. For that is what the nation-
states of Europe have done: they have superseded traditional power politics by
identifying their interests in an increasing number of fields with a wider process
of institutionalized cooperation.[13] The Italian statesman Giuliano Amato recently expressed perfectly the point I am making, although the last sentence in

the quotation that follows is unduly pessimistic when one considers that the decade that has elapsed since Maastricht has seen the introduction of the Euro, the beginnings of a genuine EU foreign policy, the successful completion of an international trade round in which the EU countries, after much internal bickering, took a common position, and a unanimously agreed decision to extend membership of the EU to most of the states in Eastern and Southern Europe that do not already belong to the Union.

> The protagonists of the construction of the Community were the nation-states who through their commitment to the European ideal satisfied their own interests. The magic of Europe, its "miracle of San Gennaro," lay in the fact that for the first time in history the satisfaction of national interests was carried on by the invention of common solutions, which then transported us beyond the solution to the specific national problem . . . a certain kind of pro-Europe rhetoric likes to deny that national interests exist. They do, and how. In Europe, problems arise when national interests fail to work the miracle, that is to say, find a common solution. For some years now, the miracle has no longer been taking place.[14]

We have been talking of the nation-states of Europe, or the member states of the European Union, as if they were somehow distinct entities possessed of a mind of their own. Of course, they are not. The "invention of common solutions" between Europe's nations has been carried on by Europe's leaders, and the "miracle" of postwar cooperation between European nation-states would not have been possible had these same leaders not managed, as the international relations theorist Arnold Wolfers predicted that postwar statesmen might, to identify themselves with both their national interests and with supranational institutions of cooperation.[15] The greatness—a strong word, but in my opinion a justified one—of the postwar generations of Europe's leaders has lain in the fact that they have remained loyal both to the interests of their individual nations and to the principle of European cooperation.

This narrative, in fact, is largely about how two generations of European leaders have performed the tricky feat of maintaining dual loyalties in circumstances in which the temptation to impose national solutions must have often been, for the big countries in particular, almost overwhelming. I am aware that this turns the narrative into something resembling traditional "great man" history, but I can see no way of escaping this terrible fate. There is a real sense in which one misses the essence of what European integration has been about if one underplays or neglects the role of national leaders in driving it forward.

TERMINOLOGY

Already in this introduction, I have used the words *supranational* and *intergovernmental* on several occasions. By *supranationalism,* I mean the belief that the nongovernmental institutions of the EC should be entrusted with greater responsibilities and powers. The Commission, the Parliament, the Court of Justice are the EU's key supranational institutions: supranationalists can be defined as those political actors who have sustained that these institutions *should* play a larger role in the life of the Community and *should* have greater independent decision-making powers. Many supranationalists, although not all, have consistently argued that the goal of European integration should even be the creation of a federal United States of Europe, although they have differed on how powerful the central institutions of the federation should be and over how many functions should be left as the exclusive preserve of the member states. When discussing such figures, I have often used the word *federalist.*

Intergovernmentalism, by contrast, is the conviction that cooperative government in Europe is difficult or impossible unless one gives decisive institutional weight to the interests and voices of the national governments. The Council of Ministers and the European Council are the two intergovernmentalist institutions of the Community. Intergovernmentalism has been the primary mode by which European institutions have functioned in the postwar period, although this has been in large part due to the presence of two nation-states—Britain and France—that were suspicious of supranationalist methods. It should be noted, however, that intergovernmentalism and its proponents are not necessarily opposed to European cooperation or integration as such.

Even knowing at any one moment what the institutions of European cooperation are called is less easy than it may seem. The term "European Community" (EC) was in common use from the mid-1960s until the early 1990s and is still often used today. But until the Maastricht treaty, the EC was officially called the European Communities, reflecting the fact that it was based upon the fusion of the Coal and Steel Community (ECSC), the Atomic Energy Community (Euratom) and the Economic Community (EEC). In Britain at least, the EC was also widely known as the Common Market until the late 1980s, and Americans even invented the term "European Common Market." After Maastricht, most people have taken to referring to the "European Union" (EU), which, strictly speaking, is the global term used to encompass European cooperation in the European Community and in the separate largely intergovernmental forums for cooperation on foreign affairs and justice and home affairs. A similar difficulty arises with the European Parliament. It called *itself* a parliament from the early 1960s onward, which was an act of effrontery since it was not directly elected and possessed neither legislative nor significant scrutiny functions. In law, however, the "Parliament" was merely the Assembly of the European Communities until the Single European Act in 1987. In this book, I have followed popular usage and used "European Community" from the 1960s to Maastricht, and "European

Union" thereafter. I have referred to the "European Parliament" only after its direct election in 1979.

NOTES

1. All the details in this paragraph are taken from the budget page on the EU's website, *Europa*, www.europa.eu.int/. Throughout this book, not least to conform to the EU's own usage, I have regarded a billion as a million millions (and not the more usual 1,000 million).

2. Regulations and directives are the most important forms of legislation within the EC. A *regulation* is a law that is (1) of "general application"; (2) binding in its entirety and (3) "directly applicable" in all member states (that is, it has no need of any enabling legislation from the parliaments of the member states but automatically becomes law shortly after its publication). A *directive* is a measure that sets broad objectives that the member states must meet within a specified date but which leaves the precise choice of means to the governments and parliaments of the member states. The distinction between the two kinds of legislation is not as large as these definitions would suggest since directives are often worded in a way that leaves little scope for adjustments. Moreover, the ECJ has ruled in several landmark cases that the fact that directives are not directly applicable does not mean that member states can be tardy or sloppy in their transformation of directives into national law. See Neil Nugent, *The Government and Politics of the European Union* (Durham, N.C.: Duke University Press, 1994), 210–11.

3. The most comprehensive general introductions to the institutions and policies of the EU are Desmond Dinan, *An Ever Closer Union* (London: Macmillan, 2000), and Nugent, *Government and Politics of the European Union*.

4. This phrase was used in the 1970 *Report on Economic and Monetary Union* (the "Werner Report") as a euphemism for the political institutions that such an economic union would need. See chapter 5.

5. The lectures were collected as *The Whig Interpretation of History* (London: Pelican, 1973). So far as I am aware, the only other scholar who has pointed out the "Whig" bias of much of the scholarship of European integration is the Oxford Central European specialist Timothy Garton Ash in his excellent essay "Ten Years in Europe," *Prospect* no. 43 (July 1999): 22–27 at 26. Garton Ash makes essentially the same point in the opening paragraphs of his short essay "Europe's Endangered Liberal Order," *Foreign Affairs* 77, no. 2: 51–65.

6. Bino Olivi, *L'Europa difficile* (Bologna: Il Mulino, 2000).

7. Quotes from Herbert Butterfield, *Whig Interpretation of History*, 40, 54, 75.

8. Andrew Moravcsik, *The Choice for Europe: Social Purpose and State Power from Messina to Maastricht* (Ithaca, N.Y.: Cornell University Press, 1998), 3.

9. J. H. H. Weiler, *The Constitution of Europe* (Cambridge: Cambridge University Press, 1999), 239.

10. See Alan S. Milward's chapter on "The Lives and Teachings of the European Saints" in the *European Rescue of the Nation-State* (London: Routledge, 1992), or Andrew Moravcsik's treatment of the geopolitical and ideological motives of the national

leaders during the EMS negotiations in *The Choice for Europe*, 301–2, where he labels the rhetoric of European unity a "deliberate deception."

11. Weiler, *Constitution of Europe*, 239.

12. Robert Marjolin, *Architect of European Unity: Memoirs 1911–1986* (London: Weidenfeld and Nicholson, 1989), 180, rounds upon "a small number of biased historians" who dispute the transformation of attitudes implicit in postwar policy.

13. Robert Kagan makes precisely this point to explain why the EU has been so alarmed by American unilateralism in the post–Cold War world. Having themselves "transcended power," Kagan argues that the EU wants to transmit "the European miracle" to the rest of the world. Inevitably, this approach is clashing with the more pragmatic policy of the United States, which is based on realpolitik and a willingness to use force to achieve international objectives. Robert Kagan, "Power and Weakness," *Policy Review*, no. 113 (June/July 2002). Quotations are from page 11 of the online edition (www.policyreview.org/).

14. "Fini e confini d'Europa," an interview with Giuliano Amato, *Limes* (January 2002): 50–51.

15. Arnold Wolfers, "The Actors in International Politics," in *Discord and Collaboration* (Baltimore: Johns Hopkins University Press, 1992), 3–24.

2

Enemies to Partners

The Politics of Cooperation in Western Europe 1945–1950

The war ended in Europe in May 1945. It left the continent's infrastructure in pieces and its peoples divided by ideological conflict and nationalist resentments. Less fertile terrain for the growth of the structures of international cooperation can scarcely be imagined. Yet by the summer of 1950, a mere five years later, the countries of Western Europe had successfully collaborated with each other, and with the government of the United States, to begin the reconstruction of their shattered economies; six of them, including France and Germany, had begun negotiations to place production of their key coal and steel industries under the control of a "High Authority" with supranational decision-making powers; in the defense field, the nations of Western Europe had allied with the United States against the threat from the Soviet Union. Astonishingly, however, this record was regarded by some to be one of failure. Too many influential intellectuals and government ministers, on both sides of the Atlantic, had hoped for the reorganization of the European nations into an authentic "United States of Europe" for such partial integration to be considered a success.

This chapter traces the growth of supranational cooperation in Western Europe immediately after 1945. It argues that five key factors prevented any of the major nations from subsiding into nationalistic solutions to the problem of reconstruction. On the other hand, there was no single factor, or combination of factors, able to constrain the nations of Europe to pool their sovereignty into a single supranational organization with wide political and economic powers.

1. The first of these factors was ideological. Many statesmen across Europe were deeply committed, in the aftermath of the war, to furthering European unity. Just months after a war in which Europe had displayed all the darkest

15

secrets of its soul, politicians of every stripe optimistically asserted the cultural unity of the continent and proclaimed the need for political union. With hindsight, it is clear that the rhetoric of building "Europe" was also a useful glue that held otherwise divergent Catholics, Socialists, Liberals and Conservatives together. Anti-democrats, be they Fascist or Communist, were opposed to European integration; being for European integration, consequently, was a badge establishing one's democratic credentials.

2. The second factor was the need for rapid economic reconstruction. The statistics of postwar devastation seem hardly credible fifty comfortable years later. Ten million homes had been destroyed in Germany: towns like Berlin, Hamburg and Essen were little more than piles of ruins. The staunchly anti-Nazi German leader Konrad Adenauer, who would become one of the founding fathers of the European unity movement in the coming decade, gave a bleak description in his memoirs of what Cologne looked like when he returned as mayor in April 1945:

> The task confronting me . . . was a huge and extraordinarily difficult one. The extent of the damage suffered by the city in air raids and from the other effects of war was enormous . . . more than half the houses and public buildings were totally destroyed . . . only 300 houses had escaped unscathed. . . . There was no gas, no water, no electric current, and no means of transport. The bridges across the Rhine had been destroyed. There were mountains of rubble in the streets. Everywhere there were gigantic areas of debris from bombed and shelled buildings. With its razed churches, many of them a thousand years old, its bombed-out cathedral . . . Cologne was a ghost city.[1]

Yet Adenauer in this grim moment nevertheless believed that "the unification of Europe seemed far more feasible now than in the 1920s. The idea of international cooperation must succeed."[2] The sheer scale of the devastation inspired a deep conviction among the first postwar generation of European leaders that there was no choice but to supersede national rivalries, if Europe was ever to return to civilized life again.

In the meantime, however, it was touch and go whether Europe could survive at all. Key hubs for the entire European economy such as Rotterdam had been blitzed into the pre-industrial age. Bridges, railways, roads and canals were blocked with the detritus of war all over the continent. There was little petrol for the few trucks and tractors still in working order. The 1945 harvest was little more than half as large as the last prewar harvest in 1938 and getting it to market was a task of surpassing difficulty. During the winter of 1945–1946, Europe's large urban areas were reduced to near-famine conditions.[3] Average per capita consumption of food in 1946 was 1,600 calories in Western Germany, 1,700 in Austria, 1,800 in Italy and just over 2,000 in France, Belgium and the Netherlands. For many city dwellers, consumption was lower than even these starkly low averages—millions of people survived on 1,000 calories a day. Only Britain and the Nordic countries managed to provide their citizens with the 2,400 to 2,800 calories consumed by the average sedentary man in a normal day—and as Europe rebuilt, few people were living sedentary lives.[4] At first, the problem of reconstruction was the arduous but practical one of digging enough coal, growing enough crops and rebuilding war-blasted railways, ports and houses. It soon became obvious to the more astute European governments, however, that complete reconstruction was more likely to be attained in a common market that would allow countries to specialize in the areas of industrial output where they enjoyed a comparative advantage. A common market would guarantee economies of scale and would mark a rejection of the economic nationalism of the 1930s whereby each and every country had sought to build up its own industries behind high tariff walls. The dazzling economic success of the United States provided a compelling argument for the benefits of a large domestic market. Robert Marjolin, the brilliant French political economist who became secretary-general of the Organization for European Economic Cooperation (OEEC) in 1948 and was a French representative on the first Commission of the European Economic Community (EEC) in 1958, wrote in his memoirs that in the immediate postwar years, "America hypnotized us, her material success was our ideal; we had almost no other aim than to bridge the gap between European industry and American industry."[5]

America wanted this too, not least because her leaders feared that the alternative would be the spread of Communism. American pressure for greater European integration—especially after the launching of the Marshall Plan in 1948—was a constant factor in the calculations of Europe's politicians. Had America lapsed back into isolationism in 1946 (an entirely possible outcome), Europe would have had to find the resources to defend itself against the USSR and to rebuild its industrial base entirely from the pockets of its citizens. In practice, this would have meant imposing a war economy, with rationing of consumer goods, onto peoples already worn out by a decade of war and hard labor. American financial aid permitted Western Europeans to enjoy the odd luxury in the late 1940s—and enabled their governments to avoid social strife. No European government, therefore, was in a position to ignore what the Americans wanted. The problem in relations with the United States was that American policymakers were apt to insist that America's economic prowess was a consequence of its organization as a federal state. As Diane Kunz has remarked: "European unity continued to appeal to Americans for several reasons, not the least of which was the conviction, tapping deep into the American psyche, that Europe's best course was to imitate the United States as closely as possible."[6] For many European leaders, including the ones most convinced of the need for European political union, full integration into a federal state was, in the 1940s, however, still no more than an aspiration.

The reintegration of Germany, even its western rump, was the fourth, and in many ways the most important, factor tending towards integration. The question of how to treat Germany after 1945 crucially divided the Western and Communist worlds, and dominated French foreign policy thinking. The French governments in this period were determined to ensure that Germany would never again pose a military threat to France and that France would have economic parity, or even supremacy, in Western Europe. Until 1948, successive French governments pursued an ambitious strategy of attempting to persuade the British and Americans to subordinate German industrial production to the needs of the French economy. France wanted her allies to allow her to substitute Germany as the economic motor of Western Europe. When, however, it became evident to France that the Russians represented a larger threat to France than Germany and that Britain and the United States were determined to reestablish West Germany as a bulwark against the Soviet Union, then France switched to a policy of encouraging the rehabilitation of Germany in the context of wider European integration. Without some such Franco-German rapprochement, no step towards European unity was imaginable, and it is for this reason that the French statesmen most responsible for seeking better relations with Germany, Robert Schuman and Jean Monnet, are regarded (and deserve to be regarded) as the founding fathers of the European Community.

By the early 1950s, in fact, France had established itself as the key political actor in Western Europe. This position ought, logically, to have belonged to Britain. The fifth factor structuring the development of Western Europe after 1945 was Britain's economic weakness and political ambivalence. Britain enjoyed moral authority after 1945 as the nation that had led the fight against Fascism, but its ability to lead the reconstruction of Europe was handicapped by its inability to reclaim its prewar position as a major importer of European industrial and consumer products. Britain did not have the dollars—and foreigners no longer wanted sterling. Britain did not have, either, the will to engage itself in schemes for European integration. Britain's politicians, both Labour and Conservative, saw Britain, in a sense quite rightly, as a world power, not a regional leader, and were dismissive of plans which required her to concede any portion, however small, of her national sovereignty to common European institutions. The Labour government elected in July 1945, moreover, was about to embark on an attempt to socialize the British economy by taking key industries (coal, the railways, iron and steel) into public ownership and greatly extending state provision of social services. The desire of continental politicians to build a common market administered by pan-European political institutions appeared to Labour's chief figures as a distraction from their core objectives.

Britain's decision to turn a cold shoulder to the Europeans has to be regarded both as a major influence upon the path taken by the rest of West-

ern Europe towards integration and as a policy misjudgment of the first order. Had the policy-making élite in Whitehall been more friendly to European integration in the late 1940s, Britain might have found herself leading
a commonwealth of European nations in the 1950s, instead of failing dismally to lead a commonwealth of former colonies. European integration
would have evolved differently had Britain been prepared to meet her
neighbors halfway—and Britain's economy would have received a salutary
dose of competition that might have prevented Britain's slide in the 1950s
and 1960s into relative economic decline. The attitude of the Foreign Office, and the British political class more generally, towards European integration in the 1940s and 1950s is testimony to the power of received ideas
to determine, or at least condition, political behavior. Politicians and their
advisers do not act in an intellectual void. They inherit a worldview from
both the institutions they direct and the society that they lead, and this set
of beliefs—whether they accept it fully or not—shapes and informs the making of policy.

THE AMERICAN VISION FOR EUROPE:
THE MARSHALL PLAN AND THE OEEC

In 1945, despite the differences of opinion over the future of Germany that
had emerged at the Potsdam conference between the Western allies and the
USSR, Europe had not yet been divided into two halves. It was not until
the end of 1947 that East–West relations broke down and what we now call
the Cold War began. Yet throughout the first two years of peace, ideological competition with Communism was an ever present factor in the calculations of European statesmen. It is usual to present this competition as being one between liberal democracy and totalitarianism. This is true, but the
meanings that have accrued to the word *totalitarian* naturally lead one to
believe that the peoples of Western Europe were united in their rejection of
the Soviet system. The fact that European (and American) leaders had constantly to remember in the postwar years was that for millions of western
Europeans, Soviet Russia represented a stirring example of economic modernization, not a ruthless dictatorship, and in the event of economic failure
in Western Europe, it was probable that the USSR would exert an attraction for millions more.

After a decade and a half of economic depression and war, Europe's voters
wanted above all else work, welfare and homes: the only question was which
political system would provide these basic social needs. In the first postwar
elections, the voters of Western Europe mostly opted for Social Democracy
(in Britain, most dramatically), or Christian Democracy (by mid-1946,
Catholic parties prevailed in Austria, Belgium, France, the Netherlands and

Italy). Yet the Communists were far from beaten. They emerged as the second party in France in the 1946 elections and the third party in Italy (and would soon emerge as the dominant party of the left in Italy, too). In both countries, they commanded key government ministries until May 1947 when they were maneuvered from power.[7] Tightly disciplined, with a huge mass membership, and a powerful role in key trade unions, Communist parties were potent political rivals to the parties of the democratic mainstream.

The newly elected governments of Western Europe thus had no choice but to provide jobs and public welfare, build houses, increase economic output and, eventually, raise levels of individual consumption. The provision of a higher standard of living was a political imperative. Such ambitious economic objectives required vast capital spending, the money for which could be raised in any or all of three ways: by diverting as much as possible of national income to investment rather than consumption; by stimulating exports to bring in money from abroad; by receiving foreign aid or investment. France, most famously, took the first course. The five-year postwar modernization plan launched by Jean Monnet in 1946 sought to direct capital investment into selected industries such as coal mining, steel, cement and transport.[8] Large segments of the French economy were taken into public ownership as the planners channeled national income towards the development of heavy industry. To a greater or lesser extent, the Netherlands, the Scandinavian countries, and Italy followed suit. Only Belgium, whose industrial base had been less damaged by the war, opted to allow relatively high levels of the national product to be spent on private consumption.[9]

Britain, as usual, was a halfway house. The Labour government did not invest as much as France in industrial development (though capital investment still took a larger share of national income than 1938), but only because its public spending plans for health and housing, in addition to its substantial military commitments in Germany and the Far East, made greater industrial investment impossible. In February 1947, the Labour government had to tell the Americans that it no longer had the resources to maintain a British army in Greece (where withdrawal of the British army would have led to an immediate Communist seizure of power). This decision, which provoked the "Truman doctrine," an American commitment to defend democracy wherever it was threatened by totalitarian subversion, also persuaded U.S. policymakers that Europe was on the verge of economic collapse. The United States had given Britain generous postwar loans (over $4,000 million) and had poured money into relief aid for the continent as a whole in the expectation that Britain would be able by the end of 1947 to act as the chief economic motor for Western Europe. This illusion was now dispelled.

The Truman doctrine speech also professed the conviction that "the seeds of totalitarian regimes are nurtured by misery and want. They spread and grow in the evil soil of poverty and strife." By the spring of 1947, there was a widespread conviction in Truman's administration that Western Europe's failure to recover from the war was providing fertile soil for communist flowers to bloom. Output dropped in Europe in the first quarter of 1947. In retrospect, this was largely due to the brutal winter weather, but in Washington pessimism reigned. A memorandum from Will Clayton, under secretary of economic affairs in the State Department, at the end of May 1947, stated baldly that Europe was "slowly starving" and on the brink of disintegration and social revolution.[10] Clayton's memorandum was seemingly decisive in persuading U.S. Secretary of State George Marshall to make his famous Harvard speech on 5 June 1947 promising that America would fund a "program to put Europe on its feet economically." For only a healthy economic economy, Marshall sustained, could "permit the emergence of political and social conditions in which free institutions can exist."

The British economic historian Alan Milward has convincingly shown that Clayton's fears were alarmist. In Milward's view, the European economies' dash for industrial growth had merely precipitated an entirely predictable balance-of-payments crisis with the United States. Europe did not have enough dollars to maintain the high-cost investment in industrialization and social services that her peoples were demanding.

This was because the rise of the totalitarian states and the war had broken the delicate mechanism of the European trading system. At the risk of oversimplifying, trade flows in pre-Hitler Europe had been largely based upon a virtuous cycle whereby Germany exported high-cost capital goods and manufactures to France, Italy, the Scandinavian countries and eastern Europe, and obtained in return foodstuffs, services, raw materials and luxury goods. All continental Europe enjoyed a trade surplus with Britain, which was able to fill the gap by virtue of the large inflows of income she received from her overseas holdings. In the 1939–1945 war, Britain liquidated her investments abroad and by 1947 had become an international debtor. Certainly, she could no longer count upon the accumulated wealth from her centuries as an imperial power to subsidize her standard of living. Germany was equally unable to fulfill her traditional role in the European economy. Most of Germany's industrial base had by 1947 either been destroyed during the war or carted off to Russia as reparations. In the spring of 1947, moreover, it was still uncertain whether the Allies would allow Germany to reestablish itself as an industrial power. Britain and America were in favor of the idea; France and the Soviet Union were vehemently opposed.

Unable to buy capital goods and manufactures from Germany, the European nations had turned to the United States for ships, airplanes, tractors, machinery, industrial plant, some raw materials they needed to maintain their ambitious investment programs. Unfortunately, they did not have much to sell the Americans in return. Most European exports to the United States were luxury goods. It takes a lot of olive oil, perfume or whisky to buy a ship or an airplane. Inevitably, Europe's trade deficit with the United States widened. France's deficit on merchandise trade with the United States increased from $649 million in 1946 to $956 million in 1947. The Netherlands' deficit more than doubled from $187 million to $431 million. Italy's more than tripled from $112 million in 1946 to $350 million in 1947. Britain, like France, had a $1,000 million shortfall in 1947.[11] Western Europe as a whole accumulated a deficit of $7,000 million in the first two peacetime years.

European governments, in short, were living far beyond their means. It is difficult to dispute Milward's argument: "In both Britain and France policy seems to have gone ahead fatalistically based upon an unspoken, perhaps unutterable assumption that the United States would . . . have to lend or give the necessary sums of hard currency to make their postwar economic policies feasible."[12]

Marshall had insisted in his Harvard address that the Europeans themselves should draw up a plan for economic recovery. Britain and France responded by calling a conference of foreign ministers in Paris in July 1947. Sixteen Northern and Western European states attended. The Soviet Union, to the relief of everybody but the satellite nations of Eastern Europe, which were compelled to follow the Soviet example, distanced herself from the Anglo-French initiative. The conference decided to establish the so-called CEEC (Committee on European Economic Cooperation) and entrusted this body with the tasks of estimating the size of Europe's economic needs and preparing a recovery program for the continent as a whole for the period from 1948 to 1952, by when, the Americans insisted, Europe should be self-sufficient. Weeks of intense—and sometimes chaotic—committee work followed. Despite intense American pressure for something other than sixteen "shopping lists," the CEEC's initial report in August 1947 essentially produced a generalized European request for $29,000 million in American aid by 1952. Michael Hogan, in his magisterial history of the Marshall Plan, states that this figure "stunned the Europeans as much as the Americans."[13]

The CEEC's opening request was a nonstarter, and the Americans told the Europeans so. However, it did compel the United States to clarify what it wanted the Europeans to do in return for the vast sums that were going to be given them. Secretary of State Marshall had been reluctant in his Harvard speech to give the impression that the United States was imposing conditions upon the European would-be recipients of her aid. Nevertheless, when the high CEEC request precipitated matters, American policymakers responded by drawing up a list of "essentials" that would have had the effect, if they had been accepted and implemented, of constructing an economic union, on American lines, in Western Europe. American policymakers urged the governments of Western Europe to devote more resources to reviving production, even if this meant cutting back on cherished social programs; to liberalize trade by slashing tariffs and by ending exchange controls; to move, once Europe had become more self-supporting, to a customs union; and, most crucially of all, to establish a "continuing European organization" with sovereign powers over the direction of the European reconstruction effort."[14]

The European reaction to this list of "essentials" was unenthusiastic. Ernest Bevin lamented the "unfortunate impression of high-handedness" left by the Americans' approach.[15] The CEEC's "preliminary findings" eventually submitted to Congress at the end of September 1947 represented a compromise. The language of the "essentials" was retained, but the Europeans insisted that economic liberalization should not cause the abandonment of social programs or jeopardize employment levels. Led by Britain and France, they refused to accept that the proposed supranational economic organization should have sovereign powers. On the other hand, they were obliged to accept a reduced aid package of just over $19,000 million. Hogan comments: "Europeans . . . sought a recovery program that would limit the scope of collective action, meet their separate requirements and preserve the greatest degree of national self-sufficiency and autonomy. Americans, on the other hand, wanted to refashion Western Europe in the image of the United States."[16]

The truth is, however, that the Americans were not in the same position as the Russians to impose their social and political model. The dollar, mighty though it was, was much less decisive than the Red Army. Just as negotiations in the CEEC reached their climax in September 1947, Britain defaulted on the terms of the $4,000 million loan extended to her in 1946 by suspending convertibility of the pound sterling into dollars. Convertibility had been introduced in August, on schedule, but Britain's hard currency reserves immediately began to ebb away at a rate of $150 million every week as foreign holders of sterling swapped their pounds for dollars. Similarly, France and Italy wobbled on the verge of bankruptcy in the autumn of 1947 and had to be rescued by a stopgap loan from the United States. Paradoxically, the profound economic weakness of the biggest Western European states was a source of negotiating strength. American policymakers knew that an economic collapse in Western Europe would only push countries like France and Italy into the hands of the Communists and that even in Britain the moderate socialism of the leadership of the Labour Party might be replaced by a more dogmatic and pro-Soviet line.

The debate in Congress over what became the European Recovery Program (ERP) illustrates the depth of American fears on this score. Although there were influential conservatives, led by Senator Robert Taft, who argued that the root of Europe's ills was its expensive experiments in socialistic legislation, and that the United States should not subsidize un-American policies such as universal health care, few seriously argued that the United States should not aid Western Europe at all. As the debate progressed, Congress became increasingly aware that retreating into isolation was not an option. Speakers who favored the Recovery Program proposed by the CEEC and the Truman administration, chief among them Senator Arthur H. Vandenberg, argued that the triumph of socialism in Western Europe would mean the end of the free enterprise system in the United States. The United States would be obliged to divert vast resources into military spending and to regulate the economy for defense purposes. America could not expect her free market economy to work in international isolation.

These arguments prevailed. In April 1948, by large majorities in both chambers, Congress authorized the first $5,000 million of recovery spending for Europe. It also established the Economic Cooperation Agency (ECA), with branches in every Western European country, to oversee the distribution of recovery plan aid. The first director of the ECA was a prominent businessman known to be strongly sympathetic to the idea of European political unity, Paul Hoffman; day-to-day relations with the Europeans was entrusted to a presidential special representative based in Paris. Secretary of Commerce W. Averell Harriman was appointed to this post.

In parallel to the ECA, the European countries set up the OEEC, the "continuing organization" which was intended to plan the division of Marshall Plan aid among its member states, as well as act as the forum for intra-European negotiations to liberalize trade. The OEEC's role in the apportioning of aid was a blow to Britain and France who would have much preferred to conduct their negotiations for ERP aid through bilateral discussions with the United States. The OEEC was nevertheless a far cry in terms of organizational powers from the supranational planning body initially envisaged by the Americans in September 1947. Essentially, the OEEC was a ministerial council of sovereign states, served by a secretariat of officials, planners and economists, and by an executive committee of civil servants from the nation-states that scrutinized the secretariat's proposals and formulated the Council's final decisions. The work of the secretariat was placed in the hands of a relatively youthful French economist, Robert Marjolin; the executive committee was chaired by a very able Foreign Office official, Sir Edmund Hall-Patch. Marjolin has written, "France and Britain called the tune in the OEEC."[17] But even France and Britain could not dictate policy outright to the other Western European states. Every country (even small nations such as Iceland and Luxembourg) had a right of veto in the Council, and no country was obliged to implement Council decisions against its will.

Despite the intergovernmental character of the OEEC, and thus the difficulty of securing unified action, Hoffman's opening address to the Council on 25 July 1948 placed a heavy responsibility upon the nascent organization. Hoffman called upon the nation-states of Europe to use the OEEC to devise and implement a "master plan of action" for the rebirth of European economic and political life. He was insistent that this plan should not be "set in the frame of an old picture or traced on an old design." Instead, he called for the OEEC nations to "face up to readjustments to satisfy the requirements of a new world." In particular, nations should avoid thinking along "the old separatist lines." Hoffman urged the Europeans to think in terms of "the economic capacity and the economic strength of Europe as a whole."[18] What the Americans ultimately had in mind for Europe has been dubbed since "the politics of productivity"—the creation of a free-trade area administered (at least in the first instance) by supranational planning bodies that would make boosting production their fundamental goal.[19] This mixture of laissez-faire and managerialism was, of course, the policy synthesis that had saved American capitalism during the 1930s and, in fact, Michael Hogan argues persuasively that U.S. policymakers were intending to export to Europe the same model of "corporative neocapitalism" that had been developed in America during the New Deal.

A "HARMONIOUS SOCIETY":
THE VISION OF THE EUROPEAN MOVEMENT

The idea of European unity has its roots in the Enlightenment and the Kantian vision of a commonwealth of states cooperating to ensure a "perpetual peace." The primary impulse for supranational government in Europe has always been the pressing need to stop members of the European family from slaughtering one other. Paradoxically, in light of the generally cautious attitude of postwar British governments towards European unification, British thinkers have always been in the forefront of this endeavor. There has been in Britain a long "dissenting tradition" of opposition to the *realpolitik* traditionally practiced by the Foreign Office.[20] British intellectuals from Tom Paine onward have sustained that the only hope for peace in Europe lay in measures that brought the peoples of Europe into closer cooperation and limited the harmful rivalries of governments. Before, during and after World War One, British liberals argued that peace in Europe depended upon an end to secret diplomacy and the creation of an international organization that would enable the nations of the world to resolve their disputes peacefully and provide a forum for planning their economic development. Similar ideas were influential in the United States and provided the intellectual ballast for President Woodrow Wilson's scheme for a League of Nations. In the 1920s, such developments as the Locarno Pact (1925), whereby the nations of Western Europe promised to resolve their differences through the League of Nations and to respect the borders established by the 1919 Versailles Treaty, were hailed as a major step towards greater European unity by its chief architects, Aristide Briand and Gustav Stresemann, the foreign ministers of France and Germany. Briand, in 1931, even advanced the idea of a European

Confederation of nation-states, although by that date many of the high hopes of the Locarno period had evaporated.[21]

The subsequent failure of the League of Nations in the 1930s did not diminish the enthusiasm of the liberal-socialist intelligentsia in Britain for internationalist solutions to the eternal problems posed by national sovereignty. The doctrine that wars broke out because of the insecurity engendered by the nature of the state system, and by the economic conflicts intrinsic to international capitalism, continued to hold sway. With a combination of prescience and almost comical optimism, British intellectuals asserted that the popular support of the dictators was largely economic in origin and could be undermined by a concerted effort to build a socialist federation among the free states of Europe—a group that was quixotically supposed to include the Soviet Union. A "New League" of socialist states, H. N. Brailsford contended in 1936, busily dedicated to raising the standards of living of its citizens by economic planning on a Soviet scale, but via British standards of parliamentary government, would set in motion a dynamic that would entice the peoples of Italy and Germany back to the path of democracy. The institutions Brailsford envisaged for the "League"—a parliament of delegates drawn from national assemblies and a technocratic central directorate—bore a remarkable resemblance to those subsequently proposed by Jean Monnet for the European Coal and Steel Community.[22]

When war broke out, schemes for European integration—which were now held to be an infallible way of inciting the suffering masses of Germany and Italy to revolt—became every intellectual's favorite pastime.[23] This hope was almost as detached from reality as the prewar vision of Joseph Stalin relinquishing the sovereignty of the Soviet Union to an assembly of social democratic worthies from the rest of Europe. But, for all their foolishness over Russia, intellectuals like Brailsford, and the political thinkers Harold Laski, G. D. H. Cole and E. H. Carr, were making a serious point that would have to be addressed once the war was over. This point was that dictatorship had thriven in the context of the Depression and the concomitant economic nationalism of the 1930s. If Europe was to avoid a return to Fascism in the future, such thinkers reasoned, its countries needed to make boosting production and the welfare of its citizens the centerpiece of their postwar economic strategy. Cooperation in this endeavor would greatly increase the chances of success. In a pamphlet written late in the war, Brailsford envisaged EEC-like institutions supervising postwar economic growth. As he perceptively understood, the key to postwar prosperity was the revitalization of Germany. If Germany's industrial prowess could be revived, it would suck in imports of raw materials, consumer goods and foodstuffs from the Mediterranean countries and Eastern Europe, setting in motion a virtuous circle of rising productivity across the continent.[24] At a time when the Allies, including the United States, were contemplating the "pastoralization" of defeated Germany (resolving the problem of postwar security by depriving Germany of its heavy industrial capacity), this understanding of how Europe would have to be rebuilt was very farsighted.[25]

Similar arguments were being made by the so-called Federal Union movement, an organization started by British academics, thinkers and churchmen at the beginning of 1939. British intellectuals associated with Federal Union, notably the educationalist W. B. Curry, the constitutionalist Ivor Jennings, and two progressive economists, Lionel Robbins and Barbara Wootton, produced pamphlets which enjoyed great intellectual influence and, by the standards of political texts, a very large sale. Curry's *The Case for Federal Union* (1939) sold 100,000 copies.[26] Jennings's *A Federation for Western Europe* (1940) included a finely drafted constitution that withstands scrutiny even today, while Wootton's *Socialism and Federalism* (1941) launched a powerful idea that socialist thinkers such as Brailsford, Laski and Cole had implicitly recognized but had never formally acknowledged: that the socialization of western economies could only come once the power of the nation-state had been superseded. Socialism could *only* be carried out on a pan-European scale.

The debate in Britain over the need for postwar European economic and political integration is important because it influenced a generation of continental intellectuals active in the resistance against Fascism. Altiero Spinelli, Ernesto Rossi and Eugenio Colorni, the imprisoned antifascist authors of the *Manifesto di Ventotene* (1941), one of the canonical documents of the European integration movement, took the debate in Britain as the starting point for their powerful appeal to the socialist movements of Europe to make the struggle against the nation-state, rather than the class struggle, the cardinal point of their political action. After the fall of Benito Mussolini in July 1943, one of the leading elements of the partisan movement in Italy, the *Partito d'Azione* (Action Party) made European unity the core of its political program. Action Party intellectuals were prominent in the *Movimento federalista europeo* (MFE), which was founded in August 1943, and contributed to the movement's journal, *L'unità europea*. Italian federalists successfully managed to diffuse their ideas. A pamphlet, *L'Europe de demain*, was smuggled into the rest of occupied Europe in 1944, and a conference of federalists, with delegations from resistance movements across Europe, was held by the MFE in Geneva in May 1944.[27]

By 1946, every country in Western Europe could boast a federalist movement of greater or lesser size—some countries, notably France, had more than one. In April 1947, these bodies federated themselves—though not, ironically, without a series of squabbles over doctrine and worries over loss of autonomy—into the *Union Européenne des fédéralistes* (UEF). The new association, which had a collective membership of some 150,000 people, declared its purpose was "to work for the creation of a European federation which shall be a constitutive element of a world federation."[28] As this declaration suggests, the UEF was not without its utopian aspects. Its main goal, however, was (an equally utopian) one that inspired intellectuals all over the continent in the early months of the Cold War—the creation of a European "Third Force" that could act as a bridge between Soviet Communism and the West European tradition of democratic socialism.[29] Intellectuals argued that European federation offered the opportunity of building a progressive socialism that would assuage Soviet fears of capitalist aggression and would, over time, lead to the totalitarian and federalist forms of socialism converging into a single democratic model. The British intelligentsia was once more at the forefront of these debates. The flagship journals of the British Left, the *New Statesman and Nation* and *Tribune,* both backed the Third Force idea, and a faction known as the "Keep Left" group was formed within the parliamentary Labour Party to oppose the anti-Russian foreign policy of Foreign Secretary Ernest Bevin.[30]

Some left-wing intellectuals—the British novelist and political writer George Orwell and Altiero Spinelli being the most famous examples—were less optimistic about relations between a United States of Europe, even one that followed socialist precepts, and Soviet totalitarianism. Spinelli, breaking decisively with the two mass parties of the Italian Left (the Communists and the Socialists), argued in 1947 that the Soviet Union regarded Western Europe as a "vital space" that it was hoping to "exploit" economically to relieve the Soviet people's misery. Spinelli argued that the USSR could not tolerate ideological competition from a successful Europe and would thus do everything possible to convert Western democracies into repressive regimes similar to its own.[31] The United States, by contrast, Spinelli argued, while it possessed "imperialist temptations and ambitions," also possessed a "sincere desire" to see Europe emerge as an independent liberal state. Insofar as there was a risk of American hegemony, Spinelli contended on many occasions, it came from the shortsighted nationalism of Europe's leaders, who refused to admit that the day of independent nation-states was over.[32]

The Keep Left group numbered only a handful of members of Parliament (MPs). The Action Party performed miserably in the 1946 elections in Italy. Federalist ideas might have remained isolated in an intellectual ghetto had it not been for the intervention in the European debate of Winston Churchill, the internationally renowned British war leader whose Conservative Party had been defeated in the general elections of July 1945. Free from the burdens of office, Churchill was free to speak out on questions of international policy. At the University of Zurich on 19 September 1946, Churchill argued that the countries of Western Europe should "re-create the European family, or as much of it as we can . . . we must build a kind of United States of Europe." According to Churchill, the rock upon which this new federation should be founded was not Britain—"We British have our Commonwealth of Nations . . . why should there not be a European group which could give a sense of enlarged patriotism and common citizenship to the distracted peoples of this turbulent and mighty continent"—but a "partnership between France and Germany." This was the only way, Churchill thought, that France could "recover the moral leadership of Europe."[33]

Subsequently, in May 1947, Churchill became the founder of the United Europe Movement (UEM), a largely British body that commanded substantial support among the traditional establishment in Britain.[34] Its 3,000 active members included numerous MPs, especially Conservatives, and many prominent academics, journalists, and clergymen. Relations with the UEF were not easy at first. The UEM was a much more conservative body whose enthusiasm for European integration was motivated at least in part—to use a phrase from another famous contemporary speech by Churchill—by the Soviet Union's decision to drop an "iron curtain" from Stettin on the Baltic coast to Trieste on the Adriatic. Where the UEF saw European federalism as an opportunity to reassure the Soviets, the UEM regarded it as a way of reinforcing Europe's ability to resist the encroachments of the USSR. Nevertheless, together with several other influential movements such as the French Council for a United Europe, the European Parliamentary Union, the Economic League for European Cooperation and the Christian Democrat *Nouvelles Equipes Internationales*, the two principal associations agreed in December 1947 to form a coordinating committee that would call a "Congress of Europe" at the Hague (Netherlands).[35]

The Congress, which was attended by over 1,200 dignitaries—including 700 parliamentary deputies—from every free country in Europe, took place in May 1948 in the immediate aftermath of the Soviet takeover of Czechoslovakia in February 1948 and the ideologically charged elections in Italy in April. In addition to Churchill, the Christian Democrat prime ministers of Italy (Alcide De Gasperi) and France (Georges Bidault) took part, as did such statesmen as Leon Blum, the Socialist prewar premier of the Popular Front government in France, Paul Reynaud, the last premier of France before the Nazi victory, Konrad Adenauer, and Paul Van Zeeland, a Princeton-educated economist and former premier of Belgium. The Communist parties of Europe boycotted the event, as did the British Labour government (although twenty-three Labour MPs attended in a private capacity). But given Britain's perennially difficult relationship with European unification ever since, it is interesting to observe the distinguished and varied character of the British delegation to the Congress: two future prime ministers, Anthony Eden and Harold Macmillan, were present, as were the philosopher Bertrand Russell, the economist Roy Harrod, the musician Sir Adrian Boult, the poet laureate John Masefield and Sir David Maxwell-Fyfe, a renowned trial lawyer.

The Congress, after an initial address from Churchill, divided into three committees—the Political Committee, chaired by another former French

premier, Paul Ramadier; the Economic and Social Committee, chaired by
Van Zeeland; and the Cultural Committee, chaired by the exiled anti-Franco
historian Salvador de Madariaga. These committees debated motions prepared by the coordinating committee and drew up three broad resolutions.
The Political Committee asserted that it was the "urgent duty" of the nations of Europe to create "an economic and political union" that would "assure security and social progress." It maintained that the "integration of
Germany in a United or Federated Europe" was the only "solution to both
the economic and political aspects of the German problem." Its main practical recommendation was the convening of a "European Assembly," composed of delegations from the national parliaments, that would act as a constituent assembly for the creation of a federal state in Western Europe. It also
proposed that a Commission should draw up a Charter of Human Rights,
adherence to which would be a precondition for membership in the European Federation.[36]

The Economic and Social Committee made a series of pragmatic immediate recommendations for economic policy. Trade restrictions of all kinds
should be abolished "step by step"; coordinated action should be taken to
"pave the way for the free convertibility of currencies"; a common program
should be established to develop agriculture; Europe-wide planning was
urged for the development of core industries such as coal and electricity generation; employment policy should be coordinated so as to produce full employment. The "mobility of labor" should be promoted to the "maximum
possible extent." In addition, it advised that these measures should be only
the prelude to an Economic Union in which capital could move freely, currencies were unified, budgetary and credit policy were centrally coordinated,
a full customs union with a common tariff was established and social legislation was coordinated to common standards. The greater prosperity engendered by these economic measures was held to be an essential precondition
for "the development of a harmonious society in Europe."[37]

The Cultural Committee recommended the creation of a "European Cultural Centre," free of all government interference, whose task would be to
promote cultural exchanges, promote awareness of European unity, encourage the federation of the continent's universities and facilitate scientific research into "the condition of twentieth-century man." A "European Institute
for Childhood and Youth Questions" was also to be established: one of its
tasks, since partially realized in the Erasmus and Socrates programs of the European Union, would have been to "encourage exchanges between the young
people of all classes in Europe, by providing finance and accommodation for
their study, apprenticeship and travel." Like the Political Committee, the Cultural Committee recommended that a Charter of Human Rights should be
drawn up and a European Supreme Court, with supranational jurisdiction,
should be established to ensure the Charter's implementation.[38]

The Congress had two main institutional outcomes. In October 1948, a unified "European Movement" was formally inaugurated in the City Hall of Brussels. The new movement's "Presidents of Honor" were Churchill, Blum, De Gasperi and the prime minister of Belgium, Paul-Henri Spaak. Before then, the European Movement had presented the texts of the Congress's resolutions to the prime ministers and foreign ministers of all the free countries of Europe and had urged them to back the creation of a European Assembly. In August 1948, with the support of the French and Belgian governments, detailed projects for unification were presented to the Permanent Commission of the Western Union.

COOPERATION BETWEEN GOVERNMENTS: THE BRITISH VISION

4 of #the 6"

The Treaty on Western Union (the Brussels Pact) had been signed in Brussels in March 1948 between the governments of Britain, France, Belgium, Luxembourg and the Netherlands. The treaty, as well as being a military alliance against the USSR, bound its participants to develop and harmonize the economic recovery of Europe and to raise the standards of living of their populations. The Permanent Commission was supposed to be the forum for such mutual cooperation between governments in the economic field.

The Treaty on Western Union was a far cry from the much greater degree of integration wished for by the European Movement, but its provisions, like the equally intergovernmental structure of the OEEC, accurately reflected how far Britain was prepared to move down the road towards supranational cooperation in the spring of 1948.

British hostility to a federal state in Europe might seem a foregone conclusion. Interestingly, however, Foreign Secretary Bevin himself had been, for much of 1947, intrigued by the notion of a European Customs Union and was seemingly prepared to acquiesce in the loss of sovereignty such an institution implied. Bevin proposed to the cabinet in September 1947 that Britain should promote some such arrangement and the idea was taken seriously enough for there to be formed an interdepartmental committee at official level with a brief to study the proposal and sum up the pros and cons from the point of view of the British economy. This committee reported in early November 1947 and gave a generally negative assessment of the value of economic union in Western Europe for the economy as a whole.[39] The committee argued that in the long run, greater economic integration in Western Europe would lead to a rationalization of British heavy industry, would expand trade and would strengthen the continent politically. However, it would also lead to damaging short-run competition for the iron and steel industry (which was the centerpiece of the Labour government's nationalization program and which was taken into public ownership in 1949) and would end Britain's advantageous trade relationship with the countries of the Commonwealth. A customs union seemed likely, moreover, to lead to a fully fledged economic union governed by supranational institutions. The notion of conferring sovereignty over the economy to an external body was even harder for a socialist government to accept than it would have been for the Conservatives. Leading Labour ministers, such as the chancellor of the exchequer, Sir Stafford Cripps, were wedded to the goal of the planned expansion of the British economy and were in no mood to subordinate their vision for British society to the economic priorities of foreigners.

In December 1947, however, the disastrous outcome of the London meeting of the Council of Foreign Ministers (CFM) placed ideas of European integration back on the agenda. The CFM had been meeting almost incessantly since September 1945 and was intended to be the forum through which the United States, the USSR and Great Britain, together with France (for European questions) and China (for Asian matters), resolved their differences over the postwar settlement. The meetings, however, became steadily more unpleasant as mutual perceptions of ideological enmity grew. The London meeting, which was preceded by a wave of vituperative Soviet propaganda against the Marshall Plan and the Western European social democrats like Bevin who were collaborating with the alleged American plan to "enslave" Europe, signaled the final inability of the wartime allies to find any agreement on the question of how to deal with the revival of Germany as an independent state (for background details, see the section on the Schuman Plan that follows). The conference ended in acrimony and left Western European politicians in no doubt that, as Bevin expressed the situation in a paper entitled "The First Aim of British Foreign Policy" to the Cabinet in January 1948, "we shall be hard put to it to stem the further encroachments of the Soviet tide" in the absence of "some form of union in Western Europe, whether of a formal or informal character."[40]

The discussion in Cabinet of this paper led to Bevin's famous "Western Union" speech to the House of Commons on 22 January 1948, which included the telling remark, "Great Britain cannot stand outside Europe and regard her problems as quite separate from those of her European neighbors." This comment had an immense impact in continental Europe where, not unreasonably, it was taken as a sign that Britain was preparing to throw her weight and prestige behind the concept of European unity. Certainly, it was the decisive impulse that led to the signature of the Brussels Pact.[41]

Actually, within the Foreign Office, there were many senior officials who saw integration in Western Europe as a golden opportunity for Britain to maintain her place in the world and who were prepared to contemplate the construction of supranational institutions if, by so doing, Britain, Europe and their colonial territories could be fused into what Michael Hogan calls a "Middle Kingdom." Only this way, officials argued with the characteristic humility of the Foreign Office, could Britain prevent itself from being reduced to the role of a pigmy between the two "semi-barbarian states on the cultural periphery."[42] Such dreams of continuing to play a world role, however, took second fiddle within the British government to more pragmatic economic concerns. The Treasury would not encompass any cession of sovereignty that might place limitations on its ability to plan the British economy or that might oblige Britain to trade more in dollars rather than sterling. The policy compromise that emerged in March 1948 was the one explicit in the creation of the Brussels Pact and the OEEC: Britain would engage with Western Europe, but would do so through rigidly intergovernmental institutions.

It is quite clear that Britain regarded her entrance into European affairs as a major development in her foreign policy, but, in fact, her attitude to European integration merely seemed niggardly to both the Americans and the Europeans and ended up antagonizing both. British behavior was "a great source of irritation" to the Americans between 1947 and 1951, but there was a limit to how tough America could get with Britain.[43] Squabbles over the powers of the OEEC paled into insignificance when compared to the wider issues of strategic policy, in which Britain was the United States' most steadfast partner. Britain had taken the lead in the spring of 1948, even before the signature of the Treaty on Western Union, to formalize military cooperation between the United States and Western Europe in a military alliance. In early 1949, these negotiations, which led to the signature in April 1949 of the North Atlantic Treaty, were at a critical stage. American policymakers were afraid that Soviet tanks would roll across the north European plain. Their only ally of any substance against this threat was Britain. Article Five of the Treaty committed its member states to regarding an armed attack against any one of them as an attack against them all. In practice, this meant that Britain and the United States were giving a guarantee that they would risk a third world conflict to defend the Rhine. As British policymakers were well aware, this stand gave Britain diplomatic leverage in other areas of policy. However briefly, the Anglo-American relationship genuinely was special in the spring of 1949.

The British had to tread relatively softly with the Americans. With their fellow Europeans, they were at liberty to be more obdurate. Britain tried to block, and when this proved impossible, to restrain, the attempts of the European movement to implement the resolutions agreed at the Congress of Europe. This was despite the fact that the other members of the Western Union were enthusiastic about pressing towards the Congress's plans to call a European assembly. In October 1948, the Consultative Committee compelled the British to acquiesce in the creation of a study group whose remit was to propose to the governments appropriate measures for the creation of a union between the countries of Europe.

The study group was composed of five British and five French representatives, three representatives from Belgium and the Netherlands, and two delegates from Luxembourg. It was chaired by the veteran French statesman Edouard Herriot. Two proposals were on the table. The first was a Franco-Belgian plan to establish a European Constituent Assembly at once. The British, by contrast, proposed the creation of a Council of European governments without any form of parliamentary supervision. In January 1949, however, Bevin agreed to a compromise by which decision-making power was to be reserved for the Committee of Ministers (as it was named), but an assembly with consultative powers was to be created in tandem. Five nations who had not signed the Brussels Pact—Italy, Ireland, Denmark, Norway and Sweden—were invited to join the new "Council of Europe."[44] This invitation, together with Italy's parallel membership in NATO—marked the end of Italy's diplomatic isolation. Her foreign minister, Count Carlo Sforza, celebrated by immediately pressing the other nations to adopt a more "federal" conception of the Council. Italy even recommended that the new body be called the "European Union." Bevin, who, with the invincible working-class British aptitude for mispronunciation, invariably referred to Sforza as "that man Storzer," dismissed Italy's bumptious diplomacy without difficulty.[45] The Treaty of St. James Palace (London, 15 May 1949) instituting the Council of Europe was, at British insistence, rigorously intergovernmental in scope.

The Council's purpose was to constitute a "closer unity" between the member states through joint action in economic, social, scientific, judicial and administrative fields. Its main institutions, the Committee of Ministers and the Assembly, were both consultative in character. The Committee of Ministers, in which each country disposed of one vote and in which votes required unanimity, was a forum for member states to debate measures proposed by the member states or the assembly, not an executive committee whose decisions were binding upon governments. The Committee had the power only to recommend measures to the governments of the member states. The Consultative Assembly, meanwhile, was able to propose items for debate by the Ministerial committee only if they were passed by a two-thirds majority. It had no legislative power whatever, and even its agenda was to a certain extent controlled by the Committee of Ministers. Paul-Henri Spaak, who was elected first president of the Assembly on 10 August 1949, later said of the Ministerial committee in particular, "Of all the international bodies I have known, I have never found any more timorous or more ineffectual."[46]

Yet the Assembly had opened its first session in Strasbourg amid scenes of great enthusiasm for European unity and to the general expectation that the Council of Europe would be the launch pad for the political and economic integration of the ten states. The assembly seized the initiative by proposing a "supranational political organization" for Western Europe; Britain refused even to contemplate this idea. It was eventually decided to entrust the task of drafting a plan for a political authority with limited but real powers to a "General Political Committee" headed by the French premier, Georges Bidault. This committee worked until mid-1950, but was unable to come up with any plan that could command the assent of the member states. In the meantime, Britain and the Nordic states had vetoed in Council motions passed by the assembly to limit the Council's power of veto and to enable the assembly to petition governments directly.

Another initiative launched by the European Movement in July 1949 had more success. This was the submission of a draft European Convention on Human Rights to the Council. After just over a year's debate and redrafting, the Convention for the Protection of Human Rights and Fundamental Freedoms was signed in Rome on 4 November 1950 by thirteen European states or authorities: Belgium, Denmark, France, Iceland, Ireland, Italy, Luxembourg, the Netherlands, Norway, the Saarland, Turkey, the United Kingdom and West Germany. Greece and Sweden signed a few weeks later. The Charter was a precise guarantee of the traditional liberal freedoms of person, property and conscience: it did not include, much to the disappointment of the Consultative Assembly's socialist delegates, specific guarantees for social rights such as the right to work. To evaluate and adjudicate if breaches of the Convention had occurred, the document created two institutions: the Commission and the Court of Human Rights. The Commission's task was to screen would-be cases according to strict criteria; the Court then judged on the merits of the case. Article 53 of the Convention committed the signatories to the Convention to "abide by the decision of the Court," although no concrete sanctions could be applied in the event of noncompliance. European states have generally tried very hard not to be cited before the Court in the postwar years. The Court's sentences have carried an explicit moral condemnation that democracies have wished to avoid.[47]

Nevertheless, by early 1950, it was evident that the European Movement's hope of leaping to a federal state in a single bound had fallen at the first fence. There would be no constitutional convention to found a "European Union." To this extent, the British, with the help of the Scandinavians and the tacit acquiescence of other important states such as France, had diverted the ambitious plans of the European federalists and imposed their vision of ad hoc cooperation between governments.

Plans for greater European unity were, however, soon to find a new outlet in the functional integration of economic sectors such as coal and steel. The second session of the Assembly of the Council of Europe was dominated by this topic. Enthusiasts for greater integration in Europe—most famously, Jean Monnet—reasoned that if the national governments would not subordinate themselves to federal political institutions, they might nevertheless agree to schemes for the transnational planning and management of key industries. Yet

it was not merely Euro-idealism that motivated this new approach. The growing economic strength and political independence of West Germany was the
decisive factor that drove the nations of Western Europe to delegate the management of heavy industry to pan-European institutions.

THE GERMAN QUESTION AND THE SCHUMAN PLAN

Any vision of the future of Europe had to incorporate Germany—her geographical position and economic potential dictated this—but no question troubled postwar statesmen more than how Germany should be governed. At the
end of the war, Germany had been divided into four zones by the Allied powers. Britain occupied the northwest part of the country. Her zone included the
large cities of Cologne and Hamburg and the Ruhr industrial belt. The United
States administered the center-south, including Frankfurt-am-Main and Mu-
nich. The French occupied the Black Forest region and the Rhineland, as well
as the Saarland, while the Russians occupied Prussia, the rest of eastern Germany and, briefly, Austria. In the spring of 1945, the Soviets transferred a vast
swathe of territory in eastern Germany to Poland. From the point of view of
administration, Berlin was a miniature replica of the country as a whole.

At the Potsdam conference (July–August 1945), the "big three" powers
reached broad agreement on how to treat defeated Germany pending a final
treaty of peace. They decided that Germany should be subjected to "denaz-
ification, demilitarization, democratization, decentralization and decarteliza-
tion."[48] Germany was to be regarded as a single economic entity, governed
by an Allied Control Commission in which each of the three powers, plus
France, would have a veto. The Allies would establish democratically elected
governments in the zones they controlled. The thorny issue of reparations—
the Russians had already looted eastern Germany of much of its industrial
plant and machinery by August 1945—was resolved by allowing each power
to take industrial equipment from the zone it occupied. The Soviet Union
would receive additional reparations from the heavily industrialized British
zone and from the zone controlled by the Americans. In return, the USSR
promised to divert foodstuffs from its (largely agricultural) zone to feed the
large cities in the West.

This broad deal never resulted in a final peace treaty. Neither Britain and
the United States nor the USSR was able to keep its word. The Soviet Union
proved unwilling to allow genuinely free democratic competition in its zone
and also reneged on its promised shipments of agricultural produce to the
West. Britain and the United States in their turn, suspended shipments of industrial plant to the USSR in the spring of 1946 for financial and political reasons. So long as the shipments continued, the western zones of Germany, particularly the densely populated industrial area controlled by the British, could

not resume production at a high enough level to buy food to feed themselves and had to rely on the charity of the occupying authorities. This was costly enough for the United States, but for economically enfeebled Britain it was an insupportable burden. In the winter of 1946–1947, British rations were cut to feed the people of Germany—hardly a popular move so soon after the end of the war. In January 1947, Britain and the United States merged their zones to create "Bizonia," which was organized as a self-governing federal state under the supervision of the occupying authorities. To the Soviet Union (indeed, to France) it must have looked as if the "capitalist" powers were re-building Germany against them.

These arguments and fears provided the background to the London Council of Foreign Ministers in November–December 1947 mentioned previously. After the breakdown of the London talks, the Cold War began in earnest. The Communist coup in Czechoslovakia in February 1948, the signature of the Brussels Pact, the April 1948 elections in Italy followed in swift succession. In this context, consolidating the West's hold on Germany became a strategic imperative. Between February and June 1948, the United States decided to extend Marshall Plan aid to Germany and to call for the formation of a West German government (an idea that was greeted with great caution by the Germans themselves, who feared—rightly—that it would lead to the dismemberment of their nation). These decisions provoked the USSR to walk out of the Allied Control Commission in March 1948. In June 1948, currency unification of the three Western zones took place and the Deutsche Mark (DM) was introduced. The USSR responded by cutting off road, rail and river transport to Berlin. Only the logistically miraculous Berlin airlift, whereby a constant stream of American and British transport planes carried foodstuffs, fuel and other necessities to the trapped citizens of the British, American and French sectors of the city, kept two million Berliners alive over the following winter. By the time the Soviet blockade was called off in May 1949, some 277,000 flights had been made and some 2.4 million tons of cargo delivered.[49]

France acquiesced in Anglo-American policy towards Germany from June 1948 onwards largely because she had no choice. America was calling the shots and had decided that European recovery and security required a strong Germany. France's agreement nevertheless marked a drastic U-turn in her foreign policy. After Potsdam, successive French governments had argued for the independence of the Rhineland from the rest of Germany (which would have provided France with a useful buffer against the revival of a strong Germany), for the internationalization of the Ruhr, and for the diversion of German coal and steel production to the French economy. The Monnet plan to reconstruct the French economy, in essence, aimed at using American money and German coal shipments to make France an industrial heavyweight in the space of five years. But the events of the spring of 1948 made several uncomfortable truths clear to French statesmen. America was intent on rebuilding Germany as a bulwark against the Soviet Union; the main military danger to France was presented by the USSR, not Germany (and, therefore, France needed to placate the Americans); some sort of deal would be necessary with the nascent West German political authorities. As the French statesman Georges Bidault, with a copious spoonful of rhetoric to help the medicine go down, told a disgruntled French National Assembly on 11 June 1948:

> We must build up Europe, and we must find some place in it for Germany. We will do all we can to create a united Europe, for this is the only way we can reconcile the countries of Europe. I wish to say that France would be wise to reconcile itself eventually with the presence of Germany in Europe and the free world, for no other reconciliation would be possible.[50]

The price for French acquiescence was a share in the direction of the Ruhr coalfield. Before 1939, a cartel of German producers had prevented France from buying the coal she needed to fuel her own steel industry. France was determined that this would not happen again. After the collapse of the CFM in London, France battled hard in negotiations between the three Western Allies on the future of West Germany to ensure that "access to the coal, coke and steel of the Ruhr, which was previously subject to the exclusive control of Germany, [should] be in the future guaranteed without discrimination to the countries of Europe cooperating in the common good."[51]

To this end, France urged the establishment of an "International Authority" for the Ruhr. But this solution was unpopular three times over. The French were unsatisfied with the substantive powers accorded to the Authority to manage German heavy industry directly; the Americans doubted its necessity; and the Germans resented the restriction of their national sovereignty over industrial policy.[52] After months of tangled negotiations, the Authority came into being in December 1948, but it was too weak to plan or control the growth of German industrial production, which then, with the active stimulation and support of the American military authorities, began to work at full capacity. West German steel production, which had been restricted to less than three million metric tons in 1947 (France produced nearly six million), surged to over nine million tons in 1949 (the same as France). In 1950, Germany produced twelve million tons; France, less than nine million.[53] The *Wirtschaftswunder* (economic miracle) that would return Germany to its position as the economic powerhouse of Europe had begun.

Contemporaneously, West Germany achieved provisional nationhood. Her Basic Law (Constitution) was adopted in May 1949, and the first West German elections took place in August of that year, resulting in a narrow victory for the Christian Democrats (CDU-CSU) who took 139 seats in the Bundestag to the 131 of the Social Democrats (SPD). The CDU formed a coalition government with the Liberals (FDP) and the moderate nationalist "German Party." The chancellor of the new German state was Adenauer, who had emerged as the leader of the CDU. A veteran politician from the Rhineland (he was almost seventy-four when he took office), Adenauer was convinced of the need for a Franco-German rapprochement: indeed, he had supported the creation of a customs union between the two countries as long ago as 1925. In two interviews with an American journalist later in March 1950, Adenauer proposed first a Franco-German political union and, when this first plan had been widely dismissed as a publicity stunt both in Germany and abroad, a Franco-German economic union, with a legislature drawn from the two countries' parliaments, and an executive "organ" responsible to the legislature. Europe, Adenauer argued, should remember how the 1834 *Zollverein* customs union had been the prelude to German unification.[54] Here, finally, was a German statesman who wanted peaceful cooperation with France, not conflict.

The Americans were also pressing hard for an improvement in Franco-German relations. American efforts to assist Europe intensified in the wake of the Berlin crisis. Marshall Plan aid for April 1949 to June 1950 was over $5,000 million; in September 1949, Congress, stimulated by President Harry Truman's admission that the United States had lost its nuclear monopoly, approved the Military Assistance Act and doled out a further $1,000 million in military aid to Europe. The quid pro quo for this largesse (of which France received more than her fair share) was the reintegration of Germany into Western Europe. In the fall of 1949, Secretary of State Dean Acheson pressurized France into normalizing relations with West Germany by the spring of 1950.[55] Improving relations with Germany became an "obsession" for French foreign minister Robert Schuman, who, as a native of Lorraine, an area of France occupied by Germany after the Franco-Prussian war of 1870, had only become a French citizen in 1919 at the age of thirty-two.[56]

Schuman gave his name to an initiative at the beginning of May 1950 that has been called "one of the key moments of the century": the plan for the creation of a coal and steel community between France and Germany.[57] This plan was the brainchild of Jean Monnet, and it bore his trademark preference for the technocratic resolution of complex political issues. Monnet approached Schuman in April 1950 proposing the internationalization of the French and German coal and steel industries. Instead of national governments setting the normative framework within which the two industries would work, a supranational "High Authority" would exercise the executive role. Schuman agreed, and Monnet and his advisers drew up the text of the declaration announcing the plan in conditions of great secrecy.[58] Adenauer and the German government obviously had to be informed, but were told only on the eve of the announcement through a personal letter from Schuman to the German chancellor, hand-delivered by a senior French foreign ministry official, that made explicit reference to Adenauer's March interviews.[59] The Americans were informed only on 7 May 1950 when Acheson visited Paris. The American secretary of state recorded his reactions in one of his memoirs:

> After a few words of greeting . . . Schuman began to expound what later became known as the "Schuman plan," so breath-taking a step towards the unification of Europe that at first I did not grasp it. . . . Schuman implored us to treat what he was about to tell us in the greatest of confidence, not to speak to any of our colleagues about it, not to send cables, or to have memoranda transcribed. For he had discussed the proposal only with the Premier (Bidault) and one or two members of the Cabinet. The next step would be to consult the whole Cabinet, and, if it approved, then to make some public statement . . . after that, France's neighbors would be approached.[60]

The reason for the secrecy was apparent. In the unsettled context of postwar French politics, untimely disclosure of the plan might have set off a damaging political crisis. Even more important, however, Schuman and Monnet were determined that the British, this time, would not sabotage the supranational dimension of the scheme. The plan would be presented as a fait accompli and only countries that acknowledged the principle of supranational government would be allowed to participate in the detailed negotiations. Their insistence on this point soothed the Americans' disappointment at being excluded from the plan's formulation. John Foster Dulles, a committed supporter of European Unity who would become secretary of state under Dwight Eisenhower just eighteen months later, described Schuman's initiative as "brilliantly creative"; President Truman himself lauded the plan as an "act of constructive statesmanship."[61] This was despite the fact that many American industrialists were worried that the putative community might be a protectionist steel cartel under another name.

Schuman secured cabinet approval the following day and on 9 May made his famous declaration. In addition to its historic proposal to "place the whole of Franco-German coal and steel production . . . under a common 'High Authority' within the framework of an organization open to participation by the other countries of Europe," Schuman's speech contained language that hinted at a more hard-bitten approach to unifying Europe. Instead of beginning, as the Congress of Europe had wanted, with a political solution to Europe's division, Schuman suggested that Europe should advance step-by-step through economic integration: "Europe will not be made all at once, or according to a single, general plan. It will be built through concrete achievements, which first create a de facto solidarity." A "wider and deeper community" would emerge once economies were more fully integrated: action on the "limited but decisive point" of coal and steel production was the best starting point since "the pooling of coal and steel production" would ensure that "any war between France and Germany" was "not merely unthinkable, but materially impossible."[62]

Beneath the high moral tone of the declaration, French national interest was alive and well. Among other things, the declaration insisted that "the task" of the High Authority would be to secure "the supply of coal and steel on identical terms to the French and German markets, as well as the markets of the other member countries." There is no doubt that France saw the Schuman Plan as the only realistic way that it could exercise continued supervision over German economic growth. Monnet had written a briefing paper for the French cabinet on 3 May that had painted a stark picture of French economic subservience to Germany in the absence of a pan-European deal. Monnet argued that the Americans were intent on building up Germany as an ally in the Cold War. Sooner or later, probably sooner, German industrial competition would present France with the grim choice of protecting its steel industry or accepting German superiority in this field. It would be better, Monnet suggested, to make a deal with West Germany while she was still weak and use the proposed High Authority to ensure that there was a balanced industrial relationship between the two countries.[63]

According to Adenauer's most comprehensive biographer, the German chancellor was initially suspicious of Monnet's motives. Monnet was the personification of international cooperation against Germany in the two wars. Might the Schuman Plan not be a subtle plot to retard German economic growth, rather than a mutually beneficial opportunity to expand production?[64] Once the two men had met each other on 23 May, this suspicion disappeared. Adenauer was impressed by Monnet's intelligence and commitment to the ideal of European unity. In their talks, he approved Monnet's insistence that nations should adhere to the plan on the basis of what Schuman had called "a leap in the dark" during questioning on 9 May. That is to say, all would-be members of the coal and steel community would begin detailed negotiations having accepted the supranational role of the High Authority in advance. Nations would have to agree to pool sovereignty if they wanted a place at the table.

It was precisely this point, as Monnet foresaw from the first, that was the sticking point for the British. Ernest Bevin was angered by the way in which the French had sprung the plan on the British, but, in truth, had little cause for complaint. In the summer of 1949, Britain had eased her balance-of-payments problems by devaluing sterling by 25 percent. This move, which naturally had a significant disruptive impact on the French economy (since it made French exports to Britain much more expensive), had been carried out in conditions of total secrecy, with only a handful of top Washington officials being informed in advance. The real cause, probably, of Bevin's rage was consciousness of the dilemma that the Schuman Plan presented for British policy. It compelled Britain to make a choice that she did not want to make and which, in some ways, she regarded as being beneath her dignity. In 1950, Britain was still, by some distance, the largest producer of both coal and steel in Western Europe. What France and Germany were proposing was, in the absence of British participation, bound to become a challenge to British supremacy in what were then the key sectors of the European economy. If Britain were not in the Community, her coal and steel would inevitably be excluded from the rapidly growing markets of Western Europe. On the other hand, if she entered the Community, her highly protected coal and steel industries would feel the full brunt of low-wage competition from the continent. The mere fact of her joining, moreover, would signal to the world that Britain was a diminished force; that she was no longer an imperial power, but merely first among equals in Western Europe.

As so often, purely contingent factors played a role. Bevin and Cripps—the key ministers, and the two most considerable figures in the government—were both critically ill (both died within a few months of the Schuman announcement) but Clement Attlee, the premier, was reluctant to substitute them at such a delicate moment. In the absence of a political lead, negotiations were carried on with Monnet throughout May 1950 by senior civil servants, at least one of whom, Roger Makins, has since been (slightly anachronistically) described as a "rabid Euro-sceptic."[65] Monnet himself appears to have found the British officials that he negotiated with to be viscerally anti-European. In his memoirs, he noted that the British seemed to have no confidence in the ability of the continental countries to resist Communism.[66]

Whatever the prejudices of British officialdom, the Monnet "talks about talks" were hardly made first priority. Hugo Young records a junior minister at the Foreign Office as saying that the Schuman Plan discussions were handled in a "curiously off-hand way" by officials.[67] Certainly, all accounts agree that the preliminary negotiations with Monnet were characterized by mutual incomprehension. The British wanted to get straight into discussions about how the Community would be regulated, asking highly technical questions about coal and steel pricing and sale; Monnet insisted that such substantive discussions were conditional upon a public declaration of willingness to accept supranational institutions and, especially, the role of the High Authority. The two leading civil servants, Sir Edward Bridges (permanent secretary to the Treasury) and Sir William Strang (permanent secretary at the Foreign Office) eventually reported to Attlee that agreement was impossible on Monnet's terms, and on 3 June 1950 the Cabinet, presided over by the deputy prime minister, Herbert Morrison, concurred. Morrison's own contribution to the debate over the Schuman Plan was famously to say: "It's no good. We can't do it. The Durham miners would never wear it."[68]

In the subsequent Commons debate on 26–27 June, Attlee stated that the British government was not willing to accept the principle that the most important and vital economic forces of the country should be transferred to "an irresponsible body that is appointed by no-one and responsible to no-one."[69]

Although Anthony Eden, the spokesman on foreign affairs for the opposition Conservatives, described the plan as a "fusion of sovereignty" rather than a loss and intimated that he was willing to accept the principle of supranational institutions "if we were satisfied with the conditions and safeguards," few on either side of the House openly dissented from the government's view that staying out was the wisest course of action. A rare exception was a man making his maiden speech—Edward Heath, the man who would eventually take Britain into the European Economic Community (EEC).

It should be noted, however, that Attlee's comment was in fact a perfectly reasonable objection to the Schuman Plan as it was originally formulated. But if Britain had been willing to concede some cession of sovereignty, she would have participated in the negotiations to create the Coal and Steel Community and would have inserted democratic safeguards into the treaty, as well as obtaining a discrete degree of protection for her coal and steel industries. This is exactly what the Dutch and Italian governments did, and Britain, who would have been offering to open her massive coal and steel industry to competition, would have been in a far stronger position to get its own way than either country.

Edmund Dell, a former Labour minister and Eurocrat turned historian, regards Britain's refusal even to join the negotiations as a disastrous misjudgment—"the British abdication of leadership in Europe." In Dell's opinion, the initial negotiations with Monnet were handled astonishingly badly: "Unprepared officials led unprepared ministers."[70] In his view—and after reading his closely researched account, it is difficult to disagree—the top civil servants convinced themselves that the plan was unacceptable both on grounds of national principle and of feasibility (Monnet's reluctance to address technical issues left its scars), and they briefed an exhausted and intellectually supine Labour government to that effect. Yet even without the historian's privileged vantage point, it ought to have been obvious to even the most insular Briton that there were powerful forces tending to the scheme's success. The plan removed the main cause of friction between Germany and France, had won the immediate and enthusiastic support of the Americans, enlarged the domestic market for the Benelux countries and was Germany and Italy's return ticket to the society of civilized nations.

But the problem was not just preoccupation with abstract issues of sovereignty, or with the plan's possibilities of economic success. Britain's politicians, as Morrison's remark illustrates, had to take public opinion into account. The *Daily Express,* then Britain's most influential mass circulation newspaper, argued on 11 May 1950 that the Schuman Plan was "a deliberate and concerted attempt to oblige us to accept the United States of Europe"— the rhetoric has a familiar ring to anybody who has lived through the heart searching provoked in Britain by the Treaty of Maastricht. But even had there not been a chauvinistic press baying against any concession to the Europeans,

it seems unlikely that a Labour government would have been prepared to surrender control over the recently nationalized coal and steel industries to a
High Authority nominated by largely Christian Democratic governments.
Labour believed it was in politics to abolish capitalism, not to make capitalism
work better. With what *The Economist* called the Labour Party's "almost phe-
nomenal gift for bad timing"—if bad timing it was—the Labour Party chose
to publish, in mid-June 1950, its official statement of policy on the European
question, a pamphlet called *European Unity.*[71] This document essentially revived the intellectual argument between progressive socialists and Federal
Union in the late 1930s and early 1940s by asserting that Britain would only
be willing to cooperate in schemes of European unification with countries
that had adopted the key socialist policies of public ownership, full employment and economic planning. Socialism came first in the order of values; Europe a poor second. Besides, the pamphlet added:

> In every respect except distance we in Britain are closer to our kinsmen in Aus-
> tralia and New Zealand on the far side of the world than we are to Europe. We
> are closer in language and origins, in social habits and institutions, in political
> outlook and economic interest. The economies of the Commonwealth coun-
> tries are complementary to that of Britain to a degree which those of Western
> Europe could never equal.[72]

Robert Marjolin—who had an excellent vantage point—insisted in his
memoirs that the Europeans would have gone "much further in the direction wanted by the Americans had it not been for the stubborn resistance of
the British to the idea of committing themselves irrevocably to the Continent."[73] At the very least, a customs union would have been formed. Given
the wide agreement on economic issues reached at the Congress of Europe,
and the enthusiasm generated by the Schuman Plan, this assessment seems
plausible. But though Britain had the power to obstruct and delay the path
of European integration, she was too much in debt to the United States to
insist on having a free hand in Western Europe. Had Britain emerged from
the war with a booming economy and her overseas investments intact,
Britain would have taken the leadership of Europe by default. Western Europe would have become as much part of the sterling zone as the Commonwealth. The other European countries would have looked to her for
loans and export markets. But Britain was as much a beggar as everybody
else and had huge demands upon the few resources that she possessed. She
was in no position to impose her vision of Europe on anybody. She retained
the power to block federalist initiatives—witness her deft emasculation of the
Council of Europe—but she was not strong enough to overcome the profound belief of both the European political class and the Washington élite
that—in Schuman's words—"le morcellement de l'Europe est devenu un ab-
surde anachronisme."[74]

This weakness became crucial in May 1950. The Schuman Plan starkly exposed the limitations of British power. Unlike the Council of Europe, it was a concrete initiative that made sound economic and political sense. The national interests of the United States, France and West Germany, and the supranationalist principles of their chief policymakers coincided. Against this array of forces, there was nothing for Britain to do but make the best of a bad job and attempt to influence the new construction from within. The Labour Party's determination not to compromise its socialist program, the ingrained mentalities of upper officialdom, deep fear of economic competition and an increasingly misplaced sense of national grandeur prevented Britain from seeing this critical fact. As Diane Kunz argues, Britain's leaders "persisted in seeing Britain lodged within three interlocking circles: with the Continent, with the Empire and Commonwealth, and with the United States. To join a European union would be to favor one relationship to the detriment of others."[75] The result of this understanding of Britain's place in the world was to ensure that British foreign policy drifted and her national influence declined. The experienced American policymaker George W. Ball, a close friend and collaborator of Jean Monnet, was surely right when he said, "Had Britain embraced the original Schuman proposal, it could have dominated the evolution not merely of the Coal and Steel Community, but also of the European Economic Community."[76]

History should not be written in the subjunctive. It is nevertheless interesting to speculate whether the subsequent sneering hostility of a large part of the British political élite to the European project can be traced back to a gnawing remorse at Britain's failure to emerge as *primus inter pares* in the 1945–1950 period. For in the following two decades, defeated France and once-Nazi Germany, putting aside their ancient rivalry, became the locus of the Middle Kingdom. Britain, after her refusal to make the "leap in the dark," carped from the sidelines and was forced to watch, both enviously and angrily, as her increasingly cooperative neighbors superseded her in economic performance and matched her in international prestige.

NOTES

1. Konrad Adenauer, *Memoirs 1945–1953* (London: Weidenfeld and Nicholson, 1966), 21–22.

2. Adenauer, *Memoirs 1945–1953*, 37.

3. See Richard Mayne, *The Recovery of Europe* (New York: Harper & Row, 1970), 29–37, for a brilliant description of the continent's economic breakdown.

4. Alan Milward, *The Reconstruction of Europe* (London: Routledge, 1992), 28–29, for the figures cited.

5. Robert Marjolin, *Architect of European Unity: Memoirs 1911–1986* (London: Weidenfeld and Nicholson, 1989), 228.

6. Diane B. Kunz, *Butter and Guns: America's Cold War Economic Diplomacy* (New York: Free Press, 1997), 50.

7. For brief details of the French Communists' fall from grace, see Frank Giles, *The Locust Years: The Story of the Fourth French Republic* (London: Secker & Warburg, 1991), 67–70. For Italy, see Paul Ginsborg, *A History of Contemporary Italy* (London: Penguin, 1990), 110–14.

8. See François Duchêne, *Jean Monnet: First Statesman of Interdependence* (New York: Doubleday, 1995), ch. 5 *passim*.

9. Milward, *Reconstruction of Europe*, 36.

10. *Foreign Relations of the United States* (FRUS), 1947, vol. 3, 230–32.

11. Figures from Milward, *Reconstruction of Europe*, 26.

12. Milward, *Reconstruction of Europe*, 50–51.

13. Michael Hogan, *The Marshall Plan: America, Britain and the Reconstruction of Western Europe* (Cambridge: Cambridge University Press, 1987), 73.

14. Hogan, *Marshall Plan*, 74.

15. Hogan, *Marshall Plan*, 79.

16. Hogan, *Marshall Plan*, 87.

17. Marjolin, *Architect of European Unity*, 195.

18. Quoted Max Beloff, *The United States and the Unity of Europe* (London: Faber and Faber, 1963), 35.

19. The phrase was coined by Charles S. Maier in his essay "The Politics of Productivity: Foundations of American International Economic Policy after 1945," in *Between Power and Plenty: The Foreign Economic Policies of Advanced Industrial States*, ed. P. Katzenstein (Madison: University of Wisconsin Press, 1978).

20. See A. J. P. Taylor, *The Trouble Makers* (London: Penguin, 1985), 13–14.

21. R. W. Seton-Watson, *Britain and the Dictators* (Cambridge: Cambridge University Press, 1938), 94.

22. H. N. Brailsford, *Towards a New League* (London: New Statesman & Nation, 1936). For a discussion of this book, see Mark Gilbert, "Foreign Policy and Propaganda in the Progressive Press 1936–1945" (Ph.D. thesis, University of Wales, 1990), especially ch. 2, "The Progressive Left and Appeasement."

23. Examples of this somewhat naïve belief are G. D. H. Cole, *War Aims* (London: Gollancz, 1939); Kingsley Martin, *100 Million Allies If We Choose* (London: Gollancz, 1940); Richard Acland, *Unser Kampf* (London: Penguin, 1940).

24. H. N. Brailsford, *The Future of Germany* (London: National Peace Committee, 1943).

25. "Pastoralization" was particularly espoused by then Treasury secretary Henry Morgenthau in 1943–1944. For Roosevelt's policy towards Germany, see Robert Dallek, *Franklin D. Roosevelt and American Foreign Policy 1932–1945* (New York: Oxford University Press, 1979), especially ch. 15, "1944: Victories and Doubts."

26. For an account of the birth of Federal Union, see John Pinder and Richard Mayne, *The Pioneers* (Basingstoke, U.K.: Macmillan, 1990), especially chs.1–2.

27. See Walter Lipgens, *A History of European Integration 1945–1947* (Oxford: Clarendon Press, 1987), 53–57 and 114–116, for a fuller account. For wartime plans for European Unity, see Walter Lipgens, ed., *Documents on the History of European Integration* (Berlin: De Gruyter, 1985), two vols.

28. Lipgens, *History of European Integration*, 376.

29. See Lipgens, *History of European Integration*, 380–85, for details of the "Third Force" concept.

30. For the "Keep Left" group, see Alan Bullock, *Ernest Bevin* (Oxford: Oxford University Press, 1985) 395–98.

31. Altiero Spinelli, *Europa Terza Forza*, ed. Piero Graglia (Bologna, Italy: Il Mulino 2000), 13.

32. Spinelli, *Europa Terza Forza*, 158.

33. Quotation based upon the text given in Uwe Kitzinger, *The European Common Market and Community* (New York: Barnes & Noble, 1967), 35–37.

34. For Churchill's attitudes on European integration, see most recently Roy Jenkins, *Churchill* (London: Macmillan, 1999), 813–19. Lipgens, *History of European Integration*, gives a short account of the formation of the UEM, 323–34.

35. This is a simplified account of a very complex set of negotiations between the various federalist groups. See Lipgens, *History of European Integration*, 657–84, for further details.

36. G. Sharp, *Europe Unites! The Hague Congress and After* (London: Hollis & Carter, 1949), 38–39.

37. Sharp, *Europe Unites!* 68–71.

38. Sharp, *Europe Unites!* 88–89.

39. John W. Young, *Britain, France and the Unity of Europe* (Leicester, U.K.: Leicester University Press, 1984), 67–68.

40. Bullock, *Ernest Bevin*, 516–19.

41. Paul-Henri Spaak, *The Continuing Battle* (London: Weidenfeld and Nicholson, 1971), 144–46.

42. These were the views of two influential Foreign Office officials, Gladwyn Jebb and Arnold Toynbee. Quoted in Hogan, *Marshall Plan*, 113.

43. Diane Kunz, *Butter and Guns*, 51.

44. See A. H. Robertson, *The Council of Europe: Its Structure, Function and Achievements* (London: Stevens, 1961), 6–7.

45. Bullock, *Ernest Bevin*, 82.

46. Spaak, *Continuing Battle*, 266.

47. This paragraph drew mostly upon Gordon L. Weil, *The European Convention on Human Rights* (Leyden: Sythoff, 1963).

48. Henry Ashby Turner, *Germany from Partition to Unification* (New Haven, Conn.: Yale University Press, 1992), 12.

49. Figures quoted in P. M. H. Bell, *The World since 1945* (London: Arnold, 2001), 93.

50. Georges Bidault, *Resistance: The Autobiography of Georges Bidault* (London: Weidenfeld and Nicholson, 1967), 161.

51. Milward, *Reconstruction of Europe*, 154.

52. Richard Mayne, *La Comunità europea* (Milan, Italy: Garzanti, 1963), 101.

53. Figures from Milward, *Reconstruction of Europe*, 367.

54. Hans-Peter Schwarz, *Konrad Adenauer: German Statesman and Politician in a Period of War, Revolution and Reconstruction*, vol. 1 (Providence, R.I.: Berghahn, 1995), 496.

55. James Chace, *Acheson* (New York: Simon & Schuster, 1998), 242–43.

56. Duchêne, *Jean Monnet*, 200.

57. Duchêne, *Jean Monnet*, 181.

58. This sentence reflects the standard account given by Monnet himself and what Milward calls his "disciples." Milward argues in *The Reconstruction of Europe*, 395–96 that there was a considerable input from the French foreign ministry. He adds that "ultimate credit for the Schuman plan must go to Schuman himself . . . he had the courage to seize the moment and translate into reality . . . suggestions and ideas which the fearfulness of others had left trembling on the brink of actuality" (396).

59. Schwarz, *Konrad Adenauer*, 504.

60. Acheson quoted in David S. McClellan, *Dean Acheson: The State Department Years* (New York: Dodd, Mead, 1976), 251.

61. Hogan, *Marshall Plan*, 367.

62. Quotation based upon the text in Kitzinger, *European Common Market and Community*, 37–39.

63. Schwarz, *Konrad Adenauer*, 510.

64. Schwarz, *Konrad Adenauer*, 509.

65. Hugo Young, *This Blessed Plot* (London: Macmillan, 1998), 56.

66. Jean Monnet, *Mémoires* (Paris: Fayard, 1971), 316.

67. Young, *This Blessed Plot*, 65.

68. Quoted Pinder and Mayne, *The Pioneers*, 120.

69. Quoted Edmund Dell, *The British Abdication of Leadership in Europe* (Oxford: Oxford University Press, 1995), 176.

70. Dell, *British Abdication*, 296.

71. Bullock, *Ernest Bevin*, 781.

72. The Labour Party, *European Unity* (London, 1950), 4.

73. Marjolin, *Architect*, 213.

74. "The chopped up character of Europe has become an absurd anachronism." Robert Schuman, *Pour L'Europe* (Paris: Editions Nagel, 1963), 19.

75. Kunz, *Butter and Guns*, 51.

76. George W. Ball, *The Past Has Another Pattern* (New York: Norton, 1982), 216.

3

Spillovers and Setbacks

From the Schuman Plan to the Common Market 1950–1958

The first half of the 1950s was characterized by both progress and setbacks for proponents of greater European integration. The Schuman Plan to integrate the coal and steel industries of France, Germany and other willing nations led to the signature of the European Coal and Steel Community Treaty in April 1951 by a core group of six nations: in addition to West Germany, Belgium, Italy, Luxembourg and the Netherlands all adhered to the Schuman–Monnet initiative. The ECSC was ratified by the parliaments of the six nations by the spring of 1952 and the new organization began operations in August 1952. It seemed as if, to quote Jean Monnet's famous address to the first ECSC assembly, "the United States of Europe have begun."[1]

Europhoria, however, was dashed by developments in the defense field. Following the outbreak of war in Korea in June 1950, the United States pushed hard not only for the rehabilitation of West Germany, but for its rearmament and integration into the defense effort of the western democracies. The rest of Western Europe, led by France, fought shy of such rapid normalization of the West German state. In October 1950, the French prime minister, René Pleven, prompted by Monnet, proposed the establishment of a European Defense Community (EDC) as a way of resolving the problem. This suggestion, which, after some initial hesitation won the enthusiastic support of the Americans, had a less fortunate outcome than the Schuman Plan. The EDC treaty was signed by the six member states of the ECSC in Paris in May 1952. Unlike the ECSC treaty, however, the EDC became the object of a political clash in the country that had originally sponsored it. In August 1954, to the despair of European federalists, a coalition of Gaullists and Communists blocked the EDC's ratification in the French National Assembly.

49

The differing fates of the ECSC and the EDC underline an important point that provides this chapter with its main theme. The nations of Western Europe were ultimately cautious about the amount of national sovereignty that they were prepared to pool in European institutions. The ECSC treaty was ratified because, compared to the original Schuman–Monnet plan, a considerable degree of supervision by national governments was built into the treaty. The EDC treaty, by contrast, would, if ratified, have represented a remarkable voluntary surrender of sovereignty by the six countries. The treaty passed effective command over national armed forces to the NATO commander in Europe, envisaged the creation of a common authority in charge of planning military procurement policy, and anticipated the birth of a European Political Community (EPC). Over the winter of 1952–1953, members of the ECSC assembly drew up a blueprint for a federal state in Europe, although their ideas did not survive the attentions of the national governments in the subsequent spring. The truth is that the EDC was a bridge too far—and not only for the French. What its failure taught European governments was that integration was easier in the economic sphere than in those areas, such as defense and foreign affairs, that went to the heart of national sovereignty, and that even within the economic sphere, national governments were not going to leave supranational institutions to operate unsupervised.

The treaty establishing the European Economic Community (EEC), signed in Rome in March 1957, reflected this lesson. The EEC treaty built upon the liberalization of trade launched at the beginning of the 1950s by the creation, under the auspices of the OEEC, of the European Payments Union (EPU), by setting up a customs union. The economic area thus created was to be governed, for the most part, through institutionally enshrined interstate negotiations, not supranational institutions. The EEC was an institutional hybrid of the OEEC and the ECSC. Yet its creation was heralded by academic theorists as being the harbinger of a harmonious state of "community" in Western Europe. The "functionalist" school of international relations, whose leading figure was the American scholar Ernst Haas, purported to have discerned, in the 1950s, an irreversible trend towards greater political integration among the countries of Western Europe. As Europe's institutions began to influence daily life across the Six, a process of "spillover" would occur; Community institutions would take on more and more responsibility and would substitute national institutions as the point of reference for political action.

This teleological interpretation of European integration (the view, in other words, that the successive negotiations undertaken by European nations to manage their economic affairs are part of a historical process that will issue in a discernible outcome) has influenced scholarly interpretations of European integration ever since. Realist theorists—the functionalists' main rivals—by contrast see no pattern in European integration, merely a series of negotiations in which the member states guardedly pool or delegate national sovereignty over areas of political and economic life in exchange for concrete economic or political gains. This chapter concludes with a discussion of the realist historian Alan Milward's attack on the functionalist school and with a full exposition and analysis of Ernst Haas's book, *The Uniting of Europe*.

THE COAL AND STEEL COMMUNITY

The treaty instituting the ECSC was signed in Paris on 18 April 1951 after an acrimonious negotiation that had required all the diplomatic skills of Jean Monnet, and a good deal of American arm twisting, to reach a conclusion. Even after the treaty was signed, the wrangling continued. The decision over where to base the High Authority envisaged by the Schuman Plan and now incorporated into the treaty was particularly fierce. Strasbourg, Turin and Saarbrücken were all mooted. The Belgian foreign minister, Paul Van Zeeland, whose commitment to greater supranational government had been so striking during the Congress of Europe, stood out so vehemently for the Belgian city of Liège at an eighteen-hour meeting of the foreign ministers in July 1951 that the Dutch delegation walked out in disgust. Luxembourg, 80 percent of whose economic production was derived from its coal and steel industries, was the compromise eventually arrived at. It was during this meeting that Konrad Adenauer (who was foreign minister as well as chancellor of West Germany) was overheard by journalists to mutter "poor Europe, poor Europe" as he stalked out of the talks for a reviving cup of coffee.[2] The pattern for all future Community negotiations involving a significant reduction of national prerogatives had been set.

The preamble to the ECSC treaty expressed sentiments in striking contrast to the jockeying for national advantage that characterized the negotiations both before and after the signature of the treaty. The "High Contracting Parties" recognized that "Europe can be built only through practical achievements which will first of all create real solidarity and through the establishment of common bases for economic development" and hence resolved to "substitute for age-old rivalries the merging of their essential interests." Their intention was to create "the basis for a broader and deeper community among peoples long divided by bloody conflicts and to lay the foundations for institutions which will give a direction to a destiny henceforth shared."

The last sentence is particularly interesting. It reflected the Monnet–Schuman thesis that by agreeing to take part in the Schuman Plan, the six nations had made an existential choice in favor of building supranational institutions in Europe (the "leap in the dark"). There was as yet no clear final goal, however. The way in which the ECSC developed would itself determine what the final shape of Europe's institutions would be.

The economic philosophy of the new organization recalled the proposals of the economic subcommittee of the Congress of Europe. The ECSC was intended to ensure the twin goals of economic liberalism and social solidarity. On the one hand, the ECSC was a pan-European effort to prevent the restoration of the prewar protectionist cartels in the coal and steel industries; on the other hand, it was a planning body charged with softening the social costs of modernizing the industries. The treaty defined the ECSC's tasks, among other things, as ensuring a steady supply of coal and steel to the market, guaranteeing equality of access to the sources of production for all consumers, monitoring prices, providing a climate that would encourage companies to expand and improve production, promoting "improved working conditions and an improved standard of living for the workers in each of the industries for which it is responsible" (art. 3e). More generally, it was to "promote the orderly expansion and modernization of production, and the improvement in quality, with no protection against competing industries that is not justified by improper action on their part or in their favor" (art. 3g). Article 4 specifically banned within the Community all import and export duties, quantitative restrictions, discriminatory deals, state subsidies and market-sharing deals between companies.

The most distinctive institution of the new Community was undoubtedly the High Authority. Consisting of nine members, it was the executive institution of the ECSC and the one "responsible for initiating and framing most of the measures needed to administer the common market."[3] Eight of these nine members were nominated by governments (France and Germany each choosing two, the other four countries nominating one); the ninth member was selected by the eight nominees. All members served six-year terms and elected a president and two vice presidents from among their own number. The first president, unsurprisingly, was Jean Monnet; his two deputies were the German Christian Democrat Franz Etzel and Albert Coppé, an "ancien ministre belge," as Monnet described him in his memoirs, who became one of Monnet's most steadfast supporters.[4] Article 9 of the treaty bound the nine members of the Authority to "exercise their functions in complete independence, in the general interest of the Community. In the fulfillment of their duties, they shall neither solicit nor accept instructions from any government or any organization. They will abstain from all conduct incompatible with the supranational character of their functions."

The full range of the High Authority's powers underlines how different an institutional beast it was from, say, the secretariat of the OEEC. Monnet's favorite way of disparaging an institution was to compare it to the OEEC, which he regarded as a byword for futility.[5] The High Authority that emerged from the ECSC treaty, while it was not the untrammeled institution

hinted at in the Schuman declaration, was a body with far-reaching independent powers. It was entitled to impose fines upon firms that broke its decisions or recommendations; it was entitled to facilitate investment by floating
loans on the capital markets and then relending the money for investment
purposes; it was empowered to soften the social costs of industrial modernization by financing vocational retraining, resettlement programs and "tide
over" allowances to workers; during times of "manifest crisis," it was free to
set production quotas in order to prop up demand. In addition to these
wide-ranging powers, the High Authority held a broad antitrust brief and
was charged with protecting the common market from anticompetitive
mergers, pricing policies or wage reductions. A somewhat ineffectual Consultative Committee of fifty leading producers, trade unionists and consumers dispensed advice to the High Authority whenever it asked for it,
which under Monnet's leadership, at least, it rarely did.

There were three principal checks on the High Authority's powers. The
strong advocacy of the Dutch during the negotiation phase ensured that
the Authority's actions and decisions were second-guessed in many areas
by the Council of Ministers, which under article 26 of the treaty was given
the task of harmonizing "the action of the High Authority and that of the
governments, which are responsible for the general economic policies of
their countries." Without entering excessively into the detail of the treaty,
the Council's approval was necessary for a broad range of policy actions by
the High Authority, especially labor issues, transport and the sale of coal
and steel products. The Council was given a limited power to set the High
Authority's agenda and exercised a tight control over its budget. The
Council, at which the national governments were usually represented by
their economics or industry ministers, thus became a powerful de facto legislature able to block (though not amend) the High Authority's initiatives.

The second political check on the High Authority was the Assembly,
which consisted of seventy-eight "representatives of the peoples of the
States" (art. 20). This formula might seem to have authorized direct elections, but the treaty's subsequent article carefully excluded this possibility by
saying that the Assembly should consist of delegations drawn from national
parliaments. The Assembly's powers were explicitly "supervisory." It had no
legislative function and hence could neither recommend measures to the
High Authority's attention nor debate and amend measures taken by the
High Authority solely or jointly with the Council. The Assembly was able to
demand oral or written replies from members of the High Authority and,
more important, possessed the power, under article 24 of the treaty, to censure the High Authority's annual report. In the event of such a motion of
censure being passed by a two-thirds majority of votes cast, the High Authority was obliged to resign *en bloc*. The Assembly was also able to intervene
in the budget process. Whenever it proposed amendments to the draft

budget agreed by the High Authority and the Council that involved no net increase in expenditure, the Council was entitled to overturn them by a qualified majority vote (voting in the Council was weighted according to production) if it so chose. Whenever the Assembly proposed amendments that increased expenditure, the Council was obliged to accept or reject them by a qualified majority vote. In a shining example of constitutional realism, the possibility that the Assembly might cut expenditure was apparently not even contemplated (art. 78a). The budget was, incidentally, funded by a levy not exceeding 1 percent on the "average value" of production within the Community, although only under Monnet's presidency (1952–1955) did it come close to raising and spending such a portion of the industries' income.

The third checking institution was the Court of Justice. The Court was originally composed of seven judges appointed by the governments of the member states for a period of six years. The treaty was explicit in stating that the judges should be people "whose independence is beyond doubt" (art. 32). The Court's powers were very precisely detailed in article 33:

> The Court shall have jurisdiction in actions brought by a Member State or by the Council to have decisions or recommendations of the High Authority declared void on grounds of lack of legal competence, major violations of procedure, violations of this Treaty or of any rule of law relating to its application, or abuse of power.

The Court, in other words, was to be a watchdog over the High Authority. Within the Community, its word was law. But its power was unidirectional: firms, citizens and the High Authority itself could not have recourse to the Court to have *national* law or administrative directives declared invalid. Despite this caveat, the Court was soon busy and settled several important complaints against the High Authority within the first few years of the ECSC's life.[6]

The novelty of the ECSC treaty cannot be disputed. The ECSC represented, in theory, a new conception of international economic governance. Instead of national governments making decisions in the short-term interest of their domestic industries, with little or no thought for the knock-on effects over their borders, the six member states were pledging themselves to make decisions in the communal interest by delegating executive powers to an independent authority subject to proper institutional safeguards. The states were merely reserving to themselves a limited right of veto over the High Authority's decisions and the right to ask for judicial review of the Authority's actions. The egoism and unpredictability of nation-states were to be substituted, in the economic sphere at least, with enlightened planning and sober bargaining in a specially created institutional forum. It was this commitment to internationalist and federalist principle, not the actual experience of the Community in its first few years of existence, which guaranteed the

ECSC the laudatory reception it enjoyed in the halls of academe. American scholars of international relations, for whom the diminution of the role of the nation-state was a primary objective, regarded the ECSC as a vindication of their theoretical ideas and conferred upon it a historical significance that it has never quite lost.[7]

The truth is more prosaic. If one looks at the activities of the ECSC between February 1953 (when the common market in coal was instituted) and February 1958 (the end of the five-year "transitional period" during which all market-deforming practices were supposed to be eliminated), one sees that the Community played a useful, though limited, role in enabling the six member states to wrestle with the social and economic problems presented by two industries of great importance. The High Authority, which Monnet presided over until 1955 when he resigned and was substituted by the senior French politician René Meyer, propped up high-cost Belgian mining areas until 1958 by imposing a "perequation" levy on the sales of cheaper German and Dutch coal (but still took the blame when the mines eventually had to be rationalized); it took on the monopoly German coal-purchasing agency with some success, winning a 1956 agreement that injected a degree of competition into this politically sensitive area; it had some success in limiting the practice of charging higher prices for the transport of imported coal and steel products; it successfully managed to obtain a generous loan from the American government and to float other loans on the American capital markets. These loans were then used for investment purposes, although the amount of ECSC investment was only a small fraction of private investment in the same period. Steel production rose by over 40 percent during the transitional period, and trade between Community members in steel products and scrap also increased greatly. These last successes, however, owe more to the general rapid expansion of the European economy in these years than to the activities of the ECSC.

On the other hand, the market for coal and steel products was still anything but free in 1958. Italy's domestic market in steel was still highly protected (Italy having won a five-year exemption in a protocol to the original treaty), and all governments still boasted an array of devices—currency devaluation, sales taxes, rebates and subsidies of all kinds—that enabled them to advantage domestic producers. The High Authority rapidly discovered that it could not establish a common market by decree. The volume of existing regulation meant that dismantling barriers to free trade was going to take time, especially in the face of procrastination from the member states. The French national coal import agency, for instance, which restricted importation permits to a handful of dealers purchasing large quantities of coal and coke and which was thus manifestly a deformation of the common market, was defended tooth and nail by the French government in the Court of Justice and in 1958 still had its powers intact. Overall, as the transitional period wore on, the High

Authority became more and more reluctant to take initiatives without the prior approval of the Council of Ministers. The worsening situation of the coal industry, which was in decline as industry increasingly switched to oil, posed severe social problems that the High Authority had neither the financial resources nor the will to handle on its own.[8]

THE DEFENSE COMMUNITY

Like the ECSC, the European Defense Community (EDC) began life as a French improvisation to the rehabilitation of West Germany. The *Bundesrepublik* had been founded, as we have seen, in August 1949, but it did not enjoy full sovereign rights at once. In April 1949, the West German government was placed under the tutelage of the so-called High Commission for Germany. This body's task was to keep a vigil over the actions of the new German government, which it did by scrutinizing each and every major decision of Adenauer's cabinet for signs of nationalist revival. West Germany was denied the right to maintain armed forces, could not join NATO or the Brussels Pact, was excluded from the United Nations. France was willing to remove Germany's pariah status in matters of coal and steel, but defense issues were altogether more sensitive for the French government, which had to placate public opinion on the question, and which had to be mindful of the French Communist Party's capacity to stir up mischief on such a delicate subject. Nevertheless, if one assumed—and both French and American policymakers did—that the Soviet Union's intentions were aggressive, the French general public's insistence on fighting the last war was a strategic disaster. The Soviet Union had a massive superiority in ground forces over the Allied troops based in West Germany and was in a position to strike across the North German plain at a moment's notice. This did not matter while the United States possessed a nuclear monopoly, but after the USSR exploded its first A-bomb in the late summer of 1949, and thus acquired a deterrent, the West's front line effectively became the Rhine. Led by Secretary of State Dean Acheson, American policymakers decided that the only logical course of action was to rearm Germany as fast as possible.[9]

The United States was unwilling to press the French too hard to accept German rearmament until June 1950, when North Korea invaded its southern neighbor. It was widely believed that North Korea was obeying Soviet orders; certainly, North Korea could not have made such a move without the Soviet government's knowledge. The similarity of Korea to Germany—a country divided between communist and pro-American halves—could not but arouse alarm in the NATO countries. The invasion seemed like a prelude to an attack on West Germany. In September 1950, at a meeting of the NATO foreign ministers, the United States committed itself to sending six fully equipped divisions to Europe, but asked the Europeans, as a quid pro quo, to drop their resistance to the militarization of West Germany. The French government, stuck, turned to Monnet for help. Monnet, working behind the scenes, reverted to a tried (though not yet tested) formula: a European Community for defense matters similar to the one then under negotiation for coal and steel. Instead of Schuman, the spokesman for Monnet's ideas was, this time, the prime minister, René Pleven.

The Pleven Plan was announced on 24 October 1950. The plan envisaged the creation of a European Ministry of Defense responsible to an assembly and to a council of national defense ministers. The Ministry of Defense would have occupied itself with organizing the administration of defense (procurement, planning, links with the war industries) not strategic questions; all national governments except West Germany would have retained separate and independent military forces. Germans would, however, have been allowed to participate in so-called integrated units, though not at more than battalion strength. American policymakers reacted with "consternation and despair" at what seemed like a French move to sabotage America's ideas for European defense. Eisenhower, who was on the point of being nominated Supreme Allied Commander in Europe said that the plan contained "every kind of obstacle, difficulty and fantastic notion that misguided humans could put into one package."[10] Naturally, he later became one of the Defense Community's most passionate defenders, although, in fairness, the Pleven Plan had been redesigned by then.

The process of redesign began in Paris between January and July 1951 when delegations from all the ECSC countries except the Netherlands (which, along with Britain, Canada, Denmark and Portugal, sent observers) agreed to create a European Authority for defense questions. Adenauer, however, was determined to extract every concession possible from the strong negotiating position he found himself in. The German leader insisted that West Germany should participate on the same basis as everybody else and that the Occupation Statute, which gave the High Commission its supervisory authority, should be scrapped. The Americans, in the meantime, were convinced by Monnet's personal diplomacy to back the scheme. They insisted, however, on explicit guarantees that the new Community would be subject to NATO at the operational level. Britain, which was governed by the Conservatives from the autumn of 1951, never thought of entering the Community, although research has shown that Anthony Eden, the foreign secretary in the new Churchill cabinet, encouraged the continental countries to press on with integration in the defense sector.[11]

Between the autumn of 1951 and the spring of 1952, two separate negotiations to abolish the Occupation Statute and to create the Defense Community wore on. At a meeting of NATO foreign ministers at Lisbon in January 1952, France finally dropped her opposition to the formation of a

German army. It was agreed that the Community would place forty-three divisions of approximately 13,000 men each at NATO's disposal, of which the Germans would contribute twelve. Despite a determined effort to block the creation of a European army by the USSR, which proposed the neutralization of Germany in a diplomatic note at the beginning of March 1952, the treaty establishing the European Defense Community was signed by the six ECSC nations (the Netherlands had chosen to come in) in Paris on 25 May 1952; the Occupation Statute was ended, *subject to the ratification of the EDC treaty*, in Bonn the following day.

The EDC treaty is worth examining in detail because it represents the largest single cession of sovereignty made by the countries of Western Europe until the Maastricht treaty in 1992. Sovereignty over defense policy was surrendered on the one hand to the EDC, which article 1 described as "supranational in character, comprising common institutions, common armed forces [article 15 specified that they would wear a common uniform] and a common budget," on the other hand to the United States, which under the treaty would have taken over the day-to-day control of all armed forces within the European theater of war. Article 18 stated that "the competent supreme commander responsible to NATO [who was perforce an American] shall be . . . authorized to ensure that the European Defense Forces are organized, equipped, trained and prepared for their duties in a satisfactory manner"; article 10 permitted member states to "recruit and maintain" independently of the EDC only armed forces that were destined for "employment in non-European territories" or were (art. 11) intended for the maintenance of "internal order." Deployment outside Europe, the treaty stressed, must not affect any nation's contribution to the common defense effort.

The Defense Community was given broadly the same institutional structure as the ECSC. A nine-member Board of Commissioners was to act as the executive branch of the Community and would report to an Assembly and a Council of Ministers. There was however, no figure corresponding to the president of the ECSC High Authority, since such an office would have been tantamount to creating a minister for European Defense and the French government fought shy of taking this step. The Council, too, was institutionally stronger than its ECSC equivalent (the Board of Commissioners would not have been able to take decisions or make recommendations without its explicit consent) and would almost certainly have become the dominant decision-making force within the Community. This institutional structure was, however, specifically stated to be "provisional" in character. Article 38 of the treaty, inserted at Italian insistence, asserted that the EDC should be a prelude to the establishment of "a subsequent federal or confederate structure." In August 1952, the Assembly of the ECSC was given the task of drawing up a blueprint for a European Political Community (EPC) that would have coordinated the foreign policies of the member states and would have gradually absorbed the functions of the ECSC and the EDC.

By March 1953, the Assembly had completed this job. It envisaged the construction of a political community that cleverly merged British parliamentary democracy with the American constitutional principle of the separation of powers. The EPC was to have consisted of a bicameral Parliament, an Executive Council, a Council of Ministers and an expanded Court of Justice. The Parliament was to have been composed of a Chamber of Peoples (a directly elected assembly) and a Senate, which would have been drawn from the national parliaments. The Senate would have had the key power of nominating, in a secret ballot, the president of the Executive Council. The president would then have had a free hand to choose a cabinet of ministers. The Executive Council, in conjunction with the Council of Ministers, would then have assumed the executive role within the Community. All its major decisions, however, would have had to be submitted and approved by the Chamber of Peoples and the Senate before being promulgated by the president of the Executive Council, who would thus have become de facto head of state. The Court of Justice would have provided the nation-states with judicial review of the constitutionality of the EPC's laws.[12]

The boldness of this vision testifies to the mind-set of the European federalists at this time. The Italian historian Bino Olivi has written that the European movement believed that "history was proving them right." In the view of the European movement, the challenge of organizing a common defense for Europe and planning Europe's economy necessitated "a great 'contractualist' effort to overcome the gradual and sectoral character of European integration in order to arrive at the political union of Western Europe."[13] Even though the member-states, in a series of meetings between their foreign ministers, immediately began tinkering with the Assembly's proposals to strengthen the role of the nation-states, it remains true that the EPC was a bold expression of the federalist ideal.

The Americans were delighted with these developments. Both Eisenhower, who became president of the United States in January 1953, and Secretary of State John Foster Dulles were committed supporters of European unification.[14] Dulles, moreover, was more willing than Acheson, his predecessor, to wield a big stick. Between 1949 and 1952, America had committed $12,000 million in military and civil aid to Europe and had placed procurement contracts worth hundreds of millions more.[15] Dulles thought (and so did Congress) that it was time that the United States was paid back by concrete steps towards political unity. Within days of taking office, Dulles was warning that America would rethink its commitment to Europe if the EDC were not ratified.

The process of ratification went smoothly everywhere except France. Getting the treaty through the National Assembly, where there was strong

Gaullist (the supporters of the Free French war leader, Charles de Gaulle) and Communist opposition, and much anti-German feeling, was a task that required strong leadership. But in Fourth Republic France, strong government was in short supply. Between May 1952 and May 1954, when the army protecting France's colonial holdings in Indochina was humbled by the Vietnamese at the battle of Dien Bien Phu, France had three premiers (Antoine Pinay, René Meyer and Joseph Laniel) who preferred to postpone ratification of the EDC treaty rather than press for its adoption. French procrastination eventually caused its senior NATO allies, Britain and the United States, to lose patience. At the Bermuda conference of Western leaders in December 1953, Winston Churchill (who had returned as prime minister after the Conservatives' narrow election victory in November 1951) harangued the French at some length and warned that they were putting the future of NATO (and hence the free world) at risk.[16] Dulles redoubled the dose a few days later, hinting that the United States would have to undertake an "agonizing reappraisal" of its defense commitments if France did not pass the EDC treaty.[17]

Matters were complicated by the French defeat at Dien Bien Phu, which drove the pro-European Mouvement Républicain Populaire (MRP) from power in Paris and led to the austere figure of Pierre Mendès-France becoming prime minister. Paul-Henri Spaak, a privileged observer, described Mendès-France in his memoirs as, de Gaulle aside, "the strongest political personality to have emerged in France since the war."[18] Mendès-France, moreover, was suspected in Washington, probably unfairly, of being a Cold War neutral. Certainly, he was not a malleable character. Dulles nevertheless determined to put the case for immediate ratification of the EDC treaty as strongly as he could. On 13 July 1954, he visited Paris, where he bluntly told Mendès-France that Congress would not "appropriate another cent" for European defense if France persisted in delaying the ratification of the treaty. He added that the United States could always opt to defend the European periphery (Britain, Spain, Greece, Turkey) and leave France to face the USSR on its own. Mendès-France responded that the National Assembly would never pass the treaty in its then form. Rejection would be a propaganda disaster. He argued that it would be better to amend the treaty to win over the more moderate Gaullists worried about the loss of national sovereignty implied by the treaty.[19]

Mendès-France put forward a list of amendments to a meeting of the EDC powers in Brussels on 19 August. Among other things, he proposed watering down the supranational dimension of the EDC by introducing an eight-year national veto over the Board of Commissioners' actions; asked that article 38 (authorizing the EPC) be deleted; requested the right to withdraw from the treaty if Germany were reunited. These amendments may have won him the support of some Gaullists in the National Assembly, but they infuriated France's partners, especially West Germany, where the government was under pressure from public opinion to get results from its controversial policy of *Westpolitik* (as Adenauer's opening to the French in 1950 was known). The German foreign minister Walter Hallstein vented his feelings at the French move by saying, "Mendès has just presented us with the corpse of Europe."[20] Paul-Henri Spaak, who chaired the meeting, wrote in his memoirs that he blamed himself for not having found a formula that would have met Mendès-France's wishes, although he argues later in the same book that the French premier was so intent on securing a "political triumph" in French domestic politics by standing up to "Europe" that a compromise may not have been possible.[21]

Mendès-France eventually allowed the EDC treaty to be debated in the National Assembly at the end of August 1954. It was rejected by 319 votes to 264 votes after a debate whose chauvinism shocked the European movement. At the risk of imposing too much order on what was a very emotional debate, opponents of the treaty used four main arguments. First, they feared that France would be swallowed up in a European superstate if they voted for the treaty. Edouard Herriot, who had been the patron of the French Council for a United Europe and had attended the Congress of Europe in 1948, proclaimed that "for us the European Community is the end of France . . . it is a question of the life and death of France." The treaty was held to be the work of a handful of technocrats (de Gaulle had darkly called Monnet "the inspirer" in a November 1953 press conference and had condemned the EDC treaty for good measure as "an artificial monster" and a "Frankenstein") who were working behind the scenes to reduce France's independence.[22] Second, French legislators worried that the proposed European army would rapidly be Germanized. Distrust of German motives was voiced openly. Third, many deputies thought that the treaty would cut France off from its Commonwealth equivalent, the French Union. Fourth, the role of national pride was a major factor. Britain had not signed the EDC treaty and the United States did not seem to expect her to. France should not lower herself to the level of what one deputy called "two defeated and three tiny countries" if Britain and America did not do the same.[23] When the result was announced, the *anti-cédistes*—Communists, Gaullists, renegade Christian Democrats and Socialists—burst into a spirited rendition of *La Marseilleise*. In response, Dulles sourly commented, "It is a tragedy that in one country nationalism, abetted by communism, has asserted itself so as to endanger the whole of Europe."[24]

In his memoirs, Jean Monnet wrote that the EDC "quarrel" had been a "harrowing split" (*déchirement*) for France.[25] But France, in a sense, was the least of the problems. Germany was left, four years on from the Pleven Plan, without statehood; the Americans, who had spent three years preaching the alarmist message that Europe faced a choice between world communism and

European unity, were bereft of ideas; the European movement had been reminded that rumors of the death of national sovereignty were greatly exaggerated. Britain, in the person of Foreign Secretary Anthony Eden, stepped
into the breach with a burst of intelligent diplomacy that managed, within a
few weeks, to integrate the *Bundesrepublik* into the West, satisfy French worries about German military revival and reengage the Americans. The British
solution was to extend the Brussels Pact to Germany and Italy. On 23 October 1954, the Brussels powers agreed to terminate the occupation of Germany, to establish a new body called the Western European Union (WEU)
with Italy and West Germany as members (in practice this meant giving the
Brussels Pact an assembly drawn from national parliaments), to permit West
Germany to join NATO and to draw up a "European Statute" for the Saarland (which had been a bone of contention between France and West Germany throughout the EDC saga). Additional protocols committed Britain to
maintaining military forces in West Germany, banned Germany from making
or acquiring certain categories of weapons (nuclear bombs, guided missiles,
capital ships) and set up an agency to monitor and audit national stocks of
armaments. The French, as the price for their acquiescence, were determined
that West Germany should know that she was on probation.

The treaty setting up the WEU retained the Brussels Pact's preamble stating that one of its goals was "to encourage the progressive integration of Europe," but nobody was fooled. Monnet later described the new body as "a
typical military alliance" and a "weak coordination structure" destined to
"vegetate," but it would be more accurate to describe it as a talking shop.[26]
Strategic planning functions were handed over to NATO, and the organization was left to act as a forum for transparency between the member states
over low-key matters of military administration. The WEU did draw up a plan
to "Europeanize" the Saarland, but it was rejected by popular referendum on
23 October 1955, and the region eventually became part of West Germany.

The power of national governments and nationalist ideology to upset the
apple cart of the European movement had, in short, been dramatically illustrated by the experience of the EDC. Monnet drew the conclusion that he
should devote his main activity to proselytizing for European unity among
the political class of the Six. Other pro-unity European statesmen concluded
that the best way of obtaining a *relance* of the European project was to work
for trade liberalization.

FROM MESSINA TO ROME

Trade liberalization was a natural outlet for the energies of supporters of European integration. Unlike defense, or even coal and steel, trade was an area
in which integration was already proceeding apace. Western European coun-

tries were buying and selling far more goods from each other. This success story was in large part due to the efforts of the much-derided OEEC. In the immediate postwar years, trade had been restricted by the payments problem. Governments, conscious of the fragile state of their economies, monitored private trade flows minutely to prevent imbalances (paid for in hard currency) from emerging. Most trade was conducted on the basis of bilateral deals between countries. As Robert Marjolin pointed out in his memoirs, such deals dampened economic growth. If France, for example, derestricted imports from Belgium and Belgium's trade balance with France moved into surplus as a result, for trade as a whole to continue to grow, Belgium had to be able to use her credit with France to buy goods from other countries.[27] Europe's producers were in effect being limited to their own, relatively small, domestic markets or to such markets abroad as their national governments could negotiate for them. Bureaucrats, rather than the market, were determining the volume of trade.

Liberalizing the market was one of the OEEC's primary tasks, along with disbursing Marshall Plan aid. The biggest step in the pursuit of freer trade brokered by the OEEC was the establishment of the European Payments Union (EPU) in September 1950. The EPU is usually described as a "multilateral clearinghouse"—in effect, a kind of bank. To join, each OEEC member state contributed a fixed quota of capital, in its own currency, equal to 15 percent of its total visible and invisible trade with other OEEC countries. The United States also contributed $350 million to the EPU's capital. Each month, the central banks of the OEEC member states were required to keep a tally of their payments to other OEEC countries and the payments of others to them. At the end of every month, they communicated this information to the EPU's agent, the Swiss-based Bank of International Settlements (BIS), which summed up the aggregate balance of payments of each of its member states and made a deposit, partly in credits redeemable in any OEEC currency, partly in gold and dollars, to the states that had an overall surplus. It made a parallel deduction from the balance of the debtor states. The member states were entitled to an "overdraft" in credits of up to 20 percent of their quota at any one time; thereafter, the Union increasingly demanded payment in gold or dollars. No country was allowed to run up debits exceeding 60 percent of its original quota. Countries with persistent balance-of-payment deficits were therefore compelled either to follow domestic austerity to reduce demand for imports or to devalue their currency—in other words, to reduce their citizens' standard of living.[28]

The EPU thus introduced an element of flexibility into European trade. Instead of a tangled thicket of bilateral deals, in which each country was careful to ensure that it did not run up too much of an imbalance with each and every trading partner, countries were freed to run deficits with countries that had products or raw materials they needed to boost production. In the meantime, the OEEC also acted as a forum for the gradual elimination of nontariff barriers such as quotas. By the mid-1950s, quotas on trade in manufactured goods had been almost abolished across the OEEC. Robert Marjolin insisted in his memoirs that without the trade liberalization set in motion by the activities of the OEEC, it was "unlikely that the Common Market would have seen the light of day."[29] Trade liberalization brought concrete, visible benefits to national economies and encouraged them to cooperate further.

There was certainly plenty to do. Although quotas on manufactured goods had been sharply reduced, tariffs on industrial goods remained very high, subsidies abounded, agriculture was jealously protected. After the debacle of the EDC, further action to boost trade seemed the most promising avenue for cooperation within the Six. The initiative was taken by the Dutch, whose foreign minister, Jan Willem Beyen, was a convinced enthusiast of free markets. In 1954, Bayen began to press for the creation of a customs union between the Six in which all forms of trade discrimination were abolished—although, as an aside, the British statesman Dennis Healey records an Italian politician saying to him at this time that he would believe in the sincerity of federalists from the Benelux countries when the Dutch "stopped growing tomatoes under glass."[30]

Bayen's proposals were flanked by new initiatives from Monnet and Paul-Henri Spaak to promote ECSC-like integration in the fields of transport and, above all, nuclear energy. On 18 May 1955, the Benelux countries submitted a memorandum incorporating both Beyen's and Monnet's ideas to the foreign ministers of the Six. The memorandum became the agenda for the foreign ministers' summit meeting at Messina in Sicily on 1–2 June 1955. At Messina, the foreign ministers rhetorically agreed that the time had come to make "a fresh advance towards the building of Europe." This advance would be achieved by progress in three fields: sectoral integration in transport and nuclear energy; "the establishment of a European market, free from all customs duties and all quantitative restrictions"; and the "progressive harmonization" of social policies.[31] A committee of governmental representatives, chaired by Paul-Henri Spaak, was charged with the "preparatory work" for these new moves towards integration.

To many in Europe, Messina seemed a damp squib. For all the rhetoric of a "European advance," the nations of the Six were plainly reserving their position until Spaak had produced concrete proposals. Monnet, however, was determined to keep the pressure on the national governments. To this end, he dedicated his energies to establishing an "Action Committee" composed of leading members of all Europe's Social Democratic, Liberal and Christian Democratic political parties, plus representatives of the organized workers. This body held its inaugural meeting in October 1955. All its founding members pledged themselves to three broad promises. First, they would each ask their own party or union to affiliate to the Action Committee and would act as delegates to the Committee on behalf of their own organizations. Second, they stated that they would use their institutional position to ensure that the Messina conference's resolution became a "real step towards the United States of Europe." Third, they would put aside all "specious solutions" to Europe's problems that were based upon "mere cooperation between governments." The Committee's founders agreed that it was "indispensable for states to delegate certain of their powers to European federal institutions." The "close association" of Great Britain with such "achievements" was greatly to be desired.[32]

In practice, the Action Committee became a lobbyist for supranational supervision and development of nuclear energy. Between its first meeting in October 1955 and the signature of the Treaties of Rome in March 1957, the Action Committee met twice (in January and September 1956). The final "resolutions" of both meetings stress almost exclusively the potential of atomic energy for the future of Europe and relegate the construction of the common market almost to a footnote. The Action Committee's reasons are easy enough to understand. Its members believed that Europe was facing an energy crunch in the near future. The "growing deficit in power supplies," they argued during their September 1956 meeting, was "the most grave and urgent problem for our countries" and exposed them to "dangerous threats to peace." Unlike the United States or the USSR, Western Europe was the "only great industrial region of the world that does not produce the power necessary to its development." Already, the Six were importing the energy equivalent of seventy million metric tons of coal per year, mostly in the form of Middle Eastern oil. By the end of the 1960s, the ECSC countries, plus Britain, were expected to import one-third of their energy needs. The September 1956 resolution stated that fuel dependency of this order would result in "insecurity and permanent risks of conflict."[33] Monnet, advised by the French scientist Louis Armand, believed that investment in nuclear energy could fill this gap, if the Six were prepared to pool their resources.

Nuclear energy did indeed occupy a central place in the discussions of Spaak's intergovernmental committee and in the bargaining between national governments that followed the submission of his committee's report in April 1956. There was, to use the jargon of the time, a *Junktim* (link) between the nuclear energy and customs union discussions. Spaak's report, which was largely written by Monnet's close collaborator, Pierre Uri, shows this. It combined the establishment of a free trade community between the Six, within which tariffs and other obstacles to trade would be gradually reduced over a period of years—that is, full implementation of the Beyen Plan—with full backing for Monnet's ideas for a nuclear energy authority (Euratom). The two new communities, the report proposed,

should be administered by commissions of government-nominated officials. The ECSC Assembly and Court of Justice would serve both of the
new organizations.[34]

The Spaak report was accepted in principle at a meeting of the Six's foreign ministers in Venice on 29–30 May 1956 after less than two hours of discussion.[35] The agreement at Venice was, however, only the starting point of
extenuated further negotiations. An intergovernmental conference was established under Spaak's chairmanship and began its work at the end of June
1956. So far as Euratom was concerned, the German government believed
that the Six should refrain from the military use of uranium. France, by contrast, made clear from July 1956 that she was determined to join the restricted "club" of nations possessing the nuclear bomb. Initially, she supported the Europeanization of nuclear energy development for both peaceful
and military uses, a position that did not go down well either in London or
Washington. France's leaders were well aware that the cost of developing nuclear programs of her own would be prohibitive.[36]

The question of free trade was even more complex. Broadly speaking, the
Benelux countries and West Germany were free traders, while France was
protectionist. Italy hovered uneasily between the two. Germany was an enthusiast for open markets in everything except agriculture. Economics minister Ludwig Erhard favored opening Europe's markets for industrial products as far and as fast as possible. Marjolin describes him as "a universalist, a
fervent advocate of total freedom of trade on a world scale."[37] Influential
sections of German business supported him by pressing for, at least, full liberalization of trade in manufactured goods throughout the OEEC.[38] Erhard,
however, could not set the tone of Germany's negotiating position. Chancellor Adenauer, who had risked much for *Westpolitik*, was, with the calamity
of the EDC fresh in his mind, not prepared to press the French government
further than she would go. The negotiation, as Marjolin (one of the chief
French negotiators) records, thus "depended on us." With France's agreement, anything was possible, "including a common market based upon the
principles of liberalism." Without France, "all roads were barred."[39] The issue thus became a question of domestic French politics. How far was France
prepared to rescind its traditional reliance on protectionism and state direction of the economy?

At any rate at first, the answer, it seemed, was not very far at all. Despite
the intergovernmental emphasis of the Spaak report, the initial reaction of
French officialdom was "icy."[40] Powerful industrial lobbies and entrenched
state bureaucracies all foresaw a loss of influence if the Spaak proposals were
accepted. The French government's official memorandum replying to the report, circulated in May 1956, insisted that liberalization of trade between the
Six would be contingent upon the harmonization of social policies. In particular, France required that equalization of pay between men and women

should be introduced across the Six; that the working week should be standardized; that the length of paid holidays should be fixed at Community level; that social security arrangements should be harmonized upward until they were on a par with the most generous system within the Community—France's, naturally. France insisted on the extension of the Common Market to cover agricultural goods—the enthusiasm of the northern Europeans for free trade tended to wane suddenly when farming, with its politically powerful producer lobbies, was under discussion—and highlighted the special difficulties that a customs union would imply for France, with its large number of dependent colonies. Marjolin notes that the agenda of all subsequent talks was chiefly concerned with the need to get France to drop its more obstructive positions.[41] France was essentially saying to the rest of the Six that it would come into the Common Market if the other countries aligned their economic model to that of France—something that Erhard, to name but one politician elsewhere in Europe, was singularly loath to do.

French reservations to the Spaak report were such that it seems almost miraculous that a compromise was eventually found. Britain, for one, believed almost to the last that no agreement would or could be reached. In retrospect, Britain was astonishingly blasé about the Messina talks and their implications. The leading British politicians were too preoccupied with Britain's global role to worry about the doings of her neighbors, and the civil servants, as in 1950, were convinced that the post-Messina talks "would not lead anywhere."[42] Britain did initially participate in Spaak's intergovernmental drafting committee, sending, at the behest of Foreign Secretary Harold Macmillan, a representative, albeit one without plenipotentiary powers. This representative, a former Oxford don called Russell Bretherton, was a mere undersecretary in the Department of Trade. Bretherton's relatively lowly rank illustrates that Britain was determined to ensure that her participation in the talks was not construed as a commitment to join a customs union, still less an endorsement of the pro-unity rhetoric of the Messina declaration. Bretherton, who was one of the most gifted British economists of his generation, made matters more complicated for Whitehall by contradicting received wisdom. The process begun at Messina, he argued, was serious, "indistinguishable from the OEEC" and likely to succeed. Whitehall refused to listen. Bretherton was recalled from the talks in November 1955. As the multiple French objections to the Spaak report became clear, Britain pinned her hopes on the collapse of the negotiations for a customs union—this would at least save her from what one senior official called at the time "the embarrassing choice" of having to decide whether to join it or not.[43]

The talks were given impetus by the disastrous outcome of an Anglo-French military adventure: Suez. On 31 October 1956, British and French troops, acting ostensibly to "separate" clashing Israeli and Egyptian forces, began air attacks on Egyptian forces guarding the Suez Canal, which Egyptian president

Gamel Abdel Nasser had nationalized in July. Seaborne and airborne landings of troops followed on 5–6 November. Both the United States and the Soviet Union (which was itself crushing the revolt against communist rule in Budapest) condemned the Anglo-French attack, and the world currency markets were spooked. A run on the pound began, and along with America's hostility to the invasion, the financial panic caused the Eden government to lose its nerve on the night of 6–7 November and concede a cease-fire, even though military objectives were being successfully achieved.[44]

The French government, which was now presided over by the Socialist Guy Mollet, was left high and dry. Only as part of a united Europe, Mollet argued, could France be on an equal footing with the Americans.[45] Marjolin, a privileged observer, says that Mollet "felt that the only way to erase, or at least lessen, the humiliation France had just suffered from the Suez affair was to conclude a European treaty quickly."[46] Mollet was encouraged in such views by Chancellor Adenauer of Germany, who visited Paris at the height of the crisis.[47] Adenauer allegedly told Mollet, "Europe will be your revenge."[48] During the chancellor's visit, France modified its insistence upon the harmonization of social and labor market policy as a prerequisite for a full customs union. She now accepted that member states would merely be obliged to do what they could to bring about such harmonization.[49] Before the end of 1956, the Germans had also conceded that France could develop an independent nuclear policy for military purposes. The way was open for the signature of both the Euratom and EEC treaties. As Winand has wryly observed, Dulles "probably contributed more to European unification by refusing to back the French and British at Suez than by vigorously pushing for the EDC."[50]

For Britain, therefore, Suez was a *dual* foreign policy catastrophe. On the one hand, she had incensed the United States, her closest ally; on the other hand, she had given an unwelcome shot in the arm to the negotiations started at Messina. Eden reluctantly resigned in January 1957, and Harold Macmillan, who was probably the most pro-European senior British politician of this period, took his place as prime minister. Now a common market genuinely looked like being created, Macmillan found himself faced with an unpleasant choice. If he did nothing, Britain would find herself outside the common tariff wall erected by the Six upon the establishment of a customs union. British industry would be able to trade less freely with such low-tariff countries as the Netherlands and Germany and would lose competitive edge to competitors from within the Six in highly protected markets such as those of France and Italy (since those competitors would no longer have to pay duties). Although Britain only sent 13 percent of her total exports to the Six (3 percent of GNP) and more than 50 percent to the Commonwealth, the Six was the fastest-growing economic area in the world and thus represented a market that the British could not afford to be driven out of.[51] On the other hand, now that the negotiations were all but completed, joining hardly seemed like an alternative either. The British could hardly expect the Six to redraft the treaties from scratch to suit British preferences.

The British squared the circle by strongly pushing a plan for a free trade agreement with the Six (see chapter 4). This plan was warmly received by such free traders as Erhard, but when de Gaulle came to power in France in the summer of 1958, all British hopes of superseding the newly instituted European Economic Community (EEC) were extinguished. Britain was glumly left to negotiate the European Free Trade Agreement (EFTA), a trade deal rather like the one signed by the United States, Canada and Mexico in the 1990s, in 1959 with the Scandinavian countries, Switzerland, Portugal and Austria.[52]

THE TREATIES OF ROME: 25 MARCH 1957

Although it attracted a great deal of contemporary attention, the Euratom treaty was less complex, and, in retrospect, much less important than the parallel treaty establishing an economic community. It identified eight main policy areas in the field of nuclear energy that would be coordinated by the new Community. Euratom was (1) "to research and ensure the dissemination of technical knowledge" by promoting and supplementing research being undertaken at national level. It was (2) "to establish and ensure the application of" common safety standards throughout the Six and (3) "to facilitate investment" in the industry. Annexe Two of the treaty made consulting the five-member Commission of Euratom obligatory whenever investment plans were being made for any aspect of the nuclear industry. Euratom was also (4) "to ensure a regular and equitable supply of ores and nuclear fuels to all users in the Community." The Commission was empowered to set up a purchasing and distribution "agency" that would have had a "right of option" on all "ores, source materials or fissionable materials" produced within the Community. In addition to these powers, Euratom was (5) to supervise the use of nuclear fuels and ensure that "nuclear materials are not diverted for purposes other than those for which they are intended"; (6) to own all "special fissionable materials" (bomb-grade uranium and plutonium) *not* intended for defense purposes; (7) establish a common market in materials, capital and employment for the nuclear industry. Its eighth and final task was to make agreements "likely to promote progress in the peaceful use of nuclear energy" with other countries and organizations. Member states were not precluded from making similar agreements on their own initiative, but the Euratom Commission was entitled to scrutinize any such proposed agreement to see if it harmonized with the aims and objectives of the new Community.

Monnet's Action Committee greeted the Euratom treaty with great fanfare. The resolution of its fourth meeting (6–7 May 1957) welcomed the signature of the two Treaties of Rome, but especially that of Euratom, as "an
event of capital importance."[53] In between the Committee's September
1956 meeting and the meeting in May 1957, a committee of three "Wise
Men," chaired by Monnet's adviser Armand (who also became first president
of the Euratom Commission), had reported. It asserted that the Six could be
producing fifteen million kilowatts (kW) of power from nuclear energy by
1967—"an electricity production greater than those of all the conventional
power stations and dams which exist today in France and Germany."[54] Such
boosterism was always going to be hard to live up to. And in fact Euratom
did not live up to the hopes of its sponsors. Like the ECSC, it lacked the resources to dominate investment in expensive nuclear power plants or to exercise a monopoly over the purchase of uranium. Its work was soon restricted
to norm setting, monitoring and brokering the actions of governments who
were, at least in the case of France, as interested in the military applications
of nuclear power as the peaceful ones. Europe, in the meantime, continued
to import more and more oil from the Middle East. In this respect, Monnet's geopolitical justification for Euratom was eventually vindicated. Dependency upon the Middle East oil supplies was destined to have dire consequences for the Six's foreign policy in the 1970s.

The EEC treaty was far more decisive for the future of European integration than Euratom. Two hundred and forty-eight articles, four annexes, nine
protocols—the size alone of the treaty testifies to the strenuous negotiation
that went into its birth, and to its scope. The treaty's protocol stated that its
signatories, being "determined" (among several other worthy objectives) to
"lay the foundations of an ever closer union among the peoples of Europe,"
had decided to create an "Economic Community." The EEC's task, according to article 2, was, "by establishing a common market and progressively ap-
proximating the economic policies of the Member States," to "promote
throughout the Community an harmonious development of economic activities, an increase in stability, an accelerated raising of the standard of living
and closer relations between the States belonging to it." The language was
identical, in short, to the discussions of the economic subcommittee of the
Congress of Europe some ten years before. It would not be the last time in
Community history that sparring nation-states left the ring of intergovernmental negotiations swathed in a comforting blanket of rhetoric about the
political and economic convergence of the member states.

The Six contracted themselves under article 3 of the treaty to eleven specific policy commitments. They would abolish all quantitative restrictions on
trade between themselves, establish a common external tariff and a common
commercial policy towards third countries and eliminate "obstacles to freedom of movement for persons, services and capital." A "common policy in

the sphere of agriculture" would be adopted, as would a common policy on transport. To these ends, the Six bound themselves both to institute a "system" that would ensure that competition was not distorted, and to apply procedures that would coordinate their economic policies and remedy "disequilibria" in their balances of payments. They further promised to "approximate" their domestic laws "to the extent required for the proper functioning of the common market." A European Social Fund and a European Investment Bank would be set up, and an "association" agreement for overseas "countries and territories" would be introduced. The common external tariff—the key provision of the customs union—was set at the "arithmetical average of the duties applied in the four customs territories [Benelux, France, Germany and Italy] comprised in the Community" (art. 19).

The timetable for this ambitious program of economic liberalization and domestic regulatory harmonization to Community norms was twelve years. This "transitional period" was subdivided into three "stages" of four years (although some slippage was both envisaged and allowed), each of which was "assigned a set of actions" that had to be fulfilled before the stage came to an end. Revenue raised by tariffs on commerce between member states, for example, would be reduced by 10 percent one year after the treaty came into force; 10 percent eighteen months later, and a further 10 percent upon the conclusion of the first four-year phase. Further precise reductions were specified for the second and third stage. Duties on individual *products* were to have been reduced by at least 25 percent during the first stage, and a further 25 percent during the second stage (art. 14). It was this article of the treaty that attracted the most attention from *The Economist*, which printed a derisive analysis in the "Notes in Brief" column of its 30 March 1957 edition. Ironically headed a "Red Letter Day for Shoppers," the paper commented scornfully that "within twelve years, if things go well, or seventeen years, if things go badly," Italians wanting to buy a Volkswagen would be able to do so at German prices. The paper, more seriously, concluded that a "liberal British influence" was needed to render the treaty more susceptible to "healthy free trade."

The Six also promised to establish a common market in "the products of the soil, of stockfarming, and of fisheries and products of first stage processing directly related to these products" within the same twelve-year framework (art. 38 [1]). The operation and development of the common market in agricultural products, however, was to be "accompanied by the establishment of a common agricultural policy among the member states" (art. 38 [4]). Article 39 [1] clarified that the objectives of this policy would be

1. To increase agricultural productivity by promoting technical progress and by ensuring the rational development of agricultural production and the optimum utilization of the factors of production, in particular labor

72   Chapter 3

2. Thus to ensure a fair standard of living for the agricultural community, in particular by increasing the individual earnings of persons engaged in agriculture
3. To stabilize markets
4. To assure the availability of supplies
5. To ensure that supplies reach consumers at reasonable prices

In other words—and the point was crucial for French negotiators—the policy in its final form would have primarily benefited the interests of agricultural *producers*, while guaranteeing *reasonable* (not world market) prices for consumers. In his memoirs, Marjolin stated bluntly: "France would never have accepted a Customs Union that did not include agriculture and did not guarantee French producers protection comparable to that which they were receiving under French law. Without a common agricultural policy, there would never have been a common market."[55] The Commission of the EEC was charged with the task of "working out and implementing" the common agricultural policy (or CAP, as it became known) by the end of the first stage of the EEC's development. The Council of Ministers, however, by unanimous vote during the first *two* stages of the transitional period, and by qualified majority thereafter, was to make all regulations, issue directives and take all decisions pertaining to agriculture (art. 43 [2]).

The Commission and the Council of Ministers were the unique institutions possessed by the EEC. Unlike the ECSC, in which the High Authority was an executive committee accountable to the Assembly (but not supervised by it) that required on many occasions the *consent* of the Council of Ministers (which thus functioned as a kind of restraining legislature), in the EEC treaty policy-making power was concentrated in the hands of the Council. While the Commission, which was composed of nine independent individuals nominated by national governments for a four-year term, had the exclusive power to propose regulations, directives or decisions and was responsible for implementing them, the Council alone could give legal force to the measures emanating from the Commission. During the first two stages of the transitional period, the Council's approval was to be by unanimous vote, thereafter by a qualified majority of twelve votes out of seventeen. Since France, Germany and Italy each disposed of four votes, Belgium and the Netherlands of two, and Luxembourg of one, the big countries would eventually need the acquiescence of at least one Benelux country for a measure that they favored. Even more important, a single big country could not exercise a veto on its own. Council amendments to Commission proposals were only possible by unanimous agreement (art. 149); a clause clearly designed to prevent denaturing compromises that would benefit a minority of member states.

The Commission, however, rapidly became a more powerful institution than had been envisaged—more potent, certainly, than the ECSC High Authority. There were three main reasons for this. The first reason was the exceptional quality of some of the individuals composing the first Commission. The first president of the Commission was Walter Hallstein, a committed European federalist who, as we have seen, had also been German foreign minister. His Commission included Sicco Mansholt, a Dutch agriculture expert who was handed the poisoned chalice of bringing the CAP into being, and the inevitable Robert Marjolin. These three men brought formidable intellectual and organizational talents to the Commission and had accumulated great experience at the top levels of international negotiation over the previous decade.

The second reason was the Commission's role as market invigilator. The EEC treaty was, among other things, the first supranational antitrust agreement. Articles 85 through 89 of the treaty clearly established that cartels were to be outlawed within the Six, and the Commission was given the task of proposing how. It took on similar responsibilities in the fields of government subsidies, the harmonization of tax policy and the implementation of common measures in the field of social provision. It was, in short, designed to be both a watchdog that barked whenever mercantilist tendencies tried to sneak into the market by the back door and a bloodhound employed to sniff them out. Since Western Europe in 1957 was largely managed along mercantilist lines, this gave the Commission plenty to do. Following on from this, the third reason for the Commission's higher than expected profile was the clear remit possessed by the new Commission. The EEC treaty set it numerous clear tasks and gave it a fixed timetable to fulfill them in. The power of proposal, in this context, became an important tool. An efficient decision-making cycle was established whereby the experts within the Commission researched and put forward new initiatives and the Council of Ministers said yea or nay. There was, in short, a Whitehall-like division between officials and politicians that could only be upset by either of the two categories deciding to invade the other's turf. The major crisis of the mid-1960s (see chapter 4) was caused by de Gaulle, on the one hand, and Hallstein, on the other, choosing to forget this simple rule.

The EEC shared the Common Assembly and the Court of Justice with the ECSC (and Euratom). The former of these institutions was as much a cipher in the new treaty as the old. The latter institution, however, gained important new powers. Whereas under the ECSC treaty, rulings of the Court of Justice could only be invoked by states objecting to the actions of the High Authority, in the EEC treaty both the Commission and member states (arts. 169–170) could ask the Court to rule that the domestic regulations of the member states were infringing the provisions of the treaty. Member states judged to be guilty were "required to take the necessary measures to comply with the judgment of the Court" (art. 171), although no explicit sanctions were available to the Court in the event of noncompliance. Article 177, moreover, empowered the Court, upon request of a tribunal or court within any of the member states, to rule whether the Treaty of Rome was being infringed by a case being decided under national law.

The crucial question raised during the Court's early judgments was whether or not these provisions empowered the Court to rule national laws and regulations incompatible with the treaty. Traditional international law holds that agreements between nation-states are binding upon the states themselves and should be implemented in good faith, but that their direct application is a matter for domestic legal procedures. In other words, a Court ruling that a provision of the EEC treaty was being violated by a specific regulation in force in a particular member-state could not by itself annul the offending regulation but merely act as judicial signal to the Community in general that one of its members was not keeping its promises. The problem with this interpretation of the Court's role, of course, was that it made enforcement of the treaty a question of politics and hence greatly multiplied the probability that the member-states, particularly the powerful ones, would permit the continuation of regulations contrary to the laissez-faire letter and spirit of the EEC treaty.

The first landmark case in the ECJ's history, *Van Gend en Loos v Nederlandse Administratie der Berlastingen* (no. 26/1962) addressed precisely this point. This was a dispute in which a Dutch company importing chemicals from West Germany was charged a higher rate of tariff, under a Dutch law of December 1959, than had been in force on 1 January 1958. The company's lawyers charged that this was a breach of article 12 of the EEC treaty, which instructed member states to "refrain from introducing between themselves any new customs duties on imports or exports, or any charges having equivalent effect, and from increasing those which they already apply in their trade with each other." The Dutch customs authorities referred the matter to the Court and asked it to decide whether article 12 (a) conferred individual rights which the domestic legal systems of the member states were bound to respect; (b) whether, in this particular case, Dutch law actually had infringed article 12. When the case came before the Court, only the Commission supported the company. The Dutch, Belgian and German governments all took the view that article 12 "was intended by the authors of the Treaty to be binding on the international plane only and that it could not be invoked directly in the national courts."[56] The advocate-general to the Court (the official charged with presenting an impartial summary of the case to the Court and with providing a preliminary opinion) by and large backed the view of the three governments, ruling that "large parts of the Treaty" (including article 12) "contain only obligations of member-states and do not contain rules having a direct internal effect."[57] The Court, citing the sentiments of the EEC treaty's preamble as evidence of the supranationalist intent of the treaty's makers, defiantly ruled to the contrary, however. According to the ruling of the seven judges:

The Community constitutes a new legal order of international law for the benefit of which the states have limited their sovereign rights, albeit within limited fields, and the subjects of which comprise not only Member States but also their nationals. Independently of the legislation of the member states, Community law therefore not only imposes obligations on individuals but is intended to confer upon them rights which become part of their legal heritage.[58]

THE UNITING OF EUROPE

When one recalls the hatreds, destruction and material poverty of Western Europe in 1945, the picture presented to the outside world by the EEC Six in 1958 was startling. In the defense field, the historic enemies, France and West Germany, were associated together in NATO and the WEU, even though nationalist fears had blocked the evolution of an overarching political community. Coal and steel production, the heart of the 1950s industrial economy, had been entrusted to an independent supranational authority and even if by 1958 the nation-states were busy reasserting their rights in this field, they were doing so as part of a Community with common stated objectives. In a more guarded way, the same six countries had elected to liberalize trade among themselves via a complex but comprehensive treaty that also provided for strictly limited but significant elements of supranational government. The Six, in crude material terms, was the fastest-growing economic area in the world. Such nations as West Germany and Belgium were restoring their traditional primacy (and leaving isolationist Britain in their wake); France, the protection-minded skeptic, was shortly to discover the benefits of free trade; still agricultural Italy, the poorest nation of the Six, was five years into its miraculous rise to the ranks of the rich industrial countries.

This felicitous picture of growing prosperity and supranational cooperation gladdened the hearts of academic theorists, especially in the United States. Since the time of the French and American revolutions, liberal internationalists have predicted (and preached) that nations that traded with one other would not fight one another either. Interdependence between nations was the key both to prosperity and peace. In the 1950s, this doctrine went by the name of functionalism, a theory that like its approximate contemporary, the hula hoop, set off from California and became a European obsession. Unlike the hula hoop, however, functionalist ideas continue to gyrate. In one form or another, they have remained the dominant explanatory paradigm among scholars of postwar integration in Europe.

The reason is not hard to find. The bible of functionalist explanation, Haas's *The Uniting of Europe*, essentially appeared to demonstrate scientifically that an unprecedented state of "political community" in which nation-states were, if not exactly banished, then at least permanently redimensioned in power and influence, was on the point of realization in the Six. Haas's book begins with a definition of the ideal types of political community and "political integration." What does it mean to say that a political community exists, or is in the process of being formed? A political community, Haas argued, would need to meet six tests before analysts could plausibly talk of its establishment.[59] First, there would have to be at least *some* "interest groups and political parties" in each nation willing to "endorse supranational action in preference to action by their national government." Haas was careful not to rule out political pluralism: skeptical parties could legitimately operate in a political community. But no political community could be said to exist if "unanimous national opposition" was present. Second, such "interest groups and political parties" would be organized "beyond the national level" and would "define their interests in terms larger than those of the separate national state from which they originate." Third, the same "interest groups and political parties" would "coalesce on the basis of a common ideology surpassing those prominent at the national level" and would, fourth, "succeed in evolving a body of doctrine common to all, or a new nationalism." Fifth, all political actors (interest groups, parties *and* governments) would "show evidence" of respect for the rule of law, by "faithfully carrying out" supranational legal provisions even when they disagreed with them. They would channel their dissent to particular provisions through the "legal avenues" open to them, rather than by threatening secession. Sixth, and most important:

> Governments negotiate with one another in good faith and generally reach agreement, while not making themselves consistently and invariably the spokesmen of national interest groups; further, community sentiment would seem to prevail if governments give way in negotiations when they find themselves in a minority instead of insisting on a formal or informal right of veto.[60]

Political integration, Haas continued, consists essentially in the process whereby "political actors in several distinct national settings are persuaded to shift their loyalties, expectations and political activities toward a new center, whose institutions possess or demand jurisdiction over the pre-existing national states."[61] It is, in other words, no other than the growth of community mindedness.

Haas was very careful to state in his opening chapter that "Political Community, as here defined, need not presuppose the emergence of a federal state . . . the constitutional form that which will qualify for the ideal type may be that of a unitary, a federal or even a confederal arrangement."[62] The interesting thing about Haas's definitions of *political community* and *political integration* is that they are entirely concerned with the *cast of mind* of the Community's political actors. A *political community*, Haas is suggesting, exists when its key political (and economic) actors think it does (and allow their belief to determine, or at least shape, their actions). When leaders from different political constituencies, different nations and different intellectual traditions share a common conviction in the necessity for and supremacy of centralized decision-making institutions; when they make "making the Community" their central preoccupation; when they are willing to suborn narrow national interests to the common good, then a political community exists, irrespective of the precise institutional form that it actually takes. Haas believed that Europe's political parties, and still more its interest groups, were still predominately "nationalist" in mentality. He was very optimistic, however, that "the expansive logic of sector integration" was propelling the Six towards the creation of a political community. This was because each new move towards integration occasioned policy "spillover" into other areas. The EEC treaty, Haas believed, was already an important "spillover" effect of the ECSC treaty and would itself compel further steps towards the supranational governance of other policy fields:

> Projecting the spill-over effect observed in the case of the ECSC, an acceleration of his process under the new treaty can safely be predicted. . . . The Assembly is bound to be a more faithful prototype of a federal parliament than the ECSC "legislature." As for the Council of Ministers, it is inconceivable that the liberalization not only of trade, but the conditions governing trade, can go on for long without "harmonization of general economic policies" spilling over into the fields of currency and credit, investment planning and business cycle control. The actual functions then regularly carried out by the Council will be those of a ministry of economics. *The spill-over may make a political community of Europe before the end of the transitional period.*[63] [italics mine]

The phrase in italics followed logically for Haas because explicit throughout his argument was the conviction that community mindedness would automatically be generated by the establishment of supranational institutions and the extension of their power and responsibilities. As central institutions took on more responsibility and power, so the political parties would compete more tenaciously to win control of them. Liberals would join Liberals across the Six in order to promote Liberal ideals through Community institutions. Socialists and Christian Democrats would do likewise. Trade unions would bargain and organize at European level, which would compel employers associations to think more supranationally in their turn. Member governments, in Haas's view, were already acting "more and more like sensitive politicians in a federal state plagued by severe regional, cultural and economic differentials."[64] They were "engaged" in the array of institutions they had created, by which Haas meant that they negotiated hard for their national interests, but would ultimately compromise rather than smash the structures of cooperation that had been so laboriously created. The Six, he

concluded, had evolved a new instrument of governance that was neither an
outright intergovernmental organization nor a federal state, but a "hybrid in
which neither the federal nor the intergovernmental tendency has clearly tri-
umphed."[65] The nation-states involved in this experiment were clearly "satisfied" with this state of affairs, although Haas left little doubt that, in the
long run, he believed that the federating principle would gradually win out
and that Europe would become an organized political community governed
by central institutions on the model of the United States. The book's last
sentence was: "The vision of Jean Monnet has been clearly justified by
events."[66]

Haas's explanation of the development of "European" institutions within
the Six was highly flattering to their postwar governments. While it is true
that functionalism as a general doctrine in political science starts from the de-
terministic presumption that political organizations evolve in response to environmental circumstances and that (in the case of Western Europe after
1945) the fact of economic interdependence between the countries of the
Six propelled political integration, a careful reading of Haas's book also
shows beyond argument that he also considered integration to be a "voluntary" process on the part of the Six's governments.[67] Ultimately, Haas was
saying that the Six's rulers had shown great enlightenment in the postwar period. Quite consciously, they had set in motion a process that would inevitably lead to the nation-states diminishing as a force and being substituted
by a political community boasting cooperative institutions. France, Germany
and Italy were no longer playing great power games (or, at least, the principles of national aggrandizement no longer invariably dictated their foreign
policy), but were groping slowly but surely towards surrendering *sacro ego-
ismo* as the mainspring of policy.

This explanation was never going to stay unchallenged once the historians
got to work on the documents. By far the weightiest alternative explanation
came from the British economic historian, Alan Milward, whose *European
Rescue of the Nation State* was first published in 1984. Haas had seen the development of European institutions as a process in which a plural number of
nation-states had collaborated to construct a protofederation, within which,
from now on, the dynamics of supranational integration would increasingly
determine the federation's future. Milward, by contrast, averred that the theoretical "antithesis" between the nation-state and the European Communities that was taken for granted in the work of functionalists like Haas, and
which has (undeniably) been such an important aspect of the EC's own
mythology, simply did not exist. The construction of European institutions
in the postwar period, Milward argued, was instead "an integral part of the
reassertion of the nation-state as an organizational concept."[68] After 1945,
the European nation-state "rescued itself from collapse," by massively increasing its powers and the scope of its activities. It established socialized

medicine and mass schooling; it nationalized key industries and it used Keynesian techniques of demand management to guarantee full employment and prosperity. The nation-state (by which Milward means the separate governments that variously managed the separate states) wanted to prove that it could deliver the goods to its citizens. The construction of Europe was part and parcel of this process since in certain areas the drive to acquire legitimacy required an "international framework."[69]

It is impossible here to do more than summarize Milward's intensely researched and meticulously argued book, but the gist of his argument is that the nation-states found "Europeanization" a useful means of guaranteeing the classic goals of nation-states throughout the ages: domestic stability, security from external dangers and prosperity for their citizens. Agriculture, Milward contends, was subsidized through the CAP as a way for nation-states to blur the costs of income support for farmers—costs that the voters of individual countries probably would not have been prepared to pay.[70] A customs union was agreed, against all odds, because the Six's economic growth was being dragged along by rapid West German economic growth. The other five were anxious both to continue to profit from the German boom and to bind Germany into the Western camp. The EEC treaty was a means of satisfying this dual objective.[71] If, moreover, we read what Milward, tongue firmly in cheek, calls the "lives and teachings of the European saints" (De Gasperi, Adenauer, Schuman, Van Zeeland and so forth), we see clearly that the central preoccupation of Europe's "founding fathers" was less pure idealism for the European cause than fear that "democracy and christianity could not be defended" against the forces of darkness unless there was a "joint economic and spiritual renewal of liberal capitalism."[72]

The corollary of Milward's argument was that the construction of the network of European institutions in place by the end of the 1950s represented a sustained "act of national will" on the part of the Six's member states. To this extent, his views are not so different from Haas's as he portrays them in the introduction to *European Rescue*. But whereas Haas's thesis both predicted and preached the withering away of the role of the nation-state in Europe, Milward's argument implied that integrationist steps would always (unless politicians radically change their behavior—a possibility his methodology does not permit him to rule out) tend to strengthen the nation-states' ability to fulfill their traditional functions.

Milward had the benefit of thirty years of hindsight, of course. But in retrospect, it is hard not to conclude that Haas was being overoptimistic in predicting the establishment of a political community, by his definition of the term, in Western Europe. States could not be progressively excluded from the equation in the way Haas anticipated. The position of the functionalist school, in fact, in hindsight seems so idealistic that Milward for one has speculated that functionalist theory was semiconsciously fulfilling its Cold War duty to American foreign policy, which saw a future United States of Europe as a "heavenly city profiled on the horizon."[73] By assuming that "integration is in some way a higher state of political organization," Milward charges, functionalists were transposing on to European history the "conventional and comforting liberal interpretation of America's own history, to which most American scholars felt it necessary to conform during the Cold War."[74]

If, however, the nation-states were the key actors pressing for measures of European integration, then integration was less a process with a predictable outcome than a haphazard game that depended for its continuance on the nation-states of the Six deciding it was in their interest to play. The second problem with Haas's methodology was that it was far too determinist. Charles de Gaulle was about to show that the concerted action of a single statesman leading a strong nation-state could impose his will on the EEC's supposed tendency to greater supranationalism. In the introduction to the *Uniting of Europe*'s second edition, Haas himself confessed that the "phenomenon of de Gaulle is omitted; the superiority of step-by-step economic decisions over crucial political choices is assumed as permanent; the determinism implicit in the picture of the European social and economic structure is almost absolute."[75] Haas consoled himself, in effect, by saying that his theory was still valid in the absence of such a figure and that even a de Gaulle had not been able to generate a "spillback" dynamic that would cause the EEC to fall apart.[76] This was true, although at the height of the 1965 "empty chair" crisis, de Gaulle's partners might have been forgiven for thinking differently. Yet implicit in Haas's notion of spillback was a third misjudgment: the idea that de Gaulle was a narrow nationalist. The challenge posed by de Gaulle to the "Monnet vision" of Europe was all the stronger because it was based upon a countervision of Europe's future that arguably was tougher-minded and more realistic than the ambitious dreams of the functionalist school.

NOTES

1. Jean Monnet, *Les Etats-Unis d'Europe ont commencées* (Luxembourg: ECSC, 1952).

2. Hans-Peter Schwarz, *Konrad Adenauer: German Statesman and Politician in a Period of War, Revolution and Reconstruction*, vol. 1 (Providence, R.I.: Berghahn, 1995), 619.

3. Political and Economic Planning (PEP), *European Organisations: An Objective Survey* (London: Unwin, 1959), 236.

4. Jean Monnet, *Mémoires* (Paris: Fayard, 1971), 438.

5. Robert Marjolin, *Architect of European Unity: Memoirs 1911–1986* (London: Weidenfeld and Nicholson, 1989), 270.

6. PEP, *European Organisations*, 242.

7. See especially William Diebold's *The European Coal and Steel Community* (New York: Council on Foreign Relations, 1960), and Arnold Zurcher's *The Struggle to Unite Europe* (New York: New York University Press, 1958).

8. The analysis owes much to the excellent chapter on the ECSC in PEP, *European Organisations*, 229–94.

9. This point is a central argument in Mark Trachtenberg, *A Constructed Peace: The Making of the European Settlement 1945–63* (Princeton, N.J.: Princeton University Press, 1999). See also James Chace, *Dean Acheson* (New York: Simon & Schuster, 1998), especially ch. 23.

10. Pascaline Winand, *Eisenhower, Kennedy and the United States of Europe* (New York: St. Martin's, 1993), 27–28.

11. Kevin Ruane, *The Rise and Fall of the European Defence Community* (London: Macmillan, 2000).

12. The best account in English of the EPC is Rita Cardozo, "The Project for a Political Community 1952–54," in *The Dynamics of European Union*, ed. Roy Pryce (London: Routledge, 1989), 49–77.

13. Bino Olivi, *L'Europa difficile* (Bologna, Italy: Il Mulino, 2000), 43.

14. In a book published in 1950, Dulles wrote:

Since disunity is so perilous and unity so precious . . . why, may we ask, does integration not happen? It does not happen because of the tradition of complete national independence has become so deeply rooted . . . vested interests have always been powerful enough to prevent peaceful change to unity. Recurrent efforts have been made to unite Europe by violence. Napoleon tried it; so did the Kaiser; so did Hitler; so, now, does Stalin. . . . The United States now has the opportunity to bring about peacefully what every western leader, without regard to nation or party, recognizes ought to be done, but will not be done unless there is friendly but firm outside pressure. The United States can and should take that opportunity and exert that pressure.

J. Foster Dulles, *War or Peace* (New York: Macmillan, 1950), 213–15.

15. Ruane, *Rise and Fall*, 47.

16. This was despite the fact that Churchill had dismissed the EDC treaty as a "sludgy amalgam." I am grateful to Philip Bell for pointing this remark out to me.

17. Quoted in Winand, *Eisenhower, Kennedy*, 50.

18. Paul-Henri Spaak, *The Continuing Battle* (London: Weidenfeld and Nicholson, 1971), 157.

19. Ruane, *Rise and Fall*, 92–93.

20. Ruane, *Rise and Fall*, 93. See also Winand, *Eisenhower, Kennedy*, 59.

21. Spaak's account of the EDC debacle is to be found in pages 159–71 of *The Continuing Battle*.

22. Quoted Frank Giles, *The Locust Years: The Story of the French Fourth Republic 1946–1958* (London: Secker & Warburg, 1991), 177.

23. Quotes are from N. Laites and C. de la Malène, "Paris from EDC to WEU," *World Politics* no. 2 (January 1957): 193–219. See also Raymond Aron, *France Defeats EDC* (New York: Praeger, 1957).

24. Quoted in Winand, *Eisenhower, Kennedy*, 62.

25. Monnet, *Mémoires*, 465.

26. Monnet, *Mémoires*, 466.

27. Marjolin, *Architect of European Unity*, 214.

28. Alan Milward, *The Reconstruction of Western Europe 1945–1951* (London: Routledge, 1984), 326.

29. Marjolin, *Architect of European Unity*, 220.

30. Dennis Healey, *The Time of My Life* (London: Michael Joseph, 1989), 115.

31. The text of the Messina communiqué is taken from U. Kitzinger, *The European Common Market and Community* (New York: Barnes & Noble, 1967), 69.

32. PEP, *Statements of the Action Committee for a United States of Europe* (London: PEP, 1969), 11.

33. PEP, *Statements of the Action Committee*, 16–18.

34. Spaak presented his report first to the ECSC Assembly on 13 March 1956; the printed report was submitted on 21 April 1956. Spaak's chairmanship of the committee was notoriously tough. On one occasion, when negotiations had slowed over the question of fruit imports, he told the committee, "I give you two hours . . . if it is not settled by then, I shall call the press in and announce that Europe won't be built after all, because we can't agree about bananas." Spaak, *Continuing Battle*, 89.

35. Spaak, *Continuing Battle*, 240.

36. Robert H. Lieshout, *The Struggle for the Organization of Europe* (Northampton, Mass.: Edward Elgar, 1999), 159–65.

37. Marjolin, *Architect of European Unity*, 281.

38. Andrew Moravcsik, *The Choice for Europe: Social Purpose and State Power from Messina to Maastricht* (Ithaca, N.Y.: Cornell University Press, 1998), 96.

39. Marjolin, *Architect of European Unity*, 281.

40. Marjolin, *Architect of European Unity*, 285.

41. Marjolin, *Architect of European Unity*, 288.

42. Hugo Young, *This Blessed Plot* (London: Macmillan, 1998), 88.

43. Young, *This Blessed Plot*, 91.

44. P. M. H. Bell, *Britain and France 1940–1994: The Long Separation* (London: Longman, 1997), 146–50. I am grateful to Philip Bell for several useful suggestions that greatly clarified aspects of the Suez crisis for me.

45. Thus Hanns Jürgen Küsters writes: "The failure of the Franco-British Suez adventure once again made France's limited role as a great power between the two superpowers abundantly clear to the Mollet government. In a quest for closer co-operation with its European partners it gave up its hesitant attitude to the Common Market in the period that followed." H. J. Küsters, "The Treaties of Rome (1955–57)," in *The Dynamics of European Union*, ed. R. Pryce, (London: Routledge, 1989) 90–91.

46. Marjolin, *Architect of European Unity*, 297.

47. See Hans-Peter Schwarz, *Konrad Adenauer: German Politician and Statesman in a Period of War, Revolution and Reconstruction*, vol. 2 (Providence R.I.: Berghahn, 1997), 240–45, for Adenauer's visit to Paris in November 1956.

48. Bell, *Britain and France*, 155.

49. Lieshout, *The Struggle*, 168. P-H. Laurent, "The Diplomacy of the Rome Treaty 1965–57," *Journal of Contemporary History* 7 (1972): 209–220; see especially 213.

50. Winand, *Eisenhower, Kennedy*, 93.

51. Moravcsik, *Choice for Europe*, 88.

52. An excellent account of Britain's Free Trade Association proposals and subsequent decision to attempt to enter the EEC is to be found in Roy Denman, *Missed*

Chances (London: Indigo, 1996), ch. 11. For a contemporary account, see Uwe Kitzinger, "Europe: The Six and the Seven," *International Organization* 14 (Winter 1960): 20–36.

53. PEP, *Statements of the Action Committee*, 22.
54. PEP, *Statements of the Action Committee*, 23.
55. Marjolin, *Architect of European Unity*, 303.
56. Anthony Arnull, *The European Union and Its Court of Justice* (Oxford: Oxford University Press, 1999), 79.
57. Arnull, *European Union and Its Court of Justice*, 81.
58. Arnull, *European Union and Its Court of Justice*, 83.
59. Ernst Haas, *The Uniting of Europe*, 2d ed. (Stanford, Calif.: Stanford University Press, 1968), 9–10.
60. Haas, *Uniting of Europe*, 10.
61. Haas, *Uniting of Europe*, 16.
62. Haas, *Uniting of Europe*, 7–8.
63. Haas, *Uniting of Europe*, 311.
64. Haas, *Uniting of Europe*, 525.
65. Haas, *Uniting of Europe*, 526.
66. Haas, *Uniting of Europe*, 527.
67. Haas, *Uniting of Europe*, xxxi.
68. Alan Milward, *The European Rescue of the Nation State*, 2d ed. (London: Routledge, 1992), 7.
69. Alan Milward, ed., *The Frontiers of National Sovereignty* (London: Routledge, 1993), 5.
70. Milward, *European Rescue*, 317.
71. Milward, *European Rescue*, 223.
72. Milward, *European Rescue*, 341. There is some truth in Milward's comments. In his essay, "Europe—Past, Present and Future," Adenauer wrote, "The integration of Europe must be achieved. I am convinced that it is the sole salvation for the Christian West." Salvation, the text made perfectly clear, was to be free from the threat of Soviet Communism. But also from war, especially between France and Germany. See Konrad Adenauer, *World Indivisible* (New York: Harper & Brothers, 1955), 49–81 at 51.
73. Milward, *European Rescue*, 13.
74. Milward, *European Rescue*, 13.
75. Haas, *Uniting of Europe*, xxiii.
76. Haas, *Uniting of Europe*, xxix.

4

In the Shadow of the General

De Gaulle and the EEC 1958–1969

Charles de Gaulle is often depicted as an ardent nationalist, a man who used France's unique position within the EEC to put a brake on the process of gradual integration begun by the ECSC and accelerated by the Treaties of Rome. There is, of course, much truth in this picture. De Gaulle was an archenemy of the supranational dimensions of the EEC treaty and certainly, by his actions, put paid to any hope that Western Europe would evolve towards the creation of a political community in the 1960s. Yet though de Gaulle did brake the momentum of the EEC at a crucial moment in its history, he also saved the new organization from premature crisis. The EEC treaty required huge alterations in the economic behavior of the member states. France, with its cosseted agriculture, heavily protected manufacturers and comparatively lavish welfare state, was the nation that was required to make the greatest adjustments of all. Without de Gaulle's personal leadership, and the institutional power devolved upon the president by the Constitution of the Fifth Republic in France, it is probable that France would not have been able to meet its obligations under the EEC treaty. Hans von der Groeben, the second German nominee to the original Commission and, like Walter Hallstein, an ardent federalist, summarized the point well when he said that the last governments of the Fourth Republic would have been willing to "exhaust the political opportunities of the Treaty of Rome," but would "scarcely have been able" to enforce the "radical domestic reforms" that the EEC treaty stipulated.[1] When de Gaulle came to power at the beginning of June 1958, France was suffering from rapid inflation and a ballooning balance-of-payments deficit. De Gaulle, once his constitutional position had been fortified, acted decisively to prepare France for the first round of tariff reductions

85

envisaged by the EEC treaty. The franc was devalued by 17.5 percent in December 1958, government expenditure was cut sharply back and taxes were raised.[2]

De Gaulle, in short, backed the EEC from the first. He merely had a restrictive interpretation of what it was supposed to lead to. De Gaulle wanted to extend the free market to agriculture, liberalize trade in manufactures gradually within the context of the customs union and preserve the Six from "Anglo-Saxon" contamination. It was to be a trading bloc, whose geopolitical policy was to be set by the French government. This concept of European unity was simply different (though, in its own way, hardly less ambitious) from that of Jean Monnet, Walter Hallstein and the European Movement. It was one that entrenched national governments, not technocrats, or pan-European institutions, as the driving force of the Community. *Une Europe des patries* was not a mere slogan for de Gaulle. But his vision of an activist Europe cutting a dash on the world stage was not one the more timid member states of the Six were prepared to go along with. Germany, Italy and the Netherlands did not regard French *gloire* as a substitute for American leadership in the fields of defense and foreign policy. They were far happier pampering their farmers.

THE EEC'S FIRST FOUR YEARS

De Gaulle's first act in defense of a restrictive interpretation of the EEC treaty was to block negotiations for a free trade agreement on 14 November 1958. Even after the signature of the Treaties of Rome, the British had pressed on, via the OEEC, with their plan to break down the EEC's common external tariff, which, in the British government's view, was an unjustifiable act of discrimination against other OEEC members. In this endeavor, they had the powerful backing of German minister for the economy Ludwig Erhard, important sections of German industry, the Dutch government, and even, though more conditionally, the Italians. Only the French were outright skeptics.

Yet the British still failed to mobilize a consensus around the creation of a larger free trade area. The main reason for this was the failure of the British government to make substantive concessions on her own account. The British put forward three main proposals. Trade in manufactured goods was to be liberalized throughout the OEEC; agricultural products were to be excluded from the agreement and Britain (hence) would be able to continue importing cheap food from Australia and New Zealand; there would be no common external tariff. Oddly, the British did not entitle their negotiating position "having your cake and eating it." Had the scheme been implemented as the British wanted, Britain would have gained twice. In the first place, Britain would no longer have faced the consolidated tariffs introduced by the EEC treaty. In the second place, as the French government immediately spotted, Britain's scheme would have allowed the British to import—for example—cheap Australian wool and then resell it in France, without customs duty, in the form of expensive sweaters. The British were striving to get access to the large market of the Six, while preserving the competitive advantage of so-called Commonwealth preference. As bait, they were dangling the prospect of easier access to Britain's large consumer market before West German industry.[3] Marjolin says dryly that the British proposals would have left Britain "at the meeting point of two preferential systems, enjoying the advantages of both."[4] De Gaulle's decision to cut short the negotiations amounted to telling the Germans to choose quickly between France and Britain. As de Gaulle correctly guessed, friendship with France was too important in Chancellor Adenauer's plans for the Germans to choose in favor of Britain. After de Gaulle's veto, the British were compelled to settle for the distinctly second-best solution of forming the European Free Trade Agreement in January 1960 with the Nordic countries, Austria, Switzerland and Portugal.[5]

The Commission welcomed de Gaulle's abrupt termination of the talks. Its fear was that the EEC might dissolve "like a lump of sugar in a cup of tea."[6] This almost certainly was Britain's political goal. One consequence of de Gaulle's decision, however, was that liberalization within the Six proceeded apace. Quantitative restrictions on intra-Community trade had been entirely suppressed by December 1961. At France's initiative, intra-Community trade barriers were lowered faster than specified by the EEC treaty, and the common external tariff, in part to reassure the United States, whose exports had been affected by growing intra-Six trade after January 1958, was set at a lower level than Britain's for industrial goods. The EEC also agreed to a large number of bilateral tariff reductions with the United States during the so-called Dillon Round of trade talks from 1958 to 1960.

This substantive progress on trade was matched in another area important for France: the renewal of the Treaty of Association between the EEC and the non-European countries and territories that had special relations with Belgium, France, Italy and the Netherlands. For the most part, these countries were France's African "dependencies" (to use the phrase then common). Article 131 of the EEC treaty said that the "purpose of association is to promote the economic and social development of the countries and territories." It envisaged two main mechanisms. First, the Six were to "apply to their trade with the countries and territories the same treatment as they accord each other pursuant to this treaty" (art. 132 [1]). In practical terms, this meant that the people of the Six had to pay more than before for coffee and fruit, especially bananas. The EEC was choosing to privilege its former colonies in Africa at the expense of Latin America. Second, the Six pledged a substantial aid package. Article 1 of the Implementing Convention attached to the EEC treaty set up a development fund that would invest $580 million over five years. Article 3 of the Implementing Convention also empowered the Commission to draw up "general programs" for financing social programs, in particular hospitals and schools, and specific "productive development projects." The general programs were almost entirely financed by France.

Initially at least, the convention with the associated countries was one of the EEC's "signal successes."[7] Between 1959 and 1962, most of the countries listed in the EEC treaty became independent, but in a sense this enhanced the EEC's role. The fact that aid was nominally being dispensed by a supranational organization rather than by the former colonial powers directly undoubtedly rendered such funds more acceptable to the African countries' new leaders. In July 1963, the Yaoundé Convention extended the original Treaty of Association and provided for a further $730 million in aid. An Association Council, composed of ministers from the Six and from the African nations, and a Parliamentary Conference provided the convention with an institutional framework.[8]

The consolidation of the Six as a cohesive customs union, German support over the FTA and the success of the Implementing Convention all put the EEC's account with the French government decisively in the black. However, these issues, while important, were a sideshow compared with agriculture. The most important single event in the EEC's first four years was the negotiation of the CAP. Failure to reach agreement on a Community-wide regime for agriculture would have smashed the common market as a whole. Yet agriculture was the thorniest of subjects. Producer groups were well organized and politically influential, farmers still constituted a decisive segment of the electorate (in 1958, agricultural workers constituted 23 percent of the workforce in France, 35 percent in Italy and 15 percent even in West Germany), agricultural incomes, depressed by a decade of falling prices, were already very low and were provoking a drift to the towns that was imperiling the rural way of life. Left to itself, agricultural employment within the Six would have shrunk quite rapidly in the 1960s as inefficient small farmers were squeezed out of business. The picture was particularly bleak in France, whose rural areas were in deep crisis by 1960. De Gaulle, making an alarmed comparison with the then acute crisis in France's colonies, warned that France would have an "Algeria on our own soil" if the problems of agriculture were not soon resolved.[9]

These factors, taken together, meant that there was no chance whatever that the CAP would reflect the liberal principles prevailing in the rest of the EEC treaty. The governments of all six countries were determined to get a deal that maximized farm incomes in their countries, minimized competition for their farmers and was a domestic vote winner. With such a starting point, negotiations on the proposals put forward by the Commission inevitably became fraught. On 9 December 1961, de Gaulle flatly warned the rest of the Community—and Germany, the main footdragger, in particular—that France would not implement the next round of tariff cuts on manufactured goods if the CAP deadline set by the Treaty of Rome were breached.[10] That deadline was 31 December 1961: in the end, an accord was only reached on 14 January 1962 after the Six decided to "stop the clock" and carry on bargaining.

The accord specified that a common market in agricultural products would be gradually introduced between 1 August 1962 and 31 December 1969. A common system of levies on foreign imports was introduced to ensure that prices were not undercut by outside competitors, and an export subsidy regime was implemented. The CAP, in other words, although fiendishly complicated in its detail, was simple in conception. The EEC intended to solve the economic and social problems of agriculture within the Six as a whole by guaranteeing artificially high domestic prices and subsidizing exports, rather than encouraging cheap food and compelling a shakeout among domestic producers.

The devil, however, was in the details. Agricultural production was divided into three main categories: grains and dairy products, pig meat and eggs, and fruit, vegetables and wines. The first of these categories was the most sensitive since the price of grain had a knock-on effect throughout the entire agricultural economy. During the seven-year transitional phase, each country would set target prices for wheat and barley production (dairy products were subsequently handled on the same basis). High-cost countries such as Germany would be entitled to impose levies at their frontiers on grain coming from other EEC members and to grant subsidies to allow their domestic producers to export production elsewhere in the Six. The target prices would gradually be reduced until prices were harmonized throughout the Community at the end of the transitional period. Thereafter target prices would be set at Community level.

To prevent target prices from falling, the Six set up the so-called Guidance and Guarantee Fund to buy surplus production from producers at the so-called support price (about 10 percent less than the target price) and to subsidize exports. No cap was placed on the amount that the Community would buy, and thus producers were essentially handed a blank check to increase harvests at the taxpayers' expense. Nobody knew in 1962 how much the CAP would cost. But it was clear that it would not be cheap. It was agreed in principle during the 1962 negotiation that costs would eventually be paid out of the Community's "own resources"—which would consist of a levy placed upon imported foodstuffs from nonmembers. In the meantime, until June 1965, the CAP was to be financed by contributions from the member states. West Germany was to pay up to 31 percent of the costs; France and Italy up to 28 percent each.

Markets in pig meat and poultry and in fruit and vegetables were less tightly regulated. The pig meat and poultry sectors were defended from foreign competition by high "sluicegate prices" (a tariff on imports). There was no Community support price regime, however, in this sector. Fruit and vegetables were to be regulated by quality standard only, and by January 1966 produce was supposed to circulate freely with member states being entitled to impose border checks to ensure that quality standards were being maintained.[11]

The CAP was anything but an attempt to find an equitable solution to the difficulties of European agriculture. At bottom, it was a crude bargain between France and Germany. France wielded the potent threat of postponing the EEC's transition to its second stage—which would have been a severe setback for German industry—in order to unload much of the vast cost of subsidizing French agriculture on to the Community as a whole. France, as Andrew Moravcsik has explained, in agriculture was "largely uncompetitive on the world market, yet competitive within Europe."[12] The CAP enabled France to dispose of its surpluses within the Six at artificial prices while building up its export trade on the back of Community subsidies. It was a major achievement for de Gaulle, and while Moravcsik arguably exaggerates when he claims that it was less the pursuit of French *grandeur* than the "price of French wheat" that subsequently persuaded de Gaulle to veto British entry into the EEC in 1963, the central place of agriculture for overall French policy cannot be disputed.[13]

THE "UNION OF STATES"

De Gaulle's determination to restore France's place in the world was shown within weeks of his taking office. In the autumn of 1958, he wrote to Macmillan and Eisenhower proposing that NATO should be put under the joint leadership of a "directorate" of the three nuclear (or, in the case of France, which exploded its first atomic bomb in December 1960, soon-to-be nuclear) powers. Both Britain and the United States rejected this proposal as diplomatically as they could.[14] The episode seems to have convinced de Gaulle, however, that France, if it wanted to exercise its rightful role on the world stage, would have to do so as the de facto head of a European "Third Force." But to perform this role, the Six needed a new layer of intergovernmental institutions capable of making decisions on major questions of foreign policy and military strategy. In the summer of 1959, de Gaulle proposed that the Six's foreign ministers should meet three times a year to coordinate the EEC's foreign policy; in September 1960, at one of his frequent policy-making press conferences, he outlined a vision of a committee of the Six's heads of government making policy in foreign policy, defense, cultural and economic fields. Below this supreme committee, de Gaulle envisaged a supporting bureaucracy of technocrats in each field and a common assembly made up of delegates from the national parliaments. He also proposed that the plan should be submitted to the peoples of Europe in a Community-wide referendum as a way of giving it greater legitimacy. In short, he was putting forward "a total change in the objectives and methods of European unification."[15] A change, it is perhaps not gratuitous to point out, that anticipated the invention of the European Council—now the main architect of policy within the European Community—by a decade and half.

After some months of bilateral discussions with France's EEC partners (the Dutch, especially, were skeptical), the heads of government of the Six held a summit meeting at Bad Godesberg on 18 July 1961 to consider de Gaulle's proposals. At Bad Godesberg, after de Gaulle had dropped his populist scheme for a referendum, the Dutch acquiesced to a final communiqué that spoke of the Six's "determination" to press ahead with "the desire for political unification implicit in the EEC treaty" by instituting "regular summits between the Six's heads of government." A committee, to be headed by Christian Fouchet, a French diplomat who had been a "Gaullist of the first hour"—one of the brave handful of officials and soldiers who had joined de Gaulle in exile in 1940—was given the task of putting flesh on to the bare bones of this statement.

Fouchet reported on 2 November 1961. He proposed the establishment of what article 1 of the treaty called an "indissoluble" Union of States. The union's aims were to "bring about the adoption of a common foreign policy"; to ensure the "continued development of their common heritage and the protection of the values on which their civilization rests"; to contribute to "the defense of human rights, the fundamental freedoms and democracy"; to adopt a common policy for defense "in cooperation with the other free nations" (art. 2). Under Fouchet's plan, the union was provided with three main institutions: the Council, the Parliament and the Political Commission (PC).

The Council's main functions were outlined in articles 5 and 6. It was to be composed of the heads of government of the Six's member states, who would meet three times a year to "deliberate on all questions whose inclusion on its agenda is requested by one or more of the member states" (art. 6). Decisions were to be made on a basis of unanimity, with member states being granted the possibility of abstention, and were to be binding upon all states that had not abstained. The Council's president was to be chosen by the member states at each meeting and was to "take up his duties two months before the subsequent meeting and continue to exercise them for two months after the meeting" (art. 5). The Council was not necessarily to have, therefore, a revolving presidency. Had de Gaulle decided that international circumstances required him to lead the union for two or even three successive summits, he would have had the constitutional right to insist upon this—and who would have dared to deny him?

Nominal parliamentary scrutiny of the Council was to be provided by the Assembly of the European Communities—upgraded in Fouchet's plan to the status of a parliament, although it would not have had legislative functions. Administratively, the Council was to be served by the PC, which was to consist of "senior officials of the Foreign Affairs departments of each member state" (art. 9). It was to be based in Paris and was to be presided over by the representative of the member state holding the presidency of the Council. The PC was to implement the union's budget, which was to be drawn up by the Council and supplied by the member states. France, West Germany and Italy would each pay 28 percent of the new union's costs; the Netherlands and Belgium, 7.9 percent; Luxembourg, 0.2 percent (art. 13).

The Fouchet plan envisaged a period of three years in which the Union of States worked in conjunction with the other European Communities. Thereafter, however, there would be a "general review" whose "main objects" would be "the introduction of a unified foreign policy and the gradual establishment of an organization centralizing, *within the Union*, the European Communities" (art. 16, emphasis mine). De Gaulle's idea, plainly, was to merge the three economic Communities into a single body (something that happened in 1965 with the Merger Treaty) and have the unified "economic" Commission report to the Council of the union in the same way as the Political Commission was intended to do. The national governments would have reasserted their primacy over the Communities' supranational institutions and France would have been in a position to assert its primacy over the other governments of the Six.[16] It is a mistake, however, to think of the Fouchet plan purely as a ruse to enhance the greater glory of France. It was a genuine attempt by de Gaulle to avert the EEC's degeneration into what Hedley Bull was subsequently to call "Civilian Power Europe."[17] De Gaulle believed that the Six could not (or, at any rate, should not) afford merely to grow prosperous behind the shelter of the American nuclear umbrella. It needed to strike out and assert a foreign policy of its own. Stanley Hoffmann provides an insightful contemporary analysis of de Gaulle's goals for Europe:

> The General, a French nationalist, is also a "European nationalist." His concern for Europe is least understood in the United States, where people tend to assume that only the "Europeans" of Mr. Monnet's persuasion really care about uniting Europe. Just as he wants to prevent France from being a mere pawn on the international chessboard, the General wants to assure that Europe—which he sees as being the mother of civilization—can again become one of the principal players after having for more than twenty years been just a stake though the fault of its own divisions.[18]

De Gaulle's scheme would have been audacious even in more settled times, but it is important to remember the dramatic context in which the

Fouchet plan was put forward. By November 1961, just weeks after the East German government had constructed the Berlin Wall, the East–West conflict had reached its tensest moment since the Berlin airlift. In the late 1950s, the Soviet Union had built an intercontinental missile force to rival that of the United States, a fact that had caused the United States to rethink its nuclear strategy from top to bottom. Would the United States be prepared to use its still superior nuclear forces in defense of Europe, if it risked a devastating Soviet counterattack? In March 1961, newly elected President John Kennedy seemed to suggest that it would not automatically use America's nuclear arsenal in Europe's defense. The doctrine of "flexible response" in substance proposed that the NATO countries in Europe should build up their conventional forces to deter the USSR and leave a monopoly on nuclear arms to the United States.[19] This was not acceptable to de Gaulle, who had already withdrawn parts of the French armed forces from the NATO command structure and who now ostentatiously carried out bomb tests in the Sahara Desert in March and April 1961. Earlier, with characteristic subtlety, he had first tested the French bomb during an official visit by Soviet premier Nikita Khrushchev to Paris. De Gaulle saw two main advantages in having independent nuclear forces. First, as he had explained to Dwight Eisenhower in 1959, even a small nuclear force had a deterrent effect—an enemy's power to kill you ten times over lost all force if he himself had been obliterated once.[20] Second, by threatening to go nuclear, France would have the leverage to ensure that the United States maintained its European commitments. On 10 May 1961, de Gaulle officially announced his intention to build a French *force de frappe*. A visit from Kennedy to dissuade him at the end of May 1961 did not mend relations, although First Lady Jacqueline Kennedy compensated by enjoying a striking social success during the president's visit to Paris.[21]

The other members of the Six knew perfectly well at Bad Godesberg, therefore, that moves towards European political union, in the context of Franco-American relations, meant signing up to a much more self-reliant vision of western European security. The Fouchet plan, had it ever been implemented, would have given de Gaulle the institutional machinery to put himself forward as the "leader" of Western Europe and would have strengthened his case for parity with the United States and Britain in the direction of NATO. It was precisely for this reason that the plan ultimately foundered. Between November 1961 and January 1962, intergovernmental talks on the Fouchet plan proceeded, with skeptics, prominent among them the Dutch, arguing that it was pointless to go ahead with political union until Britain's application to join the EEC (Britain had applied on 31 July 1961) had been decided. The original version of the plan was also watered down to ensure that the proposed union was subordinate in military matters to NATO and to underline the independence of the institutions of the three European communities. This pettifogging opposition caused de Gaulle's patience to

snap. On 18 January 1962, flushed with his victory in the agriculture negotiations, de Gaulle introduced a new draft treaty that struck out all mentions
of NATO and incorporated trade and industry (the chief prerogatives of the
EEC) into the union's responsibilities. The Five "were filled with consternation" at the French government's "blunt way of issuing ultimatums."[22] De
Gaulle's high-handed action showed only too clearly how the Union of
States would be governed if they agreed to it.

American diplomacy chose this moment to make its case. On 25 January
1962, President Kennedy presented the Trade Expansion Bill to Congress,
asking for authorization to conclude a wide-ranging free trade agreement
with Western Europe. The United States needed such an agreement, because
the creation of the Six had led to a substantial fall in American exports to the
EEC, but the primary motive was political. The "Grand Design," as
Kennedy called it, was predicated upon free trade, British membership of the
EEC and American leadership in defense matters. Its most famous evocation
came on 4 July 1962, when Kennedy made at Philadelphia what was described as the "declaration of interdependence":

> We believe that a united Europe will be capable of playing a greater role in the
> common defense, of responding more generously to the needs of the poorer na-
> tions, of joining the United States and others in lowering trade barriers, resolv-
> ing problems of commerce, commodities and currency, and developing coordi-
> nated policies in all economic, political and diplomatic areas. We see in such a
> Europe a partner with whom we can deal on a basis of full equality in all the great
> and burdensome tasks of building and defending a community of free nations.[23]

Long before the Philadelphia speech, however, American diplomats were
spreading the message that the future of the Six was with the United States.
The choice, the Kennedy administration argued, was between an "Atlantic
Community" protected by NATO, in which the United States and the Six
collaborated on equal terms, and a precarious new venture into geopolitics
with de Gaulle at the helm.

The smaller nations of the EEC had no difficulty in choosing the American option. Belgium and the Netherlands refused to bow to the French *démarche* of 18 January. Between February and April 1962, there were intense
conversations between the states, with Adenauer and the Italian premier Amintore Fanfani playing a mediating role. This mediation won concessions
from de Gaulle. On 15 March 1962, Fouchet's committee issued a text com-
paring the position of the French delegation with that of the other delegations. This text showed that the French had, in fact, moved substantially towards the common position of the Five, although substantive divergences
did remain. France agreed that a union of States called the "European
Union" would be created; she conceded that the European Union would
merely "reconcile, coordinate and unify" the policy of the member states in

foreign policy, economics, cultural affairs and defense; she said she was "desirous of welcoming" other countries of Europe into the existing European institutions; she accepted that "committees of ministers" for foreign affairs, defense, education and culture should form part of the institutional structure of the Union.

The French also yielded on the substance of article 16. It now read: "Three years after this Treaty comes into force, it shall be subjected to a review in order to consider suitable measures either for strengthening the Union in general in the light of progress already made or, in particular, for simplifying, rationalizing and coordinating the ways in which member states co-operate."[24] This was obviously completely vacuous and represented a de facto retreat (or, at least, a strategic withdrawal) by the French government from its attempt to centralize and subordinate existing European institutions into a single body under its control.

The French concessions, however, were nothing like enough to win over the Dutch, in particular. The 15 March draft of the treaty featured strong Benelux demands that the French were not prepared to accommodate. Thus, the Dutch and Belgians wanted the treaty to be clear that a common defense policy would operate "within the framework of the Atlantic alliance"; they wanted the treaty to say that it "would not derogate from the competence of the European Communities"; they said that the Six were "ready to welcome" new members. So far as institutions were concerned, they wanted a rotating presidency of the Council and the establishment of the office of secretary-general. What this figure would have done precisely is not clear from the 15 March draft, but he was to have been "independent of the governments of the member-states" and thus introduced a supranational dimension to the treaty. A further element of supranationalism was added by subjecting the actions of the Council to judicial review by the European Court of Justice. Most important of all, article 20 of the Benelux version of the treaty stated that the "general review" of the union's activities should lead to a "draft constitution" being drawn up and being submitted to the European Parliament. The review's central goal would be to institute a directly elected parliament and to introduce majority voting into the Council. At the end of the EEC's transition period (that is, in 1970), the European Union and the European Communities would be incorporated into "an organic institutional framework, without prejudice to the machinery provided for in the Treaties of Paris and Rome."

The other members of the Six and Belgium and the Netherlands, in particular, were thus advocating what amounted to a federalist charter. The central point of difference between de Gaulle and both the Americans and the Five was ultimately an unbridgeable one of principle. De Gaulle was insistent that the states of Europe had to face the challenges of the Cold War and economic development by acting together, rather than fobbing off responsibility in key policy areas to the United States and to trans-European institutions. The others were reluctant to surrender to this starkly realist interpretation of Europe's future. The Dutch eventually pulled the plug on the Fouchet negotiations on 17 April 1962, when it became clear that France would not back down on their opposition to the supranational dimensions of the European Union and would not accept delaying the implementation of the treaty until Britain had joined the EEC. De Gaulle's response was given, as usual, at a press conference. On 15 May 1962, he warned darkly that Europe was far too dependent upon the United States and dismissed the idea that Europe could be governed through supranational institutions as a fantasy worthy of the "thousand and one nights."[25] He was to dedicate the next four years to proving himself right. The failure of the Fouchet plan for a Union of States was the first act in a three-act tragedy for the hopes of the federalists. There is no doubt that de Gaulle was deeply wounded by the rejection of his scheme. He seems to have concluded that if he could not have the Europe he wanted, he would make sure that his opponents did not get their way either.

THE FIRST BRITISH NEGOTIATION FOR ENTRY

The British decision to apply for entry to the EEC had been chiefly provoked by growing evidence that the British economy was performing badly compared to its continental rivals. Britain's labor costs were rising in comparison with the EEC Six, as British business proved less able than its continental rivals to cap the inflationary pressures caused by a tight labor market. Between 1950 and 1958, Britain's economy grew at an annual rate of 2.7 percent per year: good by the standards of the 1970s and 1980s, but far behind competitors such as Germany (7.8 percent), Italy (5.8 percent) and France (4.6 percent). Even more significantly, the former "workshop of the world" was losing her prominence as an exporter of manufactured goods. Britain's export trade grew by just 1.8 percent a year in this period; Germany's by 15 percent. In 1958, Germany's economy overtook Britain in size and her share of world export trade also exceeded Britain's.[26] This precipitous decline in Britain's relative economic position caused the higher reaches of the civil service to wake up to the importance of European integration with a jolt. The snobby superiority of the postwar generation of Whitehall mandarins towards the Europeans' attempts at integration was replaced by hardheaded economic analysis. Sir Frank Lee, a senior treasury official, began insisting in the spring of 1960 that the EFTA countries, especially Britain, could not afford, without lasting economic damage, to remain excluded from the large and rapidly expanding market of the Six and should negotiate an accord between the two trade blocs that conceded the principle of a common external tariff and concessions to the European model for agriculture.[27]

Geopolitical considerations also played a key role. When Britain applied for membership, she was, to paraphrase Dean Acheson's famous words, losing an empire without yet having found a role. The policy of decolonization inaugurated by prime minister Harold Macmillan in 1959 was ending Britain's role as an imperial power. Suez had taught Britain that her much-vaunted "special relationship" with the United States was a somewhat one-sided affair. The Six loomed in the minds of British diplomats as a potential vehicle for the German domination of Europe, or else as a "Napoleonic" bloc, against which Britain was bound to organize her diplomatic efforts. According to de Gaulle, Macmillan told him in the summer of 1958, "The Common Market is the continental system all over again. Britain cannot accept it. I beg you to give it up. Otherwise we shall be embarking on a war which will doubtless be economic at first but which runs the risk of gradually spreading into other fields."[28] In December 1960, Macmillan spent the Christmas holidays drafting a Cabinet paper that represented *his* "Grand Design" for the future of British foreign and economic policy. Its key passage stated that exclusion from the "strongest economic group in the civilized world must injure us." Exclusion was "primarily a political problem" that had to be "dealt with" by making a "supreme effort to reach a settlement" while de Gaulle was in power in France. From then on, Macmillan was unequivocally committed to pressing for outright membership of the Community.[29]

Actually, it is worth underlining that Britain, in a sense, did not so much apply for membership of the EEC in July 1961 as initiate a negotiation to see whether the Six were prepared to modify the Treaty of Rome to a sufficient extent to make joining acceptable for Britain. This is not to say, however, that Britain was not prepared to make concessions to get in. Edward Heath, the chief British negotiator, made Britain's position admirably clear in his opening speech at the negotiations on 10 October 1961. Britain, Heath said, recognized that the decision to seek entry to the EEC was "a turning point in our history." He then proceeded to explain the considerations that had led Britain to take such a drastic step. In "the first place," according to Heath, was Britain's "strong desire to play a full part in the development of European institutions." When the Six had decided to press ahead with what Heath called "a more organic kind of unity" in 1957, Britain had not then felt able to take part. Exaggerating somewhat, Heath added that it had never been "agreeable" for Britain to find that she was "no longer running with the stream towards European unity." The "second consideration" propelling Britain's application for membership, according to Heath, was the "increasing realization" that "a larger European unity had become essential" in a world where "political and economic power is becoming concentrated to such a great extent." The "third factor" influencing Britain's decision was the "remarkable success of your Community." Heath stated that Britain wished to "unite our efforts with yours; and to join in promoting, through the EEC, the fullest possible measure of European unity."[30]

Heath's prefacing remarks have been quoted at length both because they represent the most unambiguously pro-European statement ever made by a leading British politician in a public setting and to provide a contrast with the clear-cut pragmatic bargain that Heath then subsequently offered the Six in the main body of his remarks. Heath stated that the British were willing to "subscribe fully" to articles 2 and 3 of the EEC treaty and accept a common tariff, the abolition of internal tariffs, a common commercial policy and a common agricultural policy *if* the Six were prepared to meet Britain halfway over "three major problems." These problems were Commonwealth trade, UK agriculture and "the arrangements which could be made for our partners in EFTA." The third of these problems was largely pro forma. The concerns of the other EFTA nations would never have dissuaded Britain from concluding an agreement with the EEC that was in Britain's national economic interest. The first two, however, were not. Heath warned that he would be misleading his listeners if he "failed to say" how deeply the British people felt about the Commonwealth. He further stated that it would be a "tragedy" if British entry into the EEC "forced other members of the Commonwealth to change their whole pattern of their trade and perhaps their political orientation." Britain, Heath warned, could not "join the EEC under conditions in which this trade connection was cut with grave loss and even ruin for some of the Commonwealth countries."[31]

On agriculture, Heath, despite having said earlier that Britain accepted the CAP, proceeded to chip away at the principles underpinning the Six's agricultural agreement. He pointed out that Britain's own system of agricultural protection provided the highly satisfactory result of cheap food for consumers and guaranteed incomes for farmers. Britain placed low tariffs on agricultural products and none at all upon those coming from the Commonwealth. Prices in the shops were therefore low. The British farming community was maintained by income support payments that amounted to about three-quarters of the industry's net income of £360 million per year. Britain, in other words, lavishly paid a relatively restricted number of people to till the land and maintain the rural community in exchange for the benefits of world market food prices for the consumers. Implementing the CAP would have overturned this state of affairs, and Heath's words made clear that the British government was reluctant to make this sacrifice. He insisted that any price rises in basic foodstuffs would have to be introduced "gradually" and hinted that the Six might contemplate reforming the CAP to adjust to British practices, rather than the reverse: "I am sure that the pooling of ideas and experience will have fruitful results; indeed, some features of our agricultural arrangements may prove attractive to you."[32]

Heath had no choice but to insist upon these conditions. Conservative Party opinion would not contemplate a policy damaging to the Commonwealth countries, especially the "white" former dominions such as Australia, New Zealand and Canada. Farmers were then, as now, one of the Conservative Party's key backers. Yet, the two key British conditions were bound to tread on de Gaulle's corns. Establishing a system of trade preferences for the former French empire and, above all, instituting the CAP were the two key concerns of the French government in October 1961. British entrance was bound to throw the main thrust of de Gaulle's economic diplomacy into doubt. For this reason, the talks soon became bogged down in a quicksand of detail. Throughout 1962, long weeks were spent in excruciating argument over New Zealand butter—or, as the jargon preferred, "temperate zone foodstuffs." The Six, in general, and the French, in particular, were insistent that Britain should adapt her domestic agriculture to the same regime as the Six and enter the CAP fully in 1970, and the British, who were under intense pressure from the Commonwealth countries, felt obliged to honor Heath's pledge not to harm trade with the former empire. A gathering of the Commonwealth countries in London in September 1962 was a public relations disaster for the British government as the prime ministers of Australia, Canada and New Zealand openly accused Heath and Macmillan of ignoring their interests. A few weeks later, the Labour Party's leader, Hugh Gaitskell, made political capital out of the Conservatives' difficulties by clearly stating that Labour was opposed to any deal that harmed the Commonwealth trade. Gaitskell, however, also raised the thorny issue of membership's constitutional implications. In a famous phrase, he claimed that British membership of the EEC would be the end of "a thousand years of history."[33]

The intransigence of both the Commonwealth nations and the French government over agricultural questions is arguably significant when one studies the causes of de Gaulle's seemingly sudden decision on 14 January 1963, after months of tedious negotiation over the minutiae of the British application, to veto British entrance. The French president's move has become something of an academic mystery story, with historians queuing to decipher de Gaulle's motives. The standard interpretation is the so-called Trojan Horse theory. This links de Gaulle's abrupt "*non*" to the so-called Nassau agreement on defense policy between Britain and the Kennedy administration on 21 December 1962. Nassau was a partial climb down by Prime Minister Macmillan from the policy of possessing an independent nuclear deterrent. Britain had intended to deliver nuclear weapons using Vulcan bombers and Skybolt missiles purchased from the United States. Shortly beforehand, Kennedy told Macmillan that he would be canceling the Skybolt project for technical and financial reasons and offered Britain instead submarine-launched Polaris missiles. There were two problems with this. First, Britain had first to build the submarines—which postponed the date of her

nuclear independence—and, second, Kennedy insisted that the new Polaris
fleet should be part of a multilateral NATO force and that Britain should be
allowed to press the button only when the highest British interests were at
stake. Macmillan, bereft of Skybolt, had no choice but to acquiesce to
Kennedy's proposal.[34] The two countries then invited de Gaulle to participate in the multilateral force under the same conditions. De Gaulle, who had
met Macmillan just a few days before Nassau, was both infuriated at not being consulted and was convinced that the British climb down was evidence
that Britain would always do the Americans' bidding. Once in the Community, Britain would become an agent for American interests and would lead
the EEC towards the broader Atlantic Community envisaged by Kennedy at
Philadelphia. As Stanley Hoffmann put it: "Slamming the door on the
British . . . seemed to him less damaging to his policy [of building a strong
and independent Europe] than the disaster represented by the entry of England, the Trojan Horse of the United States, into the Common Market and
by the formation of a loose Atlantic Community directed by and dependent
upon the United States."[35]

The standard interpretation has recently been challenged by a major work
of scholarship. Andrew Moravcsik's *The Choice for Europe*, which is both an
innovative work of theory and a closely argued historical description of the
EC's development between Messina and Maastricht, contends that de
Gaulle's decision was motivated primarily by fears for the future of French
agriculture if Britain were to be admitted. Moravcsik's view is that de Gaulle
"decided against British entry early on . . . because Britain was certain to
block generous extra financing of the CAP."[36] Moravcsik points out that de
Gaulle told the French cabinet that he had warned Macmillan that he would
not agree to British entry when Macmillan visited him *before* flying to Nassau (Macmillan's reaction was so emotional that de Gaulle told his ministers
that he had wanted to say, in the words of the song by Edith Piaf, "*ne pleurez
pas milord*"). Furthermore, Moravcsik says, de Gaulle does not anywhere cite
geopolitical or "ideational" motives for his veto either in his memoirs or in
the text of the press conference at which he delivered his veto. Moravcsik
comments:

> De Gaulle devotes almost 1,500 words to what he terms a "clear" explanation
> of his veto without mentioning any disagreement with the Anglo-Saxons over
> security issues, the Fouchet plan, political union or any other geopolitical terms
> . . . mention of the United States is restricted to concern about its overwhelm-
> ing economic influence and its purported desire, along with Britain, to promote
> European trade liberalization without a preferential arrangement for agricul-
> ture.[37]

Moravcsik is certainly right to underscore the centrality of agricultural
concerns in de Gaulle's press conference speech. De Gaulle began by assert-

ing, "We cannot conceive of a Common Market in which French agriculture would not find outlets commensurate with its production." The "entry of agriculture into the Common Market" had been a "formal condition" for French participation. Britain, however, from the beginning "had requested membership, but on its own conditions." This was especially true of Britain's agricultural regime, which de Gaulle termed "obviously incompatible with the system that the Six have set up for themselves." The question, de Gaulle suggested (and this, in fact, was the nearest he came to expressing an outright "non"), was whether Britain could place itself "within a tariff that is truly common, giving up all preference with regard to the Commonwealth." De Gaulle concluded, "One could not say" that this problem had been resolved. Would it ever be? Only Britain, de Gaulle averred, could answer that question.

Thus far, this description of de Gaulle's speech appears to confirm Moravcsik's revisionist interpretation. De Gaulle went on, however, to outline further objections to Britain's entry, which, he claimed, would inevitably be followed by the applications of other states. An influx of new members would "completely change the series of adjustments, agreements, compensations and regulations already established between the Six." In de Gaulle's view, the "eleven-member, then thirteen-member and then perhaps eighteen-member Common Market that would be built would, without any doubt, hardly resemble the one the Six have built." He went on:

> Moreover, this Community, growing in this way, would be confronted with all the problems of its economic relations with a crowd of other states, and first of all with the US. It is foreseeable that the cohesion of all its members . . . would not hold for long and that in the end *there would appear a colossal Atlantic Community under American dependence and leadership which would soon swallow up the European Community.* This is an assumption that can be perfectly justified in the eyes of some, but it is not at all what France wanted, and what France is doing, which is a strictly European construction.[38] [italics mine]

It is surely fair to suggest that Moravcsik's somewhat abstract reformulation of these words—"mention of the United States is restricted to concern about its overwhelming economic influence"—does not begin to do justice to de Gaulle's meaning, above all by not mentioning the general's evident dislike of and hostility to an "Atlantic Community." Moreover, it is not true that de Gaulle does not mention "geopolitical concerns" in his memoirs as a justification for vetoing British entry. De Gaulle in fact says that he and Macmillan spent many hours together "either alone or accompanied by our ministers" discussing the "great subject" of British membership. De Gaulle says that these conversations convinced him that Britain was not ready to "moor herself to the Continent." Later, he adds, "a certain special agreement concerning the provision of American rockets and underlining the submission of

Britain's nuclear means, concluded separately at Nassau with John Kennedy, was to justify my circumspection."[39]

Moreover, it is certainly not true that de Gaulle failed to mention "security issues" in his 14 January press conference. A substantial part of the conference was given over to whatever de Gaulle's most eminent French biographer, Jean Lacouture, described as a "disdainful rejection of . . . the Nassau accords."[40] Moravcsik appears to regard this part of the press conference as entirely irrelevant to the question of British membership and merely points out (in a footnote) that "even in response to a question on the MLF, de Gaulle does not link nuclear issues to the EC."[41] This, however, is splitting hairs. The overall thrust of the conference, and the tone of de Gaulle's comments on American strategic policy towards Europe, leaves no doubt that the general's central preoccupation in 1963 was that the countries of the EEC might lose their independence and become satellites of the United States both economically and militarily. British entrance into the Community could only strengthen this possibility, and thus it is entirely logical to suppose that de Gaulle blocked British entry for this reason. That de Gaulle feared that British entrance might also lead to a more laissez-faire approach to agriculture is also plainly true, but what is not immediately clear to the uninitiated is why Moravcsik will not admit the possibility that de Gaulle might have had two motives, the relative weight of which, as in any historical argument, is naturally open to discussion (and perhaps never susceptible to a definitive conclusion).

The answer, of course, is methodology. Moravcsik's narrow insistence upon the centrality of agriculture should perhaps be regarded as an instance of theoretical overreach: a tendency to squeeze each and every event in the Community's history into a single overarching explanation—in this case, Moravcsik's extremely stimulating theory that the driving force of European integration has primarily been the concern of national leaders to promote the interests of their domestic economic producers. Moravcsik is not alone in succumbing to this tendency to theoretical overreach: it is perhaps an inevitable consequence of attempting, retrospectively, to prove the theorems of political science by demonstrating that past events conform to them.

As the German historian Oliver Bange has shown in his meticulous reconstruction of the events surrounding de Gaulle's veto, *The EEC Crisis of 1963*, British entry was round two of the geopolitical arm-wrestling bout begun by the rejection of the Fouchet plan. On one side of the table were the British and the Americans, whose support for British entry at times spilled over almost into outright intimidation; on the other, de Gaulle. At stake was nothing other than the political organization of the West. What gave de Gaulle the strength to stand out against the intense American pressure was, ultimately, the support of Konrad Adenauer, who, Bange shows, became convinced by the summer of 1962 that Britain, for a variety of reasons, would be an uncomfortable partner within the EEC.[42] The same point is made by Schwarz in his biography of Adenauer:

> Those who spoke to Adenauer during these weeks [May 1962] gained the impression that he had made up his mind: a definite turning towards France, reserved relations with the United States, a scarcely concealed "no" to Britain's participation in political union and—this was also important— intensive efforts to achieve a *modus vivendi* with the Soviet Union.[43]

What drove "the Old Man" to take the decisive step of backing de Gaulle? De Gaulle's cultivation of Adenauer (between November 1958 and January 1963, the two men met on fifteen occasions, had 100 hours of talks and wrote to each other over forty times) was certainly one reason.[44] When Adenauer made a state visit to France in July 1962, he was hailed by de Gaulle as "a great German, a great European, a great man who is a great friend of France."[45] Flattery on this scale must have been hard to ignore. When de Gaulle made a return visit to Germany in September 1962, moreover, he aroused massive popular approval by declaring his admiration for the "great German people." In a droll aside, he added: "They must be, they are cheering me."[46] Nobody had spoken to the Germans in these tones since 1945. Adenauer also harbored serious doubts over the economic benefits Britain would bring to the Community. He was also less than impressed by the Kennedy White House. The prolonged Berlin crisis of 1960–1962 left Adenauer with the conviction that Kennedy was "a weak president surrounded by inexperienced advisors from the professorial class."[47]

Adenauer, in short, seems to have convinced himself that France had to be the keystone of his foreign policy. Backing de Gaulle was nonetheless a very bold decision to take. Adenauer gave his foreign policy a French orientation against the advice of his economics minister (Ludwig Erhard), his foreign minister (Gerhard Schroeder), most of the rest of his cabinet and the opinions of the four other EEC states. This was despite the fact that he was well aware that both Schroeder and Erhard coveted his job (Adenauer was about to celebrate his eighty-seventh birthday) and that his government was already weakened by a political scandal—the so-called *Spiegel* affair—that had led to the enforced substitution of the defense minister Franz-Josef Strauss in December 1962. Adenauer's support for the French government was given, moreover, in the most explicit manner possible—by the signature of the Franco-German Treaty of Friendship on 22 January 1963. Although the contents of the treaty had been under discussion for some months, the two countries' foreign ministries had been preparing for an exchange of diplomatic letters confirming cooperation in defense matters and youth and family affairs. The German foreign ministry staffers were so taken aback by the decision to formalize relations in a treaty that they had not brought any official treaty paper with them, nor did they have the appropriate leather folder.

A top official was dispatched at the last moment to buy something suitable in rue Faubourg St. Honoré.[48] As Bange states: "It is almost certain that if there had been someone else heading the Federal Government the treaty would not have been signed."[49]

The treaty established close military, diplomatic and cultural ties between the two countries. The heads of government were to meet each other twice a year; the foreign ministers of the two nations were to meet every three months; "high officials" within the foreign ministry were to meet every month to "survey current problems and to prepare the ministers' meeting." Similar regular contacts were to be initiated in the fields of defense, education and youth (a particular preoccupation of Adenauer's). In foreign policy, the two countries committed themselves to "consult each other, prior to any decision, on all important questions of foreign policy . . . with a view to arriving, in so far as possible, at a similar position." Such consultation would specifically deal with EEC, NATO and East–West matters, although the German parliament, upon ratification, insisted upon writing into the preamble of the treaty a commitment that such consultation would not lead to decisions incompatible with West Germany's obligations under the EEC and NATO treaties. In defense, the high commands of the two countries were to "harmonize" strategy and tactics and the governments were to "endeavor" to organize military procurement projects on a joint basis. In the field of education and youth, every effort was to be made to increase the number of young French people learning German and young Germans learning French. In terms reminiscent of the 1948 Congress of Europe, the two governments called for the institution of exchanges between "pupils, students, young artists and workers" and for cooperation in scientific research.

The Franco-German treaty was Adenauer's last major act as a statesman. Erhard, under strong American pressure, broke into open revolt against his leader and eventually, after intense party infighting, substituted Adenauer as leader of the CDU in September 1963. But the damage was already done. On 29 January, the French foreign minister, Couve de Murville, finally ended the negotiations for British entry. The Benelux governments and press squawked, but were unable to go beyond merely voicing their dissent. Macmillan was left to tell the British people in a broadcast: "What happened at Brussels yesterday was bad; bad for us, bad for Europe, and bad for the whole Free World."[50] But not bad for de Gaulle, who had revenged the defeat of the Fouchet negotiations and had asserted his primacy within the Six.

THE "EMPTY CHAIR" CRISIS AND
THE LUXEMBOURG COMPROMISE

The paradox of de Gaulle's rejection of the British application is that he might well have found the UK a welcome ally in the EEC's third major crisis of the early and mid-1960s, the so-called Empty Chair crisis. If the Fouchet crisis was about the supranational Dutch battling to stop the French's ambitions to turn the EEC into a third force, and the 1963 crisis about de Gaulle's equally strenuous opposition to the EEC's Atlanticization, the almost fatal bout of infighting which rocked the Community between June 1965 and January 1966 was motivated by de Gaulle's desire to keep decision making out of the hands of the Commission and Assembly and in the hands of the member states. Britain would unquestionably have sided with the general on this issue.

From the theoretical point of view, the "Empty Chair" crisis was the event which disproved the mechanical belief in "spillover." As Haas predicted, the successful implementation of the EEC treaty caused demands for the powers of the EEC's supranational institutions to be extended. As Haas had not anticipated, de Gaulle showed that the nation-states, at any rate France, were more than strong enough to block the centralizing impulses of the Commission.

The crisis arose directly out of a major success for greater integration. The EEC had spent most of the period between January 1963 and December 1964 wrangling over the small print of the CAP. West Germany, in particular, defended the interests of her farmers with remarkable tenacity against the Commission's desire, backed by the French government, to accelerate trade in cereals by harmonizing wheat prices throughout the EEC. West Germany had stubbornly refused to take the politically problematic step of weaning her farmers off high support prices for wheat. European agricultural protection was also obstructing progress in the so-called Kennedy Round trade talks taking place under the aegis of the General Agreement on Trade and Tariffs (GATT). West Germany had much to gain from reduced protection in manufactures, but her high agricultural tariffs were causing the Americans to balk in the negotiations.[51] In the autumn of 1964, France lost patience and set a deadline of 15 December 1964 for substantial reductions in West German wheat prices. Caught between these external pressures, and internal resistance, in an election year, from farmers' groups who feared French competition, the German government eventually agreed to reduce its target price for cereals to 425 DM per metric ton. It was further agreed that the harmonized wheat price would be introduced on 1 July 1967, not in 1966 as the Commission wanted, and that the price would be established in "units of account" (equal to $1) not national currencies. German farmers were to be compensated between 1967 and 1970 to the tune of just over 1,100 million marks from the Guidance and Guarantee Fund. Since Germany contributed only 28 percent of this fund, this enabled her to offload most of the cost of subsidizing her farmers on to the other members of the Six.[52]

These decisions opened the way for a completion of the common market. In January 1965, the Commission proposed that 1 July 1967 should become the deadline for the final removal of all intra-Community tariffs and the final harmonization of the common external tariff. Economic union, it seemed, would be realized three years ahead of schedule. Almost simultaneously, the Six, recognizing that the EEC had now outgrown Euratom and the ECSC, agreed to unify the cumbersome structure of the three communities into a single body. The so-called Merger treaty was signed in April 1965. According to von der Groeben, this move was not an unmixed blessing: "The amalgamation of functions and the doubling of staff necessitated large-scale reorganization . . . as a consequence of which the Commission lost valuable time which could have been spent on its real tasks."[53] The Merger treaty also established the so-called Committee of Permanent Representatives (COREPER), a committee of high-level officials from national governments charged with briefing the Council of Ministers on the Commission's proposals.

The agreements to complete the common market and unify the three separate Communities turned the Commission, potentially, into a major power. The question was, how would it handle this power? Would it press for increased supranational governance in Europe, or would it allow the member states to continue to take the initiative and restrict its activities to the technocratic task of making the common market work? The Commission's president, Walter Hallstein, preferred the former course of action. At the end of December 1964, he gave a speech at Chatham House in London, which read almost like a declaration of war against the Gaullist concept of Europe. Hallstein's speech was framed around a series of questions and answers. The first question was: "Hegemony or Balance of Power?" Was the EEC dominated by a single state, or did it work as the result of precarious accords between governments? Hallstein answered: neither. "No member state can impose its will on the others." Moreover, the Commission would shortly become an institutional power to be reckoned with. From January 1966, the Council of Ministers would vote by a qualified majority and, in accordance with article 149 of the EEC treaty, unanimity would be needed among the member states to amend a Commission proposal. These two key "constitutional" powers would make the Commission the "mediator" of the EEC and end forever any prospect of a single country dominating the EEC's proceedings. Hallstein posed the question of whether this fact implied a reduction in national sovereignty. Again, he responded, "no." The concept of state sovereignty was a myth, at any rate for the relatively small powers of the EEC. Europe had to learn to reach common decisions and speak with a single voice if it was to count on the world stage. To this end, the member states would be forced to recognize that economic union was not enough. More integration was needed at the political level, and Hallstein made clear to his audience that he regarded the Commission as an activist agent that would propose and promote increased integration in the political sphere. What would the foreign policy orientation of this new Europe be? Hallstein underlined that the EEC's link with the United States was fundamental to its future. He scathingly attacked, though not by name, supporters of realpolitik, arguing that a vision of international politics that reasoned in such categories was "mistaken" and "immoral."[54]

Hallstein's Chatham House speech has been summarized at some length because it gives the lie to those who heap all the blame for the "Empty chair" crisis on the shoulders of de Gaulle. It was essentially a manifesto for out-right supranationalism. Marjolin records in his memoirs that Hallstein and a majority of the Commission had decided that the moment was ripe to aug-ment the Commission's authority.[55] The issue that forced the conflict be-tween the French government and the Commission was the sensitive one of CAP financing. The January 1962 accord had specified that the CAP would be paid for by national contributions until 30 June 1965. After the 15 De-cember 1964 agreement, the Council invited the Commission to submit proposals by 1 April 1965 specifying how agriculture would be financed from 1 July 1965 until the CAP entered into operation (which was then ex-pected to be 1 January 1970, but was subsequently brought forward, as we have seen, to 1 July 1967 by the Commission). According to Marjolin, Hall-stein and Mansholt drew up the three-point plan that they subsequently sub-mitted to the Council in "utmost secrecy." The other members of the Com-mission were apparently kept "carefully out of the picture" while the proposals were being drafted.[56]

Hallstein's plan was simple in conception. From 1 July 1967, the EEC's running costs, of which farming was by far the biggest component, would be paid out of the EEC's "own resources," which would derive from the levies imposed upon non-Community agricultural imports and by the proceeds de-riving from the common external tariff on industrial goods. Since collecting fees on this scale would produce resources far in excess of what the Com-munity was already spending, the Commission's second proposal was to phase in the amount raised by industrial tariffs—a popular proposal with the Netherlands, which otherwise stood to lose the substantial income it re-ceived from charging duty on goods imported via Rotterdam and then reex-ported to the rest of the Six. Nevertheless, by 1 January 1972, the Com-mission would have been in control of all revenues deriving from the common external tariff.[57]

The Commission's third proposal was that the Assembly of the EEC should have a greater say in deciding the shape of the Community's budget. The Assembly had been pressing for a greater role in the Community's ac-tivities since 1963, but had run into a wall of (mostly French) opposition. The Commission now proposed that the existing system of deciding the Community's budget (by unanimous vote in the Council, after the opinion of the Assembly had been heard) should be replaced by a new and more complicated procedure. The Commission would send a draft budget to the

Council, which would amend it and send it to the Assembly. The Assembly
was empowered to make amendments by a simple majority vote and to send
the budget back to the drawing board—the Commission. The Commission
could accept or reject the amendments. If it *accepted* the amendments of the
Assembly, the Council could only overturn the decision if five out of six
countries voted against on a "one country, one vote" basis. In the event of
the Commission *disagreeing* with the Assembly on a specific point, the support of four countries out of six was needed by the Commission in the Council of Ministers. If a blocking majority of four could not be raised, the Assembly's version was automatically accepted.[58]

This scheme simultaneously gave the Assembly a bigger role in the
budget process and made the Commission the arbiter of the EEC's soon-
to-be-augmented revenues. As Marjolin comments, "The Commission
would become, in budgetary matters, a kind of government of the Community." The Commission would, with the assistance of a mere two states
(the pro-federalist Netherlands and Luxembourg, say), have been in a position to drive through its expenditure plans even if Italy, Germany and
France had been contrary. Marjolin regarded this as an "absurdity" and told
his colleagues so.[59] Jean Monnet's Action Committee cautiously welcomed
nevertheless the Commission's proposals at the beginning of May 1965.

The Commission's plans, however, did not go far enough for the Assembly. On 12 May, it adopted a resolution by 76 votes to 0, with ten Gaullists
abstaining, which increased its own role in the budget process still further.
Under the Assembly's counterproposals, the Commission was to have sent
its draft budget to the Council and the Assembly simultaneously. The Council was given twenty days to make such amendments as it preferred by a qualified majority vote. The Assembly was to pronounce within two months by
a simple majority vote. The Commission would then give its opinion on both
sets of proposals. It could dissent from the Parliament's text, but needed the
support of a 5/6 majority in the Council to overturn the Assembly's position. If the Council decided by a 5/6 vote to adopt neither the Assembly's
position nor the Commission's, the matter would be referred back to the
Parliament, which could, with a two-thirds vote of those present and a simple majority of its members, reinstate the Assembly's original view.[60]

This barrage of arcane detail about budgetary reform is necessary because
it underlines the fundamental character of the crisis. From 1 July 1967, the
EEC was to become an institution with substantial resources of its own. Who
would decide how the resources would be spent? The Commission and the
Assembly were each suggesting that they should control the Community's
purse strings. Both were suggesting that the member states should cede control of the EEC's financial future to its supranational institutions. It was a
challenge that de Gaulle could not ignore.

Nor did he. The Commission's proposals were debated in the Council of
Ministers on 13–15 June 1965. At this meeting, the French simply dropped

the idea that the CAP should be financed by "own resources" from 1 July 1967 and suggested that the member states should continue to fund the Community until 1 January 1970. When the Council met again on 28 June, faced with the specific task of deciding how to finance the EEC's agricultural spending before the 30 June deadline, the pro-federalist states—Italy, Germany and the Netherlands—engaged in a peculiarly self-defeating piece of brinkmanship by insisting that the Commission's proposals had to be agreed in their entirety even if this meant a delay in reaching the decision on the agricultural finance mechanism. Couve de Murville, the French foreign minister, blankly denied this was either true or possible. Newhouse, in his sophisticated reconstruction of the "Collision in Brussels," stated, "The most implacable of de Gaulle's antagonists was to be his sorely tried partner to the South."[61] Italy, as both a consistent supporter of greater supranationalism and a major loser in the existing agricultural financing mechanism, was forced into a clash with France. But looking back at this meeting of the Council, it is hard not to conclude that France's partners had decided to give the French a taste of their own negotiating medicine. Newhouse records that during the end-of-June meeting, "there was a sense of settling old scores."[62] Italy, the Netherlands and West Germany were trying to exploit France's desire for a permanent settlement on agriculture by deliberate intransigence over the financial mechanism, in the case of Italy, and by a generalized backing for an increased role for the Community's supranational institutions.

The first rule of international politics, however, is to pick your fights carefully. The gauntlet having been thrown down, France picked it up and proceeded to slap the Community in the face with it. On 6 July 1965, France withdrew its permanent representative from Brussels and announced that it would not be taking part in the Community's specialized policy committees. The empty chair policy had begun. The Five and the Commission responded to this ploy on the part of the French by throwing in the towel. At the end of July 1965, the Commission drew up an extremely complicated plan that blurred the agricultural financing issue and shelved the question of the Assembly's role in determining the budget. As Marjolin, who did most of the drafting, pointed out in his memoirs, this new proposal "gave the French full satisfaction."[63]

De Gaulle, however, decided to up the ante. A long summer silence was followed on 9 September 1965 by what is probably his second most famous press conference. On this occasion, de Gaulle spoke his mind with vehemence about federalists like Hallstein and their plans. France, he said, wanted a "reasonable" Community. That did not mean one "ruled by some technocratic body of elders, stateless and irresponsible." De Gaulle emphasized that France had only agreed to the implementation of the second stage of the EEC treaty in 1962 because her partners had finally agreed to "settle the agricultural problem" by 30 June 1965. They had not fulfilled that undertaking and had, he implied, seemingly colluded with the Commission's attempts to make itself "a great independent financial power." This fact, de Gaulle argued, had allowed the French government "more clearly to assess in what position our country risks finding itself if some of the provisions initially laid down in the Rome treaty were actually enforced." Meetings in the Council of Ministers would from 1 January 1966 be by a qualified majority. Decisions would be made on economic policy or even agricultural policy "without France's let or leave." Altering the Commission's proposals would be impossible "unless by some extraordinary chance, the six states were unanimous in formulating an amendment." The Constitution of the Fifth Republic did not permit "such a subordinate position," de Gaulle averred. Bleakly, de Gaulle concluded that the Community would no doubt get underway once more "after a period of time the length of which nobody can foresee."[64]

The Five responded more robustly than expected to this escalation of the conflict and insisted that France should respect the EEC treaty. They backed off, however, from dragging France before the European Court of Justice for having breached article 5 of the EEC treaty, which states that "[member-states] shall abstain from any measure which could jeopardize the attainment of the objectives of this treaty." Any such decision would surely have prompted de Gaulle to break with the Community permanently. At this point, however, French domestic politics intervened. A presidential election was due in France at the beginning of December 1965. All four of de Gaulle's opponents, especially the Liberal, Jean Lacanuet, and the Socialist, François Mitterrand, overtly (and, in Mitterrand's case, opportunistically, since he was allied with the anti-Europe Communists) campaigned on a pro-European platform and advocated restarting negotiations with the Five. An important French farmers' association urged its members to vote against de Gaulle. As a result, Mitterrand, who was endorsed by Jean Monnet, forced de Gaulle into a second ballot that the general only narrowly won.

The week after Christmas 1965, the French government said it was willing to attend a meeting of foreign ministers (not, it insisted, a meeting of the EEC Council of Ministers) to discuss the crisis. This meeting took place on 17–18 January 1966 in Luxembourg. Couve de Murville submitted a "decalogue" of grievances against the Commission on behalf of the French government—essentially, Couve argued that the Commission was usurping the central role of national governments and was behaving as if it were the executive arm of a federal administration. Couve added that there could be no compromise on the question of majority voting. These demands met with a strong negative reaction from the Five and the meeting was adjourned until 28 January. Before the renewal of talks, agreement was reached on a "heptalogue" of points clarifying the relationship between the Council and the Commission. The question of the retention of the veto proved more intractable. Several member states were as determined to keep majority voting as the French were to get rid of it. Negotiations continued until late in the evening on 29 January 1966. The ministers finally reached agreement by agreeing to differ. The compromise they arrived at—the "Luxembourg compromise"—is worth quoting fully if only as testimony to the subtlety of the negotiators' minds:

1. When issues very important to one or more member countries are at stake, the members of the Council will try, within a reasonable time, to reach solutions which can be adopted by all members of the Council, while respecting their mutual interests, and those of the Community, in accordance with Article 2 of the treaty.
2. The French delegation considers that, when very important issues are at stake, discussion must be continued until unanimous agreement is reached.
3. The six delegations note that there is a divergence of views on what should be done in the event of a failure to reach complete agreement.
4. However, they consider that this divergence does not prevent the Community's work being resumed in accordance with the normal procedure.[65]

France, in other words, reserved her right to repeat her obstructive actions of the previous six months if she were to be outvoted on an issue she indicated to be of major national importance. The other nations did not consent to France's right to do so, but acknowledged that she would. As the French wanted, moreover, agriculture was to be financed until 1970 through national contributions and the decision on the Commission's "own resources" was postponed until that date. The CAP, it was agreed, would come into force on 1 July 1968 at the same time as the last stage of tariff cuts on manufactured goods. Haas had been disproved. A single government, acting with determination, had been able to impose its will on the Community and ensure that the governments of the member states, not the Community's supranational institutions, were the chief decision makers of the Community. Not that the other governments were too dismayed by this fact. Marjolin says the other governments "did not want the majority vote any more than the French government did and they sacrificed it to the French with no great pain, and some even with secret relief."[66]

POSITIVE AND NEGATIVE INTEGRATION

The Luxembourg compromise left de Gaulle as the arbiter of the Community's development. France opposed Hallstein's renewal as president of the Commission in 1966 and the German was replaced by Belgium's Jean Rey from 1 July 1967. De Gaulle dismissed the second British attempt to gain membership—during the premiership of the Labour leader Harold Wilson in 1967—almost contemptuously. In May 1967, de Gaulle warned of "destructive upheaval" if Britain succeeded in entering the EEC. A visit from

Wilson in June 1967, at which the British prime minister apparently told de Gaulle that Britain would not "take no for an answer," was to little avail.[67] In November 1967, de Gaulle made clear his absolute opposition to British entry. In fairness, Britain's parlous economic state turned the general's veto into a normal act of prudence. The travails of sterling in 1967, which culminated in a substantial forced devaluation just before de Gaulle's announcement, meant that absorbing Britain into the EEC would have been a major economic risk for the other participants. Britain was no longer the haughty world power that was too dignified to lower herself to cooperating with her neighbors across the channel. She was a postimperial power who was retrenching desperately on her overseas' commitments and defense budget. She was also rapidly becoming a postindustrial power whose manufacturing industry was being outclassed by West Germany and the other countries of the Six. Two generations of economic laxness had left Britain a beggar at Europe's door: de Gaulle was not alone in believing that British membership could only weaken the EEC, not strengthen it.

De Gaulle also sat on all attempts to further supranational government within the Community. Plans for a directly elected parliament, for greater economic integration and for "political cooperation" were all put on the shelf for so long as the general remained in power. Not surprisingly, this situation of stalemate induced some academic analysts of the EEC to swing from "Monnetian" optimism to grim pessimism about the prospects for an extension of supranational government within the Six. One of the first, and certainly the most influential, academic revisers of the functionalist doctrine was Stanley Hoffmann. His seminal article "Obstinate or Obsolete: The Fate of the Nation-State and the Case of Western Europe" advanced the thesis that international relations experts had underestimated the extent to which the "national situation" of France, in particular, would lead her to reject European supranationalism once it began to impinge upon sensitive areas. The crisis in the Community, in other words, could not be attributed to the malevolence of a single individual, but was structural in character and hence could not be eliminated by the general's political or physical demise. According to Hoffmann, the defining feature of France's "national situation," by which he meant the circumstances bequeathed to a given country by its history, was that unlike West Germany, Italy or the Netherlands, France had not got over nationalism. The humiliations in Vietnam, Suez and Algeria had generated a resentful nationalism in the country's political class that had found a spokesman in de Gaulle. West Germany and Italy were allies of the United States through necessity, not choice, and hence did not feel diminished by their subordination. Nationalist France, however, was not content to settle down into a life of bland prosperity within Community institutions and beneath the shelter of the American nuclear umbrella. She was adamant that she would not accept either American leadership in foreign policy or technocratic government by Brussels in economic policy. Hoffmann pointed out that in the functionalist conception, Europe was a machine that required constant inputs of sovereignty from the Six to keep working. In the 1965 crisis, the machine, impatient at the niggardly scale at which inputs were coming in, had demanded the right to set its own targets. The nationalist reaction in France had been immediate, just as it had been in 1954 when the Americans had overstepped the permissible mark. Hoffmann, gloomily, thought that for the foreseeable future pessimism was the only rational attitude for proponents of European unity. France would not allow the machine to restart in the absence of strict controls over its fuel supply.[68]

The leading British proponent of European Unity, the economist John Pinder, took a more optimistic attitude. Writing in early 1969, after de Gaulle had been weakened by the 1968 crisis in France, Pinder suggested that economic logic pointed to a continuation of integration from the mostly "negative" integration hitherto achieved, to a greater measure of "positive" integration. By "negative" integration, Pinder meant the removal of all measures of national preference within the economic space created by the EEC treaty. By "positive" integration, he meant "the formation and application of coordinated and common policies in order to fulfil economic and welfare objectives other than the removal of discrimination."[69] Negative integration, Pinder argued, had been achieved first for four main reasons, two of which might be termed structural, the other two of which were contingent political reasons. The structural reasons were that the EEC treaty was consciously intended to be a "new deal for Europe" in which "war between the member countries would become unthinkable." Permitting national discrimination, in this context, was impossible and hence ensuring that national preferences were as far as possible eliminated had been one of the treaty's primary motivations. Second, it was quite simply easier to ban discrimination than legislate positively: "a treaty can more easily make effective the 'thou shalt not' commandments than the 'thou shalt' ones."[70]

The contingent reasons had been the presence of the "neoliberal" Erhard at the heart of the German government and the presence of de Gaulle in France. Erhard's hostility to planning and de Gaulle's "political ideology that violently rejects the idea of any authority above or outside the nation-state" had combined to place severe limits on positive policymaking. More generally, the detail and wording of the EEC treaty was far more vague when matters requiring positive integration were involved, and such vagueness gave states every opportunity to drag their feet.

Pinder was nevertheless convinced that the issue of positive integration would have to be confronted by the Six. The main argument he adduced in support of this contention was the certainty that members of the Six would, in the future, have to deal with balance-of-payments problems. By joining the EEC, countries had, at any rate in theory, renounced many of the usual array of measures available to national governments to keep their payments in approximate balance—tariffs and other protectionist measures being the most important of these. But what if (and it is clear in his context that Pinder was thinking of a hypothetical British membership of the Community) a country as a result of lax government spending, evolution in the world market, consumer propensity to spend rather than save or sheer cultural lack of economic dynamism ran persistent balance-of-payments deficits with its partners? Bereft of the protectionist option, it would have no choice but to impose austerity. But what if austerity did not solve the problem? What if the country was condemned to a lengthy period of economic stagnation? Pinder answered that there were two possible "broad alternatives."[71] First, a country could "contract out" of the Community for a while and impose emergency protectionist methods. This option, however, would prove disastrous to the Community as a whole. Second, the Community could develop "joint policies" operated by the EEC's institutions itself to boost economic growth in laggard countries—positive integration.

> Positive integration, particularly to solve the balance-of-payments problems of member countries now that their national economic defenses have been removed, may be necessary to the success and even to the survival of the Community. This may require (i) major common policies at Community level over a wide range of key subjects, including regional, social, monetary and fiscal policies with the corresponding fiscal and loan-raising powers, and (ii) the coordination of monetary, budgetary and incomes policies of the member states.[72]

Pinder's analysis, upon close examination, glossed over the fact that the member states could use currency devaluations to maintain their competitiveness and to keep their balance of payments in order. In fact, this was the very strategy that France, Italy and Britain would use for the next decade to maintain some sort of parity with an increasingly dominant West German economy—although, as we shall see, West Germany eventually rebelled against the costs to *her* economy of this economic equivalent of relying on slimming pills rather than an exercise regime.

But if one allows for this omission, Pinder was making an extremely prescient point (and was, in fact, contributing to what would be an important shift in the direction of policy). As soon as de Gaulle fell from power on 28 April 1969, the governments of the Six, including France, began to look at ways in which they promote measures of positive integration in precisely the areas of policy (regional development, social issues and monetary policy) that Pinder had identified. To this extent, Hoffmann was wrong in supposing that France's "national situation" made her hostility to integration a structural factor capable of constraining the development of the Community as a whole. But he was right in identifying the "national situation" of countries, and the perceptions of their national leaders, as being *a* key constraint on how far the EEC would be able to introduce measures of positive integration. On the one hand, as Pinder realized, economic logic might (the use of the conditional is obligatory: his argument was not determinist) push the EEC towards greater coordination, harmonization and centralization. On the other hand, nation-states with proud and complex histories were the entities being integrated. Inevitably, their leaders viewed integration through the lens of their own national circumstances and priorities: a fact that prevented the Community from unfolding according to the dictates of economic or any other form of logic, especially when, as in the 1970s, huge structural changes in the world economy were throwing those circumstances and priorities into flux. The decade that elapses between the end of de Gaulle's presidency and the introduction of the European Monetary system in January 1979, which is so often dismissed as a period of stagnation by scholars, is fascinating for this reason.

NOTES

1. Hans von der Groeben, *The European Community: The Formative Years* (Brussels: European Commission, 1985), 39.

2. See Frances Lynch, "De Gaulle's First Veto: France, the Rueff Plan and the Free Trade Area," European University Institute Working Paper no. 8/98, for background on de Gaulle's decision.

3. See Andrew Moravcsik, *The Choice for Europe: Social Purpose and State Power from Messina to Maastricht* (Ithaca, N.Y.: Cornell University Press, 1998), 164–76, for an excellent account of British economic preferences.

4. Robert Marjolin, *Architect of European Unity* (London: Weidenfeld and Nicholson, 1989), 320.

5. A contemporary account is Uwe Kitzinger, "Europe of the Six and the Seven," *International Organization* 14 (Winter 1960).

6. Von der Groeben, *European Community*, 52.

7. Von der Groeben, *European Community*, 84.

8. The best study of the EC's policy towards its former colonies since the early 1960s is Enzo Grilli, *The EC and the Developing Countries* (Cambridge: Cambridge University Press, 1994).

9. Moravcsik, *Choice for Europe*, 180.

10. Gisela Hendriks, *Germany and European Integration. The CAP: An Area of Conflict* (Oxford: Berg, 1991), 49.

11. This account of the CAP relies on European Community Information Service, *A Common Market for Agriculture* (Brussels: European Communities, 1967).

12. Moravcsik, *Choice for Europe*, 180.

13. Moravcsik, *Choice for Europe*, 7.

14. The text of Eisenhower's reply is included as an appendix in Lois Pa'
Ménil, *Who Speaks for Europe? The Vision of Charles de Gaulle* (London: W
and Nicholson, 1977), 193–94.

15. Pierre Gerbet, "In Search of Political Union: The Fouchet Plan Negotiations," in *The Dynamics of European Union*, ed. Roy Price (London: Croom Helm, 1987), 114

16. The text of the original Fouchet plan is included as an appendix in Lois Pattison de Ménil, *Who Speaks for Europe?* 195–200.

17. Hedley Bull, "Civilian Power Europe: A Contradiction in Terms?" *Journal of Common Market Studies* 21 (September–December 1982): 149–70.

18. Stanley Hoffmann, "De Gaulle, Europe and the Atlantic Alliance," *International Organization* 18 (Winter 1964): 2.

19. Arthur Schlesinger, *A Thousand Days: John F. Kennedy in the White House* (New York: Houghton Mifflin, 1965), gives excellent background to the Kennedy administration's policy towards Europe. See especially "The Not so Grand Design" and "Two Europes: De Gaulle and Kennedy." The other indispensable text on Franco-American relations in the 1960s is John Newhouse, *De Gaulle and the Anglo-Saxons* (New York: Viking, 1970).

20. Brian Crozier, *Charles de Gaulle* (London: Eyre Methuen, 1973), 533.

21. For the Kennedy visit, see Newhouse, *De Gaulle and the Anglo-Saxons*, ch. 5, "The Education of John F. Kennedy," 120–48.

22. Von der Groeben, *European Community*, 112.

23. Uwe Kitzinger, *The European Common Market and Community* (New York: Barnes & Noble, 1967), 166–68.

24. The text of the March 15 plan, with the alternative proposals of the Belgians and Dutch is included as an appendix in Lois Pattison de Ménil, *Who Speaks for Europe?* 201–12.

25. De Gaulle's press conference is quoted at length in Pattison de Ménil, *Who Speaks for Europe?* 73–76. De Gaulle's own account of the Fouchet negotiations in his *Memoirs of Hope* is disappointingly skimpy, although he does underline the important role played by Amintore Fanfani and the Italian government. The Fouchet negotiations have not been systematically treated in English since the publication of Andrew Silj, *Europe's Political Puzzle: A Study of the Fouchet Negotiations and the 1963 Veto* (Cambridge, Mass.: Harvard University Center for International Affairs, 1967).

26. Hugo Young, *This Blessed Plot* (London: Macmillan, 1998), 105–6.

27. Moravcsik, *Choice for Europe*, 171.

28. Charles de Gaulle, *Memoirs of Hope: Renewal and Endeavor* (New York: Simon & Schuster, 1971), 188.

29. See Alistair Horne, *Macmillan 1957–1986* (London: Macmillan, 1989), 256.

30. Heath's speech is extensively reported in Kitzinger, *European Common Market*, 151–63.

31. Heath in Kitzinger, *European Common Market*, 158.

32. Heath in Kitzinger, *European Common Market*, 162.

33. For a full text of Gaitskell's speech, see *The Eurosceptical Reader*, ed. Martin Holmes (London: Macmillan, 1996), 13–38.

34. For the Nassau conference, see Horne, *Macmillan*, 437–43.

35. Hoffmann, "De Gaulle, Europe and the Atlantic Alliance," 14.

36. Moravcsik, *Choice for Europe*, 189.

37. Moravcsik, *Choice for Europe*, 190.

38. I am quoting the translation of de Gaulle's press conference in Kitzinger, *European Common Market*, 185.

39. De Gaulle, *Memoirs of Hope*, 220.

40. Jean Lacouture, *De Gaulle: The Ruler 1945–1970* (London: Harvill, 1991), 359.

41. Moravcsik, *Choice for Europe*, 190.

42. Oliver Bange, *The EEC Crisis of 1963* (London: Macmillan, 2000), 63–67.

43. Hans-Peter Schwarz, *Konrad Adenauer: A German Politician and Statesman in a Period of War, Revolution and Reconstruction*, vol. 2 (Providence, R.I.: Berghahn, 1997), 615.

44. De Gaulle, *Memoirs of Hope*, 180.

45. Schwarz, *Konrad Adenauer*, vol. 2, 621.

46. Lacouture, *De Gaulle*, 341.

47. Schwarz, *Konrad Adenauer*, vol. 2, 605.

48. Schwarz, *Konrad Adenauer*, vol. 2, 672.

49. Bange, *EEC Crisis*, 157.

50. Quoted Horne, *Macmillan*, 448.

51. Hendriks, *Germany and European Integration*, 51–52.

52. Hendriks, *Germany and European Integration*, 53.

53. Von der Groeben, *European Community*, 175.

54. Hallstein's speech was subsequently printed in the *World Today*, January 1965, 10–24. All quotations are from the published text.

55. Marjolin, *Architect of European Unity*, 348.

56. Marjolin, *Architect of European Unity*, 350.

57. John Lambert, "The Constitutional Crisis 1965–66," *Journal of Common Market Studies* 4 (1965–1966): 195–228 at 202.

58. Lambert, "Constitutional Crisis," 204.

59. Marjolin, *Architect of European Unity*, 350.

60. Lambert, "Constitutional Crisis," 205.

61. John Newhouse, *Collision in Brussels* (London: Faber, 1967), 70.

62. Newhouse, *Collision in Brussels*, 108.

63. Marjolin, *Architect of European Unity*, 353.

64. Lambert, "Constitutional Crisis," 216.

65. Quoted Lambert, "Constitutional Crisis," 226.

66. Marjolin, *Architect of European Unity*, 356.

67. Young, *This Blessed Plot*, 196.

68. Stanley Hoffmann, "Obstinate or Obsolete? The Fate of the Nation-State and the Case of Western Europe," *Daedelus* 95 (Summer 1966): 892–908.

69. John Pinder, "Positive and Negative Integration: Some Problems of Economic Union in the EEC," *World Today*, March 1968, 90.

70. Pinder, "Positive and Negative Integration," 98.

71. Pinder, "Positive and Negative Integration," 105.

72. Pinder, "Positive and Negative Integration," 110.

5

Weathering the Storm

The EC during the
Economic Crises of the 1970s

The 1970s are often regarded as years in which economic crisis, British intransigence and the narrow self-interest of the member states combined to stall the motor of the integration process. Upon close examination, however, this description is untenable. These trying years for Europe were in fact characterized by a tenacious shuffle in the direction of greater integration and cooperation. If one drives the teleology of the European movement from one's mind and looks squarely at the facts, one sees that the Nine—Britain, Ireland and Denmark joined the EEC in 1973—dealt with the economic fallout of the 1973–1975 oil shock not by retreating into economic nationalism, but by striving to establish a system of relatively stable exchange rates. In his autobiography, Roy Jenkins, the British Social Democrat who presided over the European Commission from 1977 to 1981, contended that the European Monetary System (EMS) "has been the central channel from which most subsequent European advance has flowed."[1] This observation is probably true—the monetary union achieved in the 1990s would have been impossible without the experience of the EMS—but even more striking is the deep-seated change of mentality implicit in the decision to adopt the EMS in the first place. By instituting controlled exchange rates, governments reacted to the severe recession of the 1970s—the first postwar contraction of economic activity in Europe—with a measure that guaranteed that the common market was able to continue functioning and that protectionism did not gain ground.

It was concerted action by governments that achieved this result. In institutional terms, the chief innovation of the 1970s was the creation of the European Council, regular summits of the heads of state or government, which rapidly became the supreme policy-making body of the EC. Yet the supranational institutions of the EC also consolidated their position. The Court of Justice successfully asserted the supremacy of legislation emanating from the European Community over national laws and confirmed its view that the Treaty of Rome had conferred rights on the citizens of the EC's member states. The Assembly obtained the first prerequisite of parliamentary status by being chosen by direct election in June 1979. European federalists engaged in much rethinking about the future direction Europe should take. The key document in this context is unquestionably the thoughtful—but profoundly ideological—1976 report by the prime minister of Belgium, Leo Tindemans, which represented both a restatement and a readjustment of the doctrine of European movement. The fact that Tindemans's report was not immediately acted upon is relatively unimportant. By 1976, European supranationalists were well aware that Rome would not be built in a day. But they continued to believe in the rightness of the blueprint drawn up in the 1940s as a long-term objective for the peoples of Western Europe.

THINKING POSITIVE 1969-1972

The cause of the belief that the 1970s were a decade of stagnation is ultimately traceable to the fact that supporters of European federalism had hoped that the Community, post–de Gaulle, would take immediate strides towards unity. De Gaulle's successor was a man, Georges Pompidou, who had quarreled with the general and was determined to give his own imprint to French policy. Almost Pompidou's first act as president was to propose a meeting of the Six's leaders to discuss how to go beyond the degree of integration already achieved with the common market. Admittedly, Pompidou's zeal may have been prompted by the fact that he was being constrained to make concessions by the need to renegotiate (again) the financial regulation for the CAP, which was set to expire on 31 December 1969.[2]

This meeting took place, symbolically, at the Hague in the Netherlands on 1–2 December 1969. At the Hague, the gathered heads of government decided upon an ambitious program of objectives in five crucial policy areas: financing the Community, which, it was agreed, would finally be provided with its "own resources"; strengthening Community institutions, in particular the Assembly; the creation of economic and monetary union; "political unification," which the foreign ministers were asked to study; the enlargement of the Community through negotiations with such would-be entrants as Britain, Ireland, Denmark and Norway. The small print of the first of these objectives was decided in April 1970 when the Six decided that the EEC would be funded by levies on imports into the Community and by the transfer from national governments of up to 1 percent of the receipts from value-added tax (VAT). The French government ruled out, however, any suggestion that the establishment of "own resources" should lead to an increase in the budgetary powers of the Parliament.

The next three of these objectives generated detailed reports by distinguished members of the European establishment. A committee chaired by the prime minister of Luxembourg, Pierre Werner, dealt with economic and monetary union. The Werner report was presented at the end of October 1970. Its main conclusion was that "economic and monetary union is an objective realizable in the course of the present decade, provided the political will of the member states to realize this objective, solemnly declared at the Conference in the Hague, is present."[3] The report set tough immediate targets. Between 1 January 1971 and the end of 1974, it recommended that eleven specific tasks should have been fulfilled. These included making the Council of economics and finance ministers the "center of decision" for economic policy within the Community; obliging national governments to conduct budgetary policy within the guidelines laid down by the Council; introducing broad harmonization of indirect taxation and taxation upon both corporate profits and fixed interest securities and dividends across the Community. On monetary policy (the most sensitive area so far as national sovereignty was concerned), the report suggested that the Committee of Governors (an informal committee of the EC's central banks) would play a key role both in setting general economic policy and in "progressively narrowing" the "margins of fluctuation" between Community currencies by intervening on the financial markets.[4] No control over national interest rates was envisaged at this initial stage: the Committee would have had the power only to "lay down general guidelines" and to "express opinions and make recommendations" to recalcitrant nations.[5]

The second stage sketched by Werner—the word is appropriate since the report was much less detailed in this regard—would have featured "the laying down of global economic guidelines," "the coordination of short-term economic policies" by monetary and credit measures and "the progressive elimination of exchange rate fluctuations" by the Community's institutions.[6] The report left the question of a common currency open. Economic and monetary union could be "accompanied by the maintenance of national monetary symbols" (this ugly phrase is entirely typical of the report's abstract language), but it was suggested that "considerations of a psychological and political order militate in favor of the adoption of a single currency."[7]

In short, the report envisaged full power to plan the economy of the Community being transferred to the Council of Ministers and to the Commission, which would, of course, have retained its power of proposal. As the report stated: "The center of decision for economic policy will exercise independently, in accordance with the Community interest, a decisive influence over the general economic policy of the Community."[8] Such a shift of core economic responsibilities from national governments to Brussels had political implications that entailed "the progressive development of political cooperation," but the report did not specify what this might mean in concrete terms, except to underline that the "center of decision" would have to be subject to the European Parliament.[9] Werner's report was accepted in principle by the Council of Ministers in the spring of 1971, although not without many reservations being aired.

The powers of the European Parliament were the concern of a report by Professor Georges Vedel, a French political scientist, who was asked in April 1971 to propose measures of constitutional engineering to strengthen the legislative and supervisory role of the Community's parliamentary institutions. There is no need to go into Vedel's report in the same amount of detail as the Werner report, but in synthesis, it can be said that Vedel, too, proposed a two-stage extension of powers. In stage 1, he urged that the Parliament should be given powers of "co-decision" (veto) over all matters concerning the revision of the treaties, the admission of new members, the ratification of international agreements and actions taken by the Council under article 235 of the EEC treaty. He argued that the Parliament should possess powers of "suspension" over all proposals to harmonize national legislation. In a second stage, co-decision powers would be extended to the Parliament in this sphere, too.[10]

The third report to emerge in response to the Hague summit's final communiqué was actually the first to be published. The foreign ministers of the Six outlined proposals for greater cooperation in foreign policy in July 1970 and on 27 October 1970 issued a four-part plan of action to increase "political cooperation" between the states.[11] Despite some leaden rhetoric in the preamble, the plan's actual recommendations were extremely limited: it is both an instructive and an amusing task to read them in conjunction with the original Fouchet plan. It urged two fundamental objectives, neither of which would have raised the blood pressure of even a die-hard defender of national sovereignty in this sphere:

> To ensure, through regular exchanges and consultations, a better mutual understanding on the great international problems;
> To strengthen their solidarity by promoting the harmonization of their views, the co-ordination of their positions, and, where it appears possible and desirable, common actions.

In pursuit of these ends, the foreign ministers advised that they should meet "at least every six months," unless the "gravity" or "importance" of the agenda required a summit of heads of state or government. A "political committee" of government-nominated officials should meet four times a year to prepare their masters' agenda. Any issue could be on the agenda: if a subject impinged upon the remit of the European Communities, the Commission was to be invited to give its opinion. An informal "biannual colloquy" was to be held with the Assembly. Within two years, the foreign ministers were to issue a second report that assessed how much progress had been made towards political cooperation between the Six—or rather, as Britain, Denmark, Ireland and Norway had by then begun entry negotiations, between the Ten. This document, the so-called Copenhagen report, is discussed briefly later, but it is perhaps worth noting here that it made a point of referring to the "characteristically pragmatic mechanisms" instituted by the Luxembourg report of 27 October 1970. "Pragmatic" was an elegant euphemism. In foreign affairs, the Six had agreed only to talk to each other and to acknowledge that it would be agreeable if they could reach agreement when they talked.

The foregoing description of the developments set in train by the Hague summit is important background for the enlargement negotiations, which began in earnest at the end of June 1970, following the surprise victory of Edward Heath's Conservatives in the British general elections of that month. The would-be entrants were striving to join a club that had great ambitions for its future. Swallowing the Treaty of Rome was now just part of the problem. Europe intended to become an economic union with strengthened centralized institutions and a common currency. Heath's task was to show his continental counterparts—especially France—that Britain was prepared to go along with such a major expansion in the EEC's activities. Heath, largely from genuine European idealism, but in part because he envisaged rebuilding Britain's chronically "depressed areas" with EC cash, was both willing and able to make such a commitment.

It is also true that Britain was desperate to join on almost any terms. OECD figures for 1970 show clearly how far Britain had slipped behind the Six in economic terms. British GNP, which in 1950 had been two-thirds as large as the collective product of the Six, was now less than one-quarter. GNP per head, which had been almost exactly double that of the Six in 1950 ($940 versus $477) had declined to three-quarters of the average for the Six ($2,170 versus $2,557). Exports from Britain to the Six had increased from $800 million in 1950 to $4,200 million in 1970—but the cash increase disguises the fact that both figures represented about 2 percent of GNP. In the same period, trade among the Six had risen from $3,000 million to $43,000 million. Britain's official reserves of hard currency had actually declined since 1950: the Six's had increased tenfold.[12] In his book *Missed Chances*, Sir Roy Denman, a senior Foreign Office official who was part of the British negotiating team, comments wryly: "No sensible traveler on the sinking *Titanic* would have said, 'I will only enter a lifeboat if it is well scrubbed, well painted and equipped with suitable supplies of food and drink.'"[13]

The negotiators on the other side of the table were, of course, well aware of the pessimistic mood engendered by Britain's dismal economic performance and were able to exploit it to drive a hard bargain. There were three main areas of difficulty in the negotiations, and Britain was obliged to make major concessions in all three. These areas were imports of dairy produce from New Zealand and cane sugar from the West Indies, fishing rights and the size of the British contribution to the Community budget. Of these, the last was the most important. The French government initially insisted that Britain should contribute to the budget, from the beginning, on the same basis as any other member state. Since Britain was a major importer of non-Community agricultural produce (especially from New Zealand), she would have had to pay, under the terms of the agreement on financing the Community reached in April 1970, substantial sums into the Community and would have received (since the EC's budget was dominated by the CAP and Britain had a small agricultural sector) relatively little in return. In all, Britain would have been paying over a fifth of the Community's budget.

Britain's counterproposal was that she should pay 3 percent of the EEC's budget in the first instance and gradually increase that figure year by year. This suggestion prompted President Pompidou memorably to declare: "The British have three qualities among others: humor, tenacity and realism. I have the feeling that we are slightly in the humorous stage."[14] The issue was eventually resolved with a compromise that did not fully satisfy the British negotiating team but which was as good, given her "weak" bargaining position, as she could reasonably have hoped to get.[15] Britain's contribution would rise eventually to approximately 19 percent of the budget over five years from a starting point in 1973 of just under 9 percent. The underlying assumption of this deal, however, was that agriculture would have a diminished role in the EC's budget and that Britain would benefit from Community subsidies to help regional regeneration. So long as agriculture dominated the EC's expenditure, the British budgetary question was a mine waiting to explode. It was in fact agreed that the budget deal could be renegotiated if an "unacceptable situation" arose later in the 1970s. Mrs. Thatcher was to make full use of this concession (see chapter 6).

The compromise over the budget issue (and New Zealand imports, which were granted preferential access to the Community for a transitional period) was reached only after a May 1971 summit meeting between Pompidou and Heath. The British prime minister appears to have removed any lingering suspicions about Britain's European vocation from the mind of the French president, although Heath's account of the meeting leaves little doubt that he was pushing at an open door.[16] Thereafter, the negotiations, on everything except fish, that most intractable item in any international negotiation, proceeded smoothly and reached a successful conclusion in June 1971. Britain promised to harmonize her food prices up to Community levels by "1 January 1978 at the latest" (Act of Accession: art. 52) and to abolish her duties on EEC products in four stages between 1 January 1973 and 1 July 1977 (art. 32). The Common tariff was also to be introduced in progressive stages and was to come into full force on 1 July 1977 (art. 39).

The question of entry to the "Common Market," as, in Britain, the EC was invariably called until the mid-1980s, immediately became a political battlefield. British politics is perhaps the most partisan in the democratic world, with cross-party collaboration being almost unknown. Over entry to the EC, however, the tribal loyalties broke down. "Europe" was—still is—a question that transcended differences of class or economic philosophy and proved able to unite Marxist left-wingers with die-hard Conservative nationalists such as Enoch Powell in a crusade against membership.[17] It also united the "sensible center" of British politics—progressive conservatives, social democrats, liberals—in a way that unnerved the leadership of the Labour Party in particular. Britain was bedeviled by enough industrial, social and public order problems in the early 1970s to make the idea of a "great coalition" of moderates drawn from all three of the traditional parties seem anything but outlandish.

This ability of the European issue to upset traditional allegiances was shown in October 1971 when the House of Commons debated and voted upon the terms of entry obtained by the government. The motion passed by the seemingly large majority of 356 to 244 on 28 October, but this figure disguised an almost unprecedented breakdown in party discipline. Led by Roy Jenkins, who was then deputy leader of the Labour Party and a former chancellor of the exchequer, 68 pro-European Labour MPs defied a three-line whip, opportunistically imposed by party leader Harold Wilson, to vote for the terms of entry. Thirty-seven Conservative MPs voted against the motion—the Heath government's majority was 27. Had the Labour rebels obeyed the whip, Heath's European policy, *and* his government, would in all probability have been in ruins. As Denman recalls, "All the jeering xenophobia of the Labour Party bubbled to the surface" once the result was announced. In an ugly atmosphere of intimidation, Jenkins, the turncoat, was called a "fascist bastard" by irate left-wing backbenchers.[18]

Victory in the October debate did not mean that Heath's troubles were over. The Treaty of Accession was signed on 22 January 1972, but the treaty still faced ratification in the Commons. Heath could no longer count on the Labour rebels. As Jenkins puts it, "The Labour Europeans had signed up not for the duration but one quick engagement."[19] The second reading of the European Communities bill on 17 February 1972 was passed by a majority of just eight votes. Several of the subsequent ninety-two votes on the legislation were carried by even narrower margins before the third reading passed by a majority of 301 to 284 on 13 July 1972. Only the steadfast support of the six Liberal MPs, and a number of "old and bold" Labour abstainers, provided Heath with the necessary majorities. It seems likely, however, that had the government ever been defeated, Jenkins and a sufficient number of centrist Labour MPs would have broken party discipline to rescue the bill—a move that, had it happened, would have anticipated the formation of a Social

Democrat party in Britain by a decade. The bill received the royal assent (capital letters seem incongruous in this context) on 17 October 1972. It had occupied thirty-nine days of debate in 1972 and ten days in 1971: in all, the Commons debated British accession for 173 hours.

Britain, along with Ireland and Denmark (but not Norway, whose opposition to the EC's fishery policy had caused her to reject membership in a referendum in September 1972), entered the EEC on 1 January 1973. Even before formal accession, however, the three new member states were invited to Paris to take part in a major summit confirming the relaunch of the Community. The entry of the Three had been welcomed tepidly in France, where Pompidou had taken the "wholly unnecessary step" of calling a referendum on 22 April 1972 over the issue of enlargement.[20] Only 36 percent of eligible voters bothered to cast a ballot. Pompidou, in the company of the idealistic German chancellor, Willi Brandt, nevertheless hoped to reignite enthusiasm for the EEC by setting out an ambitious program of reforms.

The declaration issued by the heads of state and government at the end of the conference on 21 October 1972 certainly marked a qualitative leap in the Community's political position.[21] It presented the EC as a self-confident organization of states that was rapidly evolving into an authentic political community and was taking a coherent and independent approach to the world's major problems. As the preamble to the declaration said, "Europe must be able to make its voice heard in world affairs, and to make an original contribution commensurate with its human, intellectual and material resources." The Nine committed themselves to the fundamental principles of democracy, to the establishment of monetary and economic union, to an "improvement in the quality of life as well as the standard of living," to "increase [their] effort in aid and technical assistance to the least favored people," to the development of international trade and to the promotion of détente with the countries of Eastern Europe. Most strikingly of all, the Nine stated:

> The construction of Europe will allow it, in conformity with its ultimate political objectives, to affirm its personality while remaining faithful to its traditional friendships and to the alliances of the Member States, and to establish its position in world affairs as a distinct entity determined to promote a better international equilibrium, respecting the principles of the Charter of the United Nations. The Member States of the Community, the driving force of European construction, affirm their intention to transform before the end of the present decade the whole complex of their relations into a European Union.

Talk is cheap, of course, but this lofty vision of the Community's future—which uniquely managed to combine Gaullism, European federalism and Brandtian progressivism in a single formula—was backed up by a sixteen-point plan for action. In the field of economics, the Nine committed themselves to the Werner report's timetable, to coordinated policies for fighting inflation, to obtaining greater stability in the world's currency markets. Specifically, they pledged themselves to create a "European Monetary Co-operation Fund" by April 1973 that would have the task of reducing the margins of fluctuation among the Nine's currencies. The Nine further agreed to give a "high priority" to correcting the "structural and regional imbalances that might affect the realization of Economic and Monetary Union." To this end, they agreed to set up a regional development fund before the end of 1973. The establishment of this fund had been the British government's chief priority for the summit.[22]

Similar firm pledges were made to establish a program of action in the field of employment and vocational training (by January 1974) and the environment (by July 1973). Somewhat fuzzier promises were made to "establish a single industrial base" by action to promote high-technology industries, conversion of declining industries and the harmonization of company law. The Nine also affirmed—most nebulously of all—that they would formulate a common energy policy.

In foreign affairs, they committed themselves to increase the quantity and improve the quality of their aid to the developing nations; to the "progressive liberalization" of tariff and nontariff barriers via the GATT; to establish a common commercial policy towards the countries of Eastern Europe from 1 January 1973. The Nine pledged themselves to take a coordinated position in the ongoing Conference on Security and Cooperation in Europe—a negotiation that eventually led, in 1975, to the Helsinki Declaration on Human Rights. The foreign ministers of the Nine would meet four times a year, instead of twice, and would produce, by 30 June 1973, a second report on "political cooperation."

Finally, the nine heads of state or government made several suggestions for the "reinforcement of institutions." These were something of a damp squib compared to the rest of the declaration, since they largely consisted of minor procedural improvements. The final paragraph of the declaration, however, did request the institutions of the Community to draw up a report, before the end of 1975, on how to transform the EC's existing institutional structure into a European Union.

Reviewing the declaration of the nine heads of state or government at Paris, it is hard not to assent to Edward Heath's judgment that "overall, the summit provided the impulse for the next stage of the Community's development," though opinions will differ on his view that it was a "tragedy" that the Nine were unable to follow through on most of the pledges they had made.[23] Certainly, his belief that the Paris agenda might have had concrete results if "President Pompidou, Chancellor Brandt and myself, the three men who created the enlarged EEC, had remained in power" will strike many as excessively self-regarding.[24] The Nine were knocked off course (as Heath himself elsewhere acknowledges) by the economic forces unleashed by the

October 1973 oil shock and by the perennial instability of the world's currency markets. These forces were to make something of a mockery of the proud hopes of the Paris summit. Above all, they were to cancel all hopes that economic and monetary unification was just around the corner.

MONETARY TURMOIL 1971–1974

The optimism of the Paris summit with respect to monetary union flew in the face of the experience of the Nine on the currency markets since the publication of the Werner report. At the beginning of the 1970s, the industrial economies were characterized by a set of imbalances that made the conduct of macroeconomic policy extremely difficult. The United States, whose economy was growing rapidly as a result of high government spending on the Vietnam War, had become a large net debtor towards the rest of the industrialized world. Her domestic consumption boom had led to an outflow of dollars as Americans bought freely from Europe and Japan, compounding an already present deficit largely caused by investment overseas by American companies.[25] The EC, as the world's second largest market, was a particular beneficiary of this private American investment. This outflow of dollars mattered since the postwar system of fixed exchange rates had been underpinned since the July 1944 Bretton Woods conference by the United States' commitment to buy back the dollar holdings of other countries in gold at the fixed price of $35 per ounce. The United States was thus established as the anchor of the financial system. At the time, with the U.S. economy running record trade surpluses, and the rest of the world desperate for dollars, nobody regarded this as a particularly onerous burden. But by the early 1970s, doubts were beginning to grow that the greenback could keep its value. Policymakers became acutely aware that if foreign countries decided to swap their accumulated dollars for bullion, the United States would run the risk of a run on Fort Knox. Central bankers and private investors around the world held far greater amounts of dollars than the United States could pay in gold (the EC member states alone held about $16,000 million in their central banks) and they were beginning to become skittish at the United States' persistent failure to balance its books.[26]

The outflow of dollars presented major domestic problems for the EC countries, and for West Germany, the largest beneficiary, in particular. Large and persistent trade and investment surpluses were potentially inflationary and required states to take measures—tax increases, credit controls—to mop up excess liquidity in the economy. At least, this was the settled view of the West German government and the fanatically anti-inflation German central bank, the Bundesbank. Germany had endured one of the worst inflations of all time in the 1920s and the consequent loss by the German middle class of its savings had been one of the key factors that had propelled the Nazis to power. West Germany's 1949 Basic Law therefore made price stability a constitutional imperative. West Germany's belief was that the U.S. government ought to reduce the high levels of public and consumer spending within the American economy, even if this meant slower economic growth for the United States and the world in general.

The Nixon administration took a different view. Nixon's treasury secretary, the Texan John Connolly, argued instead that countries such as Germany and Japan were exploiting the relative openness of the American economy to amass artificial trade surpluses. The solution, in his view, was for the United States to follow a policy of import restrictions on foreign goods, for America's allies to take on more of the costly burden of their own defense and for the Europeans and the Japanese to loosen restrictions on economic activity within their domestic economies. The resulting overall increase in economic growth would suck in American exports and would eliminate the core problem of the United States' persistent current account deficit.

At Camp David on 15 August 1971, President Nixon elected to end dollar convertibility for gold, impose a hefty "temporary surcharge" upon imported goods and to give tax breaks for investment in plant and machinery "made in the USA." This decision, which was taken without consultation with America's principal trading partners, signaled to the rest of the world—and specifically to the currency markets—that the U.S. government intended to solve its balance-of-payments problems by allowing the dollar to float downward and, if necessary, by protecting its economy against foreign goods. In 1971, a preelection year, the U.S. administration simply was not prepared to take the political risks associated with reducing demand sharply. Rather than raise taxes on profits, income and consumption—the price of gasoline being the most glaring example—the Nixon administration was choosing to offload its problems on its partners. As Kunz says, "Nixon decided to put the domestic economy first and let the international chips fall where they might."[27]

From the European point of view, the impact of the American action both emphasized the logic of the Werner report's call for a single Community currency and threw in sharp relief the substantial obstacles in the path of any such development. Nixon's suspension of convertibility predictably led to a general strengthening of European currencies. But this strengthening was not symmetrical. That is to say, some currencies, notably the DM, quickly increased in value more than others. This was in part because there was simply more demand for instruments denominated in these currencies, in part because central banks followed divergent policies. France, for instance, preferred to limit the rise of the franc against the dollar by selling francs on the currency markets and by imposing exchange controls on the movement of capital. This move naturally improved France's competitiveness against West

Germany since a weaker currency was a de facto trade barrier that decreased the cost of exports from France and made its imports more expensive. In October 1971, the West German finance minister, the notoriously verbose Karl Schiller, publicly (and pithily) attacked France for following "Colbertian" policies.[28]

Nixon's *démarche* had, therefore, both opened up cracks within the Community and threatened to cause a breach in transatlantic relations.[29] Faced with the prospect of a major trade war in which everybody would be a victim, the industrialized nations sensibly backed away from the brink. On 17 December 1971, a meeting at the Smithsonian museum in Washington of the so-called Group of Ten largest economies agreed to across-the-board revaluations against the dollar in exchange for the suspension of the import surcharge. The Japanese, the Germans and the Swiss sacrificed most of all: they all revalued their currencies by more than 13 percent against the dollar's value in May 1971. The Germans raised the mark by an overall 4.75 percent against a basket of all major currencies; the Dutch and the Belgians raised the guilder and the Belgian franc by 3.25 and 3.75 percent, respectively. The British and Italians revalued, by contrast, only 1.75 percent by this measure, and the French by a token 0.25 percent.[30] In order to take some of the tension out of exchange rate movements, the Smithsonian meeting also diluted the idea that currencies were to have fixed parities. Instead, currencies would be free to fluctuate up to 2.25 percent above or below a "central value" against the dollar before central banks intervened in the currency markets. This device became known as the "tunnel."

It was a device that did not fully satisfy the West German government and the governments of those EC countries like the Netherlands that could boast strong currencies. Their currencies were soon drifting up towards the roof of the tunnel, while other countries, notably France and Italy, lagged behind. Accordingly, on 7 March 1972, the EC Six, joined two months later by soon-to-enter Britain, formed the "Snake within the tunnel." EEC states promised to restrict fluctuations between their own currencies to just 1.125 percent above or below their central value by intervening on the currency markets to shadow the DM. The Snake was thus an attempt to lash the EEC's currencies together like boats in a harbor that would rise and fall together as the dollar tide advanced and ebbed.

The institution of the Snake was on balance a victory in the lengthy debate over the right way to achieve monetary unification for the so-called economist approach. Briefly, some theoretical economists and finance ministry officials, of whom Schiller had been the most vocal, had sustained that a common European currency would only be introduced after a trial period of policy convergence. Historically weak currencies such as the pound sterling or the French franc (until the early 1970s, the Italian lira was regarded as a comparatively strong currency) would have to prove to the currency markets that they could live with a hair shirt on before the fusion of currencies could be attempted. The Snake, at any rate in theory, provided this discipline. It was premised upon the idea that its members would match the public austerity that made the German DM or the Swiss franc such attractive safe havens for international investors—although the Bundesbank was concerned that it might do the opposite and lead to Germany diluting her own policies to meet the more lax standards of her Community partners. As events soon showed, several member states were in fact not equally willing (or politically able) to keep station when the financial waves got rough.

The opposing school of thought to the "economists," the so-called monetarists, had consistently held that Europe should simply fix currencies at a mutually agreed rate. It should then deal with the social and economic consequences of the abolition of exchange rate freedom by greatly increasing the Community's central budget and its power to channel funds to the less competitive regions of the Community. This was the thinking underlying Edward Heath's hope that Community membership would be a means of regenerating Britain's depressed areas.

Britain's economic weaknesses, in fact, were such that she was not economically robust or politically stable enough to stick to the regime imposed by the Snake. Sterling joined the Snake in May 1972, just as gloomy balance-of-payments figures, and the unconvincing figure of Chancellor Anthony Barber, unleashed a storm of speculation against the pound. Britain quickly spent a huge portion of her reserves in a vain bid to stay tied to its new European partners. She failed. On 23 June, the pound, together with the Irish punt, was forced to float free (and promptly plunged, although high British inflation soon eroded any competitive gains that devaluation was able to give British industry). Subsequent capital movements away from the dollar compelled Bonn to impose controls on the purchase of German bonds by foreigners. This decision led to the acrimonious resignation of Schiller from the finance and economics "super ministry" and his substitution by his acerbic rival Helmut Schmidt.[31]

This catalogue of currency crises makes the blithe tone of the October 1972 Paris summit slightly bewildering. How were Europe's leaders able to look forward to intensified monetary cooperation in line with the recommendations of the Werner report when they had spent over a year being buffeted by the currency storm unleashed by Nixon's decision to suspend gold convertibility? The inability of Britain to protect the value of its currency, the magnetic attraction of the DM for international investors, the jealously guarded institutional power of the Bundesbank, the preference of the French for managing the franc in such a way as to boost the balance-of-trade surplus hardly augured well for monetary integration. Yet the commitment to an integrated currency was undoubtedly a powerful one. In March 1973, the dollar dived again, shattering the floor of the tunnel. Six EC states—West Germany, the Netherlands,

France, Belgium, Luxembourg and Denmark—jointly floated upwards against the dollar; only Italy could not keep up with the pace and was forced to drop out. Solomon is clear that the decision to float as a group reflected the European countries' "aspirations for European unity."[32] Willi Brandt, indeed, boasted at the time that the cohesion shown by the six EC states during the March 1973 currency crisis was proof that "consensus of opinion within the European Community, which has formed around the nucleus of Franco-German solidarity, is only a hand's breadth from becoming a reality." Europe, Brandt drew the conclusion, should not remain a "study in abstract architecture" but needed to "qualify as a political community also."[33]

So long as France formed part of the Snake, such aspirations for European Union retained some residual force. The oil shock in the autumn of 1973, which quadrupled the price of crude to $11 a barrel, put paid however to France's membership. Unable to contain speculation against the franc, France left the Snake in January 1974, although she temporarily rejoined in 1975–1976. In December 1974, meeting in Paris, the Nine bowed to the inevitable and consigned the Werner report's timetable for monetary unification to the Greek *kalends*.

The inability of Britain, France and Italy to peg their currencies to the DM reflected investors' fears about inflation in those economies. Any kind of fixed or semifixed exchange rate regime between states is impossible to maintain if there are gross disparities in inflation rates since high-inflation countries are bound to suffer an incremental loss of competitiveness—and thus risk losing markets and jobs to their less profligate trading partners. As Peter Ludlow has felicitously remarked, the inflation performance of the Community states in the mid-1970s bore more resemblance to the final classification in a Western European subgroup in the World Cup qualifying competition, with Germany at the top and the United Kingdom and Italy no less securely at the bottom, than to an association of more or less equal states progressing harmoniously and happily towards union.[34]

At bottom, this uneven level of economic performance was a question of domestic political stability. Brandt's belief that consensus was beginning to prevail within the Community was disconcertingly erroneous. The EC was in fact split along ideological lines. In the north of Europe, especially Germany and the Netherlands, politics was based upon broad acceptance by all political forces, including, crucially, the trade unions, of a social market economy in which private enterprise coexisted with high levels of state-provided health care, insurance and social security. In Britain, France and Italy, such consensus over the fundamental character of the polity did not exist. In all three countries, political forces committed to the state direction of the economy were a key variable in the equation. Italy had been wracked by violent strikes and labor unrest since the "hot autumn" of 1969: its successful Communist Party, which was exercising a de facto veto over government policy by the early 1970s, actually represented a force for comparative moderation in industrial disputes. The Heath government in Britain was brought down in 1973–1974 by striking miners and power workers who swept away successive attempts by government, industry and the union leadership to negotiate a binding national incomes policy. The Labour government headed by Harold Wilson (1974–1976) subsequently followed a doctrinaire policy of boosting public spending, nationalization (the taking of whole industries into state ownership), appeasing union pay demands and imposing crippling levels of taxation on the better off (the marginal tax rate reached 83 percent for the highest incomes). These policies provoked a flight of capital, sky-high inflation and a series of sterling crises. In October 1976, the British government, like many Third World countries since, was obliged to beg for a substantial loan from the International Monetary Fund. The Fund lent Britain the money, but insisted on deeply unpopular cuts in public spending as the price of its generosity. In France, the opposition Socialists and Communists formed the "Union of the Left" in 1972. Its platform, despite long-awaited guarantees from the Communists on democracy and human rights, nevertheless promised the state control of the economy via public ownership of the banks and the introduction of high-cost measures of social welfare. In all three countries, in short, inflation-fighting measures of the kind that appealed to the Bundesbank were a recipe for calamitous levels of social unrest. It was this fact, above all others, that took monetary unification off the agenda.[35]

FOREIGN POLICY FAILURES AND THE TINDEMANS REPORT

The level of political instability in Western Europe and the acrimony induced by the falling dollar were the main reasons that Henry Kissinger—then national security adviser in the doomed Nixon administration (Kissinger became secretary of state in September 1973)—decided to make 1973 the "Year of Europe" for American foreign policy. In a speech given in New York on 23 April, Kissinger argued that a new era in transatlantic relations was dawning. Western Europe's economic revival and economic unification was "an established fact"; the USSR had reached "near-equality" in the military balance of power; Japan had emerged as a "major power center." New problems, such as "insuring the supply of energy" were coming to the fore. Europe's "new generation" was less committed than their parents to "the unity that made peace possible and to the effort required to maintain it." By the time President Nixon made a scheduled tour of European capitals at the end of 1973, Kissinger wanted the United States and its allies to have worked out a new "Atlantic Charter" in which the Europeans committed themselves to making a bigger contribution to the West's cause. Kissinger emphasized that the United States supported European unity—but expected "to be met in a spirit of reciprocity" in trade matters. The United States would not withdraw unilaterally from Europe—but, in turn, expected "a fair share of the common effort for the common defense."[36]

In his memoirs, Kissinger insisted that the U.S. government had "conceived the speech as a summons to a new period of creativity among the industrial democracies."[37] In Europe, however, this initiative was greeted with a "thundering silence" in European capitals by statesmen who could see no reason why the United States should want to rejig the basis of Atlantic alliance.[38] When, in June 1973, the Nixon administration signed the Soviet-American agreement on the prevention of nuclear war and intensified détente between the superpowers without so much as consulting the Europeans—who, after all, had most to lose if better U.S.-Soviet relations led to American troop withdrawals—relations became still more chilly. French foreign minister Michel Jobert was especially angered by Kissinger's snub.

Europe's commitment to a common foreign policy, however, only made a complicated situation worse. The Nine met in Copenhagen on 23 July 1973 and decided to ask their senior foreign ministry professionals to prepare a document for the attention of the Nine's foreign ministers in September. In keeping with their desire to present a common front in foreign policy questions, the EC countries—even Britain—drew up their response to the Atlantic Charter speech without consultation with the Americans, transmitted their (somewhat vacuous) response to the United States via the Danish foreign minister (Denmark was chairing the Council of Ministers) and then refused to have any bilateral or informal conversations with the United States on the issue. It is clear from his memoirs that Kissinger regarded this attitude as a deliberate bid by the Europeans—and in particular the French—to take advantage of President Nixon's domestic travails to assert its foreign policy independence from the United States.[39] It is at least as likely, in fact, that the episode illustrates the empirical limits of the EC's common foreign policy. The EC was trying to reproduce the internal process of foreign policy formulation typical of a federal state like the United States (Kissinger's own proposal, after all, was the result of internal debate and discussion of which the Europeans knew little or nothing), while remaining a collection of sovereign nation-states.

Tensions between the United States and Europe only intensified in October 1973 when Syria and Egypt attacked Israel in an attempt to recapture territory lost during the 1967 "Six-Day War." OPEC's decision to boycott those Western countries that supported Israel in the conflict—the United States and the Netherlands were singled out—tightened the screws still further. Europe was placed in the uncomfortable position of having to choose between its American ally and the suppliers of what had become since the late 1950s its main source of energy generation.[40] The governments of the

Nine chose to back the Arabs. Having first almost unanimously forbidden the United States to make use of European bases for military flights to Israel, the EC's foreign ministers declared on 6 November 1973 that Israel should give back the territory it had held since 1967 and should "respect the legitimate rights of the Palestinians." This position was in line with several UN resolutions on the Palestinian question, but in the circumstances of the time, the EC's stand "conveyed the implication that when faced with the economic, social and political consequences of a sustained oil embargo the Nine had chosen the path of appeasement at any price."[41]

Proponents of greater political cooperation noted, however, that the Nine had for the first time reached a common position on a major issue of foreign policy. The December 1973 Copenhagen summit, building upon the Luxembourg report on political cooperation discussed earlier, underlined this novelty by asserting the Nine's "common will to see Europe speak with one voice" in foreign affairs. Specifically, the summit announced that the Nine intended to press ahead with a dialogue with the oil producers in order to achieve a "global regime" that would balance economic development in the producer countries with a stable oil supply for the industrialized world at "reasonable prices." The Arab countries welcomed this conciliatory approach.

As a respected French commentator subsequently pointed out, the diplomatic crisis provoked by the oil shock "revealed the gap between the ambitions proclaimed for Europe and its capabilities for real action."[42] By backing the Arabs so openly, in a conflict that had in the meantime escalated into a Cold War crisis, the EC had chosen, to use an Americanism, to play hardball with the United States. Certainly, it had more than lived up to its aspiration in the 1972 Paris summit to "establish its position in world affairs as a distinct entity determined to promote a better international equilibrium."

The American response was blunt. In December 1973, speaking just before the Copenhagen summit, a hostile Kissinger stated, "Europe's unity must not be at the expense of the Atlantic Community."[43] Kissinger, prompted by Helmut Schmidt, subsequently proposed creating a consumers' organization of the largest industrial nations, whose members would pool their oil reserves and would coordinate their responses to any further price hikes by the OPEC producers' cartel.[44] In February 1974, the largest industrial countries gathered in Washington, D.C., to discuss the American scheme.

The Washington conference was a shambles from the European point of view: Bino Olivi records that "nobody who attended [the conference on energy] will easily forget the grim spectacle of disunity and disorder in the Community's ranks."[45] American speakers from President Nixon down linked energy matters to questions of national security and drove home the point that isolationism was likely to gain ground in the United States if Europe persisted in appeasing the Arab countries.[46] Nobody was so vulgar as to threaten troop withdrawals from Europe openly, but the message was clear. This hard American line split—as it was clearly intended to—the French (the keenest supporters of EC–OPEC negotiations) from the Germans and resulted in an embarrassing row between Jobert and Helmut Schmidt, who openly accused the French government of putting Europe's relationship with the United States in jeopardy.[47]

In the end, every EC state except for France joined the American-sponsored International Energy Agency in November 1974. Earlier, in June 1974, the Nine also acknowledged that the United States would be informed and consulted during the formulation of any major European foreign policy initiative.[48] Kissinger had, in effect, browbeaten eight EC member states into toeing the American line. The political outcome of the oil shock was, in other words, reminiscent of the Fouchet negotiations. Europe was not yet ready for the French vision of an independent European foreign policy. The Nine had seized upon the oil crisis as a way of establishing its credentials as a force to be counted in world politics. However, at the first whiff of grapeshot, their ranks had scattered.

By the end of 1974, therefore, the grand design of the Paris summit, of achieving a European Union by the end of the 1970s, was looking somewhat battered. Monetary unification was a nonstarter, hamstrung by the inability of the Nine's governments to agree upon common macroeconomic policies to combat inflation and by the fragile state of social peace in some member states. The objective of a common foreign policy had proved unworkable on its first trial. Europe was looking more than ever like a mere loose collection of reluctant neighbors whose geographic proximity and economic ties compelled them to endure a minimum degree of pannational cooperation in trade questions.

At the December 1974 Paris summit, the governments of the Nine addressed this gloomy state of affairs in two ways. First, in a move that must have caused a smirk of satisfaction to pass across the face of the shade of Charles de Gaulle, they agreed to formalize their occasional summits under a new name—the European Council. The new body would meet three times a year and while not formally part of the EC's machinery would provide the EC with an agenda-setting forum. Second, the Nine asked—some might think somewhat belatedly—one of their number, the then prime minister of Belgium Leo Tindemans, to "define what was meant by the term European Union." Tindemans was given a year to fulfill this onerous task.

The Tindemans report, which was sent to the European Council on 29 December 1975, represented a major act of rethinking by a keen supporter of a federal Europe. Widely dismissed at the time as timid, the report was in fact a shrewd assessment of the limits to integration in Western Europe and an intelligent guide to the direction that further measures of integration would have to take. European Union, Tindemans argued, implied that "we present a united front to the external world" in "all the main fields of our external relations," including foreign policy. It implied that Europe would have a common economic and monetary policy, and that Europe would institute regional development programs to "correct inequalities in development and counteract the centralizing effects of industrial societies." It implied "social action" to "encourage society to organize itself in a fairer and more humane fashion" and to protect Europeans' civil rights. To achieve these tasks, European Union implied institutions "with the necessary powers to determine a common, coherent and all-inclusive political view, the efficiency needed for action, the legitimacy needed for democratic control."[49]

Tindemans's understanding of European Union was thus a restatement of the socially responsible market liberalism that had informed the debates of the Congress of Europe in 1948. His report was not original in terms of federalist doctrine. It was much more original in terms of tactics. Tindemans envisaged a "step-by-step" approach to European unification and essentially placed the onus upon the governments of the member states to launch initiatives through the newly established European Council.[50] Specifically, in the field of foreign policy, Tindemans recommended that the meaningless distinction between "political cooperation" and "Community business" should be abolished. He further proposed that the EC should gradually take a common position on aiding the less developed world and should improve relations with the United States by the simple device of the European Council's delegating one of its members to pursue clarificatory talks with the U.S. government. The member states should cooperate among themselves in the European Council to hold down defense costs and monitor crises—Portugal was a particular worry at that time—within the European region.[51]

In the field of economic and monetary unification, Tindemans presciently and practically suggested that monetary integration might be advanced by allowing those countries that were capable of economic and monetary union to press ahead, using the Snake, as a starting point. The Snake, which was not, strictly speaking, a Community mechanism, only regulated its members' external monetary policy. Tindemans hoped that members of the European Council would, consulting at all times with nonmembers, proceed to coordinate their internal monetary policy (money supply), their budgetary policy and their strategies to combat inflation.[52]

Tindemans was anxious to make Europe "a more discernible reality" to its people.[53] He advocated the introduction of a European passport, free movement across frontiers, the simplification of procedures for refunding medical expenses, increased student exchanges and the harmonization of educational qualifications. In general, the EC, prompted by the European Council, should try to give Europe its "social and human dimension."[54] A "European Foundation," to be partly financed by the Community, should be created by the European Council to fund and promote "the ideal of society" inherent in the European project.

Tindemans also advocated limited, but shrewd, reforms to the institutional structure of the EC. At Paris in December 1974, the Nine had agreed, despite British and Danish reservations, to permit the direct election of the European Assembly. Tindemans approved this decision and made several cautious recommendations for extending the Assembly's powers. The Assembly should gradually be given a "power of proposal" by allowing it, in the first instance, to address resolutions to the European Council. It should take a higher public profile by staging "state of the union debates" twice a year to which prominent national politicians should be invited. Voting by qualified majority, Tindemans argued, should become the norm for the Council of Ministers. The European Council should appoint the president of the Commission, who would appoint the rest of his colleagues in consultation with the Council. The Assembly would gain the right to approve the new Commission in a formal vote of confidence, and the Commission itself—which since the defeat of Hallstein had stagnated under the presidencies of Jean Rey (Belgium), Franco Maria Malfatti (Italy), Sicco Mansholt (Netherlands), and Francois-Xavier Ortoli (France)—would become a more activist body in line with what Tindemans regarded as the intentions of article 155 of the EEC treaty.[55]

Europe's federalists would have preferred Tindemans to present a draft constitution for Europe: plainly, his recommendations fell far short of this. His report was still strong beer, however, for the Nine, who bashfully refused to swallow its contents at a gulp. Tindemans's report was on the agenda for the four meetings of the European Council subsequent to its submission. No concrete action resulted. Instead, the member states would take a number of cautious sips over the next fifteen years until, with the Treaty of Maastricht, a Europe very similar indeed to Tindemans's prescriptions was actually enacted.

THE EUROPEAN MONETARY SYSTEM

The first such sip was the creation of the European Monetary System (EMS). Essentially a revised and more inclusive version of the Snake, the EMS was brought into operation in January 1979 by exactly the methods that Tindemans had prescribed for further advances in integration: by diplomatic initiatives on the part of the member states within the European Council. More accurately, it was brought into being by the actions of certain key political leaders. Writing history in terms of "great men" and their decisions is distinctly unfashionable nowadays, but in the case of the EMS, it is difficult to do otherwise. Something like the EMS may well have been introduced in time, but without the imaginative leadership exercised by Helmut Schmidt, who had succeeded Willi Brandt as chancellor of the Federal Republic in May 1974, Valery Giscard D'Estaing, who had become president of France in the same month, and Roy Jenkins, who became president of the European Commission in January 1977, it is difficult to believe that such an ambitious scheme could have overcome the many vested interests opposed to it in the late 1970s.

Schmidt was the chief driving force. Schmidt's powerful intellect seems to have become engaged in the question of monetary unification out of pique with the weak performance of the new American president, Jimmy Carter, whom he describes as "idealistic and fickle" in his memoir *Men and Powers*.[56] At least in part, Schmidt was alarmed by what he regarded as Carter's amateurish foreign policy. Early on in his administration, Carter tried to prevent Germany from selling nuclear technology to Brazil, decided to go ahead with production of the neutron bomb (and then changed his mind) and adopted a confrontational line on the Soviet Union's human rights abuses. All these policies were judged to be aberrant by Schmidt.

Mostly, however, Schmidt was infuriated by the Carter administration's studied neglect of the dollar. In the first half of 1977, the dollar resumed its slide in the currency markets. By mid-1977, it had skidded to DM 2.35 and would decline to below DM 2.0 by the end of the year and DM 1.76 by September 1978 (in August 1971 it had been worth DM 4.20). Nobody knew where the dollar's fall would stop. As Jonathon Carr has written, the dollar "seemed not so much to be floating as drowning."[57] The risk was that the OPEC countries, whose coffers were by now awash with dollars, would stash their newly acquired wealth in European currencies and in the DM in particular.[58]

As usual, the problem was the American trade deficit, which topped $31,000 million in 1977. The Carter administration reiterated the standard American position that its deficit was due to the overly cautious policies of the European economies and urged the Europeans to act as a "locomotive" for growth. In *Men and Powers*, Schmidt dismissed this theory as a "Loch Ness monster" that "surfaced from the depths" whenever the dollar was in difficulty.[59] Throughout 1977, West Germany came under intense international pressure to stimulate its economy and cut its substantial trade surplus by sucking in imports. At the May 1977 summit of the leading industrial nations, Schmidt, against his better judgment, was forced to pledge that Germany would aim for 5 percent growth in its economy—a target that was impossible without increasing inflationary pressures within the economy.[60] From the point of view of exasperated European finance ministers and central bankers, especially in West Germany, the cause of the dollar's weakness was rather the lack of political will in Washington to take the politically divisive decision to curb domestic American consumption, in particular of energy. According to

Roy Jenkins, Schmidt's central role in the decision to launch a monetary initiative in Europe was essentially a reaction to his growing conviction of American incompetence. It gave Schmidt "some escape from his frustration at knowing better how to run the world than Carter or Brezhnev or Callaghan [British prime minister 1976–1979], but mostly feeling himself inhibited by his country's past from trying to do so."[61]

Andrew Moravcsik provides a useful supplement to this essentially psychological explanation of Schmidt's motives by pointing out the economic benefits for Germany of the EMS: "The primary purpose of the initiative was to dampen DM appreciation by helping weak currency countries impose macroeconomic discipline rather than either devalue or impose trade restrictions."[62] As in the early 1970s, the DM strengthened against the dollar disproportionately in 1977–1978. The franc and the lira floated down with the dollar; sterling strengthened, but by significantly less than the DM. Even the Scandinavians devalued. The dollar's slump, in short, was pricing German industry out of its main markets.[63] The EMS, by this analysis, should be interpreted as an attempt to reduce Europe's exposure to the fluctuations of American policy by encouraging trade, on fair terms, within a select club of countries.

Other countries regarded the imposition of a monetary straitjacket in Europe as beneficial for their economies. Certainly, Giscard's strong support of the scheme was motivated by this conviction. When Giscard became president of France, he initially tried to impose austerity in order to combat soaring inflation rates. The ensuing surge in unemployment—to what was then regarded as the unacceptable figure of almost one million—panicked his government, which pumped subsidies into troubled industrial sectors. But this largesse was a temporary blip in policy. Giscard, like an increasing number of statesmen across Europe, had lost faith in the power of the state to deliver economic growth without inflation. As he wrote in a stimulating 1976 book of prescriptions for French democracy, economic activity was like the human organism: "If each breath we draw, each step we take, had to be the result of conscious decision, illness would soon follow."[64] The trouble with the French economy, Giscard contended, was that the "brain"—the state—was trying to do too much.

When, in August 1976, Jacques Chirac, Giscard's prime minister in France's semipresidential system, resigned over policy differences, Giscard turned to a man, the former European commissioner Raymond Barre, whom he knew to share his economic liberalism fully. In September 1976, Barre introduced a tough program of tax increases and public spending cuts designed to take demand out of the economy. France had embarked upon the road of making herself authentically competitive as an economy, instead of relying on currency devaluation to do that job for her. Measures of monetary integration could only help this program. They lashed France to the

German economy (taking away any temptation to dilute Barre's policies)—and gave the French government an opportunity to depict its painful reforms as a necessary sacrifice. It was both idealism *and* realism that led Giscard to state unambiguously that France's "number one task" was to make economic and monetary unification a reality.[65]

In the case of Roy Jenkins, pressing for greater monetary unification was a means of launching his presidency of the European Commission, as well as a deeply held intellectual conviction. Jenkins had become president of the Commission as a result of his impressive leadership of the "Britain in Europe" campaign during the 1975 referendum on EC membership called by Prime Minister Harold Wilson—although Jenkins had originally strongly opposed the idea of a referendum when Labour was in opposition and had even resigned the deputy leadership of the party over the issue.[66] The referendum had been Wilson's way—and, probably, was the only way—of reconciling the war to the knife within the government between "pro-marketeers" like Jenkins and the "anti-marketeers" of the left who, in many instances, wanted Britain's withdrawal from the Community to be the prelude to the imposition of a socialist siege economy.

The pretext for the referendum was the somewhat cosmetic "renegotiation" of Britain's terms of entry obtained by Wilson in March 1975, the terms of which were openly rejected by a substantial minority of the cabinet, by the party's National Executive Committee and by a special conference of the Labour movement in the spring of 1975.[67] On 5 June 1975, after a lengthy campaign, the country voted on whether or not to stay in the Community. The turnout was low by general election standards—64.5 percent—but the debate over the issues that had preceded the vote had been intense and wide-ranging. In his memoirs, Jenkins says, with little hyperbole, that during the referendum "the nation debated its future in a way that it had not done for a long time past, at least since the 1945 election."[68] To the surprise of many observers, the majority in favor of staying in was strikingly large: 67.2 percent said "yes." Jenkins, who had worked tirelessly for a "yes" vote and had put the case for a positive vote in the final televised debate, emerged from the campaign with his already considerable standing as a statesman enhanced.

Jenkins was first sounded out for the presidency of the Commission, on the initiative of Helmut Schmidt, in January 1976. When he failed to succeed Wilson as leader of the Labour Party (and hence prime minister) in March 1976, he indicated his willingness to do the job and was formally appointed by the European Council in June 1976.

Jenkins did not begin his new job well. He was quickly brought face-to-face with some Euro-realities—the first and foremost being that "in Brussels, outside a narrow field of coal and steel and agricultural decisions . . . nothing much happened unless a majority of governments could be persuaded to join in leaning on the lever."[69] By mid-1977, his performance was being belittled by *The Economist*, which seems to have jolted him out of a self-pitying mood of gloom and despair. At the end of July 1977, he decided that his presidency needed a theme and that that theme would be economic and monetary union.[70]

Jenkins's commitment to monetary union was first systematically aired in public in Florence on 27 October 1977 during the first Jean Monnet lecture at the European University Institute. His speech advanced a powerful intellectual case in favor of economic and monetary union in Europe. In synthesis, Jenkins argued that economic growth would increase, with beneficial knock-on effects on the Community's potentially catastrophic unemployment rates, and worldwide currency stabilization could be achieved, if the EC had the courage to merge its individual national currencies into one.[71] Drawing upon the recently published work of a Community-sponsored committee of academic economists, he also sketched a fascinating picture of the political implications of monetary union. Jenkins envisaged a "multitiered," confederal Europe whose heart was a central government, small by the standards of major federal states such as the United States or Germany, which was spending about 5 to 7 percent of gross Community product. This central administration would occupy itself with "those aspects of external relations where intercontinental bargaining power is called for"; a much-increased regional aid policy; high-tech industries such as aerospace; politically sensitive industries like steel, shipbuilding and textiles. A common energy policy would also be required.[72]

Jenkins was under no illusion of the "political implications" of what he was saying. He was proposing as great a step forward in the degree of integration as the "last generation" of European leaders had faced when they signed the Treaties of Rome. His justification for doing so might have come out of a realist textbook on international relations:

> Do we intend to create a European union or do we not? . . . There would be little point in asking the peoples and governments of Europe to contemplate union, were it not for the fact that real and efficient sovereignty over monetary issues already eludes them to a high and increasing degree. The prospect of monetary union should be seen as part of the process of recovering the substance of sovereign power. At present we tend to cling to its shadow.[73]

Jenkins's Florence speech was initially dismissed as Euro-rhetoric by a skeptical press. Certainly, it represented a bold departure from the prevailing "economist" position on achieving economic and monetary union. Jenkins was arguing, in effect, that political willpower should substitute for the gradual, painstaking alignment of the Nine's economies—although his insistence on a relatively small central government for the Nine marked him off from most "monetarists," too. The commissioner for economic affairs, his predecessor as president of the Commission, Francois-Xavier Ortoli, was far more cautious. A lengthy and somewhat scholarly document on "The Prospect of Economic and Monetary Union" submitted by the Commission to the 5–6 December 1977 meeting of the European Council reflected Ortoli's views rather than Jenkins's by calling for a gradualist five-year program of economic convergence.[74] The Council itself approved the Commission's document "with satisfaction," but it is doubtful that the leaders of the Nine had, at this stage, engaged with the arguments in any detail.

By December 1977, therefore, the Nine had accepted that monetary union, like good health and fine weather, was in principle a good thing. But they had certainly not committed themselves to pursuing the economic policies that would be necessary to bring it into being. Jenkins says in his biography that "reproclamation of monetary union had done well in providing me with a message, but I was far from confident that it was going to provide Europe with a monetary advance."[75] What turned Jenkins's vision into at least partial reality was the intervention of Helmut Schmidt. On 28 February 1978, Jenkins had a routine meeting with the German chancellor. Schmidt startled Jenkins by stating that if the Union of the Left were defeated in the forthcoming March 1978 elections in France, he would propose in response to the dollar problem "a major step towards monetary union; to mobilize and put all our currency reserves into a common pool, if other people will agree to do the same, and to form a monetary bloc."[76] This decision represented a significant change of direction for Schmidt, who had greeted Jenkins's original speech with skepticism, saying that he was in favor in principle of economic and monetary union but "not if it meant German inflation going to 8 percent."[77]

Having committed himself to pursuing greater integration in the monetary field, Schmidt proceeded with singular individualism to formulate his ideas. His cabinet, the Bundesbank and most of the governments of the EC, including Britain, were kept in ignorance of his thinking until the Copenhagen European Council on 7–8 April 1978. Only Giscard was let into the secret during a meeting at Rambouillet on 2 April, at which the two leaders, "like two dramatists preparing a performance in which they themselves were to be the most important actors," carefully plotted out the strategy and tactics they would use at the summit.[78] At Copenhagen, Schmidt proposed, emphasizing that he was speaking in a purely personal capacity, that the EC should back up the Snake by creating a European Monetary Fund, similar to the International Monetary Fund, with member states pooling approximately 15 to 20 percent of their reserves to provide cash for interventions in support of economic restructuring in member states' economies. He further suggested that EC currencies rather than dollars should be increasingly used instead of dollars for interventions on the exchange markets and that the so-called European Unit of Account (EUA, the instrument used by the EC to calculate members' contributions and farm prices) should become a proto-currency. EC states should settle their debts to each other in EUAs and should issue debt denominated in this notional "Euromoney."[79]

The other European leaders, Britain's James Callaghan aside, welcomed Schmidt's proposal with varying degrees of comprehension and enthusiasm. Schmidt's proposal, which by now had been elaborated upon by a duo of trusted advisers, was formally adopted—and publicized for the first time—at the subsequent Bremen summit in June 1978. In a coup for the French government, the EUA was renamed the "European Currency Unit," or Ecu, at Bremen. The Ecu, Giscard smugly revealed, had been a coin in medieval France.

Between June and December 1978, Schmidt's proposal, which was itself a more pragmatic and limited conception of economic and monetary union than Jenkins's, was nibbled away in the meetings of the finance ministers and central bankers. The final version, agreed at the Brussels European Council on 4–5 December 1978, jettisoned the idea of a European Monetary Fund and limited itself, essentially, to widening the membership of the Snake and fine-tuning its mechanisms. The core element of the new EMS was the exchange rate mechanism (ERM), which, at any rate in theory was to be based upon the Ecu. The Ecu was defined as a "composite currency" whose value was determined by merging together the currencies of the member nations according to a complex formula based on three criteria: percentage of gross Community product contributed; percentage of Community exports; overall size of the economy. Members of the new system would be obliged to limit fluctuations of their currencies to within 2.25 percent above or below their par value against the Ecu. Italy, however, was allowed to join in a special "band" that allowed the lira to fluctuate as much as 6 percent above or below par for a limited period of time. The same offer was made to Britain, which refused to join, and to Ireland, which broke its postindependence currency union with Britain and joined at the same 2.25 percent rate as everybody else. Italy and Ireland's adhesion was only secured after they obtained, in the course of an ill-tempered debate during the Brussels summit, a trivial increase in funding from the EC's regional aid fund to help their economies adjust to the rigors of the new system.

The Ecu's role, however, was more nominal than real since, at the behest of the Bundesbank, the "central rate" was to be used to "establish a grid of bilateral exchange rates" between participating currencies. In other words, member states' central banks, as well as monitoring their currencies' standing against the Ecu, had also to ensure that they did not breach the 2.25 band against all other participating currencies. The rules of the Snake, in other words, had been slightly loosened. To suit an increased membership, a slightly wider margin of fluctuation was now being permitted. But the member states were still signing up to a system in which they were obliged to tie their currencies to the value of the mark. If the mark continued to rise against the dollar, the rest of Europe's currencies would rise against the dollar too and the member states would therefore tend to trade between themselves more, strengthening the Community as an economic force.[80]

This point is very important. Giscard accepted the idea of a bilateral grid of exchange rates during a Franco-German summit in Aachen in September 1978, which was accompanied with a great deal of pomp and ceremony. Giscard and Schmidt visited the tomb of Charlemagne, and Giscard famously said, "Perhaps when we discussed monetary problems, the spirit of Charlemagne brooded over us."[81] This ostentatious "Euro-claptrap," to use the words of one of the EC's most outspoken and well-informed critics, has been interpreted as being a mere device to help sell the EMS in France.[82]

There is no doubt some truth in this, but it is too reductive. Schmidt was, as usual, thinking long term. According to his biographer, the German chancellor "urged skeptics" to see the EMS "in the political context of the next fifteen or twenty years." He did not regard the niceties of the EMS as "technical monetary questions," but as "political, economic and psychological matters of the first importance."[83] The EMS *was* enabling Germany to stem the tendency of the mark to overshoot in value, and it *did* provide the franc with a potential framework for austerity (although the version agreed at Brussels left plenty of room for countries to drop in and out of the system and for periodical revaluations of the member currencies). To this extent it was in the domestic political interests of both countries. But, at least in the minds of its creators, the EMS was laying the foundations for a European economy that was less vulnerable to outside shocks. One can see why they regarded such an achievement as one that transcended narrow national interests.

The EMS eventually got under way, three months behind schedule, in March 1979 after a somewhat futile squabble with France over its effects on farm prices. Britain did not join: the Labour government believed, with the characteristic defeatism of the British political class in the 1970s, that without the weapon of competitive devaluation, British industry would never be able to withstand the full force of continental competition and unemployment would rise to politically unsustainable levels. When the Conservatives, under the leadership of Mrs. Thatcher, won the May 1979 election, they were skeptical of entry for the opposite reason: they wanted a virile pound in order to squeeze inflation from the British economy. As Roy Jenkins dryly remarked in his biography: "In fact under both of them Britain enjoyed for several years a higher rate of unemployment and inflation than any participating country."[84]

BEYOND THE COMMON MARKET

The EMS was a far cry from the plans of the Werner report at the beginning of the 1970s. The Nine were not using a single currency, nor were centralized institutions in Brussels carrying out macroeconomic policy. The national governments and the central banks of the nine member states continued to be Europe's main economic actors. Yet it was not a negligible event either. The Nine (or eight out of the nine) had, with varying degrees of enthusiasm, signed up to the notion that Europe's economic future lay, at any rate in economic terms, in becoming West Germany writ large; an association of social market democracies trading freely among themselves and committed to budgetary austerity. This commitment was not yet permanent: France had not definitively relinquished the model of the socialist command economy—as the first Mitterrand presidency was about to show—and Italy had certainly not relinquished budgetary profligacy. But the EMS represented a major act of identification with a vision of European economic organization that had been an implicit goal for the countries of western Europe since the Congress of Europe.

This progress towards greater integration on the economic front was matched by a gradual and, in retrospect, significant consolidation of the legal status of the Treaty of Rome by the Court of Justice. *Van Gend en Loos* (see chapter 3) had established that the treaty conferred rights directly upon the citizens of the member states and that member states were infringing those rights when they passed laws that did not conform with the EEC treaty. The implication of this position was that Community law took precedence over national law. Insofar as Dutch law already acknowledged the primacy of international law over national law where the direct effectiveness of international law could be shown to exist, for the Netherlands at least the question was now settled. There were, however, other EC states—for example, Italy—where there was a constitutional presumption of the primacy of national law. In *Costa v. Enel* (case 6/64), a case in which a lawyer from Milan refused to pay his electricity bill because he considered that the Italian government had infringed several provisions of the EEC treaty when it nationalized the electricity industry, the Court of Justice ruled, contrary to the arguments put forward by the Italian government, that it was fully entitled to decide whether the law nationalizing the power industry was in conflict with the EEC treaty. The Court argued that by signing the EEC treaty the member states had made "a permanent limitation of their sovereign rights, against which a subsequent unilateral act incompatible with the concept of the Community cannot prevail."[85] None of this helped Signor Costa, however, since the Court also ruled that the Italian government had not in fact breached the treaty.

In the 1970s, this principle of primacy for Community law was reinforced by two other major cases. In *Internationale Handelgesellschaft v. Einfuhr und Vorratsstelle Getreide* (case 11/70), the ECJ, responding to a German Court that regarded an EC regulation incompatible with the German Constitution, controversially ruled that the "validity of a Community measure or its effect within a member state cannot be affected by allegations that it runs counter to either fundamental rights as formulated by the Constitution of that state, or the principles of a national constitutional structure."[86] In *Amministrazione delle Finanze dello Stato v. Simmenthal* (case 106/77), the ECJ clarified the procedural implications of the doctrine of primacy by insisting that national courts, whenever they were faced with a conflict between a national norm and a Community measure had the duty to give "full effect" to Community regulations without waiting for new legislation, or the rulings of national courts of appeal, to resolve the question for them.[87] This ruling was intended to guarantee the efficacy of Community legislation in countries like Italy, where governments might otherwise have kept the offending norms on the statute books pending an appeal to the country's Constitutional Court, or the death of the plaintiff, whichever might be the sooner. The ECJ was not prepared to let countries with byzantine legal systems use procedure as a backdoor form of protectionism.

Nor, indeed, was it prepared to allow legislative lethargy to block the uniform application of Community legislation. Case 148/78, *Pubblico ministero v. Ratti*, is a good example of the ECJ's attitude in this regard. Signor Ratti, a manufacturer of solvents and varnishes, had packaged and labeled his products in accordance with guidelines contained in two EC directives, which the Italian government had not yet transformed into Italian law. The Italian authorities prosecuted him for not following Italian law in this area. The ECJ ruled that a member state "may not rely, as against individuals, on its own failure to perform the obligations which the directive intends," although it exonerated the Italian government over the directive on varnishes, since the deadline for implementation had still not expired.[88]

One final case from the 1970s should be cited to show the ECJ's willingness to interpret the EEC treaty in defense of the citizen. *Defrenne v. Sabena* (case 43/75), in which a Belgian air hostess sued the national airline because she was being paid less than male stewards doing the same work, led the ECJ to rule that "the principle of equal pay forms part of the foundations of the Treaty." Article 119 of the treaty was unambiguous on this point. The ECJ, moreover, citing article 117 of the treaty, which says improving working conditions and a rising standard of living for workers is a goal of the Community, meant that pay could not be leveled down, but had to be leveled up.[89]

The net effect of the ECJ's case law between 1964 and 1978 (of which this is a mere summary of the highlights) was, in retrospect, immensely significant. In the first place, it prevented the member states from undermining the liberalizing thrust of the EEC treaty by domestic legal cavils. Member states could not pretend that the treaty's provisions, or legislation passed in accordance with the treaty's procedures, did not have a direct effect on the citizens of the member states, nor could they lawfully obstruct the *effectiveness* of EC regulations and (well-worded and appropriate) directives with national principles, practices and procedures. In the second place, in Weiler's words, it meant that "Community norms that produce direct effects are not merely the law of the land, but the 'higher law' of the land."[90] The EEC treaty had obtained "an authority similar to that of a constitution in a federal system."[91] The European Community, in other words, was not an alliance or association of states united together for a common purpose, but a community of states bound together by a legal framework that conferred rights upon the states' citizens. It was a polity, albeit one of a unique kind.

By comparison with the ECJ, the European Assembly registered an only modest increase in its powers and status in the 1970s. Nevertheless, the institution did secure the gain that it had been most adamantly pressing for since its very formation: direct election. The Paris summit of December 1974 conceded the principle of direct election (which had been implicit in article 138 of the EEC treaty and for which the Assembly had been actively pressing since 1960). With a nod to the Vedel report, the summit communiqué also stated that "the competence of the European Assembly will be extended, in particular by granting it certain powers in the Community's legislative process." The Tindemans report, as we have seen, backed this suggestion. But the failure of the EC to make progress on a common foreign policy and to achieve monetary union in a sense robbed proponents of a larger role for the Assembly of their strongest argument: the need to make the Community's procedures more democratic and more transparent. Had the EC evolved during the 1970s into the European Union envisaged at the 1972 Paris summit, or even the more limited confederal vision evoked by Roy Jenkins in his Jean Monnet lecture, the case for a genuine European legislature armed with powers of scrutiny, veto and proposal would have become unanswerable. But as David Marquand argued at the time, "Although large numbers of critically important decisions are now taken by the Community authorities, integration has not yet gone far enough to make the undemocratic nature of the system either obvious or intolerable."[92]

In September 1976, the foreign ministers of the Nine approved the European Elections Act. The Assembly was enlarged from 198 members to 410, and a five-year term between elections was agreed. Seats were distributed to the member states with little regard to the relative size of national electorates: Britain, Federal Germany and Italy, whose electorates were all just over 40 million voters, were fairly given eighty-one seats apiece—but so was France, whose electorate was only 33.3 million. The Netherlands, with twenty-five seats for 9.3 million voters, could feel hard done by in comparison with Belgium (6.3 million and twenty-four), Ireland (2.1 million and fifteen), Denmark (3.5 million and sixteen). Luxembourg's mere 200,000 voters were given six representatives in the revamped Assembly.[93]

Article 5 of the act permitted members of the Assembly to belong both to their national parliaments and the European body. Member states were free to draw up their own electoral systems for the vote pending a proposal from the Assembly itself for a uniform electoral procedure. Since these provisions revised certain articles of the EEC treaty, the member states were obliged to submit the European Elections Act to national parliaments for ratification.

In most countries, ratification was a formality. In Germany, both the Bundesrat and the Bundestag legalized the act unanimously in June 1977; a few months earlier (February–March 1977), the two chambers of the Italian parliament had been almost equally unanimous. The "small countries" ratified the act without serious problems. In Britain and France, however, ratification became the center of a major political debate over the threat supposedly posed by direct election of the European Assembly to national sovereignty. Gaullist and Communist opposition meant that the French government was only able to ratify the European Elections Act by making it a vote of confidence.[94] In Britain, ratification took until 1978 and was only passed after a clause was included stating that "no treaty providing for any increase whatever in the powers of the Assembly will be ratified by the United Kingdom unless it has been approved by an Act of Parliament."

There was also a major battle in Britain over the choice of electoral system. The strong anti-Europe faction within the Labour Party meant that premier James Callaghan was reliant on Conservative votes for the passage of the European Elections Act, and the Conservatives' price was retention of the British first-past-the-post electoral system. Direct elections did in fact have to be postponed from the spring of 1978 to 10 June 1979 as a result of this British reluctance to embrace any form of proportional representation and the consequent need for the U.K. Boundaries Commission to design eighty-one new Euro-constituencies.

The election campaign itself disappointed supporters of European federalism by being predominately "local" in tone. In Britain, in particular, the poll was regarded as a postscript to the dramatic electoral victory of Mrs. Thatcher in the general elections of May 1979. In Italy, the national election took place the previous week and the two polls inevitably merged into a single campaign. In France, the election became a referendum on the EMS and granted both the Gaullists and the Communists a platform for a frenzied denunciation of the European project—hardly the advertisement for European unity that the federalist movement wanted. The Communists' electoral manifesto said that the country's leaders wanted "France, dismembered and weakened, to be integrated and drowned in a West European conglomeration led by Federal Germany, and ultimately controlled by the United States."[95] Jacques Chirac, the Gaullist leader, not to be outdone, ranted too against "this Europe which is dominated by Germano-American interests."[96]

Turnout varied from country to country. There was 90 percent turnout in Belgium; well over 80 percent in Italy. At the other extreme, turnout in Britain was just 33 percent. Overall, a respectable 60 percent of eligible

European citizens voted. The newly elected Assembly certainly reflected the full diversity of political opinion within the Nine. The Socialists, with 109 seats, narrowly beat the European Peoples' Party (Christian Democrat: 105) to become the largest contingent in the Assembly. The British Conservatives, who took sixty seats, allied with four Danish right-wingers to provide the next largest group. Communists, Liberals and Gaullists completed the list of major formations within the Assembly. The ideological lineup of the new Assembly, however, was less important than the fact that there was a large majority of Euro-federalists in almost every grouping. The European Parliament, as it now began to be known, would become in the early 1980s a hotbed of activity for more rapid movement towards European political and economic integration and for an increase in its own powers.

These supporters of European federalism, in the European parliament and outside, were largely responsible for establishing the myth that the 1970s had been a decade of failure for the Community. As Moravcsik has remarked, this characterization is "true only from a federalist perspective that focuses on the institutional centralization of administrative and democratic decision-making."[97] True, the Community had not lived up to the aspirations of the Hague and Paris summits. But politics is the art of the possible, and the wish lists of October 1972 were never going to be attained in the international environment engendered by American domestic crisis, the oil shock and the collapse of Bretton Woods. What in retrospect is surprising is that Europe survived—survived, moreover, with much of its idealism intact. None of the Nine withdrew from the Community, none established a socialist siege economy, eight signaled their intention to "deepen" their economic cooperation in the EMS, all of them accepted a strongly supranational interpretation of the EEC treaty in relation to national law. Three new members joined the Community (and stayed in it); the new members would shortly be joined by three former Mediterranean dictatorships who regarded the EC as a force that could stabilize and protect their fragile democracies.

The seventies, in short, were, to quote Moravcsik once more, a "decade of both consolidation and innovation."[98] If the Gaullist interlude had taught that European integration would not be delivered by the inexorable workings of European institutions, the 1970s illustrated that "European Union"—whatever that phrase meant (and Tindemans's redefinition of the phrase was not the least achievement of the 1970s)—would not be enacted by the fiat of enlightened national leaders. Yet the 1970s also underlined that Europe's national leaders, working through institutionalized summit meetings, could make substantive progress towards achieving fuller economic integration. The necessity for enhanced economic integration, moreover, seemed evident. If Europe were to insulate herself even partly from an unstable global economy, she had to trade more within her own boundaries—

a goal that implied broad agreement over macroeconomic fundamentals. This latter lesson was still imperfectly learned in 1979, but between 1979 and 1986, the commitment to freer intra-Community trade, sound money and budgetary rigor that was implicit in the EMS bargain became the policy of choice for most of the Community. This agreement on fundamentals was reached, however, only after it had flirted with a form of doctrinaire socialism that was antithetical to Community principles, and after Britain's new leader had slammed her handbag on the table and demanded her money back.

NOTES

1. Roy Jenkins, *A Life at the Centre* (London: Macmillan, 1994), 490.

2. For a very clear statement of Pompidou's general attitudes to European unity, see the transcript of a press conference given by the French president on 21 January 1971 in Paris. Pompidou argued in favor of a European "Confederation," driven by the national governments, who would decide all major questions by unanimity in the fashion of a coalition government at national level. He dismissed (then widespread) plans to turn the Assembly into a "real parliament" as "entirely worthless" in the absence of a "true" European government. For the text, see the Italian periodical *Relazioni internazionali*, 30 January 1971, 115–16.

3. The "Werner Report," supplement to *Bull. EC*, no. 11/1970, 14.

4. "Werner Report," 28.

5. "Werner Report," 28.

6. "Werner Report," 28.

7. "Werner Report," 26.

8. "Werner Report," 12.

9. "Werner Report," 13.

10. The "Vedel Report," supplement to *Bull. EC*, no. 4/72.

11. The "Luxembourg Report" of EC Foreign Ministers. *Bull. EC*, no. 10/70.

12. Kitzinger, *Diplomacy and Persuasion* (London: Thames & Hudson, 1973), 29.

13. Roy Denman, *Missed Chances* (London: Indigo, 1996), 223.

14. Edward Heath, *The Course of My Life* (London: Hodder & Stoughton, 1998), 372.

15. Denman, *Missed Chances*, 234.

16. Heath, *Course of My Life*, 366–72.

17. Good examples of anti-European pamphlets (indeed, one great speech aside, they remain the best documents British Euroskeptics have produced) are (Conservative) J. Enoch Powell, *The Common Market: The Case Against* (London: Elliot Right Way Books, 1971) and (Labour) Douglas Jay, *After the Common Market: A Better Alternative for Britain* (London: Penguin, 1968). An excellent example of pro-EC literature is Hugh Thomas, *Europe: The Radical Challenge* (London: Weidenfeld and Nicholson, 1973).

18. Denman, *Missed Chances*, 240–41.

19. Jenkins, *Life at the Centre*, 332.

20. P. M. H. Bell, *Britain and France 1940–1994: The Long Separation* (London: Longman, 1997), 225.

21. The communiqué of the 1972 Paris summit of EC leaders is to be found in *Bull. EC,* no. 10-72.

22. Heath, *Course of My Life*, 388.

23. Heath, *Course of My Life*, 392.

24. Heath, *Course of My Life*, 395.

25. Ironically, this investment by U.S. corporations was seen as a major threat to Europe's future in a book that was very influential throughout Europe, Jean-Jacques Servan-Schreiber's *La Défi Américaine* (Paris: Editions Denoel, 1967), published in English as *The American Challenge* (London: Penguin, 1969). One of Servan-Schreiber's main fears was that "if we allow American investments to enter freely under present conditions, we consign European industry . . . to a subsidiary role, and Europe herself to the position of a satellite" (33).

26. Franco Garino, "Dopo i provvedimenti economici di Nixon," *Relazioni internazionali*, 5 September 1971, 873–74, states that the EEC member states had total reserves of $37,099 million at the end of July 1971. Forty-four percent of these holdings were in dollars. West Germany's holdings were $17,664 million, 61 percent of which were in dollars.

27. Diane Kunz, *Guns and Butter: America's Cold War Economic Diplomacy* (New York: Free Press, 1997), 218.

28. Robert Solomon, *The International Monetary System 1945–1981* (New York: Harper and Row, 1982), 196.

29. William Diebold, "The Economic System at Stake," *Foreign Affairs* 51, no. 1 (1972): 170–72.

30. Solomon, *International Monetary System*, 209–10.

31. Jonathon Carr, *Helmut Schmidt: Helmsman of Germany* (London: Weidenfeld and Nicholson, 1985), 69–70.

32. Solomon, *International Monetary System*, 233.

33. Brandt's views appeared in the op-ed columns of the *New York Times*, 29 April 1973.

34. Peter Ludlow, *The Making of the EMS* (London: Butterfields, 1982), 8.

35. For the role of the PCI in Italy, see Paul Ginsborg, *A History of Contemporary Italy 1945–1988* (London: Penguin, 1990), chs. 9–10. For Britain, see Alan Sked and Chris Cook, *Post-War Britain* (London: Penguin, 1984), chs. 10–12. The memoirs of Labour chancellor Dennis Healey, *The Time of My Life* (London: Michael Joseph, 1989), chs. 19–20, are very useful for an understanding of the British crisis. The program of the French Socialist and Communist parties was published, with a preface by François Mitterrand, as *Changer La Vie* (Paris: Flammarion, 1972).

36. Henry Kissinger, *Years of Upheaval* (London: Weidenfeld and Nicholson), 152–53.

37. Kissinger, *Years of Upheaval*, 153.

38. James O. Goldesborough, "France, the European Crisis and the Alliance," *Foreign Affairs* 52, no. 3 (1974): 547.

39. Kissinger, *Years of Upheaval*, 192–94.

40. Fiona Venn, "International Cooperation versus National Self-Interest: The United States and Europe during the 1973–1974 Oil Crisis," in *The United States*

and the European Alliance since 1945, ed. Kathleen Burk and Melvyn Stokes (Oxford: Berg, 1999), 71–98 (here, 72–73).

41. Henri Simonet, "Energy and the Future of Europe," *Foreign Affairs* 53, no. 3 (1975): 451.

42. Françoise de la Serre, "L'Europe des neuf et le conflit Israélo-Arabe," *Revue Française de Science Politique* 24, no. 4: 804.

43. Goldesborough, "France, the European Crisis and the Alliance," 543.

44. Helmut Schmidt, *Men and Powers* (New York: Random House, 1989), 163.

45. Bino Olivi, *L'Europa difficile* (Bologna, Italy: Il Mulino, 2000), 160.

46. Venn, "International Cooperation versus National Self-Interest," 86.

47. Goldesborough, "France, the European Crisis and the Alliance," 539.

48. See the section on "European Political Cooperation," in *Bull. EC*, no. 6/74, for an account of the meeting of the EC foreign ministers in Bonn on 10 June 1974 at which this decision was reached. See also Richard McAllister, *From EC to EU: An Historical and Political Survey* (London: Routledge, 1997), 98.

49. The "Tindemans Report," supplement *Bull. EC*, no. 1/76, 12–3.

50. Tindemans Report, 30.

51. Tindemans Report, 16–18.

52. Tindemans Report, 20–21.

53. Tindemans Report, 28.

54. Tindemans Report, 29.

55. Tindemans Report, 29–32.

56. Schmidt, *Men and Powers*, 181.

57. Carr, *Helmut Schmidt*, 138.

58. Ludlow, *Making of the EMS*, 71.

59. Schmidt, *Men and Powers*, 273.

60. Ludlow, *Making of the EMS*, 74–76.

61. Jenkins, *Life at the Centre*, 473.

62. Andrew Moravcsik, *The Choice for Europe: Social Purpose and State Power from Messina to Maastricht* (Ithaca, N.Y.: Cornell University Press, 1998), 253.

63. Ludlow, *Making of the EMS*, 73.

64. Valery Giscard D'Estaing, *Towards a New Democracy* (London: Collins, 1977), 100.

65. Giscard, *Towards a New Democracy*, 140.

66. See Jenkins, *Life at the Centre*, 327–49, for the internal struggles within the Labour Party over the referendum.

67. Peter Byrd, "The Labour Party and the European Community 1970–1975," *Journal of Common Market Studies* 13 (1974–1975): 476–78.

68. Jenkins, *Life at the Centre*, 418.

69. Jenkins, *Life at the Centre*, 459.

70. Jenkins, *Life at the Centre*, 461–63.

71. Roy Jenkins, "Europe: Present Challenges and Future Prospects," *Bull. EC*, no. 10/77, 7.

72. Jenkins, "Europe: Present Challenges and Future Prospects," 12–13.

73. Jenkins, "Europe: Present Challenges and Future Prospects," 13.

74. European Commission, "The Prospect of Economic and Monetary Union," *Bull. EC*, no. 10/77, 22.

75. Jenkins, *Life at the Centre*, 470.

76. Jenkins, *Life at the Centre*, 470.

77. Jenkins, *Life at the Centre*, 467.

78. Ludlow, *Making of the EMS*, 89. See also David Storey, "The Launching of the EMS: An Analysis of Change in Foreign Economic Policy," *Political Studies* 36 (1988): 397–412, for a meticulous account of how and why the EMS was adopted.

79. Ludlow, *Making of the EMS*, 92.

80. For a clear explanation of how the EMS was supposed to work (and how it subsequently failed to work as intended), see Dennis Swann, *The Economics of the Common Market: Integration in the European Union* (London: Penguin, 1995), ch 7.

81. Ludlow, *Making of the EMS*, 182.

82. The quotes are from Bernard Connolly, *The Rotten Heart of Europe* (London: Faber and Faber, 1995), 17, and Moravcsik, *Choice for Europe*, 301–2.

83. Carr, *Helmut Schmidt*, 145.

84. Jenkins, *Life at the Centre*, 484.

85. Quoted Anthony Arnull, *The European Union and Its Court of Justice* (Oxford: Oxford University Press, 1999), 97; Renaud Dehousse, *The European Court of Justice* (London: Macmillan, 1998), 42.

86. Quoted Arnull, *European Union*, 98. The German Supreme Court has never accepted this principle and in 1994 warned in *Brunner v. the Treaty on European Union* that it had a general responsibility for monitoring breaches of the rights guaranteed in the Basic Law by EC institutions. See, Arnull, *European Union*, 102–5.

87. Dehousse, *European Court of Justice*, 44–45.

88. Quoted Arnull, *European Union*, 118.

89. See Arnull, *European Union*, 460–67, for a discussion of the case. Ms. Defrenne was involved in three sex discrimination cases before the ECJ in all.

90. J. H. H. Weiler, *The Constitution of Europe* (Cambridge: Cambridge University Press, 1999), 22.

91. Dehousse, *European Court of Justice*, 43. The quotation is in the context of the *Simmenthal* case, but it reflects his wider view.

92. David Marquand, *Parliament for Europe* (London: Cape, 1979), 88.

93. European Commission, *A Parliament for the Community*, October 1977, 29.

94. Geneviève Bibes, Françoise de la Serre, Henri Ménudier and Marie-Claude Smouts, *Europe Elects Its Parliament* (London: Policy Studies Institute, 1980), 2–3.

95. Bibes et al., *Europe Elects Its Parliament*, 32.

96. Bibes et al., *Europe Elects Its Parliament*, 39.

97. Moravcsik, *Choice for Europe*, 312.

98. Moravcsik, *Choice for Europe*, 312.

6

The 1992 Initiative
and the Single European Act

Between 1979 and 1986, the European Community, after looking briefly as if it were in terminal paralysis, regained the sense of rapid momentum it had possessed before de Gaulle and the adverse economic conditions of the 1970s. The Single European Act (SEA: 1986) was the largest single step towards fuller economic and political integration in Europe since the signature of the EEC treaty in 1957. By the terms of the treaty, the newly expanded twelve-nation EC—Greece joined in 1981; Spain and Portugal, in 1986—accepted a crucial dilution of national sovereignty by permitting qualified majority voting (QMV)—weighted voting in which bigger countries such as Britain or Germany possessed more votes than smaller nations such as Luxembourg and Denmark (though fewer than they ought to have possessed had the votes been weighted according to population)—in the Council of Ministers on all questions relating to the completion of a genuinely free internal market in manufactured goods and services. Until 1986, the "Common Market" was not fully liberalized insofar as a host of restrictive nontariff practices obstructed trade between the member states. The great achievement of Jacques Delors, the heavyweight French finance minister who became president of the Commission in January 1985, was to place the elimination of such practices at the heart of Europe's agenda.

Delors, however, could never have pulled off this signal diplomatic victory had he not been assisted by a profound change in the intellectual climate among the European political élite. The period of 1979 through 1986 saw the emergence of a new consensus among Europe's political leaders that economic growth could only be attained by greater liberalization and increased competition within a Europe-wide market. The Reaganite and Thatcherite "revolutions" in Britain and the United States doubtless were partly responsible for

155

the adoption of this economic philosophy, although both Christian and Social Democrat European leaders flinched from the social consequences of the dogmatic free market capitalism espoused by Thatcher. But the impulse that led to the SEA lay much deeper than the "Anglo-Saxon" democracies' marriage with the doctrines of the Chicago School. The root of the SEA was ultimately the one that had underlain the movement towards European economic integration since the 1940s: the belief that establishment of a large domestic market on the American model would stimulate steady economic growth. Even during the 1970s, trade between the Nine had continued to grow despite the effects of the recurrent monetary crises.[1] The oil shock of 1979–1981, when prices of crude tripled in the space of a year, and the subsequent attempt by the United States to squeeze inflation out of its domestic economy by raising interest rates to record levels, which spilled over into Europe by driving up the price of the dollar and thus causing European inflation to rise, brought in its wake a period of economic stagnation and rising unemployment in the Community.[2] While the causes of this stagnation were external, the Nine's sluggish response to the Gulf States' oil hikes and the Federal Reserve's tight money policy seemed to indicate that the Nine, for so long an area of extraordinary economic vitality, had become complacent and inflexible. "Eurosclerosis" became the favorite description of the European economy for gung-ho Reaganites celebrating the revival of American economic performance in the early 1980s. By the mid-1980s, Europe's leaders were ready to make liberalizing Europe's economy a political priority.

The leaders of Germany (Helmut Schmidt until 1982, when he was replaced as chancellor by Helmut Kohl) and Italy (the key figure here is Bettino Craxi, who by 1983 had dragged his once Marxist Italian Socialist Party into the political center and had himself become prime minister) would doubtless have negotiated and signed something like the SEA sooner had they regarded the conditions to be ripe. Traditional Europhile free traders like the Dutch would certainly not have opposed greater deregulation. Measures to eliminate nontariff barriers were, in any case, a logical continuation of the philosophy underlying the EMS—the removal of trade-distorting structures. In 1979, moreover, a significant judgment by the European Court of Justice, the so-called *Cassis de Dijon* case, where the ECJ affirmed that the eponymous French liquor could be freely sold in West Germany even though its alcohol content was too low for it to be classified as a spirit under German law, had undermined the common practice of using product standards as a way of obviating Community competition. But the political obstacles in the path of a policy of economic liberalization at Community level were substantial. In the early 1980s, three complex issues— the implications of French domestic policy, the question of British contributions to the Community budget, and enlargement to the Mediterranean countries, especially Spain—dominated the Nine's agenda and left statesmen (and one formidable stateswoman) with little time for major initiatives.

FRANCE SEES THE LIGHT

In the case of France, the issue was the left's defiant and, with the benefit of hindsight, quixotic attempt to build "socialism in one country." Raymond Barre's austerity programs provoked a backlash among the French electorate in 1981. First, Giscard d'Estaing was defeated in May for the presidency by the Socialist candidate François Mitterrand, and then, once Mitterrand had exercised his presidential prerogative to dissolve the National Assembly, the Socialists and Communists won a large majority in the ensuing general elections. The declared objective of Mitterrand's first government, which was headed by Pierre Mauroy and contained several Communists, was to stimulate growth in the French economy while increasing the already generous social benefits enjoyed by French workers. This strategy flew in the face of any objective analysis of the French economy's principal weaknesses. Most economists thought that France was already living beyond her means. Throughout the postwar years, France had been loading its productive economy with excessive social burdens. A unionized workforce had won itself generous pay raises and governments of all colors had legislated for costly levels of social benefits. Boyer states: "From 1970–84 French production costs grew faster than those of its competitors."[3] In the 1970s, moreover, France had begun to fall behind Germany and other European countries in the production of high-added-value products for export. These twin failings had led to sliding profits among major French companies, and to a decline in the amount of business investment. The oil shock in 1979 compounded these problems by sharply raising production costs and reducing profits still further.

The Mauroy government essentially tried to overcome these problems by boosting domestic demand and centralizing the power to make investment decisions in the hands of the state. The poorest households benefited from a policy of "redistributive Keynesianism" worth about 2 percent of GDP; taxes were raised on the wealthy and on business; the state nationalized a large number of key companies and banks.[4] The result of these policies was a predictable increase in imports, since the majority of French consumers had more francs in their wallets. But France's industrial partners, who were in the midst of a recession, did not buy more French goods in return. The trade deficit was 95,600 million francs in 1982—far higher than the budget had predicted.[5] State ownership of the commanding heights of the economy, moreover, dismally failed to solve the investment shortfall. Business investment actually fell by 2.5 percent in 1982, which had a knock-on effect on GDP growth.[6]

France's growing balance-of-payments deficits and sluggish growth provoked capital flight and a downward lurch in the value of the franc: an event that had European-wide implications since it meant that France was reneging on her commitment, within the EMS, to maintain stable exchange rates.

France formally devalued the franc in both October 1981 and June 1982. The devaluations were, moreover, very considerable in size. The franc lost 8.5 percent of its value in October 1981 and 10 percent in June 1982, although in this latter case, Germany insisted upon a wage freeze in France as the price of her agreement. As Connolly puts it: "The combination of the ERM and the out-and-out Socialist phase of Mitterrand's government had led to almost total French monetary subjugation to Germany."[7]

Further sales of francs on the currency markets followed in the spring of 1983. At the risk of oversimplifying, Mitterrand's France was faced by March 1983 with an unfudgeable choice between the EMS and its ideological commitment to building an economy founded upon socialist principles. The PSF *might* have elected to solve France's trade deficit by imposing a siege economy, with high tariff barriers in place against both the rest of the world and France's Community partners, but such a strategy entailed "rejection of the EEC," which was the rock upon which French economic policy had been founded for the previous thirty years.[8] Plenty of Mitterrand's closest advisers advocated this course. They were resisted by the finance minister, Jacques Delors, who had become genuinely convinced that the warm bath of currency protectionism could only drain the French economy of what vitality it still possessed. Delors won the argument—just. In exchange for one final devaluation of about 10 percent, Delors was authorized—by Mitterrand, but in a sense by the Germans, who were dictating terms—to implement cuts in public spending, raise taxes on personal consumption and reduce taxes on business. Connolly is being deliberately provocative when he calls the March 1983 devaluation "a sort of monetary 1940," but the accuracy of his analysis is hard to dispute.[9] By March 1983, the French government had lost control of much of its sovereign power to make economic policy.

The lesson was not lost on Mitterrand, who was far from an expert on economics, but who knew everything there was to know about the exercise of power. Mitterrand, who had treated the EC with lofty disdain at the height of his government's experiments, suddenly rediscovered his European vocation and became an ardent proselytizer for further integration. It is hard not to suspect that Mitterrand reasoned that France would *regain* some measure of economic and political sovereignty if she pushed for greater political integration within the EC. France had, in short, an impeccably "realist" reason for wanting to see greater integration take place.

Her major European partners, headed by West Germany and Italy, had done their best to keep the European flame burning in France's absence. Shortly after the third French realignment within the ERM, in June 1983, the Ten (Greece had entered the Community in 1981) signed a "Solemn Declaration" on European unification at the Stuttgart European Council (in EC law such declarations are regarded as statements of intent but are not legally binding). This declaration was the somewhat tortured outcome of the so-called Genscher–Colombo initiative. Launched in January 1981 by the German foreign minister Hans-Dietrich Genscher during a speech in Stuttgart that recalled the objectives of the Tindemans report to the attention of the member states, the initiative was immediately seconded by the Italian government. In November 1981, Genscher and his Italian counterpart, the highly respected Christian Democrat Emilio Colombo, presented to the European Parliament (and subsequently to the European Council) a draft "European Act" with an appended "Statement on Questions of Economic Integration" that made a strong case for a severely limited, but nevertheless significant, increase in the degree of supranationalism within the Community. The draft Act, for example, attached a very high importance to political cooperation, stating that one of the EC's central "aims" should be to "act in concert in world affairs so that Europe will be increasingly able to assume the international role incumbent upon it by virtue of its economic and political importance." Institutionally, it proposed that the European Council should become the "source of political guidance" for the Community and its central decision-making body. On the Parliament, the draft European Act was somewhat timid. According to the Act's proposals, the Parliament was to be given a much higher public profile, although it would have remained a chamber that scrutinized and debated the proposals of the governments of the member states rather than an out-and-out legislature. The Commission was referred to as the "guardian of the treaties" and as the "driving force of European integration," and it was suggested that it should advise and support the European Council on all matters, including foreign policy, with which the Commission would be "closely associated." Within the Council of Ministers, the draft Act attached "decisive importance" to the reform of procedures to allow more majority voting. Genscher and Colombo suggested that a member state wishing to veto a given proposal should be made to produce a written statement of explanation. A veto would only be accepted if a member state invoked its "vital interest" in two consecutive Council of Ministers' meetings. The statement on economic matters was less concrete in its prescriptions. It did affirm, however, that the common market should be "brought to completion" and that the member states should "strive" to obtain "increasing convergence of their economies."[10]

Without the full cooperation of Britain and France (not to mention an increasingly Euroskeptic Denmark), there was never any hope that Genscher and Colombo would put political integration back on the Community agenda. Between November 1981 and June 1983, the draft Act was whittled down to size by a "prolonged negotiation" that brought the proposals, by June 1983, "back within the confines of treaty orthodoxy."[11] In particular, the idea of promoting more frequent majority voting in the Council of Ministers simply vanished from the final text in the face of concerted hostility from Greece and Ireland as well as the three countries mentioned earlier. The section on the Parliament, moreover, offered such diluted increases in its role that the Parliament passed a motion on 9 June 1983 openly expressing its dissatisfaction. In one regard, however, the Solemn Declaration laid down an important pointer for the Community's future strategy. It indicated the "completion of the internal market" and the "elimination" of nontariff barriers as the most plausible area for concerted Community action in the near future along with reinforcing the ERM.[12] France's damascene conversion to the European cause in March 1983 made this objective a workable one.

In retrospect, the Solemn Declaration's importance was entirely symbolic. The German-Italian venture should be seen less as a "missed opportunity" to secure an advance in European unity than as a restatement of first principles by Bonn and Rome.[13] The early 1980s were arguably the nadir of the EC's fortunes. Summit after summit ended in public acrimony and political indecision as the British fought relentlessly for a reform in Community financing. It is hard to imagine that two hardheaded statesmen of the caliber of Genscher and Colombo genuinely thought that the time was ripe for an Act that possessed even limited supranational overtones. The purpose of the Genscher–Colombo initiative was surely to indicate to Paris and London that two at least of the "big countries" had not lost faith with the European project.

THE BRITISH BUDGETARY QUESTION

Between 1979 and 1984, the British budgetary question (or "bloody British question," to use Roy Jenkins's *bon mot*) was Banquo's ghost at almost every meeting of the European Council. Mrs. Thatcher wanted "her money back" and would not let the Community progress until she had been compensated. The nature of the problem is quite straightforward to describe. Throughout the 1970s, the EC budget grew rapidly, from just over 4,000 million units of account in 1973 (when Britain entered the EC), to 14,400 million in 1979, when Mrs. Thatcher came to power. While this sum was still less than 1 percent of the EC's economic output, two countries, Germany and Britain, were paying far more into the Community than they were getting out. In Britain's case, this shortfall amounted to nearly 1,400 million Ecu in 1979 (the Ecu fluctuated in value between £0.62 and £0.66 in 1979–1980). Worse, in the absence of a budget agreement, Britain's net contribution was scheduled to overtake Germany's in 1981–1982 and to rise to over 2,000 million Ecu per year.[14] Britain was in short, when Mrs. Thatcher took office, on the verge of becoming the EC's paymaster—though, as Thatcher points out in her memoirs, Britain was only the seventh richest country in per capita income.[15]

Britain's excessive contribution was a consequence both of the way in which the Community was financed and of the way in which it spent its money. The Community received 1 percent of the money raised in sales taxes (VAT) by the member states; received the proceeds of levies on incoming agricultural products and the proceeds of tariffs on extra-Community imports. A combination of political funk and historical trading patterns made this an extremely unsatisfactory formula for Britain. Britain's VAT returns were not as high as other EC countries since Britain for political reasons had refused to tax food, books and children's clothes—but the Community calculated the amount due according to a standardized formula, and thus Britain had to contribute a greater proportion of her VAT revenues to Brussels. More seriously, Britain continued to import large quantities of products from the Commonwealth and the rest of the world. True, British trade with the rest of the EC increased substantially in the 1970s—rising from £6,300 million in 1972 to £37,300 million in 1979.[16] But trade with the Community still represented less than half of Britain's total trade. Britain had to pay in a considerable sum in levies and import duties to the Community budget.

This would not have mattered so much had Britain been benefiting from EC payouts. But she was not. By 1979, the EC was spending almost three-quarters of its budget on the CAP. Britain, with its limited agriculture sector, received relatively little (£500–600 million a year by the early 1980s) in subsidies and price support funds. Britain had been the largest single beneficiary from the European Regional Development Fund (ERDF), receiving 28 percent of all funds committed by the fund until Greece's accession, and 23.8 percent thereafter. But the ERDF was a pale shadow of the considerable investments that would subsequently be made by the Community in the 1980s and 1990s via the structural and cohesion funds. Between 1975 and 1981, Britain received a measly £720 million.[17]

Britain, in short, was paying lots in, but not taking much out. For many Community officials, this was the membership fee that Britain had to pay if it wanted to be in the club and be part of an area of growing economic prosperity. Obviously, if everybody insisted on treating the Community budget as a ledger in which incomings and outgoings had to be exactly balanced, there would be no point having a Community at all. Moreover, the sums involved were regarded by some as being insignificant. Britain's GDP in 1979 was about £250,000 million; her EC contribution, therefore, was only a small fraction of her total economic activity.

The intensity with which Mrs. Thatcher pursued her campaign to get "her money" back therefore seems to have caught her EC partners by surprise. But it should not have. The danger that Britain would end up being a major contributor had always been recognized. As we have seen, Britain had in fact been promised that she would be given a rebate should an "unacceptable situation" arise during the entry negotiations. Mrs. Thatcher also had sound political reasons for taking a tough line with Europe. Her government began implementing controversial cuts in programmed public spending as soon as it came to power. In part for ideological reasons, in part because Britain's public finances were in their usual mess, Thatcher's cabinet lopped £6,500 million from planned spending in 1980–1981, but were still faced with a public sector borrowing requirement of almost £10,000 million.[18] In the face of a spending squeeze of this magnitude, using British money to keep French farmers in the bucolic idyll to which they had become accustomed was politically indefensible. As Mrs. Thatcher argued in October 1979: "I can't play Sister Bountiful to the Community while my own electorate are being asked to forego improvements in the fields of health, welfare, education and the rest."[19]

The Dublin European Council, on 29–30 November 1979, was "the occasion for Europe's first encounter with Mrs. Thatcher in full flood." During dinner on the first day, Thatcher spoke for four hours "without pause, but not without repetition" about the British budget problem. Helmut Schmidt pretended to sleep; Giscard looked on in unfeigned horror; Francesco Cossiga of Italy "wrung his hands."[20] In retrospect, the negotiations were little more than a high-stakes game of poker. The other member states were initially prepared to offer Mrs. Thatcher £350 million a year (about 600 million Ecus); she stood out for a full refund. The British government had two cards up its sleeve. In the last resort, it possessed the option of withholding its VAT contributions (in her memoirs, Mrs. Thatcher records that "even the possibility" of this action—which was of dubious legality—caused "satisfactory anxiety in the Commission").[21] The British government could also be—and was—obstreperous in the Community's agricultural committee by threatening to veto price rises. Britain could, in short, threaten to bankrupt the Community and squeeze the incomes of the agricultural constituencies of the other member states. On the other hand, if Britain overbid, there was a real risk that the other eight members would make her an offer and tell her to take it or leave the Community.

Neither side gave ground at Dublin, or during the first months of 1980. It gradually dawned upon Mrs. Thatcher's fellow leaders, however, that she was not going to be outbluffed. At the end of April 1980, at a meeting of the European Council in Luxembourg, the Eight threw in their cards. Britain was made a substantial offer of a rebate worth 2,400 million Ecus for 1980–1981. To the amazement of the gathered European leaders, Mrs. Thatcher rejected the deal, throwing the Community into potentially its worst crisis since 1965. It was one bluff too many, however. The French and the Germans refused to be "handbagged" any further. Under pressure from the Foreign Office, Thatcher grudgingly accepted an almost identical bargain (worth an estimated 2,585 million Ecus over the two years) negotiated at a meeting of the foreign ministers a month later.[22] Ironically, in both 1981 and 1982, the British contribution turned out to be far lower than anticipated, although in 1983 the issue returned once more to the forefront.[23]

It is interesting to note, in retrospect, how the debate over the British contribution swiftly became an exercise in haggling, rather than a discussion of first causes. The British budgetary question simply would not have been an issue had the Community been prepared to contemplate a systematic rethink of the CAP, whose abuses were shouting out for reform by the beginning of the 1980s. Yet the "Comprehensive Agreement" reached with the British carefully stated (paragraph seven) that the Community, despite pledging itself to "structural changes" to eliminate "unacceptable situations" for any member state, would not "call into question" the "basic principles of the common agricultural policy."[24] The Commission attempted to sketch out what this commitment might mean in a document, *Reflections on the Common Agricultural Policy*, published at the end of 1980. Here, after saluting the achievements of the CAP, the Commission made a case for capping the amount of agricultural production by instituting a system of levies on excess production. It was "time to act," the Commission concluded boldly.[25]

Some such reform was urgently needed. In the early 1980s, the CAP's central design flaw was blatantly obvious: it used price fixing both to maintain farm income and to balance supply and demand.[26] There was constant political pressure to keep farm prices high (in order to keep peasants on the land and to buy rural votes), but higher prices naturally gave an incentive for higher production, which generated huge food surpluses that the Community had to buy, albeit at the lower guarantee price. Charging farmers for overproduction—which was given the somewhat Orwellian name of "co-responsibility"—was one way of combating the rocketing increases in the CAP's budget and the accumulation of the hugely unpopular "wine lakes" and "grain mountains" to which such purchases naturally led.

In May 1983, the Commission, backed by the member states, went further and attacked, for key products such as milk and grain, the core principle of the CAP by imposing caps on the *amount* of production for which the guarantee price would be paid. Farmers no longer possessed an unlimited license to produce at the taxpayer's expense. This reform to the CAP was the main achievement of the hapless Luxembourger Gaston Thorn, who replaced Roy Jenkins as president of the Commission in 1981.

What nobody at the Commission was suggesting was a more market-oriented approach to agriculture. In a host of ways, the CAP's interventionism produced negative outcomes. Subsidies, far from enriching Cornish hill farmers or Sardinian shepherds, went disproportionately to already wealthy cereals farmers from northern Europe, since their yields— helped by large doses of chemical fertilizers and other environmentally damaging practices—had risen faster than anybody's. European consumers, who were being denied access to beef from the Argentine, bananas from Ecuador and wheat from Canada, had to pay higher prices than necessary in the shops. EC-subsidized exports of grain, meat and sugar were the source of endless trade friction with the United States, Australia and South America.[27] The CAP had not even eliminated domestic subsidies by national governments for farmers. The wild currency fluctuations of the 1970s had made a nonsense of the original idea of common agricultural prices almost as soon as the CAP came into force. As a result, from the early 1970s onwards, countries had been allowed to pay equalizing payments called "monetary compensatory amounts" (MCAs) to farmers to ensure that rivals from weak currency countries did not seize an "unfair" advantage. The French, in particular, were also using a vast range of illegal aids to subsidize agriculture: of fifty-one such subsidies identified by the Commission in 1980, thirty-nine were being employed by the French government.[28]

A 1982 study of the CAP stated bluntly: "A decade and a half of empirical evidence has confirmed that as an economic policy for the Community as a whole the CAP was irrational."[29] A policy can be irrational, however, and still have plenty of backers. In the case of the CAP, its supporters were politically powerful farmers' lobbies and the national governments of large agricultural exporters, especially France, Ireland, the Netherlands and Denmark. It was simply more expedient for Europe's leaders to pay Mrs. Thatcher off than to stop the CAP budget's remorseless growth—growth that the 1983 measures slowed but did not stop. Similarly, despite the vital political importance of EC membership as a bolster for the still fragile democracies of Portugal and Spain, negotiations were long delayed by fears that the Iberian countries would provide unwelcome agricultural competition and place the CAP under intolerable strain.

MEDITERRANEAN ENLARGEMENT

Greece, Portugal and Spain all applied for EC membership during a two-year arc in the mid-1970s. Greece, whose military dictatorship crumbled in 1974 after the debacle of the Turkish invasion of Cyprus, formally applied in June 1975; Portugal, under the leadership of the Socialist Mario Soares, applied in March 1977, as soon as its own democratic transition had stabilized. Spain, the largest and most problematic of the three would-be entrants, was the last to apply in July 1977. Until the Spanish Socialist Party (PSOE) took power in October 1982, Spain's domestic political instability precluded her from pursuing membership with full vigor.[30]

The three Mediterranean countries presented, as the Commission recognized, both a challenge and an opportunity for the EC. In the superb documentation prepared by the Commission for the Copenhagen European Council meeting in April 1978 a clear picture of the chief difficulties consequent upon enlargement emerges.[31] These were:

- *Economic imbalances:* All three would-be entrants had smaller per capita GDP than any member state. This was a particular problem in the case of Portugal, whose income per head, at purchasing power parity, was estimated by the Commission to be just $1,504—much less than 50 percent of the per capita incomes of every existing member state except Italy ($2,742) and Ireland ($2,512). Spain ($2,384) and Greece ($2,309) did better by this measure. The relatively good performances of Greece and Spain, however, disguised enormous regional differences. Cities such as Athens, Madrid and Barcelona enjoyed "European" standards of living; the more rural regions of both countries were as poor as Portugal. The Commission's overall assessment was that the Three possessed a "stage of development lying mid-way between the less-developed countries and the industrialized countries."[32] If the Three entered, it was clear that the rest of the Community was going to have to dig deep into their pockets to pay for infrastructure improvements and to soften the economic costs of entry. It was also assumed that all three countries would become large net exporters of labor once citizens from the Three were at liberty to move throughout the Community: a politically sensitive issue at a time of rising unemployment. Large numbers of Greeks and Portuguese were already working in France and Germany.
- *Agriculture and fisheries:* All three countries had substantial, none-too-efficient agricultural sectors. The number of people employed in agriculture in the Community would increase by 55 percent if the Three were admitted; agriculture represented 16.6 percent of GDP in Greece, 11.8 percent in Portugal, and over 10 percent in Spain. Admission of the Three raised the specter of deeper wine lakes, a citrus fruit *sierra* and overproduction of olive oil. French and Italian producers would face cheaper competition in these areas, as would Irish and British trawlermen, who would have to open their fishing grounds to the gigantic Spanish fleet.
- *Trade and industry:* All three countries specialized in manufacturing sectors—textiles, chemicals, footwear, food processing—that were already problem industries for the Community. Until the early 1970s, Spanish industry in particular had sheltered behind a formidable array of formal and informal trade barriers. A 1970 agreement between the EC and Spain had allowed Spain considerable freedom to maintain trade barriers and, as ever, this residual protectionism had enabled the Spanish government to postpone politically unpopular structural reforms to the economy. There were serious worries that Spain's coddled industrial sector would not be able to cope with membership of the Common Market. All three countries possessed worsening current account deficits as their imports of increasingly expensive oil outweighed their surpluses in manufactured exports and "invisible" earnings such as

tourism. All three countries had suffered from high rates of inflation throughout the 1970s. Portugal and Spain's rate of price increases had been even worse than Britain and Italy's dismal performance; Greece's had been on a par. The currencies of all three Mediterranean applicants were thus seen as unpromising potential members of the EMS.

- *Institutional questions:* The Commission warned that "with twelve members, the institutions and decision-making procedures will be under considerable strain and the Community will be exposed to possible stalemate and dilution unless its practical *modus operandi* is improved."[33] The only way around this problem was to extend qualified majority voting and to weaken the unanimity principle enshrined in the Luxembourg compromise. Deciding how many Council of Ministers votes each country should have, and how many seats in the Assembly, was also no easy matter. Spain was a large country in terms of population (36.2 million), but its total GDP, at the then exchange rate, was not much larger than the Netherlands', which had twenty-two million people fewer. Greece and Portugal were entitled to the same weighting as Belgium (all three had just under ten million inhabitants), but their contribution to the Community's economy was far lower. The Commission was insistent that, as a general principle for regulating such matters, "the Community must . . . avoid any appreciable shift in the existing balance, based on a combination of demographic factors and political considerations, between member states."[34] But this was easier said than done.

There were, therefore, a large number of question marks hovering over enlargement to the new Mediterranean democracies. The Commission nevertheless urged the member states to make the negotiations a priority, arguing that "the challenge of enlargement can and must be the start of a new Community thrust towards the objectives set by the authors of the treaties."[35] Its view appeared to be that by anchoring the Three in the Community, democracy would be safeguarded in the applicant states—and the EC itself would obtain a new lease on life as it altruistically sought to bring the Three's levels of development up to rich-country standards.

Despite this high-flown aspiration, negotiations only proceeded quickly with Greece, which signed a treaty of accession on 28 May 1979. Greece was given, with allowance being made for the usual battery of exemptions, five years beginning on 1 January 1981 to implement the *acquis communautaire* (the accumulated legacy of EC law). Greek tariffs and quotas were to be gradually reduced on EC products by January 1986; the Community's agriculture regime (and prices) was to be phased in over the same period; the drachma was to be added to the "basket" of currencies used to calculate the value of the Ecu. The Greek government was to designate which regions would qualify for regional aid under the ERDF. Except for steel products, the member states promised to eliminate all tariff discrimination against Greek products from 1 January 1981. Greece was given five votes in the Council of Ministers, twenty-four seats in the Parliament, and was allowed to nominate one commissioner and one justice on the Court. In return for this generous settlement, the EC, mindful of the prospect of a wave of migration, insisted that there should be a seven-year suspension of freedom of movement within the Community for Greek nationals.[36]

Spain and Portugal's accession, by contrast, was still unresolved in 1981 when Mitterrand came to power. The Community seemed to quail at the challenge presented by Spanish entry in particular. The Commission's "Opinion on Spain's Application for Membership," submitted to the European Council at the end of November 1978, was distinctly more gloomy about Spanish membership than it had been earlier in the year. While it was formally favorable to Spanish entry, its opinion largely concentrated on pointing out the "scale and complexities of the problems arising from Spain's accession."[37] The opinion made, moreover, a number of suggestions—the immediate introduction of VAT and a longer transition period for agriculture than industry—that caused "consternation" in Spain, where industrial leaders responded by saying "yes to membership, but not at any price."[38] Spain's grave political problems, which culminated in a tragi-comic attempted coup by reactionary army officers in February 1981, hardly strengthened its cause.

There were two other major obstructions, however. The first was French hostility to Spanish entry. Under Giscard d'Estaing, French worries about Spanish agricultural competition, and the likelihood that Spanish entry would lead to a net reduction in the size of the subsidies paid out to French farmers, bogged down negotiations. By the end of 1981, there had been twenty-five negotiation sessions, including nine at ministerial level, but no single chapter of the accession accords had been completed.[39] This was despite the fact that France had a substantial trade deficit with Spain and could only benefit from an opening up of the Spanish market. French obstruction lessened after the election of Mitterrand—on 22 March 1982, six chapters of the accession instruments were agreed in a single marathon bargaining session—but did not disappear entirely. However, when Spain elected a Socialist government that had placed membership of the Community at the heart of its manifesto, the new prime minister, Felipe Gonzales, hoped that "Socialist solidarity" would weaken France's hard-line defense of her national interests.[40] He was swiftly disillusioned.

It was not until Mitterrand's conversion to a pro-European stance in the spring of 1983 that Spanish and Portuguese entry became a genuine possibility. But it was still clear that the French government would not let the Iberian democracies in at the cost of her farmers' incomes. The June 1983 Stuttgart European Council offered a glimpse of hope when, following a successful visit to Bonn by Felipe Gonzales, Germany (who would have to shoulder most of the financial burden) proposed increasing the Community's share of VAT revenues from 1.0 to 1.4 percent, but explicitly linked any such increase to a successful resolution of the enlargement question.[41] The Spanish foreign minister at the time, Fernando Morán, subsequently called Helmut Kohl's intervention "una gran contribución alemana al proceso."[42] But Britain's agreement had to be obtained for any such move, and Mrs. Thatcher was unbending in her determination to limit Britain's EC contribution, which was rising again, to "fair" levels. The December 1983 European Council in Athens was dominated by the budget crisis and ended with the member states being unable even to agree upon a final communiqué.

The crucial act of political will, which made enlargement to the Iberian countries certain, came only at the Fontainebleau summit (25–26 June 1984), when the gathered European leaders committed themselves to resolving all the thorny technical problems associated with enlargement within three months—after first resolving the budget problem. This ambitious timetable was not respected—not least because Greece, of all countries, made its "yes" to enlargement conditional upon the institution of "integrated Mediterranean programs" from which it could benefit—but the summit's decision did give decisive impetus to the negotiating process. Mitterrand visited Madrid immediately after the summit for talks with Felipe Gonzales.

Spain and Portugal finally signed their treaties of accession in March 1985. The terms were less generous than the treaty with Greece had been, although the Iberian countries were allowed a longer transitional period than Greece to adjust to membership. Beginning on 1 January 1986, a seven-year transitional period was agreed for the full reduction of all tariff barriers and quotas imposed by the Iberian countries on industrial products. For agricultural products, the transitional period was seven years for Spain and ten years for Portugal. Unlike the Greek case, this accord was to be reciprocal: Spanish wine growers and citrus fruit producers were not allowed immediate access to the Community market but had to wait for the EC's own tariffs to be gradually eliminated over the same time span. Spanish and Portuguese citizens, like the Greeks before them, had their freedom of movement within the Community suspended for seven years; access to northern fishing waters was also to be restricted for the same period. Spain was awarded eight votes in the Council of Ministers; Portugal, five. Sixty deputies were to be elected to the European parliament by the Spanish electorate; Portugal was awarded twenty-four MEPs. With these additions, the Parliament reached the unwieldy size of 518 members. Three new portfolios were created on the Commission, with Spain being awarded two places, and Portugal one.[43] Overall, membership of the EC did not offer Spain and Portugal the prospect of overnight prosperity. It did, however, symbolize the return of the two states to the democratic mainstream after nearly fifty years at the margins. Both states would prove capable of grasping the political opportunities presented by EC membership with both hands.

THE 1992 INITIATIVE AND THE DOOGE COMMITTEE

The decision to approve the entry of Spain and Portugal into the Community was not the only decision of importance taken at Fontainebleau. First, the Community's leaders finally defused the British question. The preceding Brussels European Council in March 1984 had ended in disarray, when Mrs. Thatcher's demands for a guaranteed British refund, and her refusal to be fobbed off with a temporary five-year arrangement worth 1,000 million Ecu each year, had enraged the French and Italians. Mitterrand openly warned Britain that she should not assume that the rest of the Community would wait forever. A Europe *à deux vitesses* (two-speed Europe) was thinkable. Moravcsik has plausibly argued that this threat of exclusion was taken seriously by the British.[44] At Fontainebleau, the Community's by now desperate need for a bigger overall budget (to pay for an enlarged CAP) coincided with some unexpected flexibility from a seemingly chastened Iron Lady. After a day and a half of talks, Britain was guaranteed 1,000 million Ecu for 1984 and an automatic 66 percent refund thereafter in return for supporting an increase in the Community's "own resources" from 1 percent of VAT revenues to the 1.4 percent suggested by the Germans at Stuttgart the year before.[45] This refund would be guaranteed so long as the 1.4 percent rate remained. Since Britain possessed a veto over any alteration to this figure, the deal was very acceptable for Thatcher, who had got most of what she was asking for.[46]

The summit also took the key decision to relaunch the project of European Union—for which the Parliament had been pressing—by appointing two ad hoc ministerial commissions. The first, which was to deal with the question of the "Europe of Citizens," was chaired by the Italian politician Giuseppe Adonnino. The second, on institutional reform, was chaired by an Irishman James Dooge.

Fontainebleau in fact ended with an effusion of hope for the future of the Community from the gathered leaders, including Mrs. Thatcher—although she does not mention this lapse in her memoirs. A document presented by the British government to the European Council on the subject of the future of the EC clearly illustrates that Britain, its budget problems resolved, was prepared to be a good citizen of the Community. Britain pressed for immediate action to "harmonize" market-deforming standards and practices in order to create a "true" single market; urged the abolition of frontiers and all obstacles to the movement of people, capital or goods; spoke of the need for a "common approach" in foreign affairs and claimed the Ten should show their "political will" on the world stage. It even recommended more frequent use of QMV.[47]

There was, in fact, enough harmony among the gathered leaders for them to agree on replacing Gaston Thorn with a front-rank French politician, Jacques Delors. The Council realized that if rhetoric was to be turned into substantive progress, it needed to appoint a heavyweight figure from a big country who would not be overshadowed by the national leaders. Delors, a technocratic figure who had also served a term in the European Parliament before becoming Mitterrand's finance minister, was the ideal choice: so much so that the Germans, who might have expected to nominate a candidate of their own, were among his strongest supporters. The Commission that Delors and the national governments assembled in the next months was a highly competent body, which could boast among its number such experienced Eurocrats as Lorenzo Natali of Italy, who had served as vice president of the Commission since January 1977, and Claude Cheysson, who had served in the Commission under Ortoli, Jenkins and Thorn. Yet the member of the Commission who had most impact was a newcomer. Lord Arthur Cockfield was a British businessman who had been secretary of state for trade and industry under Mrs. Thatcher. Delors appointed him as commissioner responsible for the internal market, the liberalization of which was made the centerpiece of the new Commission's agenda for 1985.

In retrospect, it can be seen that the time was ripe for an initiative in this field. The leaders had committed themselves to it in the Solemn Declaration; the British government, so wary usually of initiatives with a "European" flavor, was deregulating its own economy with vigor and had an ideological stake in promoting the abolition of the nontariff barriers; freer trade within the Community offered the prospect of boosting sluggish economic performance and getting unemployment down from the socially dangerous levels (the Community average had soared to above 11 percent during the recession of the early 1980s) to which it had risen. Business groups, the most important of which was the so-called European Round Table, were also lobbying hard for a reduction in nontariff barriers to trade and for enhanced measures of deregulation.[48]

There had also been an important judicial stimulus for reform. In the *Cassis de Dijon* case (no. 120/78), the ECJ ignored the German government's imaginative defense that under German law Cassis was too strong to be classified as a wine, but too weak to be spirits and held that a product lawfully produced and marketed in one member state should normally have access to the others, unless compelling reasons of health and safety could be adduced to the contrary.[49] Quite apart from winning the esteem of German drinkers who liked to tinge their white wine with a dash of black currant, the ECJ, by its ruling also "created a simple standard for resolving trade disputes."[50] This, in turn, weakened the member states' previous resistance to the notion that there should be harmonized standards at Community level, for "mutual recognition would lead to national measures being applied to national products only, while goods produced in member-states with less stringent requirements would have to be admitted freely."[51] One can exaggerate, however, the extent to which the Court's ruling opened the trade barriers within the EC. In the aftermath of the *Cassis de Dijon* ruling, the Thorn Commission drafted legislation in a wide range of areas to achieve common product standards, but the readiness of member states to evoke the Luxembourg compromise meant that most of it never reached the statute books. In the meantime, Germany continued to ban imports of foreign beer by invoking its time-honored beer purity laws, Italy rejected all pasta that was not made with hard grain, and Belgium insisted that margarine should be sold in cubes, not rectangles.[52]

Cockfield's major personal contribution was to devise a way to bounce the member states into living up to their rhetoric on the single market and free trade. Upon becoming commissioner for the internal market, Cockfield bundled together the numerous proposals for legislation piled up by the Thorn Commission into a single white paper, *Completing the Internal Market*, which contained nearly 300 detailed proposed regulations and directives.[53] The document also had a clear and compelling rationale (Cockfield called it a "philosophy"), which was that the EC should become a "space without barriers." Customs posts and border controls, the physical symbols of the Community's continued division, should be torn down. But so should the invisible restrictions on trade in goods and services that were equally effective at segregating national economies.

The individual chapters were concerned with specific physical, technical and fiscal barriers that needed to be abolished if the overall objective of a barrierless Community was to be attained by 1992, the target date set in the document. In the meantime, the document insisted, member states should conduct trade on the basis of mutual recognition of national standards and should not allow the absence of a European norm to affect the import of any product. A thirty-five-page annex to the document set out detailed timetables for the approval by the Council of Ministers of each individual piece of legislation: in order to speed up the process of harmonization, Cockfield proposed that the Community should not attempt to "harmonize or standardize at any price."[54] Rather, it should try to "approximate" national standards by reducing differences to an acceptable level.

Completing the Internal Market was more than a mere memorandum on technicalities, however. It concluded with a self-consciously rhetorical flourish that sought to underline its historical importance. In every politician's favorite cliché, the Commission claimed, "Europe stands at the crossroads."

The Community could either press ahead with the plans outlined in the document or "drop back into mediocrity." The free movement of goods, which the white paper intended finally to achieve, was "the indispensable precursor" for a more historic objective: "European unity." Failure to implement a single market in goods, services and people within 1992 would be to "offer the peoples of Europe a narrower, less rewarding, less secure, less prosperous future than they could otherwise enjoy."[55]

Cockfield and Delors were well aware, of course, that Europe's statesmen were perfectly capable of subscribing to such lofty sentiments about Europe's future, while defending national interests tooth and nail. To reduce the risk that the national governments would be briefed against the proposals of the white paper by their respective civil servants, the Commission distributed the document just two weeks before the Milan summit on 28–29 June 1985. The Commission, in short, was painting the national governments into a corner and giving them no scope to renege on their past rhetoric.

The skill and dedication that Cockfield had brought to the task of completing the single market gradually lost him the esteem of his patroness. In her memoirs, Lady Thatcher describes Cockfield as "a natural technocrat of great ability and problem-solving outlook." She adds, however, that he "was prisoner as well as master of his subject." It was "all too easy" for him to "go native" once he got to Brussels and move from "deregulating the market to re-regulating it under the rubric of harmonization."[56]

Thatcher's immediate wrath was directed against Cockfield's proposals to harmonize indirect taxes throughout the Community. Cockfield's defense—that article 99 of the EEC treaty required such harmonization since varying tax rates could distort the market by advantaging countries with low tax regimes—provoked a glacial encounter between the British prime minister and her appointee. It concluded with Cockfield telling Thatcher that she should have read the treaty before she signed it. Thatcher replied, "I did not sign anything"; to which the brave (or foolhardy) commissioner responded that she had been minister in the government that had signed. This remark was greeted with a furious silence.[57] Tax harmonization was one aspect of the white paper that did not survive the subsequent negotiating process. Thatcher subsequently explained her position in her memoirs: "Competition between tax regimes is far more healthy than the imposition of a single system . . . in any event, the ability to set one's own levels of taxation is a crucial element in national sovereignty."[58]

Thatcher and the British government had also begun to cool on other aspects of the project launched at Fontainebleau. The Dooge committee on institutional reform was dogged by British intransigence. The Fontainebleau communiqué had rashly compared it to the 1956 Spaak committee, and hence it had been burdened with the expectation that it would present proposals for a radical transformation of the Community's institutions and practices. Pressure for a supranationalist turn in the Community's institutions had been growing for some time. In 1983, the European Parliament, ably instigated and managed by the veteran Italian federalist Altiero Spinelli, drafted a "Treaty on European Union" for the attention of the Ten's governments. This treaty was formally approved by the Parliament on 14 February 1984 and was submitted to the Fontainebleau summit for reaction.

The draft treaty envisaged a greatly empowered European Parliament, effectively equal in status to the Council of Ministers (art. 16); a president of the Commission empowered to choose his own commissioners, albeit after consultations with the national governments (art. 25); a political structure that gave the institutions of the Union "exclusive competence" in single market issues (art. 47) and competition policy (art. 48). The Union was to have "concurrent competence" (which meant that the member states could "continue to act so long as the Union has not legislated" in the fields of economic and monetary union, "sectoral" policies such as transport, research and technology, industry, and energy, social and health policy. The Community's budget, instead of being the object of endless wrangling between the member states in the European Council, would be worked out by the Commission and then decided by an intricate process in which the Parliament would have had the final word (art. 76). Only in foreign policy did the treaty fight shy of advocating substantial further integration. For this reason, ardent federalists in the European movement described the draft treaty as a merely "prefederal" document, but this description underestimates the clarity and scope of Spinelli's blueprint.[59]

None of the member states were prepared to countenance anything like this degree of political integration. The Parliament's proposal was not on the agenda at Fontainebleau. But some countries (the Benelux nations, Italy, Germany) were more willing than others to implement some of the Parliament's proposals. These British, backed up by the Danes and the Greeks, were much less enthusiastic. The divergent positions were reflected in the report of the Dooge committee to the 29–30 March 1985 meeting of the European Council in Brussels. The committee agreed that Europe's "priority objectives" were "a homogeneous internal economic area," "promotion of the common values of civilization" and the "search for an external identity," but were divided over the means. The committee wanted "efficient and democratic institutions" for the EC, but had quite different interpretations of this phrase. The argument raged in particular around the question of whether formal veto power would be retained or dispensed with by member states for all but "exceptional cases." Denmark was determined not to give up her formal veto power in the Council; Britain, while recognizing the need for greater majority voting, was equally opposed to relinquishing her sovereign power to say no. A majority of the committee approved the Parliament's suggestion that the president of the Commission should be able to put forward his own list of potential commissioners, but Britain insisted that the national governments should retain that right. The majority of the committee favored an increase in the Parliament's powers of "joint decision making," among other reforms, seeing this as a way of making the Parliament a "guarantor of democracy in the European system": Britain merely urged the Parliament, within its existing treaty powers, to "make a more effective contribution." In all, some thirty-seven different points of dissent were entered as footnotes to the text agreed by the majority.[60]

The British and Danes were actually on the horns of a particularly uncomfortable dilemma. Both wanted to press ahead with market liberalization, but neither regarded the EC as a federal state in embryo. For both, the EC was and would remain an association of sovereign nation-states. But market liberalization was impossible while the veto remained. Once Cockfield's white paper became public knowledge, the dilemma sharpened. Britain, despite Thatcher's reservations about tax harmonization and her suspicion of pan-European directives, welcomed the laissez-faire thrust of the Commission's proposals and expected to do well from them. But the white paper, in the absence of QMV for single-market legislation, manifestly offered almost 300 opportunities to use the national veto unless the member states compromised their sovereign rights.

Nevertheless, at the Milan summit, Britain and Denmark stood by their blank refusal to surrender the veto. The British suggestion, that there should be a "gentleman's agreement" that QMV would be used for single-market issues and that member states should have to defend any use of the veto by giving a public statement of their reasons, found little favor among the rest of the Community, who perhaps reflected that one of the gentlemen was a lady of strong convictions. The impasse was broken by Italian prime minister Bettino Craxi and his foreign minister, the perennial Giulio Andreotti, who realized that article 236 of the EEC treaty allowed them to call, by a simple majority vote, an intergovernmental conference to discuss the amendments to the treaties proposed by the Dooge committee. The Dooge committee had itself recommended that its recommendations be discussed by a conference of this type. With the support of all the member states except Britain, Denmark and Greece, Craxi put the matter to the vote. Mrs. Thatcher found herself in the unusual position of being "bulldozed" into doing the will of others, but was compelled to acquiesce.[61]

THE SINGLE EUROPEAN ACT

Mrs. Thatcher's decision to accept the *diktat* of the majority at the Milan European Council paid off handsomely. It is widely agreed that Britain was more successful than any other country in writing its agenda into the language of the final treaty. During the intergovernmental negotiations that took place in the autumn of 1985, Britain skillfully adopted a more flexible position on the use of the national veto—accepting much greater use of QMV—but in return drove a very hard bargain over the single market. Cockfield's white paper, with the exception of its tax provisions, was written into the treaty as Thatcher wanted. In her memoirs, Thatcher makes her negotiating stance perfectly clear:

> I had one overriding positive goal. This was to create a single common market. . . . British businesses would be among those most likely to benefit from an opening up of others' markets. For example, we were more or less effectively excluded from the important German insurance and financial services markets where I knew—as I suspect did the Germans—that our people would excel. . . . The price which we would have to pay to achieve a single market with all its economic benefits, though, was more majority voting in the Community.[62]

The internal market was defined in article 13 of the SEA as "an area without internal frontiers in which the free movement of goods, persons and capital is ensured" and the Community committed itself to "progressively establishing" this area by 31 December 1992. Article 18 made clear that legislation necessary for the achievement of this objective would be decided by QMV in all matters except "fiscal provisions" and matters relating to "the free movement of persons" and "the rights and interests of unemployed persons." Thatcher was determined, in other words, that passport controls would be retained for incomers into Britain and that a majority of member states would not compel her to introduce costly social benefits for the small army of unemployed people her policies—in the opinion of many—had caused. However, other European states with higher standards of social, health and safety, environmental and consumer protection than Britain insisted in their turn that harmonized legislation would "take as its base a high standard of protection." The right of member states to invoke "public interest" grounds, under article 36 of the EEC treaty, as the basis for blocking imports was diminished by making any such decision subject to the Commission's verification and approval. The Commission and other member states would also have the right to ask the ECJ to review any "improper use" of article 36.

Article 17 of the SEA amended article 99 of the EEC treaty to ensure that proposals to harmonize "turnover taxes, excise taxes and other forms of indirect taxation" would henceforth be decided by unanimous vote in the Council of Ministers. Mrs. Thatcher had got her way on this issue, too.

Thatcher also took grim delight in frustrating the hopes of the more supranationalist-minded Europeans. In her memoirs, she awards first prize for overambition to Jacques Delors, who wanted the SEA to revive the

Community's commitment to European monetary union. Britain, aided by Germany and the Netherlands, resisted this ambition tenaciously. Article 20 of the SEA inserted a new amendment into article 102 of the EEC treaty on "cooperation in economic and monetary policy." The words "Economic and Monetary Union" only appeared afterwards, in brackets. Article 20 merely committed European leaders to "cooperate with each other in accordance with the objectives of article 104 of the EEC treaty" (which requires each member state to pull off the enviable balancing act of ensuring "the equilibrium of its overall balance of payments and to maintain confidence in its currency, while taking care to ensure a high level of employment and a stable level of prices"). It did, however, open up the prospect of an intergovernmental conference being called in the event of further developments in the economic and monetary field becoming necessary. This gave Britain a de facto veto over the evolution of the EMS into anything more ambitious (since treaty changes suggested by an IGC had to be approved unanimously), but Thatcher would have cause to rue this concession.

Second prize for overambition in Mrs. Thatcher's book went to the Italian government, who wanted to give the European Assembly (or Parliament as it was for the first time explicitly referred to in a Community treaty) powers of legislative "co-decision" in keeping with the recommendations of the Parliament itself in the February 1984 draft treaty on European Union. There was never any prospect of the British government (but here Thatcher was not alone) accepting the transformation of the European Parliament into a "real" parliamentary assembly with legislative powers. In the SEA, the Parliament gained two new powers. First, it was given the right of assent over all treaties of enlargement and association made by the Community. Second, article 149 of the EEC treaty, which conferred advisory powers on the Assembly, was replaced by article 7 of the SEA, which introduced the so-called cooperation procedure for some ten articles of the revised EEC treaty. About two-thirds of the proposals in the Commission's "internal market" white paper were to be decided by this new approach.[63]

The cooperation procedure gave Parliament the right, within three months of the Council of Ministers' approving a piece of legislation, to amend the Council's "common position" or even to deny its consent—albeit by an "absolute majority of its component members," not just a majority of those present. The Council retained the right to override the Parliament's veto with a unanimous vote. Amendments were to be dealt with by the Commission and the Council together. The Commission was empowered to harmonize the Parliament's text with the Council's and was free to accept or reject the Parliament's suggested amendments. The Council then voted by a qualified majority (which, with the accession of Spain and Portugal meant at least fifty-four votes out of a possible seventy-six) on the revised text, though it was entitled to incorporate parliamentary amendments rejected by the

Commission by a unanimous vote. If the Council wished to amend the Commission's revised text, it had to do so unanimously. There was no further recourse to the European Parliament.

Far, in short, from turning the Parliament into a real legislature, the SEA, if anything, strengthened the role of the Community's *executive* in the legislative process. This point was subsequently stressed by the European Parliament when it debated the SEA in January 1986. The distinctly unenthusiastic motion proposed by supporters of the SEA perceptively pointed out that the act had transferred substantial legislative responsibilities from elected national parliaments to the unelected Commission and to national governments.[64] Since 1986, it has been objectively true that in many crucial areas of policy EC governments need to concern themselves more with building a winning coalition within the Council of Ministers than with winning over backbenchers in their own national parliaments. The fact that most EC legislation is made during intransparent bargaining sessions between national executives and the Community central administration is the root cause of the EC's (now EU's) notorious democratic deficit. Arguably, it has also been a major contributing factor in the generally acknowledged decline in status of national parliamentary institutions in the EC states. Voters are well aware that the real action takes place in Brussels—but can do little or nothing to influence developments there.

The introduction of the single-market clauses, the wider adoption of QMV, the safeguarding of member states' veto power over tax questions, the adoption of the cooperation procedure and the suggestion that economic and monetary union might be resolved by a further intergovernmental conference constituted the major elements of novelty in the SEA. But the treaty also contained a series of related articles on social policy, economic and social cohesion, research and technological development, and the environment. In retrospect, it is clear that Mrs. Thatcher thought she was turning the Community into a market economy administered by national governments. Most of the other heads of state or government thought, by contrast, that they were creating a *social* market economy, on the Rhineland model, that would evolve into a more tightly knit political Community with the passage of time.

Thus article 21, which amended article 118 of the EEC treaty, obliged member states to "pay particular attention to encouraging improvements" in health and safety matters and urged them to make "harmonization of conditions" their objective in this area. The Commission was instructed to prepare directives establishing minimum requirements for gradual implementation in the social policy field, although the act was careful to state that such directives should "avoid imposing administrative, financial and legal constraints in a way which would hold back the creation and development of small and medium-sized undertakings." This commitment to harmonized health and safety initiatives, in conjunction with article 18's explicit call for high levels of protection in these areas, was to become one of the major sources of Mrs. Thatcher's subsequent alienation from the EC and its works. The Commission and most of the member states tended to regard this article as legitimating Community action in the general sphere of social policy. The commitment of such countries as Denmark, France and the Netherlands to top quality standards in social policy was absolute. Such countries were afraid that laissez-faire countries like Britain would steal a cost advantage once the market became truly free. But they were also alarmed that harmonization might level down standards to British or American levels: to avoid this fate, article 21 specifically provided for member states introducing "more stringent measures for the protection of working conditions" if they wished.

Economic and social cohesion, at the behest of the Greeks, became a Community priority. Article 23 of the treaty amended article 130 of the EEC treaty by introducing a commitment to "reducing disparities between the various regions and the backwardness of the least-favored regions." The member states were to "conduct their economic policies" with this aim in mind. Overall, the language of the new clauses expressed the fears of the Mediterranean countries—including the two Iberian democracies which, being on the point of entry, had participated in the negotiations—that the internal market, unless it was tempered with rapid investment to enable them to catch up, would only heighten the economic superiority of the richer northern countries.

The environmental provisions of the SEA (art. 25), by contrast, reflected a fear on the part of the richer countries, that boosting economic growth, as the internal market promised to do, meant more pollution and a lower quality of life. They laid down as a principle that Community action on environmental issues should ensure "the polluter should pay" for the pollution caused: a dictum that opened up the prospect of the Commission introducing legislation to tighten fuel emission targets or to compel recycling. It was agreed, however, that on environmental regulations, that although QMV would be used "to define those matters on which decisions are to be taken," the Council of Ministers would make final decisions by a unanimous vote.

The lengthiest provision in the SEA was article 31 on European political cooperation. To a very great extent, the member states reiterated the positions they had taken since the early 1970s. They promised to "endeavor to formulate" common foreign and defense policies; to "ensure that common principles and objectives are gradually developed and defined"; to "endeavor to avoid any action or position which impairs their effectiveness as a cohesive force in international relations." Much of the complex machinery coordinating foreign policy discussions between the member states was now formalized into words (and a permanent secretariat of officials seconded from the foreign ministries of member states was established). Yet the integration of foreign policy making remained in its infancy. Despite this fact, final ratification of the SEA, which was signed in February 1986, was held up until July 1987 because an Irish citizen, Raymond Crotty, argued successfully in the courts that the Irish constitution would have to be changed by referendum before the clauses on political cooperation could be approved.[65] The Irish electorate dutifully did change the constitution, though less than half bothered to vote.

The SEA was only signed, let alone ratified, after some embarrassing argument. In January 1986, the Danish parliament passed a motion rejecting, by a narrow majority, the text of the act and urging its government to renegotiate terms. This demand was obviously impossible, and so Denmark instead held a hastily organized referendum on the SEA on 27 February 1986. When the Danes voted, the SEA passed with a 56 percent vote in favor. By then, nine countries had formally signed the treaty at a ceremony in Luxembourg on 17 February; Italy and Greece grouchily opted to wait until the result of the Danish referendum and eventually signed on 28 February. The Italians were at pains to underline their "deep dissatisfaction" with the SEA as a worthwhile step towards European integration. Foreign Minister Andreotti, upon signing, placed an official record of dissent in the annals of the intergovernmental conference: in his view, "objective analysis of the results of the conference showed that the SEA was merely a partial and unsatisfactory response to the need for substantial progress." The Italian government was particularly alienated by the conference's refusal to give powers of codecision to the Parliament.[66]

At the signing ceremony, other advocates of stronger European institutions did their best to put a good face on the results of the conference. Hans van den Broek, the Dutch foreign minister and president of the Council of Ministers in the first half of 1986, said the SEA possessed the merit of striking a balance between "the possible and the desirable"; Frans Andriessen, a vice president of the Commission, described the SEA merely as "the embodiment of what is feasible in Europe" and expressed his wish that the member states had displayed "more courage in their commitment to the completion of the internal market and the enhancing of the monetary dimension."[67]

The European Parliament made even these effusions of faint praise seem like eulogies. Altiero Spinelli said dismissively, "The Council has produced a mouse, a miserable, still-born mouse." In another cutting remark, Spinelli recalled Hemingway's *The Old Man and the Sea*, where the sharks strip the flesh from the giant marlin caught by the fisherman, and said, "They have left us with the bare bones."[68] A significant minority of MEPs wanted to make a symbolic vote of rejection; eventually, however, the Parliament approved the treaty by passing a motion that asserted that the intergovernmental conference had been "undemocratic" in keeping the Parliament "at arm's length" throughout the negotiation and described the SEA as being "very far from constituting the genuine reform of the Community that its people need." The Parliament urged the member states and the Commission to "exploit to the very limit the possibilities offered by the Single Act."[69]

There is no evidence that Mrs. Thatcher understood the depth of this delusion with the SEA, nor indeed that she ever took the language of the SEA's initial articles, which spoke of "making concrete progress towards European unity," seriously. As Hugo Young has written, the rhetoric of European unity was for the British government simply "Euro-guff, or Euro-twaddle, a bizarre, cultish worshipping at the altar of Jean Monnet, which would mercifully never get anywhere near full transubstantiation into the body of revealed and meaningful law."[70] Mrs. Thatcher would pay heavily in the coming years for this elementary failure to see that the SEA was, for the majority of member states, not an end, but very much a beginning.

EVALUATING THE SINGLE EUROPEAN ACT

There is little doubt, in retrospect, that the doom and gloom that accompanied the signing of the SEA was more angst over dashed expectations than a lucid appraisal of the Act's significance. True, faced with the task of governing an enlarged Community that was attempting to perform a hugely multiplied number of tasks at a Community level, the member states had shrunk during the IGC from instituting parliamentary democracy on a continental scale and had chosen to make more policy in negotiations among themselves. However, what is surprising—bewildering is perhaps the correct word—is that anybody should have thought that the federalist option stood even the remotest chance. From a British perspective, it is fascinating to read the conclusion on the SEA of the standard Italian history of European integration, Bino Olivi's excellent but passionately pro-federalist *L'Europa difficile*: "The intergovernmental conference's attempt to arrive at a treaty instituting European Union had failed; the contents of the SEA were inadequate and piecemeal [*inorganico*], less comprehensive than even the most pessimistic predictions on the eve of the talks."[71] This is a good example of how historical writing is inevitably permeated by the author's own values and hopes. That the objective of the IGC might actually be European Union presumably never crossed Mrs. Thatcher's mind. And what crossed Mrs. Thatcher's mind counted a good deal more during the negotiations than any number of draft treaties from the European Parliament.

But the inescapable fact that was missed in the immediate recriminations over the outcome of the SEA negotiation was that the member states *had* committed themselves to completing the internal market and that even the states most traditionally jealous of their national sovereignty had been willing to relinquish their right of veto in a wide range of policy areas. The case of Britain is particularly striking. Mrs. Thatcher, in pursuit of the economic gains she believed market liberalization would bring for Britain's competitive financial services sector, had approved a document that allowed Britain's European partners to make law applicable to British citizens without, at any rate in theory, the consent of the British government. As Hugo Young has written, the Single Act "surrendered sovereignty, accelerated momentum . . . it seemed to signal Britain's open-eyed engagement with the dominant culture of the Community."[72]

More generally, the SEA was, to use Pinder's terminology, a massive advance in the degree of negative integration present in the Community; but it also opened the prospect, if the political will existed, of pursuing positive integration in the fields of monetary policy, health and safety and economic cohesion. This was not small beer. It was wildly unrealistic of European federalists to expect the Iron Lady to give any more. The SEA may have been a lowest common denominator agreement, but the common denominator was a high one. Britain conceded an immense amount in order to get more.

The mere fact that all twelve member states had put their names on a document of the SEA's importance was in itself an achievement that few, if any, academic commentators would have predicted in the late 1970s or early 1980s. Probably the best work of scholarship on the EC in these years was a book by the British international relations theorist, Paul Taylor. Significantly entitled *The Limits of European Integration* (1983), Taylor's book argues in essence that the EC had since the early 1970s settled down into little more than a collaborative association of nation-states. The EC in the early 1980s was almost the opposite of the functionalist Community predicted by Haas. Supranational institutions like the Commission had waned in importance, while intergovernmental institutions like the European Council had waxed. The presidency of the Council of Ministers had become a key role, with individual governments using their presidency to obtain a share of the Commission's agenda-setting function. Despite the direct election of the European Parliament, European political parties had not formed; this reflected the fact that Community consciousness at popular level was nonexistent.[73] The EC was, in short, a useful institutional facilitator of interstate cooperation, but it was not a significant political actor in its own regard.

According to Taylor, the causes of this loss of impetus were inherent in the nature of the project. The ideology of the European movement had posited a "United States of Europe," with centralized institutions and an open economy, to which every democratic European country could belong. But centralizing power in Community institutions had run into the predictable problem of persuading recalcitrant national institutions to give up power. Moreover, there was too great a diversity in the member states' economic and social circumstances for everybody to be included comfortably into a single formula. Policies such as the EMS and the CAP were constantly being amended to take national circumstances into account and had become denatured as a result. Expansion of the Community to include Britain meant that the Community had lost the "dominant core" of France and Germany as a driving force.[74] The Community's efforts and energies had increasingly been diverted towards satisfying British objections to its existing practices rather than pressing on towards greater integration. The only way out of this situation of blockage, Taylor argued, was to allow "Europe à la carte." This was to permit the practice of partial agreements between the member states so long as a specified minimum of states approved.[75] There would be no obligation on any member state to accede.

Taylor's recommendation reflected the frustration felt by many pro-European academics, policymakers and politicians in the early 1980s. Britain's behavior over the budget, France's flirtation with a siege economy, France and Greece's watchfulness during the entry negotiations for the Iberian democracies had bred a mood of resignation. Openly pro-integration, Taylor could see in 1983 no other way of regenerating "a stronger sense of Community."[76] If partial agreements were permitted, he argued, there would probably be rapid movement towards economic and monetary union, a passport union, abolition of frontier controls and the introduction of common welfare policies in a select group of states. Other countries could join when and if they were ready: in the meantime, they could pass "parallel legislation" in their national parliaments whenever a particular regulation struck them as worthwhile.[77]

The SEA proved that the EC could make one last collective leap forward. It did not disprove Taylor's overall thesis; the Schengen and Maastricht treaties, which are discussed in the next chapter, were only possible because the Community renounced a set menu for all its diners. Taylor's idea of "Europe à la carte," moreover, has since been dignified with the name of "enhanced cooperation" and written into the Treaties of Amsterdam (1997) and Nice (2001). But, while negotiating the SEA, all the Twelve did eventually agree upon the same, admittedly restricted, list of courses—much though some of them wanted to taste the splendid, but possibly indigestible, desserts being offered by the European Parliament. Why? What persuaded the national governments to abandon the negativity of the early 1980s and contemplate the substantial reduction in national sovereignty implicit in the SEA?

The SEA was, in retrospect, the outcome of a unique set of circumstances. These were : (1) Britain, having resolved the budgetary question, was both relatively open to EC initiatives and ideologically inclined towards free markets; (2) completing the single market, especially after the *Cassis de Dijon* ruling, was an objective that had wide appeal among the member states on economic grounds; (3) France, having experimented with an overambitious form of domestic socialism, placed European integration at the heart of her policy as a way of regaining some degree of economic sovereignty; (4) the enlargement of the Community to the new democracies of the Mediterranean made institutional reform desirable; (5) the leaders of Germany and Italy, in particular, showed a strong propensity to test the limits of European integration and push for significant renunciations of national sovereignty to Community institutions. Germany, moreover, backed her rhetoric with hard cash. By allowing France to devalue the franc within the EMS and by paying for the British budget rebate, Germany prevented these two more acrimonious partners from wrecking the Community altogether.

Exceptional political leadership also played a crucial role. Two politicians in particular stand out. Margaret Thatcher's preference for free markets and her underestimated personal pragmatism overcame her abhorrence of surrendering national sovereignty and ensured that an agreement was reached between the Twelve. But her willingness to compromise was limited and ensured that the process of integration remained firmly in the hands of the national governments—even if those governments soon found themselves with their hands full. Jacques Delors convinced Mitterrand in 1983 that France could not go back on her postwar choice of participating in a wider European market. When he became president of the Commission, Delors showed subtle political judgment in making the completion of the internal market, rather than monetary and economic union, the flagship of the Commission's proposals and charismatic leadership in selling the Commission's ideas to the national governments. Hugo Young has said, rightly, "The Single European Act . . . was a fusion between the visions of Margaret Thatcher and Jacques Delors."[78] The Iron Lady has never lived this uncomfortable fact down.

Although Delors and Thatcher shared a belief in the value of free markets, their intellectual companionship ended there. The internal market, in the view of Delors, required a social dimension, with high levels of welfare protection, if it were not to be a mere charter for business. It also required a mechanism to prevent the competitive devaluation of currencies—the last major barrier against imports available to member states. These issues would ignite the conflagration in relations between Britain and the rest of the EC that would dominate Community politics between 1988 and 1990 and would lead to Mrs. Thatcher's ousting in November 1990 as leader of the Conservative Party. They would also be the most controversial elements of the Maastricht treaty (February 1992), which at once superseded the SEA as the most important addition to the corpus of Community law since the EEC treaty.

NOTES

1. See David R. Cameron, "The 1992 Initiative: Causes and Consequences," in *Euro-Politics*, ed. Alberta Sbragia (Washington, D.C.: Brookings Institution, 1993), 23–74 at 38–39, for figures on the growth of trade between EC member states.

2. For an accessible contemporary account of the effect of the rise of the dollar on the world economy, see Robert Solomon, "The Elephant in the Boat? The United States and the World Economy," *Foreign Affairs* 60, no. 3 (1981): 573–92.

3. Robert Boyer, "The Current Economic Crisis and Its Implications for France," in *The Mitterrand Experiment*, ed. George Ross, Stanley Hoffman and Sylvia Malzacher (Cambridge: Polity Press, 1987), 44.

4. Peter Hall, "The Evolution of Economic Policy under Mitterrand," in *The Mitterrand Experiment*, ed. George Ross, Stanley Hoffman and Sylvia Malzacher (Cambridge: Polity Press, 1987), 54–56.

5. Alain Muet, "Economic Management and the International Environment," in *Economic Policy and Policy-Making under the Mitterrand Presidency*, ed. Howard Machin and Vincent Wright (London: Pinter, 1985), 73.

6. Muet, "Economic Management," 73.

7. Bernard Connolly, *The Rotten Heart of Europe* (London: Faber and Faber, 1995), 28.

8. Hall, "Evolution of Economic Policy," 63.

9. Connolly, *Rotten Heart of Europe*, 30.

10. All quotes from the text of the draft "European Act" presented to the London European Council, November 1981. The act is included as appendix A in Pauline Neville-Jones, "The Genscher–Colombo Proposals," *Common Market Law Review* 20 (December 1983): 657–699 at 685–90.

11. Neville-Jones, "Genscher–Colombo Proposals," 657.

12. The text of the Solemn Declaration is in the *Bull. EC*, no. 6/83, 24–29.

13. This is the conclusion of Gianni Bonvicini, "The Genscher–Colombo Plan and the Solemn Declaration 1981–83," in *The Dynamics of European Union*, ed. Roy Pryce, (London: Routledge, 1989), 186.

14. Germany was the biggest contributor in 1979, giving 1,510 million Ecu. Britain was second with 1,373 million. The big gainers were the Netherlands (320 million), Ireland (641 million) and Denmark (495 million). For the full figures, and the method of calculation, see Joan Pearce, *The Common Agricultural Policy* (London: Royal Institute of International Affairs, 1981), 102.

15. Margaret Thatcher, *Downing Street Years* (London: HarperCollins, 1993), 63.

16. European Commission, *Britain in the Community 1973–83: The Impact of Membership* (London: European Communities, 1983), 7–11.

17. European Commission, *Britain in the Community*, 63.

18. Thatcher, *Downing Street Years*, 52.

19. Thatcher, *Downing Street Years*, 79.

20. Roy Jenkins, *A Life at the Centre* (London: Macmillan, 1994), 498–99.

21. Thatcher, *Downing Street Years*, 79.

22. *Bull. EC*, no. 5/1980, 7–10.

23. Geoffrey Denton, "Re-structuring the EC Budget: Implications of the Fontainebleau Agreement," *Journal of Common Market Studies* 23 (December 1984): 123.

24. *Bull. EC*, no. 5/1980, 9.

25. European Commission, "Reflections on the Common Agriculture Policy," *Bull. EC*, supplement 6/80, 17.

26. Pearce, *Common Agricultural Policy*, 1.

27. Pearce, *Common Agricultural Policy*, 59–61.

28. Pearce, *Common Agricultural Policy,* 48.

29. Pearce, *Common Agricultural Policy,* 9

30. For the domestic policies of Spain's fledgling democracy, see Kenneth Maxwell and Steven Spiegel, *The New Spain* (New York: Council on Foreign Relations, 1994).

31. European Commission, "General Considerations on the Problem of Enlargement," *Bull. EC,* supplement 1/78 (1978a); "Economic and Sectoral Aspects: Commission Analyses Supplementing Its Views on Enlargement," *Bull. EC,* supplement 3/78 (1978b).

32. European Commission, 1978b, 22.

33. European Commission, 1978a, 15.

34. European Commission, 1978a, 15.

35. European Commission, 1978a, 17.

36. The European Communities, *General Report 1979* (Brussels: European Communities, 1979), 211–215.

37. The European Commission, "Opinion on Spain's Application for Membership," *Bull. EC,* supplement 9/78, 19.

38. Paul Kennedy, "Spain's Relations with the European Community 1962–1986" (unpublished manuscript, University of Bath, England, p.t.kennedy@bath.ac.uk). For a detailed study of Spain's relations with the EC, see Juio Crespo Maclennan, *Spain and the Process of European Integration* (London: Palgrave, 2000).

39. Kennedy, "Spain's Relations," 11.

40. Bino Olivi, *L'Europa difficile* (Bologna, Italy: Il Mulino, 2000), 231.

41. Antonio Alonso, *España en el Mercado Común. Del Acuerdo del 70 a la Comunidad de Doce* (Madrid: Espasa Calpe, 1985), 173–75.

42. Fernando Morán, *España en su sitio* (Barcelona, Spain: Plaza y Janés/Cambio 16, 1990), 305.

43. *Bull. EC,* 3/85, 7–9.

44. Andrew Moravcsik, "Negotiating the Single European Act: National Interests and Conventional Statecraft in the European Community," *International Organization* 45 (Winter 1991): 36.

45. Denton, "Re-structuring the EC Budget," 123–25.

46. Despite the widespread belief that Britain's budget contribution was small beer, the eventual rebate negotiated by Mrs. Thatcher was sufficient to pay for "the entire family doctor service in Britain." See Hugo Young, *This Blessed Plot* (London: Macmillan, 1998), 323.

47. "Europe: The Future," paper produced for the Fontainebleau European Council by the British government, reproduced in the *Journal of Common Market Studies* 23 (September 1984): 73–81.

48. The European Round Table included the chief executives of such important multinationals as FIAT, Philips, Unilever, Thyssen Steel, Bosch Electronics, as well as industrialists from firms based in countries outside the EC (e.g., Volvo, Ciba-Geigy) and it published a series of influential pamphlets in the early 1980s specifically directed at the political élite.

49. The *Cassis de Dijon* case, strictly speaking, ought to be called *Rewe-Zentral AG v. Bundesmonopolverwaltung für Branntwein.* It is easy to see how the French name caught on. For academic discussions of *Cassis,* see Martin Shapiro, "The European Court of Justice," in *Euro-Politics,* ed. Alberta Sbragia (Washington, D.C.: Brookings

Institution, 1992), 123–56; Karen J. Alter and Sophie Meunier-Aitsahlia, "Judicial Politics in the European Community: European Integration and the Pathbreaking *Cassis de Dijon* Decision," *Comparative Political Studies* 26 (January 1993): 535–61.

50. David R. Cameron, "The 1992 Initiative: Causes and Consequences," in *Euro-Politics*, ed. Alberta Sbragia, (Washington, D.C.: Brookings Institution, 1992), 53.

51. Renaud Dehousse, *The European Court of Justice* (London: Macmillan, 1998), 92.

52. Richard Griffiths, in Keith Middlemas, *Orchestrating Europe* (London: Fontana, 1995), 92–93.

53. European Commission, *Completing the Internal Market* (Luxembourg: Com (85) 310).

54. *Bull. EC,* 6/85, 18.

55. European Commission, *Completing the Internal Market*, 55.

56. Thatcher, *Downing Street Years*, 547.

57. Lord Arthur Cockfield, *The European Union: Creating the Single Market* (London: Wiley Chancery Law, 1994), 56.

58. Thatcher, *Downing Street Years*, 553.

59. The complete text of the Parliament's proposals is to be found in *Bull. EC,* no. 2/84, 7–26.

60. The Dooge Committee's report is to be found in *Bull. EC,* no. 3/85, 102–11.

61. Thatcher, *Downing Street Years*, 551.

62. Thatcher, *Downing Street Years*, 553.

63. Juliet Lodge, "The European Parliament from Assembly to Co-legislature: Changing the Institutional Dynamics," in *The European Community and the Challenge of the Future*, ed. Juliet Lodge (London: Pinter, 1989), 69.

64. *Bull. EC,* no. 1/86, 9–10.

65. The strange case of Mr. Crotty is discussed in William Nicholl and Trevor C. Salmon, *Understanding the New European Community* (Hemel Hempstead, U.K.: Harvester Wheatsheaf, 1994), 50.

66. *Bull. EC,* no. 2/86, 10.

67. *Bull. EC,* no. 2/86, 8.

68. Quotes from Olivi, *L'Europa difficile*, 301.

69. *Bull. EC,* no. 1/86, 10.

70. Young, *This Blessed Plot*, 337–38.

71. Olivi, *L'Europa difficile*, 301.

72. Young, *This Blessed Plot*, 338.

73. Paul Taylor, *The Limits of European Integration* (London: Croom Helm, 1983), 298–300.

74. Taylor, *Limits*, 302–4.

75. Taylor, *Limits*, 305.

76. Taylor, *Limits*, 307.

77. Taylor, *Limits*, 308.

78. Young, *This Blessed Plot*, 332.

7

The Maastricht Compromise

The Single European Act deliberately created a space. The question that arose between 1986 and the signature of the Treaty on European Union in February 1992 was what would be built upon the terrain cleared by Cockfield and Delors. Margaret Thatcher, true to her laissez-faire instincts, wanted the space to be developed by the free market, without central planning and with the minimum of regulation. Jacques Delors, the quintessential French planner, was disinclined to adopt this solution. He thought in terms of constructing a towering edifice: a European federal state that would substitute the national governments in most areas of policymaking. At the Maastricht meeting of the European Council in December 1991, the Twelve finally opted to build themselves a distinctly lopsided three-pillar structure that no architect would ever have designed. The Treaty on European Union, or, as it is familiarly known, the Maastricht treaty, should be regarded as a hard-fought compromise that blended a genuine impulse towards a greater supranational organization of Europe with the need to safeguard the interests and preferences of the member states.

The impulse for supranationalism very largely came from Germany. Reunification in 1989–1990 unambiguously established Germany as first among equals in the Twelve. Germany had eighty million people—over twenty million more than Britain, France and Italy—and was the natural leader of the newly liberated countries of eastern Europe. The unambiguous support of the Bush administration for unification showed that Washington regarded the new Germany as the key element in its European policy. For the first time since the early 1950s, the prospect of Germany breaking free from French tutelage in Europe became a reality—or seemed a reality to anxious diplomats in London, Paris and Warsaw. The strengthening of European integration represented by the

Maastricht treaty represented in this context a symbolic affirmation that Germany intended to continue its postwar commitment to pooling sovereign power with the other countries of western Europe. Germany would become even more "European."

At the same time, the Maastricht negotiations and events post-Maastricht illustrated that the European Community would be more "German" than ever before. The great innovation of the Maastricht treaty—monetary union—was achieved by transferring the principles and practices of German monetary policy onto a continental scale. Much of the subsequent suspicion and popular hostility to the Maastricht treaty in Britain, Denmark and France can be traced to dislike of this prospect. The British Euroskeptics, the more alarmist of whom aired semiracial theories about the German desire for domination in Europe, were only the most extreme examples of this widespread preoccupation. Such theories naturally deserve only ridicule. But it would be unhistorical not to underline that 1989 to 1993 saw a major shift in the Community's center of gravity. Since Maastricht, the most important country within the EU has been united Germany, not France. Germany cannot get everything it wants in EU negotiations, but nothing meaningful can be achieved against German opposition.

THE "PAQUET DELORS" AND THE DELORS REPORT

The Single European Act was expected to lead to a substantial increase in the Community's economic output. A Commission-sponsored report into the "costs of non-Europe" asserted in 1987 that the 1992 initiative, if fully implemented, would lead to a noninflationary boost of at least 7 percent in the gross economic output of the Community (GCP) by 1993 and to the creation of five million jobs. Microeconomic factors such as the abolition of frontiers and the harmonization of technical standards would provide a stimulus of between 2.2 and 2.7 percent, while gains from greater efficiency as the single market caused firms to restructure and find economies of scale could be expected to add a further 2.1 to 3.7 percent. The 1992 measures could thus be expected to produce, by themselves, one-off gains of over 4 percent of GCP—and perhaps far more. However, the report pointed out that such microeconomic gains were not the end of the story. Governments could, if they wished, invest the extra wealth generated by the 1992 initiative into growth-enhancing macroeconomic measures such as reducing taxation, improving infrastructure or retiring public debt. The final figure of 7 percent growth was arrived at after taking such measures into account.[1]

Such claims were somewhat controversial with professional economists, who tended to believe that the expected benefits of the single market had been systematically overstated. Nobody disputed, however, that the 1992 initiative was likely to increase economic activity within the Community. The question was—for what end? Delors was not disposed to regard economic growth as an end in itself. As George Ross has written, "The Delorist vision saw the market as an indispensable allocator of resources, decision-maker and source of economic dynamism. The market by itself could not, however, guarantee equity, a moralized social order, or full economic success."[2] Delors's primary concern between 1987 and 1990 was to ensure that the gains of the single market were fairly shared out.

Delors was concerned first that shortcomings of infrastructure and investment would fatally hamper the efforts of the Community's least-developed regions to compete in the single market. Second, Delors believed that a properly functioning market required a single medium of exchange. He had been convinced by a close friend, the influential Italian economist Tommaso Padoa-Schioppa, that the Community's economy was endangered by an "inconsistent quartet." The four points of this quartet were (1) free trade; (2) stable exchange rates within the exchange rate mechanism; (3) autonomy of domestic monetary policy; and (4) the end of restrictions upon the movement of capital within the space created by the SEA. Padoa-Schioppa's argument, stripped to its essentials, was that these four conditions could not coexist stably without monetary union.[3]

Third, the benefits of the single market, in Delors's view, had to lead to a net increase in welfare and social cohesion. The "domaine social" was of paramount importance for him. Raised in the "personalist" tradition of the French philosopher Emmanuel Mounier, Delors profoundly rejected the vision of human society promoted by laissez-faire liberalism.[4] If the single market merely identified Europe with rising profits for big business and a transfer of production to countries with lower standards of social protection, the European project as a whole would be discredited. As he said in a 1988 book: "There is no sense in competition developing to the detriment of the standards of social protection and the working conditions upon which the European economic model is founded. Europe will not be built if the workers do not feel involved, if social progress is not part of its final objectives."[5]

The Delors Commission acted swiftly in 1987–1988 to address the first two of these concerns. The question of geographical cohesion was dealt with in February 1987 when the Commission presented the "Paquet Delors"—in effect, a five-year plan to increase the amount the Community spent, via its so-called structural funds, on regional development. In all, Delors's package of measures envisaged spending about 60,000 million Ecu before the end of 1992; funding for the regions would by then account for one-quarter of all the Community's expenditure. Most of the new spending (63 percent) was to be concentrated on so-called Objective 1 regions (Ireland including Ulster, most of Spain, Portugal, Greece, southern Italy, Sardinia and Corsica), where economic activity was much lower than the Community average. A lesser proportion of the new money (12 percent) was to be directed at Objective 2 regions that had been hard hit by industrial decline. Areas "fully eligible" for Objective 2 status included South Wales, northwest England, the Walloon provinces of Belgium, the Saarland, Genoa and the Basque country.[6] Delors somewhat immodestly stated that "the sums invested in the first of these objectives are comparable to those mobilized by the Marshall Plan."[7] The remaining 25 percent was to be spent on measures for alleviating long-term unemployment, providing youth training and modernizing agriculture in certain designated parts of the Community.

Overall, the Delors package represented a substantial voluntary transfer of wealth from Europe's rich heartland to its much poorer fringes. Ireland, Spain and Portugal, in particular, have much to thank Delors for, although they owe at least as much to German chancellor Helmut Kohl. Delors's set of measures for regional development could only be paid for by capping growth in agricultural spending (which was opposed by the French) and by increasing the amount of the Community's "own resources" (which was resisted by the British). Had Kohl not been prepared to underwrite the costs of this latest expansion in the Community's budget, the Paquet Delors would have failed. As it was, it was only approved in February 1988 after several heated meetings of the European Council.

Delors's second concern, economic and monetary union, was addressed at the Hanover summit of the Twelve in June 1988, when the gathered heads of state and government, after some deft preparatory work by Helmut Kohl, voted to allow him to chair a committee that would include the governors of all the Twelve's central banks and that would have the specific remit of drawing up a concrete proposal for the introduction of monetary union.[8] The central bank governors were thus not being asked to give their opinion on *whether* a single currency was desirable, but on *how*, technically, such a currency might be introduced. Pressure for a single currency had been growing throughout the 1980s. France and Italy, to name but two countries, had complained bitterly in 1987 about the economic costs of shadowing the Deutsche Mark in the EMS. Influential members of the German government, including the foreign minister, Hans-Dietrich Genscher, believed that it was in Germany's interest to take the lead on the issue of monetary unification since the alternative—a return to floating currencies—might prove harmful to German industry. Delors capitalized upon this sentiment to put the issue on the agenda—although, once again, he needed the support of Kohl. Yet, despite the high-profile political support for the Committee, involving the central bankers was a must. As Tommaso Padoa-Schioppa has written, "had the Central Banks been excluded . . . [from the Delors committee] . . . they might have taken a more negative view of the prospects of monetary union." In that case, the Italian economist added, it would have been "more difficult" to "produce the document that played, both technically and politically, a role comparable to the Spaak report on the Common Market."⁹

The Delors Committee was by no means plain sailing for the president of the Commission. He was by no means a technical expert on monetary policy and had to work intensely hard in order to be up to scratch on the subject.¹⁰ He had, moreover, to deal with the openly rude attitude of the Bundesbank's chairman, Karl-Otto Pöhl, who considered that he had been tricked into participating by the German government and who was determined to ensure that the Committee would either fail or else would recommend what would amount to the reproduction on European scale of the institutions and practices of German monetary policy. Pöhl switched off his earphones and read a newspaper when Delors gave his opening speech in French. Delors dealt with this obstreperous approach by playing "a modest role throughout."¹¹ His style was "to depoliticize discussions by focusing on very precise technical points, to define the exercise as technocratic."¹² He even spoke in English. Gradually, Pöhl became more cooperative.

Pöhl did not bend significantly on questions of substance, however. The Bundesbank position during the Delors committee was based around three cardinal points. First, monetary union would require a central bank, with a board composed of independent central bankers, that could set interest rates without political interference and that was mandated by statute to keep inflation low. Second, monetary integration should not precede general economic convergence: would-be members should have met precise macroeconomic targets for inflation, budget deficits and currency stability. Third, there should be no fixed timetables that might lead to political pressure for a fudge of the economic criteria for membership. EMU would start when there were enough countries ready to start and not a moment before.¹³

Perhaps to Pöhl's surprise, the Bundesbank's conditions were in substance accepted by the other members of the committee. The Delors Report was published in April 1989 after some eight meetings of the committee. Delors himself supervised the published text very closely: Joly Dixon, the member of his cabinet responsible for monetary policy, has said, "There wasn't a phrase in the final paper which he didn't author."¹⁴ The report advised that the Community should move to EMU in three stages. The first stage would begin on 1 July 1990. By then, all the EC's countries would be members of the ERM and would cooperate, through existing institutions, for an unspecified amount of time, to achieve convergence of the main economic indicators. All remaining controls on cross-border capital movements would be abolished in line with the single-market initiative. Currency realignments within the ERM would still be possible at this stage. Stage 2 would see the formal establishment of what was called in the report the "European System of Central Banks," which would be independent of national governments and other EC institutions. This body would take over the day-to-day running of the EC's existing arrangements for coordinating monetary policy and would plan its own eventual transformation into a central bank. The Council of Ministers would set *nonbinding* guidelines, by qualified majority voting, for the member states' budgetary policy at this stage. Exchange rate adjustments, while legally possible, would be regarded as "last resort" measures at this stage. Stage 3 would imply the fixing of exchange rates, compulsory macroeconomic policy guidelines, set down by the Council of Ministers and the European Parliament, to avoid stability-threatening budget imbalances by individual member states and the centralization of hard currency reserves and monetary policy in the hands of the ESCB. A single currency would preferably be introduced at this stage.[15]

The conformity of the Delors report to the Bundesbank's preferred model is evident from this summary. Governors from the other banks, and Delors, knew that the Bundesbank's prestige in Germany as the constitutionally enshrined defender of the value of the DM was such that the German political and business élite would never countenance its substitution unless the Bundesbank itself was satisfied with the anti-inflation credentials and monetary soundness of the proposed Community institutions. Pöhl was thus in a position to say, "take it or leave it." But the peculiar character of the Delors committee should be remembered. The governors were acting in a personal capacity, not as the representatives of the member states, and were thus free to draw up a scheme that appealed to their own broad economic philosophies—which naturally tended to place a premium upon sound money. All accounts agree that Pöhl's conditions were agreed to with remarkably little opposition. Even the British representative, Robin Leigh-Pemberton, who owed his job to Mrs. Thatcher's patronage, was seemingly convinced that the report made good sense. His decision to sign the report, however, "took great courage."[16] Mrs. Thatcher, who had underestimated the risk that the Delors committee would actually lead to a joint recommendation by the central bankers to the European Council, had now awoken to the dangers to national sovereignty presented by the Delors report and was furious at what she regarded as Leigh-Pemberton's betrayal. As Delors had presumably anticipated all along, such an authoritative statement that EMU was possible gave momentum to the idea of implementing it. At the first EC summit after the publication of the report, in Madrid at the end of June 1989, the heads of government agreed to adopt the Delors report as the basis for an intergovernmental conference, though they postponed the decision on when the conference would actually start.

Mrs. Thatcher, making the best of a bad job, acquiesced in this decision and committed Britain to membership of the ERM. She did, however, reserve Britain's right to choose for herself when the economic conditions were ripe for entry to the ERM (and not be constrained by the July 1990 deadline) and emphasized that Britain's adherence to the first stage of the process outlined by the Delors report should not be construed as an indication that Britain was prepared to sign up to the second and third stages as well. Paragraph 39 of the Delors report states, "The decision to enter upon the first stage should be a decision to embark on the entire process." As two British journalists wrote: "Taking the first bite committed the diner to swallow the whole meal."[17] Mrs. Thatcher was indicating at Madrid that she intended to scrutinize the exotic foreign food on offer to her with care and attention and would pick from the menu only the items she was sure she would like. It should be said, however, that even this compromise position had been forced upon the Iron Lady by domestic political considerations. In the days immediately before the Madrid summit, her chancellor, Nigel Lawson, and foreign secretary, Geoffrey Howe, who had been pressing her to join the ERM throughout her third government, had jointly threatened to resign if she did not make a specific commitment to entry.[18] Howe had also publicly stated that he had not given up his hopes of eventually becoming prime minister. At Madrid, Thatcher had therefore to choose between provoking a potentially fatal split in her cabinet and breaking the harmony of the Madrid summit. It was really no choice. On the single currency, she could always fight another day.

THE BRUGES SPEECH

The remainder of the Twelve could hardly have been under any illusions that proceeding towards EMU would mean a fight with the British prime minister that would be at least as intense as the clash between Gaullist France, the Commission, and the other member states in the 1960s. They had known for nearly a year what Mrs. Thatcher's vision of the future of the Community was. In the summer of 1988, Delors, newly confirmed for a second term as president of the Commission, had told the European Parliament that before long he expected that "80 percent" of legislation affecting the Community's citizens would be made in Brussels, not the national parliaments. He had compounded this daring candor by appearing as a guest of the British Trade Unions Congress in August 1988 and promising that social protection and employees' rights would be a primary concern of his second presidency. The Congress, battered by nine years of Thatcherism, greeted Delors's speech with a standing ovation.[19] It was a deliberate challenge that Mrs. Thatcher could not ignore.

Nor did she. On 20 September 1988, she delivered a speech entitled "The European Family of Nations" to the College of Europe in Bruges. The "Bruges speech," as it is familiarly known, is unquestionably one of the most memorable tirades in contemporary political history—and would have been more memorable still had a panicked Foreign Office not succeeded in editing out some of the more inflammatory passages of the first draft. But the speech is not merely a tirade. It presents a carefully constructed alternative vision for the development of the EC that the subsequent evolutions of the Community in the 1990s have not entirely eclipsed.[20]

The most important point to underline about the Bruges speech is that it was not a nationalist rant. If anything, it was internationalist in tone. The speech's main thrust was to warn the EC that it was becoming "a narrow-minded, inward-looking club" and was in danger of equating the strengthening of the EC's institutions—at the expense of the sovereignty of the member states—with the construction of European identity. For Thatcher, the EC was merely one manifestation of European identity among many. European identity was above all a cultural and historical concept, signifying adherence to a broadly similar set of values based upon the rule of law, Christianity, and the shared experience of exploring, colonizing and, "yes, without apology," civilizing much of the world. European identity was also intimately connected to the shared experience of the many wars European nations had fought against each other. In these wars, Britain had always "fought to prevent Europe from falling under the dominance of a single power." If liberty was today one of Europe's core values, this was largely due to the efforts of Britain: "Only miles from here in Belgium lie the bodies of 120,000 British soldiers who died in the First World War. Had it not been for that willingness to fight and to die, Europe would have been united long before now—but not in liberty, not in justice." In the light of her cultural understanding of European identity, Thatcher stressed that the countries "east of the Iron Curtain" were also "European" and, crucially, so was the United States. The Atlantic Community, Thatcher stressed in her peroration, was "Europe on both sides of the Atlantic." Thatcher believed—with considerable justification—that Delors was ideologically hostile to the free market values symbolized by the United States. One of the most important themes of the whole speech was that Britain would never permit the institutions of the EC to be built in rivalry with the relationship individual European nations, Britain above all, enjoyed with their cousin across the Atlantic.

It would be an exaggeration to say that the main body of the speech portrayed the EC as the latest power attempting to dominate Europe, but Thatcher did leave no doubt in her audience's mind that the Commission—and supporters of a federal Europe in general—were overstepping the mark. Thatcher proposed five "guiding principles" for action: "willing cooperation between sovereign states"; "encouraging change"; "Europe open to enterprise"; "Europe open to the world"; "Europe and defense." Her vision for the EC was one in which sovereign nation-states cooperated, within the framework of the EC, to inject a dose of free market principles into the CAP, to build upon the SEA by accelerating the liberalization of trade within the Community and the ending of state protectionism in such industries as telecommunications and banking, to adopt a liberal common policy in the ongoing "Uruguay round" of trade talks (see chapter 8), to maintain and strengthen Europe's defense in partnership with the United States. It was a program of practical steps—all of which, quite objectively, did need addressing—and, at the same time, a very British appeal "not to let ourselves be distracted by Utopian goals."

It was a speech, moreover, that drew three lines in the sand. The first such line was a rejection of any concept of supranational government in Europe. The single most memorable sound bite in the speech was: "We have not successfully rolled back the frontiers of the state in Britain, only to see them reimposed at a European level, with a European super-state exercising a new dominance from Brussels." The second was an assertion of the British state's right to police its borders: it was a "matter of plain common-sense that we cannot totally abolish frontier controls if we are also to protect our citizens from crime and to stop the movement of drugs, of terrorists, and of illegal immigrants." The third was a warning that Britain would not adopt the Rhineland "social market" model of capitalism. The EC did not need "new regulations which raise the cost of employment and make Europe's labor markets less flexible and less competitive." Britain "would fight attempts to introduce collectivism and corporatism at the European level."

These three anathema were not chosen casually. They were the areas in which the Commission and the more actively integrationist of Britain's European partners were most intent on pooling or delegating sovereignty. When Mrs. Thatcher made her speech, the Delors committee was about to illustrate that most of the other member states had few qualms about bequeathing one of the core functions of national sovereignty to a supranational institution. The second area, the abolition of border controls, was already proceeding via the so-called Schengen agreement between the Benelux countries, Germany and France. In June 1985, in pursuit of a decision made in principle by the June 1984 Fontainebleau summit, these countries had agreed that they would gradually diminish frontier checks on vehicles crossing their borders—including vehicles from other Community countries or even nonmember states. Despite some of the problems that arose from this policy—the Netherlands had, for instance, much more liberal drugs laws than the other Schengen countries and the accord facilitated the circulation of soft drugs purchased in Dutch cities—the original five were determined to press on with this policy. In June 1990, they signed a full-blown treaty, subsequently ratified by the national parliaments, that confirmed that they would abolish all internal borders before 1 January 1993 and that made provisions for joint policing of the frontierless zone thus created. The Schengen "group" also committed themselves to gradually harmonizing their laws on immigration, asylum, drugs and other issues.

The Schengen group's commitment to open borders was obviously an approach that presented many problems for other EC countries: the issue of IRA terrorism alone rendered it impracticable for any British government, at any rate in the late 1980s. But Mrs. Thatcher, in the Bruges speech, was just as intent on underlining a point of principle. In her view, immigration, asylum and drugs were issues that would be decided at Westminster in perpetuity. Moreover, her commitment to the free movement of peoples throughout the single market was not to be taken to mean that she believed movements of people should be *unmonitored*. Deciding who could, and who could not, enter Britain was a sovereign right of the Westminster Parliament that could not be surrendered.

The third area excluded by the Bruges speech from Community action, social policy, went to the heart of the Thatcherite "revolution" in the British economy. Since 1979, Thatcher had been engaged in the deregulation of British business. By the late 1980s, British business had the least onerous level of welfare provision in the EC. Millions were working on short-term contracts without guaranteed rights to training, holidays or pensions; maternity leave was ungenerous and paternity leave unheard of; there was no minimum wage or limit on working hours; state unemployment compensation was meager; layoffs and plant closures were regarded as management decisions, not—as elsewhere in Europe—social disasters requiring government intervention; the trade unions had been squashed by a series of laws that limited their right to picket and to organize, let alone take part, via German-style supervisory boards, in the management decisions of major companies. For the rest of the Twelve, Britain's position was both unethical and an unfair competitive advantage—so-called social dumping. Despite the blunt warning of the Bruges speech, the Commission, supported more or less keenly by the other member states, pressed ahead in 1989 to put social rights at the heart of the EC's agenda.

The outcome of this Commission activity was the Community Charter of Basic Social Rights for Workers, a "solemn declaration" of principle that was presented in its final form to the December 1989 Strasbourg European Council and was approved by all the member states with one entirely predictable dissenter.[21] The charter identified twelve broad rights that everybody working in the EC ought to possess. These were (1) the right to freedom of movement. EC citizens should be able to move from one country to another and take up jobs on the same terms (social security, tax and so forth) as locals; (2) the right to employment and fair remuneration; (3) the right to improved living and working conditions; (4) the right to adequate social protection against unemployment, illness and so forth; (5) the right to freedom of association and collective bargaining; (6) the right to vocational training throughout the worker's career; (7) the right of men and women to equal treatment not only in pay, but in education, training, social protection and career opportunities; (8) the right to worker information, consultation and participation; (9) the right to health and safety protection in the workplace; (10) the right to protection of children and adolescents; (11) the right of the elderly to a pension providing a decent standard of living; (12) the right of the disabled to be given opportunities for work training and social rehabilitation. In short, the "harmonious vision" underlying the member states' attitude to social policy throughout the postwar period was alive and well. Mrs. Thatcher, less beholden to the European movement's traditions, bluntly described the social charter as "quite simply a socialist charter."[22]

The Commission followed up the social charter with an action plan of recommended directives and other measures. The problem facing the Commission, and those member states that wanted to turn the charter into binding law, was that the Commission lacked the clout to overcome British objections. Article 100 of the EEC treaty provided for harmonization of national laws that affected the creation of a single market. If the Commission could plausibly contend that widely differing standards of social protection were antithetical to the creation of a common market, it was free to propose legislation. Unfortunately, at any rate from the Commission's point of view, during the SEA negotiations, laws concerning the rights and interests of employed persons had been specifically singled out as belonging to a category that required unanimous, not qualified majority, voting. Only health and safety legislation could be passed by QMV and could therefore avoid a British veto. In 1990, under the guise of introducing health and safety measures, the Commission proposed draft directives to ensure minimum standards across the Community in the rules concerning the employment of part-time workers, the length of the working day and the duration of maternity leave. Britain, who was faced with the most systematic legislative changes—and by far the largest bill—for introducing this legislation, took the directive on part-timers all the way to the ECJ and strongly resisted the other two in the Council of Ministers. Ultimately, all three directives were implemented, but, in a sense, the British government had made its point. It would fight any social policy legislation tooth and nail. Obviously, against such animus, there was little prospect of the principles of the social charter ever being turned into a coherent body of law. The only way to enact the principles of the social charter was to change the treaties (or wait for a change of government in Britain).[23]

By the time of the Strasbourg summit in December 1989, then, Britain was fighting the rest of the Community on several fronts. Britain was opposed to giving up its currency, opposed to surrendering its right to police its own border, opposed to turning the single market into a social market. It was increasingly obvious, however, that Britain would have few or no allies she could count upon in any of these struggles. At Strasbourg, in addition to welcoming the social charter, the Twelve took the decision to begin an intergovernmental conference on EMU in December 1990.

GERMAN UNIFICATION AND ITS CONSEQUENCES

Strasbourg was the first European Council since the breaching of the Berlin Wall and the "velvet revolution" in Czechoslovakia. At Strasbourg, the Twelve decided to establish a European Bank of Reconstruction and Development (EBRD) to help finance the economic recovery of the nations of Eastern Europe. But more generally, the collapse of Communism gave new impetus to the movement towards the political integration of Europe. At the end of 1989, the EC was lurching rather than marching towards further integration. Most of the member states were prepared, seemingly, to take the huge steps of handing control over monetary policy to a committee of unelected central bankers and to make most social policy a question for intergovernmental negotiation in the Council of Ministers (as opposed to a matter for debate in the national assemblies of the member states) but were not very forthcoming on what parallel steps there would be to ensure democratic supervision of the decisions thus transferred to the Community level.

The collapse of Communism, and the subsequent reunification of Germany, an event whose inevitability became clear in the early spring of 1990, starkly underlined this asymmetry. Convinced federalists now urged the national governments to give the EC a political dimension that would enable it to "act as a stronger unit" and to fill the vacuum left by the end of the Cold War.[24] The European Parliament, which had never digested the refusal of the member states to discuss its draft constitution for a European Union during the SEA negotiations, began agitating for a political dimension to the IGC as early as November 1989. In an unusual event, some 250 MEPs and delegates from the various national parliaments met in Rome on 27–30 November 1989 for a European "assizes" in which proposals to strengthen the Community's central institutions, notably the Parliament, were debated. In March 1990, the Parliament's ideas took shape in the so-called Martin I report, in which a committee chaired by the Socialist deputy David Martin proposed that the treaties should be revised to include European political cooperation (foreign policy), strengthened Community competence in social and environmental policy, systematic use of QMV in the Council of Ministers, European citizenship and a substantial increase in the power of the Parliament.[25] The Martin II report in July 1990 made concrete proposals for treaty revision in all these areas.

Important though the Parliament's pressure was, the most powerful impulse for greater political integration was the behavior of the president of France, François Mitterrand. French foreign policy was initially anything but welcoming to the prospect of German unification, not least because West Germany itself did not initially pay enough attention to French sensibilities. Helmut Kohl's Ten-Point plan to deal with the collapse of East Germany, announced on 28 November 1989 and envisaging the creation of a "contractual community" between the two Germanies that would gradually advance to confederal status, was not cleared with the French government in advance. Mitterrand visited Soviet leader Mikhail Gorbachev on 6 December, arousing memories of the Franco-Russian "Entente" against Germany, and immediately after Christmas 1989, Mitterrand visited East Germany, giving the feeble posttotalitarian regime of East Germany a much-needed boost of credibility. On 31 December 1989, Mitterrand called for the construction of a European confederation that included the newly liberated states of Eastern Europe. This proposal put a cat among the pigeons. The president of France appeared to be suggesting that German unification was so menacing an event that the EC was no longer an adequate institutional vehicle to restrain an enlarged Germany.[26]

German unification, as the eminent German historian Karl Kaiser has explained, was an issue that raised four major concerns. How could worries about the power of a unified Germany be assuaged? How could Germany be unified while remaining in Western structures of integration? NATO membership was a particularly knotty issue. How could unification be achieved without the imposition of restrictions on German sovereignty? Last but not least, how could unification take place without the convocation of a major international conference featuring all Germany's wartime adversaries?[27] The solution to this last question was, in February 1990, to institute the so-called 2+4 talks between the two Germanies acting in concert and the four major wartime allies (Britain, France, Russia and the United States). At the risk of oversimplifying, the solution found to the other three questions—at any rate so far as the nations of western Europe were concerned—was ultimately accelerated integration of the European Community. Germany would be allowed to reunite so long as it promptly pooled much of its new power in the institutions of a strengthened European Union.

The main architect of this strategy was Chancellor Helmut Kohl. In a key speech in Paris on 17 January 1990, he invoked a metaphor much used by Konrad Adenauer and stated that "the German house must be built under a European roof." This speech was followed up by a series of meetings and telephone calls with Mitterrand, in which the two leaders and their staffs worked out a plan of action.[28] Kohl also kept in close touch with Delors and promised to put his weight behind proposals for political unification. Following the March 1990 elections in East Germany, which Kohl's Christian Democrats, by turning them into a referendum on unity, won easily, Kohl and Mitterrand moved quickly to put European political integration on the EC's agenda. On 19 April 1990, a week before a meeting of the European Council in Dublin, Kohl and Mitterrand jointly wrote to the Irish prime minister, Charles Haughey, to urge the convocation of a second IGC on political union "parallel with" that on EMU. They further urged that the preparatory work for the IGC on EMU be accelerated with the objective of ratifying any changes made by the two IGCs before January 1993. At a rapidly convened second summit in Dublin in June 1990, the Twelve decided to adopt this suggestion. The summit communiqué spoke of the need to transform the Community "from an entity primarily based on economic integration and political cooperation into a political union."[29]

The Mitterrand–Kohl initiative stimulated dark, atavistic fears among the British governing class. While Thatcher did eventually cooperate fully in the 2+4 talks, the prospect of German unification prompting further European integration seems to have unhinged the British prime minister and her circle of close advisers. In July 1990, a British newspaper, the *Independent on Sunday,* published the leaked minutes of a seminar held some months previously between Mrs. Thatcher and half a dozen British and American academic experts on Germany. The minutes, it is generally agreed, were more a reflection of the prime minister's deepest concerns than a summary of the scholarly expertise offered to her by the seminar's participants. They identified "angst, aggressiveness, assertiveness, bullying, egotism, inferiority complex and sentimentality" to be the essence of the German national character. Astonishingly, the minutes implied that "the way in which the Germans currently used their elbows and threw their weight about in the Community" suggested that "a lot still had not changed" from the days of Hitlerism.[30] A few days before the *Independent on Sunday*'s scoop, the *Spectator,* a right-wing magazine strongly identified with the Conservative leader, had published an interview with Nicholas Ridley, the minister for Trade and Industry. Ridley was Mrs. Thatcher's closest cabinet ally, one of the few senior Conservatives whom the Tory leader regarded as "One of Us." In the interview, Ridley described European integration as "a German racket designed to take over the whole of Europe." The magazine cover announcing the interview caricatured Helmut Kohl as (a somewhat portly) Hitler.[31] Ridley was forced to resign in the ensuing public outcry, although the prime minister was plainly sorry to see him go.

One does not have to be a Germanophile, or a passionate supporter of European integration, to regard Thatcher and Ridley's diagnosis of the threat posed by German unification as embarrassingly puerile. But, in the light of the principles of the Bruges speech, it is easy to understand why Mrs. Thatcher lapsed into such a mood. From the point of view of the London government, it must have seemed as if events were suddenly skidding hopelessly out of control. At Dublin, in addition to the commitment to political union, the rest of the Twelve had dismissed Britain's own economically sophisticated plan for a so-called hard Ecu as a substitute for a single currency. The hard Ecu scheme proposed, in effect, to reverse the direction of the monetary integration suggested by the Delors report. Instead of instituting, as Delors had essentially proposed, a central bank that would issue a single currency, Britain proposed that a new "European Monetary Fund" should issue a common "parallel" currency that would eventually be managed by a central bank. This currency would be the Ecu. The Ecu would have a permanently fixed value against each of the currencies of the Twelve and bank notes denominated in Ecu would be freely redeemable in any Community country. Citizens of the Community and businesses would thus be able to get used to working with a common currency and, eventually, a climate of opinion favorable to giving up the individual national currencies might assert itself. At that point, the EMF could officially be transformed into a central bank.

From Mrs. Thatcher's point of view, the advantage of this plan was the use of the conditional tense. For the foreseeable future, British citizens *would* buy their daily bread in pounds and pence, but in the future they *could* choose to adopt a single currency for the sake of simplicity. The decision, however, was not one the government, or the EC, *should* take just yet—and it became plain that Mrs. Thatcher thought that it was a decision that *ought* never to be taken.[32] At Dublin, however, the hard Ecu was regarded by Britain's partners as a complication that would only lead to unnecessary delay in the achievement of monetary union.

After Ireland, the presidency of the EC passed to Italy. Just before the first Rome summit of the Italian presidency, Britain joined the ERM at a parity of 2.95DM to the pound. Mrs. Thatcher went to Rome seemingly expecting to be congratulated for having kept her word. Instead, pressed by Chancellor Kohl, the Italians organized the so-called ambush in Rome. Eleven out of twelve states committed themselves to starting stage 2 of the EMU process on 1 January 1994, thus setting a specific deadline for moving towards currency union. Britain flatly refused to accept this development. The final communiqué also made equally specific commitments to transforming the Community into a Union, extending the number of areas of competence in which the new Union could act, empowering the European Parliament by adding to its legislative powers and precisely defining European citizenship. It added that a consensus had emerged on the need for a common foreign and defense policy for the Community. After each of these commitments, the final communiqué was punctuated with an asterisk indicating that the British government reserved its position pending the debate due to take place in the IGC.[33]

The Rome summit thus left nobody in any doubt that the battle announced in the Bruges speech was about to be joined. It would be Britain against the rest. No politician can ignore public opinion, and the British tabloid press was boiling up into a froth of hysteria equaled, in modern times, only by the 1982 Falklands War. At the press conference immediately after the summit, responding to Jacques Delors's comment that the EC would have a single currency by 2000, Mrs. Thatcher promised that she would use the government's majority in the House of Commons to block ratification of any treaty that was not in British interests. The *Sun* newspaper, in a moment of inspired chauvinistic

wordplay, shrieked in approval, "Up Yours, Delors! " Speaking in the House of
Commons two days later, Mrs. Thatcher made the same point tersely and with
passion. She claimed that the Commission was trying to "extinguish democracy" and create a federal Europe by the back door: "If you hand over your sterling, you hand over the powers of this parliament to Europe." In front of a
House hypnotized by the "sheer force of her presence," she declared that her
answer to Europe's federalists was, "No, no, no!"[34]

The British negotiating position in the IGCs was thus clear. Had Mrs.
Thatcher remained as British prime minister, there could have been no Maastricht treaty—or else, the other member states would have been driven to establish some new treaty arrangement superseding the EC altogether and excluding Britain. But Mrs. Thatcher did not remain as prime minister. Her
intransigence after Rome was the last straw for Sir Geoffrey Howe, who had
been demoted by Thatcher after the Madrid summit and who now resigned
from her government, citing the need for Britain to be "at the center of the
European partnership" as his reason for going. Howe's resignation speech
was a masterpiece of controlled fury, which unquestionably wounded
Thatcher's authority over the party.[35]

Howe's departure brought to the surface a growing dissatisfaction within
the Conservative Party with Mrs. Thatcher. Never popular with the party's
aristocratic grandees, for whom she was a lower-middle-class upstart with
dangerously radical ideas, Thatcher had been tolerated while she was successful. In 1990, however, her star was beginning to wane. It had become
evident that the much-vaunted economic boom of the late 1980s, which had
led to soaring inflation and house prices at giddy levels, was about to give
way to a painful bout of economic retrenchment. Other policies, such as the
introduction in 1989 of a deeply unpopular poll tax to finance local government, had gone badly awry. Now, the Conservative leader appeared to be
alienating herself from the European mainstream. In November 1990, most
Conservative MPs still favored Howe's preference for engagement with Europe to Thatcher's strident rejection of Europe and all its works.

Thatcher's opponents therefore rallied around the candidature of Michael
Heseltine, a noted supporter of European integration and former defense
minister, when he challenged Mrs. Thatcher for the leadership of the Conservative Party shortly after Howe's resignation. Heseltine received 152
votes in the contest, Thatcher 204. The party's somewhat arcane rules
stated, however, that to avoid a second ballot, the winner in the first round
had to receive 65 percent of the votes cast. Thatcher was a mere four votes
short. Her failure to win the first ballot provoked a polite rebellion within
her cabinet, with many ministers hinting that if she fought on she would lose
their support. Thatcher resigned and in a second ballot, the chancellor of the
exchequer, John Major, beat Heseltine and the foreign secretary, Douglas
Hurd, to become leader of the party and hence, given the Conservatives'

majority in the House of Commons, prime minister. Had just two of Heseltine's supporters voted for Thatcher, the result might have been regarded as a vindication of Thatcher's policy on Europe, and the rest of the EC might have had to deal with a revitalized British prime minister in the two IGCs— an instructive reminder of the importance of contingency in political events.

Although there were other important reasons why Mrs. Thatcher had lost the confidence of her party, Europe was the touchstone issue. The decision of the EC to proceed towards further economic and political integration, in short, had caused the fall of Britain's most powerful peacetime prime minister of the twentieth century. And though John Major immediately asserted that he wanted Britain to be "at the very heart of Europe," the scars left by Mrs. Thatcher's downfall within the Conservative Party ensured that the British government was obliged to negotiate during the IGCs with one eye always on domestic public opinion and the opinion of the Thatcherites in the parliamentary party and in the cabinet. For a large part of the Conservative Party and press, Europe was now an issue that went deeper than party loyalty. The pro-Europeans had stabbed their beloved leader in the back; they would destroy any government that compromised British sovereignty. Major's room for maneuver during the IGC negotiations was thus correspondingly slim.

THE "HOUR OF EUROPE"

The two IGCs were very different from each other. The IGC on EMU, which could work from the template of the Delors report, was relatively smooth going, although this is not to say that there were not moments of hard bargaining between the governments before a final text emerged— there were. Three issues were crucial: when would the European Central Bank be established? What would the criteria of national economic performance be to qualify for EMU and how rigorously would they be enforced? How would the British question be resolved? Britain fought hard, but fruitlessly, during the negotiations for there to be a generalized right for member states to opt out of EMU before the introduction of a single currency.[36] This idea found little support for obvious reasons. Nobody was going to sign up to a treaty that would have allowed Germany to back out before the Bundesbank's authority was surrendered. In November 1991, the Community's finance ministers agreed that the treaty would contain a specific provision regarding Britain, although the final formulation was left to the decisive Maastricht summit of the heads of government in December. On the other two questions, Germany for the most part got her way.

The IGC on political union, which began in the "Rome II" European Council in December 1990 with no more than a vague list of topics (citizenship, foreign policy, institutional reform, the social charter) for debate, was altogether more acrimonious. The Commission and such enthusiastic proponents of European federalism as Belgium, Germany, Italy and the Netherlands pushed hard at various times for radical and far-reaching reforms that would have established the EC's *vocation fédérale* beyond argument, but the opposition of France and, above all, Britain, to any treaty changes that overturned the essentially intergovernmental character of the EC was a powerful obstacle blocking such moves.

Franco-British objections extended to the form (not just the substance) that the new treaty would take. The Commission and the more enthusiastically integrationist member states preferred the forthcoming treaty to be a "tree." By this, they meant that any innovations would be incorporated, on the model of the single-market clauses of the SEA, into the existing treaty texts as new chapters. France and Britain, by contrast, were insistent that the new treaty should be built around three "pillars," the so-called Greek temple approach. The first of these pillars was the existing EEC treaty, as amended by the SEA and reinforced by the inclusion of EMU. The second pillar would be justice and home affairs; the third, foreign policy. The last two would remain areas of intergovernmental cooperation over which the Commission and the Parliament could exercise no authority.

In the end, the Greek temple won this argument, but it was not without a struggle. Luxembourg, which presided over the Council of Ministers in the first half of 1991, presented a draft treaty on European Union in April that reflected the pillar structure. This first draft was criticized severely by a narrow majority of the member states. On 20 June, accordingly, Luxembourg presented a second version that retained the pillar structure, but, as a compromise, contained a good deal more federalist rhetoric in the preamble. The treaty, it was claimed, "marked a new stage in the process leading gradually to a Union with a federal goal" and included a clause stating that in 1996 a new IGC would be called with the aim of "strengthening the federal character of the Union."[37]

It was a compromise that satisfied neither the "federalist camp" nor the Thatcherite right of the Conservative Party in Britain. The Belgian parliament passed a motion on 27 June 1991 insisting that "European integration must lead to a Union with a democratic system and a federal structure" and rejecting what it called the "tripartite structure" invented by the Luxembourg presidency; Mrs. Thatcher, by contrast, spoke in the House of Commons of a "conveyer belt towards federalism" and a hue and cry began in the anti-European press in London. In September 1991, the Dutch, instigated by Delors, started their presidency of the Council of Ministers by presenting an overtly federal draft that demanded hugely increased powers for the European Parliament and that, in line with the tree approach, incorporated foreign policy into the draft treaty.[38] Only the Belgians supported this initiative, which plainly came too late in the negotiations to be feasible, and both

Dutch diplomacy and the Commission emerged somewhat humiliated from the experience. After September 1991, the pillar approach was the only one possible.

Delors's insistence on making foreign policy an integral part of the Community framework was linked to the EC's generally lamentable performance during the Persian Gulf and Yugoslavian crises during 1991. As David Buchan has written, Yugoslavia represented a "tragic failure" in which the Community ended up "aggravating the crisis it was supposed to solve."[39] It is in fact a measure of the immensity of the challenges facing the EC's leaders in 1991 that the two IGCs—themselves hugely important developments that required the member states' full attention—were often overshadowed during the year by the twin foreign policy crises dominating the headlines. Both in the Gulf and in Yugoslavia, the EC proved quite unable to frame a common policy and stick to it (or, in the case of Yugoslavia, make it stick).

In the case of the Gulf crisis, which blew up in August 1990 when the Iraqi leader Saddam Hussein invaded neighboring Kuwait, the EC initially acted unanimously to impose economic and technical sanctions on Iraq. The EC also spoke with one voice in warning the Iraqi dictator that any attempt to "harm or jeopardize" the safety of the citizens of EC countries in his power (there were several thousand, mostly workers in the oil industry) would provoke a "united response from the entire Community."[40] The EC also pledged substantial sums in aid to the frontline states most directly menaced by the Iraqi army (Egypt, Turkey, Jordan). This common front soon began to unravel, however. France managed to get its hostages out separately by a murky unilateral deal; Germany tacitly backed a piece of freelance diplomacy by the veteran German statesman Willi Brandt who flew to Baghdad shortly after the October 1990 Rome European Council had decided that the individual states would not negotiate separately for the release of their hostages.[41] The aid money promised so generously in August only trickled out. It took the EC until October before a package worth two billion dollars was agreed by the EC's finance ministers, and then Britain held up matters further by insisting that its substantial commitment to the military buildup in the Gulf meant that it should be exempted from contributing to such payments. The Greeks even apparently tried to get their partners to charge interest on the loan to Turkey![42] It was not until the new year that aid money began to get through. As the prospect of war began to loom in January 1991, France took a wholly independent line from its Community partners. On 14 January 1991, France proposed that the crisis could be resolved, after an Iraqi withdrawal from Kuwait, by a Middle East peace conference. Her Community partners were less outraged by the content of this plan than by the fact that France did not deign to inform any of them in advance. The EC foreign ministers had met that morning and had the right, under the rules of political cooperation, to expect that they would be consulted.

When war broke out, the EC countries, Britain and France excepted, were able to contribute little of substance to the military effort and France, which was not integrated into NATO's command structure, was the source of a good many problems for the American-led operation. Germany was handicapped by its Basic Law from deploying troops outside the NATO area of command. In the end, she sent a token force of air personnel and some fighter aircraft to Turkey. Even this limited step was controversial in Germany, where public opinion was strongly opposed to the use of force against the Iraqis. The German government had to content itself with checkbook diplomacy: it has been estimated that Bonn paid as much as one-third of the final cost of the war. Italy similarly had to contend with a vociferous minority of hostile public opinion—which included the Church—and a constitutional provision against going to war. Italy's parliament eventually agreed to participate in an "international policing operation" and dispatched three warships and a fighter squadron to the Gulf, where the airmen in particular took an active operational role and suffered one loss. Spain sent warships to the Gulf, but removed them when the fighting started. Spanish politicians and public opinion were in the forefront of those opposing the campaign of aerial bombardment against targets within Iraq.. The Dutch navy played an active role in the fighting, but the Netherlands' contribution was necessarily small. In general, while most EC countries provided money for Desert Storm (as the military operation was named), helped with ancillary tasks such as minesweeping and medical care and permitted refueling for American bombers and transport aircraft, the Community's military contribution, Britain and France always excepted, was negligible. Insofar as the ability to project military force is one of the classic distinguishing features of a genuine state, Europe's more gung-ho federalists were forced to recognize that in this regard at least a united Europe did not yet begin to exist.

Delors's desire to integrate foreign and defense policy into the Community framework started from this fact. In a speech to the International Institute for Strategic Studies (IISS) in London in March 1991, Delors made a lucid presentation of the Commission's internal discussions on foreign policy questions in the light of the "object lesson" of the Gulf War.[43] Delors argued that the war against Iraq had shown that "once it became obvious that the situation would have to be resolved by armed combat, the Community had neither the institutional machinery nor the military force to allow it to act as a community." He appealed for the Community to "shoulder its share of the political and military responsibilities of our old nations." The Commission's preferred way of doing this was to resurrect the Western European Union (WEU). The WEU had bumbled along innocuously since its creation in the wake of the debacle of the EDC in 1954, but during the Gulf crisis it had suddenly emerged as a forum for separate European discussion of defense questions. The Commission, backed by the French government, now began to see the WEU as a potential cornerstone for a European foreign and defense policy. Delors, in his speech to the IISS, asserted that the EC could "take over" the "mutual assistance" clause of the 1948 Treaty of Brussels (see chapter 2) and incorporate it into the EC treaty framework.[44] The European Council would decide broad foreign policy guidelines by unanimous vote, but specific actions would then be decided by qualified majority voting in the Council of Ministers. Delors was insistent that the Americans, who had voiced worries that this creation of a European defense identity would swiftly become a rival to NATO rather than a reinforcement, need have no fears. The new Europe would be willing "to shoulder a larger burden than before"—which had to be in American interests.

This, of course, was a moot point. The Americans were unconvinced. Delors's speech prompted the United States to reiterate three conditions that its chief defense spokesmen had already presented as limitations upon a future European defense structure: first, there should be no European caucus within NATO; second, that non-EC members of NATO (such as Norway, Turkey) should not be marginalized; third, no European defense structure alternative to NATO should be established.[45] Britain strove during the political union negotiations to find a middle way between the Delors position and the American stance by suggesting that the WEU—kept resolutely free from any entanglement with the EC—might become a forum for European cooperation in NATO "out-of-area" operations like the Gulf War. In the jargon, the WEU would be a "bridge" to NATO, which would remain the chief forum for defense cooperation between the countries of western Europe.

The Americans' suspicion of an independent European foreign policy were fueled by the attitude of the French government, and Delors personally, during the so-called Uruguay round of international trade talks that had begun in 1986. By the end of 1990, the talks were sinking into a bog of mutual recrimination over agriculture, textiles and so-called audiovisual services (television and films). The member states were divided over what line to take during the trade talks, with some countries, notably Britain and the Netherlands, favoring freer trade and other nations (France, above all, but also Portugal, which had a quarter of its industrial workforce employed in the textiles industry) taking a harder line. In France, at least, the determination was strong to preserve the amount of subsidies paid to farmers through the CAP and to fight for the retention of the October 1989 "television without frontiers" EC directive that obliged the member states to "ensure, where practicable and by appropriate means," that "a majority proportion of their transmission time, excluding the time appointed to news, sports events, games, advertising and teletext services" were reserved for "European works."[46] French opinion spilled over into a froth of anti-Americanism in 1990–1991 over farming and television, with accusations of Anglo-Saxon cultural imperialism being cheerfully flung about by politicians and intellectuals of both the right and left. Delors himself fanned the flames. At a press conference after the Rome II European Council in December 1990, Delors accused the Americans of treating the EC "as if it had the plague" and said that he would not be "an accomplice to the depopulation of the land."[47] It was hardly the ideal moment for Delors to be hinting at European foreign policy independence.

The EC's failure during the Gulf conflict to act as a Community, mixed with the excitement generated by the ongoing political union negotiations, and resentment against perceived American high-handedness during the trade talks are the most plausible causes of the EC's misguided attempt from the spring of 1991 to settle the brewing crisis in Yugoslavia. As Ross writes: "Yugoslavia . . . was the first real test since the Gulf War of the EC's capacities to act internationally. Much was at stake. The test would be seen as a measure of the Community's ability to practice a common foreign and security policy."[48] Given its track record, one might have expected the EC to approach the boiling cauldron of Yugoslavia, with its ethnic hatreds, historical feuds and post-Communist economic collapse, with some prudence.

Instead, the Community plunged in knee deep. It decided that it would back the effort of the president of the Yugoslav federation, Ante Markovic, to preserve Yugoslavia as a "confederation of sovereign republics, akin to the European Community of the Balkans."[49] In April 1991, in pursuit of this goal, the first of many EC "troikas," representing past, present and future EC presidencies (in this case, the foreign ministers of Italy, Luxembourg and the Netherlands), went to Belgrade and offered a substantial aid package to the Yugoslavs. In retrospect—but not only in retrospect—this policy of dangling carrots before the republics of Yugoslavia was doomed to failure from the beginning. Comparatively wealthy Slovenia and ultranationalist Croatia were too determined to split away from a federation that they regarded as Serb-dominated. Moreover, it was obvious that Serbia would not allow these two republics to defect from the federation without first attempting to safeguard the considerable Serb minorities in Croatia. On 30 May 1991, Serbian leader Slobodan Milosevic warned, on the eve of a visit to Belgrade by Delors and Luxembourg premier Jacques Santer, that Croatia would have to surrender the territories inhabited by ethnic Serbs if it wanted independence.[50] Civil war was therefore inevitable unless the republics could be prevented from fighting by the intervention of a superior military force. The carrot of economic aid was manifestly not enough; Europe needed—if it wanted to get involved in the Balkans at all—to wield a big stick as well. But Europe had no stick to wield. All Delors and Santer could offer was aid and closer relations, provided Yugoslavia remained a federation with a single market, currency and central bank; a single army; a single foreign policy and a system of guarantees for human rights. In the prevailing political climate in Yugoslavia in the spring of 1991, these requirements were simply utopian.

When Slovenia and Croatia did declare independence, at the end of June 1991, and fighting broke out between the Serb-controlled Yugoslav army and the insurgent republics, the EC appeared monumentally unaware of its limited ability to influence the conflict. Jacques Poos, the Luxembourg foreign minister, and president of the Council of Ministers for a few more days, notoriously proclaimed, "This is the hour of Europe. It is not the hour of the Americans."[51] He might have done better to preserve a dignified silence. Neither an EC-imposed arms embargo on Yugoslavia, nor the so-called Brioni Agreement, which was signed on 7 July and bound the warring parties both to effectuate a cease-fire and, by 1 August, to begin serious talks about their future relations, managed to stop the fighting for any length of time. EC observers were to be allowed into the war zones of Slovenia and "possibly also Croatia." Dressed in white, which won them the sobriquet of "the ice cream men," these brave individuals (they were unarmed and unescorted; several were killed) were ideally positioned to monitor the repeated breaches of the Brioni accords by all parties throughout the summer of 1991. On 1 September, the EC negotiated what was called at the time "a window of opportunity." The EC threatened the Serbs, whose brutality had by now led to their being widely regarded as the villains of the piece, with "international action" unless they agreed to a new cease-fire and agreed to allow EC monitors into Croatia. A peace conference, chaired by Lord Peter Carrington, an internationally respected British diplomat, began on 7 September at the Hague.

At this point, the Community's role in the crisis became bogged down in the internal political dispute over the status of the WEU. France had proposed in August that an EC peacekeeping force be sent to the Balkans under the auspices of the WEU—a suggestion that was transparently designed to promote her agenda in the ongoing IGC. The British, in part because their experience in Northern Ireland had taught them that it was easier to send troops into a trouble spot than get them out, in part because they did not want the WEU to take on excessive importance, were implacably opposed. The Germans, who were staunchly pro-Croat, cautiously backed the French. Since, however, there was no question of German troops being sent to the war zone, this stance struck many as hypocritical. The whole debate was in any case somewhat hypothetical, since everybody agreed that there was no question of such troops being committed to *enforce* a settlement that was not acknowledged by all the parties. This lack of political will—and military clout—fatally hamstrung the peace plan proposed by Lord Carrington on 18 October 1991. Backed by the United States and Russia, the plan proposed independence for all Yugoslavia's republics on the basis of the existing frontiers in tandem with comprehensive guarantees for safeguarding the human rights of ethnic and national groups who found themselves on the wrong side of a border. The plan was simply disregarded on the ground, where the Serb minority within Croatia were fighting for union with the Serb motherland and were not willing to accept the restitution of a Croat rule they both feared and despised.[52]

By mid-November, as negotiations for what became the Maastricht treaty drew to a close, the Community began the process of disengaging from the Yugoslavia conflict. From November 1991 onward, the UN and, increasingly, the United States, became the chief outside mediators in the Balkans' crisis. Community action (or inaction) in Yugoslavia had, by the time the heads of government met in Maastricht on 9 December 1991, undermined "any credible common foreign and security policy."[53] The much-vaunted foreign policy pillar of the Treaty on European Union amounted to no more than a feeble set of hopes and half-promises. In the defense field, the Twelve agreed (art. J4) that the common foreign and security policy "shall include all questions related to the security of the Union, including the eventual framing of a common defense policy, which might in time lead to a common defense." The WEU was requested to "elaborate and implement decisions and actions of the Union that have defense implications," but the policy of the Union would "not prejudice" the obligations of "certain member states under the North Atlantic Treaty and [shall] be compatible with the common security and defense policy established within that framework."

The treaty only paid lip service to a common foreign policy, too. While article J1 of the treaty bound the states to "define and implement" a common foreign and security policy and to "refrain from any action that is contrary to the interests of the Union or likely to impair its effectiveness as a cohesive force in international relations," nothing in the treaty explained how the member states would be made to do this. Neither the European Council nor the Council of Ministers was empowered to deal with crises, or take strategic decisions, by a qualified majority binding on all the member states. Article J2 merely prescribed that "member states shall inform and consult one another within the Council . . . in order to ensure that their combined influence is exerted as effectively as possible by means of concerted and convergent action." After Maastricht, the Twelve agreed that geographical "proximity" should be the key criterion for so-called joint action by the member states. The Twelve would try to formulate a common foreign policy toward those areas—Eastern Europe, the Balkans and the Middle East— that most directly impinged upon them.[54]

Before the treaty had even been signed, however, Germany illustrated with embarrassing clarity how far rhetoric about "concerted and convergent action" actually extended by unilaterally recognizing the independence of Croatia and Slovenia. Germany had been pressuring the rest of the Community to recognize the two breakaway republics since November and on 16 December 1991 had persuaded the rest of the Twelve to recognize, by 15 January 1992, the independence of *any* of the Yugoslav republics that could meet a series of tests concerning their policy toward human rights, guarantees for minorities, democratic government, commitment to the peaceful negotiation of border disputes and so on. The president of the French Constitutional Court, Robert Badinter, was charged with drawing up a balance sheet of the republics' performance by these standards and with making recommendations. Without waiting for Badinter's findings, and in the face of warnings from top UN officials and the government of Bosnia-Herzegovina about the certain bloody consequences recognition would have elsewhere in Yugoslavia, Germany proceeded to recognize Slovenia and Croatia on 23 December 1991, although as a sop to the rest of the Twelve Germany stated that diplomatic relations would only begin on 15 January.[55]

Germany's action was presumably dictated by the well-founded fear that Badinter would not give semifascist Croatia a passing grade. In fact, when the French lawyer reported in early January, he approved only Slovenia and Macedonia. The Community proceeded anyway to recognize the sovereign status of Slovenia and Croatia, but did *not* recognize Macedonia, because the Greeks, who were nervous about Macedonian irredentism, were opposed.

The EC, after spending more than six months trying to hold Yugoslavia together, then wholly endorsed the U.S. policy of dismantling the federal Yugoslavian state. Bosnian president Alija Izetbegović was informed that Bosnia would be recognized, too, if a simple democratic majority of Bosnians voted for independence. Peace in Bosnia had been maintained for the previous forty years by subordinating a majoritarian view of democracy to the constitutional need to preserve the ethnic power balance between the Muslims, Croats and Serbs that comprised Bosnia's population.[56] If Bosnia declared independence, without first allowing its predominately Serb areas to secede, its Serb community, backed by Serbia itself, was bound to revolt. Sure enough, once the referendum had been held on 1 March 1992, and a majority obtained for independence from Belgrade, fierce clashes swiftly began in rural districts. Once the EC and the United States had recognized the new Bosnian state on 5 April 1992, the conflict escalated and rapidly became the most barbaric military campaign seen in Europe since the downfall of the Nazis.

Yugoslavia was clearly a tragedy waiting to happen. Its surging cultural and ethnic hatreds meant that civil war was always a possibility. Yet, it is hard to deny that the EC's interventions made a bad situation worse. As Simon Nuttall has written, the EC aspired to be the *deus ex machina* of the Yugoslav crisis; the god that descends from the clouds in a Greek tragedy and sets all to rights.[57] And, indeed, its early attempts to broker a peace can be seen as well-intentioned and far from futile. But gods possess overwhelming force and the will to use it. The EC had neither. Far from being godlike, during the Yugoslav crisis, the EC more closely resembled a harassed and overcivilized teacher struggling to separate school-yard bullies. Unable and unwilling on

principle to clip the Yugoslavs around the ear, the EC was reduced to pleading ineffectually for good behavior from the sidelines until its most powerful
member state decided the farce had gone on long enough. The authority
with which Germany acted in December 1991 was a potent reminder to the
rest of the Twelve of the need to bind united Germany tightly within European institutions.

THE MAASTRICHT TREATY

The treaty that emerged from the two IGCs and from the last-minute negotiating scramble between Europe's leaders during the Maastricht European
Council on 9–10 December 1991 was a constitutional lawyer's delight—and
something of an unreadable nightmare for any normal human being.[58] Yet,
difficult though it was to understand, it soon became clear to public opinion
in Europe that Maastricht represented an unprecedented voluntary cession
of national sovereignty. Every member state except Britain and Denmark in
principle relinquished its long-term right to make its own monetary policy
(and, in the short term, committed itself to meeting austere and deflationary
economic targets); every state except Britain acknowledged that it would
abide by common Community standards in the field of social policy. Individual Europeans, long used to thinking of themselves as Belgians,
Spaniards, Italians or Germans, discovered that they had been transformed—
as it seemed, overnight—into citizens of a European Union (EU). Maastricht was, in reality, less an international treaty than a tentative constitutional act negotiated by traditional diplomatic means. Little effort had been
made either to discover whether the citizens of the new Union actually
wanted the innovations of the treaty, or even to explain what the innovations
were and why they were necessary. The Treaty on European Union was presented as a fait accompli by the political class of the Twelve. Unsurprisingly,
the voters in several countries of the Community—notably Denmark and
France—subsequently decided to punish such presumption (see chapter 8).

   This widespread sense that Maastricht had been imposed upon the peoples
of Europe was, in fact, somewhat ironic since one of the main concerns of
the treaty was to render the institutions of European integration less remote
from the citizen. The treaty's preamble stressed (art. A) that the decision to
establish a Union would mark "a new stage in the process of creating an ever
closer union among the peoples of Europe, in which decisions are taken as
closely as possible to the citizen." The buzzword during the negotiations was
subsidiarity. With the Maastricht treaty, the EU had defined the areas of policy that were the competence of supranational institutions. In future, as article 3b insisted, the Community would take action "only if and in so far as
the objectives of the proposed action cannot be sufficiently achieved by the

Member States and can therefore, by reason of the scale or the effects of the proposed action, be better achieved by the Community."

The principal innovation of the Maastricht treaty was economic and monetary union. Articles 3, 4 and 102 through 109 of the EEC treaty were substantially amended to incorporate the new provisions relating to EMU and a lengthy fifty-three-article protocol establishing the statute of the "European System of Central Banks and of the European Central Bank" was also attached to the treaty. Additional protocols laying down the precise "convergence criteria" of economic fundamentals that member states would have to meet in order to qualify for monetary union were also attached. In substance, the contracting parties agreed that they would move toward EMU in three stages. Stage 1 was held to have begun on 1 July 1990; stage 2 was to start on 1 January 1994, in accordance with the decision of the October 1990 Rome summit. In stage 2, a European Monetary Institute (EMI) was to be established. The EMI was a central bank only in embryo. Its statute—set out in a separate protocol attached to the treaty—conferred upon the EMI the task of coordinating the member states' monetary policy, but it did not give the new institution the power to interfere in the decisions of the member states' central banks. The EMI's key task during stage 2 was to monitor, in conjunction with the Commission, the progress being made by the member states toward meeting the convergence criteria in advance of an examination in 1996 of their progress.

There were five criteria in all. Would-be members

- were restricted from running annual government deficits of more than 3 percent of GDP at market prices;
- could possess a national debt no greater than 60 percent of GDP;
- were bound to keep inflation within 1.5 percent of the average of the three "best-performing member states" for a full year prior to the examination;
- could boast a currency that had "without severe tensions" respected the "normal fluctuation margins" of the ERM for at least two years; and
- had maintained for a full year an average nominal interest rate on their long-term government debt that did not exceed by more than 2 percent the average of the three best-performing member states.

In theory, failure to meet these criteria could lead to the offending country facing financial penalties "of an appropriate size" imposed by the Council of Ministers (art. 104c). The treaty allowed for some flexibility in meeting the first two of these targets, however. Failure to meet the 3 percent annual deficit criterion could be condoned if the offending state had managed to get its deficit down "substantially and continuously" to a level that did not much exceed the 3 percent reference value; alternatively, if a usually prudent state had exceptionally and temporarily exceeded the target, allowances could be made (104c). Exceeding the permitted total of national debt could be forgiven if the debt/GDP ratio was "sufficiently diminishing and approaching the reference value at sufficient pace" (art. 104c).

If seven out of twelve member states could meet these five criteria, the European Council could choose to move to stage 3 of EMU in 1997. In the event that an insufficient number of countries were still unable to meet the convergence criteria, however, the treaty allowed for a delay of one year in the move to stage 3. If, however, at the end of 1997, a critical mass of seven countries had still not been achieved, the virtuous remainder were legally obliged to press on with stage 3 from 1 January 1999, to take the "irrevocable step" of fixing the relative value of their currencies and, eventually, to introduce a common currency. The only way, therefore, that the member states whose macroeconomic fundamentals were basically sound, such as Germany and the Netherlands, could wriggle out of their commitment at Maastricht was to take the irrational decision to run their economies in deliberate breach of the convergence criteria. By contrast, the only way countries such as Italy, whose annual budget deficit was over 9 percent of GDP and whose accumulated public debt was over 120 percent of GDP, could hope to meet the standards set by the convergence criteria was to tread unaccustomed paths of austerity pretty rapidly.

Britain and Denmark were the only exceptions to the iron rule of irrevocability.[59] Britain was specifically given the privilege of "opting in" to stage 3 "by a separate decision of its government and Parliament." British national honor had been saved, but, as Forster argues, "the outcome of the year-long negotiations was more like a stay of execution than a permanent reprieve from confronting the issues involved in EMU."[60] The question to join or not to join would become over the next few years an open wound in the body of the British body politic, and in particular in the Conservative Party. But it is difficult to see what alternative Prime Minister Major had. Major had to satisfy both his Thatcherite wing (and with an election due in 1992, he could not possibly take any step that would split his party) and handle his European partners' perfectly reasonable reluctance to allow Britain special privileges. The opt-in formula allowed everybody to save face and was something of a personal triumph for the prime minister.

In stage 3 of EMU, the European Central Bank (ECB) and the European System of Central Banks (ESCB) would be finally established. The ESCB was to be composed of the ECB and the central banks of the member states. Its primary objective was to conduct monetary and exchange rate policy in such a way as to maintain price stability—although, interestingly, this concept was not precisely defined. Its independence from political interference was to be absolute. Article 7 of the ESCB's statute (and art. 107 of the treaty) stated that "neither the ECB, nor a national central bank, nor any member of their decision-making bodies shall take or seek instructions from Community institutions or bodies, from any government of a member state or from any other body."

The ESCB, as a general principle, was to be governed by the decision-making bodies of the ECB. These were the Governing Council and the Executive Board. The latter of these bodies was to consist of a president, a vice president and four other members, all appointed for an eight-year term by the European Council. The Executive Board was to be responsible for the implementation of monetary policy in accordance with "the guidelines and instructions laid down by the Governing Council," which was to be composed of the members of the Executive Board and the governors of the *participating* national central banks. Since the decisions made by the Governing Council would obviously affect the economies of the nonparticipating states, a further body, the General Council, was created. Composed of the central bank governors of all the EU's member states, plus the president and vice president of the ECB, the General Council was nevertheless a largely advisory body. It had no right or power to influence interest rate decisions.

The politically sensitive task of raising or lowering interest rates was the key duty of the Governing Council. Each member of the Governing Council was to have one vote, with decisions being made by a simple majority.

The ESCB's powers also included the right to set minimum reserve requirements for banks and other credit institutions established in member states and "exclusive right to authorize the issue of bank notes within the Community" (art. 16 of the Protocol). They did *not* include exclusive power to conduct exchange rate policy. Article 109 of the treaty divided this responsibility between the ECB and Ecofin, the Council of Economics and Finance Ministers. Ecofin was empowered to "conclude agreements for an exchange rate system for the Ecu in relation to non-Community currencies" by unanimous vote and could, by qualified majority vote, set the "general orientation" of exchange rate policy. Thus, if the member states of the EU decided in the distant future to improve international monetary coordination by establishing an accord limiting the permitted fluctuation of the Ecu against the dollar and yen, the ECB would have to conduct its exchange rate policy in line with the member states' decision—even if this decision seemed likely to raise inflation.[61]

Overall, the IGC on EMU had produced an agreement that reflected German principles of monetary rigor. Tough macroeconomic targets had been set for would-be members; national central banks would remain independent until stage 3 of the process and would be freed by statute from domestic political interference; the new ECB would be institutionally mandated to deliver low inflation. German policymakers were not entirely happy, however. The decision to set a definitive date for stage 3 of the EMU process raised the suspicion—correctly, as it turned out—that political pressure to fudge the convergence criteria to allow as many countries as possible to join would be immense as stage 3 drew near. But since this concession had been put on the table at Maastricht by Chancellor Kohl, who saw it as a symbolic way for Germany "to demonstrate . . . its will to bind itself to Europe," doubtful German voices could do little more than mutter.[62] It is almost certainly true, too, that Germany's negotiators thought that the convergence criteria could not possibly be blurred enough to allow Italy—the real problem case, since Greece was not even a member of the ERM to enter.

Germany's insistence on insulating the ECB from political pressure, while understandable, unquestionably added to what commentators were beginning to call the EC's "democratic deficit." Objectively, there were good grounds for saying that the statute for the ECB-ESCB agreed at Maastricht was too little accountable to democratic institutions able to supervise their activities. Unlike both the Bundesbank and the U.S. Federal Reserve, the ECB-ESCB was not subject to the power of a national legislature able to amend—or threaten to amend—its statutory powers.[63] The statute establishing the ECB was a treaty between the member states of the European Union and thus could only be altered by all the member states acting in concert together—a distinctly unlikely hypothesis. The only nod in the direction of accountability contained in the Protocol was the requirement that the ECB should publish quarterly reports and make a full annual report on its activities to the other organs of the EU. The president of the ECB was to present the annual report to the European Parliament, which could then debate it. ECB officials could also be asked to testify about their activities before the various committees of the Parliament. It was a very thin democratic veneer. The Parliament had no power to amend the Bank's statute or to censure the Bank's governing institutions and officials. In short, the nations of the new Union had potentially contracted out the immensely sensitive task of steering growth in economic output to a small clique of professional bankers whose training, culture and personal convictions strongly predisposed them to make monetary stability a first priority. It was, in retrospect, a remarkable thing for the heads of government to do. For if the ECB's pursuit of monetary stability at all costs were to depress economic activity and lead to economic stagnation, the people who would "carry the can" for the resulting unemployment would continue to be Europe's politicians.

The ECB-ESCB was by far the most important institutional innovation in the Maastricht treaty, even though, in 1991, it remained something of a mirage by comparison with the omnipotent Bundesbank. Nevertheless, significant new powers were granted to the European Parliament. The Parliament finally obtained the right to co-decision or veto it had been denied in the SEA—and for a surprisingly large number of policy areas, although crucial issues such as agriculture, external trade and competition policy continued to remain outside its purview. The European Parliament was nevertheless now to have the final say on all legislation dealing with the free movement of workers, the provision of services, culture, education programs such as Community-financed student exchanges, consumer protection, trans-European infrastructure, the Community's highly complex programs to stimulate scientific research and development and, most important of all, measures harmonizing national legislation for single-market purposes.

Under co-decision, the Commission and the Council of Ministers had first to reach a common position on a measure before submitting it to the Parliament. The Parliament could either actively approve the measure or make no decision on it. In either case, the measure would become law. If, however, an actual majority of the Parliament (not just a majority of those voting) were opposed, the measure would be sent to a conciliation committee composed of an equal number of representatives from the national governments and from the Parliament. If this committee failed to find a common text acceptable to the Parliament, the measure as a whole was held to have failed. A similar procedure was followed when measures were merely amended, not rejected outright, by the Parliament.

The Parliament also obtained the right to *request* the Commission to submit new policy proposals (though not the right to propose measures itself); it was also charged with the task of establishing a uniform law for its own election—although its choice would be subject to a unanimous vote in the Council of Ministers—and won the right to approve any changes in its own size or composition. The Parliament was given the important new power of being able to pass an initial vote of confidence in a new Commission, and the Commission's own term of office was extended to five years in order to coincide with the life span of the Parliament. In sum, insofar as the Maastricht treaty strengthened the supranational institutions of the Community, it did so by giving new authority to the Community's legislature, rather than its executive (the Commission).

The European Council was formally brought into the Community's decision-making structure for the first time. Article D of the Common Provisions to the treaty stated that the Council was to "provide the Union with the necessary impetus for its development and shall decline the general political guidelines thereof." Since the Common Provisions are not, strictly speaking, part of the treaty itself, the European Council's actions were not subject to the jurisdiction of the ECJ, which itself gained the power at Maastricht (art. 171c) to fine member states that were failing to comply with its rulings: in effect, the authority to find a member state in contempt of court. Earlier, in 1988, the ECJ had been strengthened by the creation of a "Court of First Instance" to help it cope with the huge growth in cases in the wake of the SEA. Last, and probably least, a consultative Committee of the Regions was set up to provide subnational tiers of government a voice in the policymaking process (art. 198).

The number of policy areas in which policies were decided at Community level increased. The Commission was given powers to propose common policies in certain well-defined areas of education, culture, environment, health, transport and telecommunications policy. The right of the Community to pass legislation by QMV on workers' rights and other measures of social protection, which Britain could not accept and which almost caused the collapse of the summit, was the subject of a special protocol, signed by the other eleven member states, to the treaty, which thus gave Britain an opt-out to add to its opt-in on monetary union.[64] When one considers that Britain had ensured that there was no reference to the Union's *vocation féderale* in the treaty either, and that foreign policy decision making was left firmly in the hands of the member states, the triumphant comment by a British government spokesman that the Maastricht summit was "game, set and match" for Britain becomes comprehensible, though it was much resented by Delors and other European leaders. Major returned to London to a laudatory reception from even the most anti-European British newspapers—though that did not stop them from subsequently demonizing the treaty as a sellout of British national sovereignty.[65]

A final feature of the Maastricht treaty that deserves extended discussion is the inclusion of Justice and Home Affairs (JHA) as the second pillar. The Treaty on European Union agreed that strictly intergovernmental cooperation was to proceed on a wide range of areas. The Twelve agreed that asylum policy, border issues, immigration questions, drug addiction, international fraud, judicial cooperation in both civil and criminal matters, customs cooperation and the sharing of police intelligence were all matters of common interest and could be the object, assuming the unanimity of the member states, of joint action by the member states. To this end, a JHA Council of Ministers was established after Maastricht.

In the 1990s, JHA, after a slow start, has been one of the growth areas of European cooperation. The Union "rather grandly" affirmed, in the 1997 Treaty of Amsterdam (see chapter 8) that one of its core objectives was to become "an area of freedom, security and justice."[66] By this, the member states meant, specifically, freedom of movement, security from cross-border crime and judicial cooperation between national legal systems in criminal and civil cases. Quite a lot has been done in the first two of these areas. By the end of the 1990s, the Schengen Treaty, with its small library of related accords and agreements, had been adopted by almost all the member states (Britain and Ireland remain outside, although Iceland and Norway, despite not being members of the EU, participate) and had been incorporated into the first pillar of the Treaty on European Union. Just as in the United States, it is now possible for a non-European citizen to fly into any airport within the Schengen area and, once admitted, have absolute passport-free liberty of movement from one member state to another. Increased freedom of movement, of course, potentially benefits criminals more than honest citizens. As a consequence, in 1995, the member states agreed to establish Interpol, an information clearinghouse to facilitate cross-border inquiries into specific crimes (drugs, illegal immigration, money laundering), which began work in October 1998. Interpol's remit has been further added to since 1998 in response to the growing frequency of cross-border crime, and since 9/11 cooperation against terrorism has given a further incentive to construct common policies in the sphere of citizen security. The substitution of the lengthy process of extradition with the introduction of a "European arrest warrant" has been mooted and should soon become law.

MAKING SENSE OF MAASTRICHT

The Maastricht treaty left the EU as a remarkable hybrid polity of an entirely new kind. It was not a federal state, but a unique confederation with a complex and original structure of government. The political scientist Alberta Sbragia made a successful effort to translate the EU's institutional structure into American terms in her book *Euro-Politics:*

> For Americans to begin to grasp the differences in institutional structure between the United States and the Community, they need to imagine a collective presidency composed of governors, who make the strategic decisions on the development of the constitutional and political system (the European Council); a cabinet (the Commission), which exercises a monopoly over policy initiation as well as considerable leadership, but which is chosen by the states' governors; a very strong Senate (the Council of Ministers), comprising top political leaders chosen by the governors and having the right to amend or veto all proposals made by the cabinet; and a weak House of Representatives (the European Parliament) elected by voters but having the right neither to initiate nor veto most policy proposals.[67]

This unique institutional structure is what this chapter has called the Maastricht compromise. Moreover, by the end of the 1990s, when monetary union had been satisfactorily completed, one could add to the comparison a powerful Federal Reserve (the European Central Bank) composed of national central bankers and accountable for its actions to no directly elected body. It is worth underlining just how great the institutional innovation had been since the Fontainebleau European Council in June 1984. In the early 1980s, the EC had been an intergovernmental organization primarily concerned with agricultural questions—which meant, inevitably, that it spent much of its time arguing over opaque matters of trivial importance. It had pretensions to higher things, but the gap between the rhetoric of European federalists and the reality of the EC's institutions was immense. Less than eight years later, scholars were talking of the "European Union" as a polity of a new kind that would exercise a growing influence and importance in world politics. This was exaggerated, but the transformation described in this chapter *was* remarkable. It must, in fact, be regarded as one of the most important developments in world politics in the latter half of the twentieth century. The question is: what prompted this undeniable speed-up in the pace of integration? What led the Twelve to strengthen the Community's supranational institutions so markedly?

The answer to this question is a combination of national self-interest, supranational idealism and geopolitical realism. Scholars like Andrew Moravcsik are surely right to stress the importance of self-interest in the decision to press ahead to monetary union.[68] Europe's nations wanted monetary union not just because it would make the single market more efficient, though that was a consideration, but because it would enable them to regain a measure of monetary sovereignty from the Bundesbank. The German government was prepared to concede this demand, from fear that countries such as France and Italy would otherwise leave the EMS, but the price of this concession was that the Delors report and the eventual Maastricht treaty subjected would-be members of monetary union to German levels of macroeconomic discipline and institutional independence.

The fact that the member states, Britain and Denmark excepted, acquiesced in this startling formal abdication of sovereignty in such a sensitive area cannot be fully explained, however, without making reference to the European idealism of the leaders who were in charge of the negotiating process. Key leaders were convinced that this, finally, was the "hour of Europe." Dyson and Featherstone, in their huge and intricate account of *The Road to Maastricht*, come to the conclusion that the "vital" element in the monetary union negotiation was that Andreotti, Delors, Kohl and Mitterrand regarded themselves as "Europeans of the heart." These and other European leaders were convinced that "it was necessary to make concessions to sustain momentum towards European political unification and make it irreversible."[69]

But underlying the need to make concessions was not just an ideological leaning towards supranational government. The Maastricht treaty, like the Schuman Plan, was also made with an eye to the changing geopolitical realities of the continent. It was motivated by a deep conviction that the fall of the Berlin Wall and the unstoppable surge towards the reunification of Germany had transformed Europe. In the face of the prospect of the reestablishment of a reunited Germany at the heart of the continent, Europe's leaders felt they had no choice but to conclude an institutional bargain that would anchor Germany into the West.[70] As a result, they hastily tacked on a series of innovations in the political sphere to a treaty on economic union to which most of them were already willing in principle to subscribe.

The German government led the rush. Helmut Kohl and other members of the German political élite at times seemed more alarmed than anybody about the geopolitical challenge reunited Germany posed. Indeed, Germany's commitment to the political unification of Europe did not end with the Maastricht treaty. In December 1992, Germany solemnly amended article 23 of its Basic Law (Constitution) to make the completion of a European Union bound to "democratic, legal, social and federal principles" the official goal of the German state. History should not be written in the subjunctive, but there can be little doubt that if the Berlin Wall had not fallen at that precise moment in 1989, the IGC on political union would not have been put on the table with such abruptness by Kohl and Mitterrand. Monetary union was already a huge and potentially hazardous step forward for the Community. Delors himself seemingly thought that Maastricht had been overambitious. He told Charles Grant: "We shouldn't have made a treaty on political union, it was too soon" and argued that the Community should have made a treaty on monetary union together with a "small treaty" clarifying the role of the EC's main institutions. Delors—somewhat disingenuously, given his own role as an "inspirer"—blamed the governments' own "excessive ambition" for the Community's having gone too far, too fast.[71]

Yet since Maastricht, the European Union's member states have, if anything, raised the bar of their collective ambitions. One might have expected the 1990s to be dominated by a collective effort to digest the huge changes explicit in the Maastricht treaty. Instead, led by Germany, the Union has sought both to "deepen" its existing powers (that is, to increase the range of activities decided by the Union) and to "widen" its membership to encompass the new democracies of Central and Eastern Europe—a decision that has raised fundamental questions about the ability of the Union's current institutions to cope with a future large influx of new members that should be regarded as at least as radical a step as the decision to press for monetary and political union in 1989–1990. Far from being a decade of quiet digestion, the ten years that have passed since the signature of the Maastricht treaty have been characterized both by further nibbling at the delicacies still remaining on the high table of national sovereignty and an acute bout of Maastricht-induced stomachache.

NOTES

1. See Paolo Cecchini, *1992: The Benefits of a Single Market* (Aldershot, U.K.: Wildwood House, 1988), for a summary of the research findings.

2. George Ross, *Jacques Delors and European Integration* (Cambridge: Polity Press, 1995), 18.

3. Tommaso Padoa-Schioppa, *The Road to Monetary Union in Europe* (Oxford: Clarendon, 1994), 4.

4. Mounier's philosophy has come under fire in recent years for its alleged antidemocratic tendencies. See Zeev Sternhall, "Emmanuel Mounier et la Contestation de

la Démocratie liberale dans la France des Années Trente," *Revue Française de Science Politique* 34 (December 1984): 1141–80.

5. Jacques Delors, *La France par L'Europe* (Paris: Grasset, 1988), 70.

6. For the "Paquet Delors," see Gary Marks, "Structural Policy in the European Community," in *Euro-Politics*, ed. A. Sbragia (Washington, D.C.: Brookings Institution, 1992), 191–224, esp. 206–7.

7. Delors, *La France par l'Europe*, 54.

8. Kenneth Dyson and Keith Featherstone, *The Road to Maastricht: Negotiating Economic and Monetary Union* (Oxford: Oxford University Press, 1999), 335–42.

9. Padoa-Schioppa, *Road to Monetary Union*, 8.

10. Dyson and Featherstone, *Road to Maastricht*, 716.

11. Andrew Moravcsik, *The Choice for Europe: Social Purpose and State Power from Messina to Maastricht* (Ithaca, N.Y.: Cornell University Press, 1998), 435.

12. Dyson and Featherstone, *Road to Maastricht*, 715.

13. Dyson and Featherstone, *Road to Maastricht*, 343.

14. Ross, *Jacques Delors and European Integration*, 82.

15. *Report on Economic and Monetary Union in the European Community* ("The Delors Report") (Luxembourg: European Communities, 1989). For an acute discussion of the report, see Niels Thygesen, "The Delors Report," *International Affairs* 65, no. 4 (Winter).

16. Dyson and Featherstone, *Road to Maastricht*, 609.

17. Nico Colchester and David Buchan, *Europe Relaunched: Truths and Illusions on the Way to 1992* (London: Hutchinson, 1990), 171.

18. Margaret Thatcher, *Downing Street Years* (London: HarperCollins, 1993), 709–12, describes a "nasty little meeting" with Howe and Lawson that amounted to "an ambush before Madrid." For further detail, see Philip Stephens, *Politics and the Pound: The Tories, The Economy and Europe* (London: Papermac, 1996), 117–19.

19. Charles Grant, *Delors: Inside the House that Jacques Built* (London: Brealey, 1994), 88–89. The evening before, at a dinner in his honor, the most important union leaders had moved him to tears by singing "Frère Jacques."

20. Margaret Thatcher, "The European Family of Nations" (the Bruges Speech), in *The Eurosceptical Reader*, ed. Martin Holmes (London: Macmillan, 1996), 88–96. All quotations in these paragraphs are from this source.

21. The European Council stated that the Social Charter reflected their "sincere attachment to a model of social relations based on common traditions and practices," *Bull. EC*, no. 12/89, 11.

22. Thatcher, *Downing Street Years*, 750.

23. See Mark Wise and Richard Gibb, *Single Market to Social Europe* (London: Longman Scientific, 1993), 190–96, for a discussion of the three directives.

24. Richard Corbett, "The Intergovernmental Conference on Political Union," *Journal of Common Market Studies* 30 (September 1992): 272.

25. Corbett, "Intergovernmental Conference," 273.

26. Enrico Martial, "I giochi dell'Unione politica europea," *Il Mulino*, no. 4/91: 638.

27. Karl Kaiser, "Germany's Unification," *Foreign Affairs* 70, no. 1 (1991): 186.

28. Dyson and Featherstone, *Road to Maastricht*, 376–77.

29. *Bull. EC*, no. 7/90, 9.

30. *Independent on Sunday*, 15 July 1990, 1.

31. Hugo Young, *This Blessed Plot* (London: Macmillan, 1998), 362.

32. Young, *This Blessed Plot*, 364. Stephens, *Politicians and the Pound*, 162.

33. *Bull. EC*, no. 10/90, 16–19.

34. Stephens, *Politics and the Pound*, 182.

35. See Stephens, *Politics and the Pound*, 182–85, for Howe's resignation.

36. Anthony Forster, *Britain and the Maastricht Negotiations* (London: Macmillan, 1999), 60–68.

37. Corbett, "Intergovernmental Conference," 280. The draft treaty prepared by the Luxembourg presidency and the subsequent first Dutch draft are included in F. Laursen and S. Van Hoonacker, eds., *The Intergovernmental Conference on Political Union* (Dordrecht, The Netherlands: Nijhoff, 1992). This is a useful collection of documents relating to the political union negotiations.

38. Charles Grant, *Delors: The House that Jacques Built* (London: Brealey, 1994), 195.

39. David Buchan, *Europe, The Strange Superpower* (Aldershot, U.K.: Dartmouth Publishing, 1993), 67.

40. Trevor Salmon, "Testing Times for European Political Cooperation: The Gulf and Yugoslavia 1990–1992," *International Affairs* 68, no. 2 (1998): 246–47.

41. Salmon, "Testing Times," 247

42. Buchan, *Europe*, 35.

43. Quoted in Ross, *Jacques Delors and European Integration*, 97–98.

44. Ross, *Jacques Delors and European Integration*, 97–98.

45. Forster, *Britain and the Maastricht Negotiations*, 113.

46. Quoted in Youri Devuyst, "The European Community and the Conclusion of the Uruguay Round," in *The State of the European Union: Building a European Polity*, ed. Carolyn Rhodes and Sonia Mazey (Boulder, Colo.: Lynne Rienner, 1996), 457. The text of the directive is to be found in the *Official Journal of the European Communities*, 17 October 1989, 23–30.

47. Quoted Grant, *Delors: The House that Jacques Built*, 172. Delors was subsequently accused of trying, at the behest of the French government, to wreck the Uruguay round in November 1992. The commissioner for trade, the Irishman Ray MacSharry, briefly resigned when Delors allegedly told him that the deal he had negotiated on agriculture would certainly be vetoed by the French government. Only massive pressure on Delors from the British, Dutch and German governments got the talks back on track again and got MacSharry his job back. See Grant, *Delors: The House that Jacques Built*, 174–180.

48. Ross, *Jacques Delors and European Integration*, 168.

49. Jonathon Eyal, *Europe and Yugoslavia* (London: Royal United Services for Defence Studies, 1993), 4.

50. Eyal, *Europe and Yugoslavia*, 13.

51. *New York Times*, 29 June 1991, 4.

52. By asserting the principle of unchanged territorial boundaries, the EC was plainly backing the Croats against the Serbs. It is true, however, as Stanley Hoffmann has pointed out, that the Yugoslav government's position at the Hague conference was illogical. It wanted self-determination for all peoples (and hence the right of Serb-majority areas of Croatia and Bosnia to secede and join Yugoslavia), but made an exception for the Kosovo, the historic heartland of the Serbs, since it now had a large ethnic majority of Albanians. Stanley Hoffmann, "Yugoslavia: Implications for

Chapter 7

Europe and European Institutions," in *The World and Yugoslavia's Wars*, ed. Richard H. Ullman (New York: Council on Foreign Relations, 1996), 97–121 at 104–5.

53. Ross, *Jacques Delors and European Integration*, 169.

54. Buchan, *Europe*, 46.

55. For a very able article frankly presenting the German perspective, see Wolfgang Krieger, "Towards a Gaullist Germany? Some Lessons from the Yugoslav Crisis," *World Policy Journal* 11, no. 1 (Spring 1994): 26–38. Krieger plausibly argues (p. 30) that Bonn wanted "to demonstrate that Germany could impose its will on its European partners with respect to foreign policy decisions—despite the huge concessions Germany had made at Maastricht."

56. See Misha Glenny, *The Fall of Yugoslavia: The Third Balkan War* (London: Penguin, 1993), 164–66.

57. Simon Nuttall, "The EC and Yugoslavia: *Deus ex machina* or *Machina sine Deo*," *Journal of Common Market Studies*, Annual Review of 1993, 32 (August 1994): 23.

58. There are several good, clear introductions to the Maastricht treaty. R. Corbett, *The Treaty of Maastricht: From Conception to Ratification* (London: Longman, 1993) and Andrew Duff, John Pinder and Roy Pryce, *Maastricht and Beyond: Building the European Union* (London: Routledge, 1994), are good starting places.

59. Denmark, like Britain, was given the right to opt out of the third stage of EMU. Following the rejection of the treaty by Danish voters in June 1992 (see chapter 8), Denmark also negotiated a battery of opt-outs in defense and foreign policy from the EU treaty. These opt-outs were approved by the Edinburgh European Council in December 1992, where Denmark also explicitly committed herself to not entering the third stage of EMU. See *Bull. EC*, no. 12/92, 25–26.

60. Forster, *Britain and the Maastricht Negotiations*, 72.

61. Peter B. Kenan, "The European Central Bank and Monetary Policy in Stage Three of EMU," *International Affairs* 68, no. 3 (1992): 466.

62. Dyson and Featherstone, *Road to Maastricht*, 441.

63. Kenan, "European Central Bank and Monetary Policy," 467.

64. This creative solution was invented by Delors's aide, Pascal Lamy, and the Dutch chairman, Ruud Lubbers, and was sold to the governments by Delors in a febrile series of late-night bargaining sessions. See Grant, *Delors: The House that Jacques Built*, 201–2.

65. For press comments, see Young, *This Blessed Plot*, 433.

66. The quotation is from John Pinder's handy little textbook, *The European Union: A Very Short Introduction* (Oxford: Oxford University Press, 2001), 104.

67. Alberta Sbragia, *Euro-Politics* (Washington, D.C.: Brookings Institution, 1992), 5.

68. Moravcsik, *Choice for Europe*, ch. 6, 379–471. Moravcsik treats the negotiations on political union as a "sideshow" (p. 447) when compared with monetary union. This enables him to downplay the importance of federal ideology and the geopolitical concerns raised by German reunification.

69. Dyson and Featherstone, *Road to Maastricht*, 749.

70. The argument that Maastricht was essentially a diplomatic response to the huge political and strategic questions raised by German unification is very ably argued in Michael J. Baun, "The Maastricht Treaty as High Politics: Germany, France and European Integration," *Political Science Quarterly* 110, no. 4: 605–624.

71. Quoted in Grant, *Delors: The House that Jacques Built*, 208.

8

Europe since Maastricht

The decade that has elapsed since the Treaty of Maastricht has been a tense one that has raised more questions about Europe's future than answers. The many intellectuals and politicians who hoped that the Treaty on European Union would be a staging post for a quick transition to greater political integration have been disappointed. Two further treaties, those of Amsterdam (1997) and Nice (2001), have been negotiated without the institutional balance established at Maastricht being greatly altered. On the other hand, during the 1990s, four major developments have posed the problem of the EU's *finalité*—final institutional form.

These developments are, first, the successful introduction of the single currency, named the Euro in 1995, which began to circulate in 2002 in all but three of the EU's member states. As long ago as 1979, the British politician and commentator David Marquand argued that to transfer control over monetary policy to "an unelected committee of Platonic Guardians, accountable only to their own consciences, is clearly a fantasy and a rather unattractive fantasy at that."[1] But this is precisely what the statute of the ECB has done. Can decisions of macroeconomic policy be left in the hands of an institution so wholly free of political control? Second, the enlargement of the Union to encompass the new democracies of Central and Eastern Europe is posing hard questions for the EU. There are moral, cultural, economic and geopolitical reasons for the entry of these states, but the problems associated with their membership are both endless and difficult to resolve. Countries such as Poland, the Czech Republic, Hungary and the Baltic states are bastions of European culture and history, but their agricultural sector is large and inefficient and their populations relatively poor. Key EC policies, such as the CAP and the funds for regional development, will have to be radically redesigned

225

when the eastern Europeans join. Most challenging of all, the EU's institutional structure will also have to alter. A further influx of member states (Austria, Finland and Sweden joined in 1995, taking the EU's membership to fifteen) will render the current decision-making process, with its consensual structures, impossibly cumbersome.[2] Third, the question of the EU's "democratic deficit" has become a political issue. The Treaties of Maastricht and Amsterdam have ensured that new law in a very wide range of policy areas is made by Community institutions rather than national parliaments, which increasingly rubber stamp decisions taken by the EU at Brussels. There is no doubt that the "Europeanization" of policy is proceeding apace. But there are evident problems with this. The Commission, including its president, is selected by the national governments, rather than elected; the European Parliament is elected, but its procedures are opaque; voter turnout in European elections has declined sharply in recent polls and the Parliament's debates, while keenly frequented by corporate lobbyists, strike no chord with ordinary Europeans. The lawmaking process at EU level is in general so abstruse that European citizens have no understanding of how the rules and regulations that increasingly govern their lives are made.

For all these reasons, the establishment of federal European institutions is now emphatically on the agenda. The creation of a bicameral Parliament, with the addition of a European Senate composed of representatives from the member states' parliaments, is widely advocated by influential figures; so is the direct election of the president of the Commission. Other commentators envisage the creation of a "two-speed" Europe, with a hard core of states arrayed in a federal state with a strong central government, and with other, more sovereignty-conscious states remaining outside.

Fourth, world events are also pushing in the direction of change. The disappearance of the Soviet threat and the emergence of a "unipolar" world, with the United States as the sole military superpower, have brought home to many members of the European political class that their values and interests, while fundamentally similar to those of the United States, also differ in important and significant ways. Trade questions, the environment, the Arab-Israeli conflict and most recently Iraq are all areas of contrast between the two economic superpowers. But in foreign policy, America usually speaks with one voice, while Europe, on the big questions, often speaks with as many voices as it has member states. For this (and several other) reasons, foreign policy has commanded an increasingly central role in the internal EU debate since the late 1990s. As a leading British analyst has commented, "There has been more progress on European security and defence issues since 1998 than in the previous 50 years."[3] But the "Europeanization" of foreign policy is fraught with an obvious constitutional significance that eludes more mundane matters such as environmental policy or social policy. If the power to make alliances or to go to war was to be decided at Brussels by the foreign ministers of the member states acting upon the proposals of the commissioner with responsibility for foreign affairs, then national sovereignty in Europe, at any rate as it is traditionally understood, would, to all intents and purposes, have disappeared. The counterargument is that the member states will be much more able to promote their interests on the world stage if they act collectively. As Jacques Delors said as long ago as 1988: "Building Europe, in the current state of world forces, amounts to reasserting our capacity to act autonomously. In building Europe, we shall discover the degree of liberty necessary for us to have 'a certain concept of France.'"[4]

At the Laeken European Council in December 2001, a 105-strong "Convention" of Europe's great and good, to be chaired by Giscard d'Estaing, was charged with exploring the possibilities for institutional reform in advance of an intergovernmental conference on the Convention's findings. All the evidence suggests that the European Union will face a defining moment in its history within the next few years.

ADOPTING THE EURO

The introduction of a single currency on 1 January 2002 was greeted with great fanfare in all of the twelve participating countries. But the introduction of Euro banknotes, with their distinctive representations of Europe's rich architectural tradition, and coins, for which each participating country was allowed to choose its own designs, was only the last step of a lengthy and troublesome journey. The introduction of the single currency has dominated the life of the EU since Maastricht. The Euro has made its way into the pocketbooks of the Union's citizens only as a result of a series of political decisions to keep the single-currency project on track. Had the Maastricht treaty's provisions been implemented to the letter, the Euro would not now be in use by 300 million Europeans for their daily affairs.

The plan to introduce a single currency first survived the two-stage implosion of the EMS in the summers of 1992 and 1993. Insofar as one of the key criteria for membership of the single currency was an ability to remain "without severe tensions" within the "normal fluctuation margins" allowed by the EMS, the project of a single currency ought legally to have been consigned to the scrap heap by August 1993.

The origin of the EMS's difficulties was German domestic policy. After reunification in 1990, the Kohl government, worried that millions of East Germans would come looking for a better life in the west, made a number of decisions designed to boost economic growth in the former Communist regions. East Germans were allowed to exchange a large part of their savings for marks at a "one-for-one" ratio. This decision fueled a consumer boom as

East German consumers spent their new wealth on consumer goods. It was moreover becoming apparent that bringing the East German economy up to western European standards needed more investment by the German state than could safely be raised from taxation. More public borrowing would be necessary. This combination of policies, obviously, brought inflation in its wake. The German state was stoking economic demand with money that its citizens in the east had not earned. Starting in September 1991, the Bundesbank, with its statutory duty to keep inflation low, responded by raising interest rates to almost 10 percent—more than double the rate prevailing in the United States, which was easing monetary policy to offset the effects of the recession then taking place in the U.S. economy. As John Major explained with engaging simplicity in his memoirs, this surge upwards in German interest rates ensured that "a sea of money sloshed from Wall Street" and into the European money markets in search of higher returns. The DM absorbed the lion's share of this money and began to appreciate on the money markets, even against the French franc and other European currencies whose inflation rates and balance-of-payments figures were far healthier than the corresponding German ones.[5]

But this situation reversed the logic of the EMS. The EMS had been designed to export low German inflation to the rest of Europe; it now began to export high German interest rates to the rest of the Community. The demands of the criteria for monetary union meant that other member states were obliged to keep their currencies pegged to the soaring mark by raising their own interest rates. Germany was, in effect, being spared some of the losses in competitive edge that its domestic policy choices may have led to had a system of floating currency rates been in force. It was only a question of time before the other member states began to resent paying for German reunification with their own unemployment. The Kohl government's inflationary domestic policies, in conjunction with the rigidity of the Maastricht treaty, had, in short, placed a ticking bomb beneath the edifice of the EMS— and, potentially, the whole Maastricht project.

The prevailing mood of post-Maastricht Euro-euphoria, however, was such that doom-mongers obtained little hearing. The markets reasoned that the EU was on a "glidepath" to EMU and were thus prepared to keep buying bonds paying high rates of interest in francs, lire, pesetas and other currencies. They reasoned that they would make "capital gains on the bonds, with no risk of currency depreciation."[6] When, on 2 June 1992, a narrow majority of Danes (50.7 percent) rejected the Maastricht treaty in a national referendum, the picture changed. Although Delors was quick to say that the Danes' vote was a problem for Denmark, not for the EU, and the Lisbon meeting of the European Council (26–27 June 1992) reaffirmed the national leaders' determination to press on with ratification, the undeniable reality was that the Danish electorate had thrown doubt over the future of monetary union. But if EMU was doubtful, would Spain, Italy and other member states have the stomach for the politics of austerity implicit in the Maastricht convergence criteria? Might they not allow their currencies to devalue against the DM in the traditional way, rather than undergo the pain of getting their public finances in order? Money started to flow out of the peseta and lira and was only stanched, in the case of Italy, by the announcement of a massive package of austerity measures in July 1992.

Sterling also started to come under pressure. Britain, of course, possessed an opt-out from EMU, but the Conservative government of John Major, which had just been narrowly reelected in April 1992, had made membership of the EMS the linchpin of its economic strategy. Unwisely, Major boasted at the beginning of July 1992 that sterling would in time become the "anchor" of the system.[7] In the midst of a deep recession brought on by the popping of the 1980s property bubble, Britain was in no stronger position than was Italy to defend her currency with high interest rates.

François Mitterrand added to doubt over the future of EMU when he announced in the wake of the Danish result that France, too, would decide Maastricht's fate by referendum on 20 September. Mitterrand's motives are unclear. He may have hoped to relaunch the ratification process by obtaining a popular endorsement for the treaty. In the view of one commentator, however, Mitterrand simply acted "impetuously and unwisely."[8] The opinion polls showed supporters of a "no" vote growing in strength as the summer progressed. The referendum campaign was tinged with a strong element of popular anti-Germanism. Indeed, supporters of a "yes" vote were reduced to arguing that Maastricht was necessary to keep Germany under control. The prominent Conservative politician Edouard Balladur argued in *Le Monde* in August that "the rejection of the Treaty . . . will simply allow Germany to act as it desires, without taking heed of its neighbors or partners, without being constrained by any set of European rules in its role as a military, economic, financial and monetary power in the center of the continent."[9]

Under pressure, Mitterrand made a bad situation worse on 3 September 1992 in the course of a televised debate with the Gaullist politician Philippe Séguin. When Séguin made the reasonable point that the Maastricht treaty transferred crucial economic decision-making functions to unaccountable "technocrats," Mitterrand stated baldly that the ECB would be subject to the control of the European Council.

This astonishing public repudiation of a key provision of the ECB's statute angered the Bundesbank's new chairman, Helmut Schlesinger. Two days later, at a meeting of EU finance ministers and central bankers in Bath, England, Schlesinger refused to ease the pressure on the pound and the lira by reducing German interest rates. After British chancellor Norman Lamont had asked for a reduction for the fourth time, Schlesinger had to be restrained from walking out by the German finance minister.[10] Had he left, the other central bankers present would have walked out, too. The repercussions for the French referendum of the central bankers publicly refusing to bow to political pressure would have been immense. Almost certainly, the French electorate would have voted the treaty down. As it was, the French recorded a "*petit oui.*" By a margin of 51 percent to 49 percent, they approved the treaty. It was a "soberingly thin endorsement."[11]

Schlesinger's stand had dire consequences for the EMS. Germany's refusal to cut interest rates provoked a currency crisis of 1970s dimensions. The lira came under intense pressure and was only propped up by massive intervention in the market by the Bundesbank and the Banca d'Italia. Such intervention was unsustainable in the long term. Accordingly, on 12 September, the lira was devalued by just over 7 percent and the Bundesbank, hoping to make the devaluation stick, made a nominal cut in interest rates. It was too little, too late, not least because Schlesinger publicly warned that he could not exclude further devaluations. On 16 September, "Black Wednesday," the lira, the pound, the peseta were battered by waves of selling. The British government spent more than £15,000 million in a desperate attempt to prevent the pound from dropping below its permitted margin of fluctuation, then raised interest rates twice (from 10 to 12 percent and from 12 to 15 percent) and then threw the towel in as the markets paid no attention to its efforts.[12] Interest rates were slashed and the pound was allowed to float.

The Economist, which had said on 29 August that the British were "fond" of "talking about currency crises," but had jauntily assured its readers that "this one hardly makes the grade," headlined its 19 September edition with a single word: "Mayhem."[13]

By February 1993, the pound had lost 20 percent of its former value against the mark. The lira was similarly savaged and followed sterling out of the system: it fell from 750 lire to the mark to over 900 in the space of a few weeks. The Spanish peseta escaped with a 5 percent devaluation. In subsequent days, the Irish, Danish and even French currencies came under attack. But the Bundesbank was stauncher in defense of the franc than it had been of the pound, and the attacks were repelled.

The September 1992 currency crisis led a number of influential figures to fly the kite of a two-speed Europe, in which a core group of countries—Germany, France and the Benelux countries being the obvious candidates—would press ahead with rapid monetary union. Indeed, in the light of the Bundesbank's hostility to the single currency in the 1980s, one does not have to be a twin brother to Machiavelli to wonder whether this was not the German bank's political objective all along. More generally, it reminded Europeans that "the removal of currency fluctuations within Europe has underpinned Project 1992."[14] The goal of genuine single market was not ultimately compatible with volatile currencies. For hard-pressed British and Italian industrialists, Black Wednesday was a day of rejoicing. They could now export more cheaply to the members of the EMS while benefiting from a de facto tariff on imports. As a direct result of the *disfatta* of expulsion from the EMS, Italy now began a period of record trade surpluses. The question was how long their trading partners would put up with such a state of affairs without resorting to protectionist measures that would put the single market—the Community's raison d'être—into doubt.

The EMS lasted—with periodical bouts of turbulence—until the end of July 1993. By then, the new center-right government in Paris, which "desperately needed lower interest rates to stimulate recovery and tackle unemployment," was pleading behind the scenes for a policy of interest rate reductions on the part of the Bundesbank.[15] The meeting of the Bundesbank Council (its governing body) on 29 July 1993 was expected to deliver such a cut, not least because German industry, too, was being throttled by the central bankers' tight money policy. Newspaper speculation predicted a cut of as much as 1 percent in the days preceding the meeting. Instead, no reduction occurred. The French and Belgian francs, the peseta, the Danish krone and all the other currencies left in the system crashed uncontrollably upon the news. Impotent in the face of the markets, the EU's finance ministers decided to preserve the ERM, but to widen the fluctuation bands of the participating currencies to 15 percent above or below their central rate. In effect, they put a fig leaf in front of the nakedness of their return to floating exchange rates. They also affirmed their common commitment to the principle of monetary union and to ensuring that their economies met the convergence criteria.

And yet arguably the most important criterion for membership had just been abandoned. Nobody could with a straight face pretend that 15 percent fluctuation margins were "normal." At Maastricht the intention had been that all member states would shadow the DM closely in the run-up to EMU. Moreover, the economic cost of the EMS had to be counted in other ways. The economic slowdown caused by high interest rates was boosting welfare spending and the cost of servicing member states' national debts. This meant that public spending was ballooning as a percentage of GDP and that the member states were thus running deficits in excess of the 3 percent permitted by the convergence criteria. The rapid accumulation of new debt meant that several countries now ran the risk of failing to keep their national debts below the 60 percent specified in the Maastricht treaty.

These problems worsened in 1994. In 1995, the Commission estimated that unless the member states adopted more austere public spending policies, tiny Luxembourg, with its 900,000 inhabitants, would be the only country certain to meet both the deficit and national debt criteria by 1997. Germany and France would probably, but not certainly, squeeze in; no other country except Britain (who hardly counted) could meet both criteria, and several were expected to meet neither.[16]

These economic difficulties were the reason why the December 1995 European Council held in Madrid chose to postpone the third stage of monetary union to 1999, as the Maastricht treaty permitted. The same summit also made several more positive decisions, however. The would-be currency was to be named the Euro (the only option seriously considered was the Florin). It was decided that Euro notes and coins would circulate by January 2002 "at the latest" and that the decision on the fitness of potential member states would be made "as soon as possible in 1998."[17] Member states wishing to participate in monetary unification therefore had just over two years to get their house in order.

In 1996, the German government and Central Bank, determined to ensure that member states maintained strict financial discipline even after qualifying for membership of the Euro group, insisted upon the adoption of a "Stability and Growth Pact," which was presented to the Dublin European Council in December 1996 by the Community's finance ministers.[18] By the terms of the pact, every EU member state committed itself to aiming for "a medium-term budgetary position of close to balance or in surplus." Every EU member state would submit annual "stability programs" to the Commission, which would flag problem cases. Countries running a budget deficit of over 3 percent of GDP were to be potentially subject to "agreed sanctions" of 0.2 to 0.5 percent of GDP unless their deficit had been provoked by an "unusual event" beyond their control, or else was due to a "severe economic downturn" that had caused a fall of more than 2 percent in GDP.[19]

The Stability and Growth Pact was widely regarded as too draconian ever to be used. Indeed, its rules have been applied flexibly, not least because during the economic downturn of 2001–2002 big countries like Italy, France and, by a predictable historical irony, Germany itself have found it difficult to keep their deficit spending beneath the 3 percent limit. Many economists argue in any case that the pact makes poor sense in theory. During times of slow or negative economic growth, member states need to be free to stimulate their economies with deficit spending. Partly as a reflection of these worries, the Dublin European Council also established a "stability council" of Euro-zone finance ministers that would meet to "complement" the work of the ECB.

For most of the member states, the 1998 deadline merely condemned them to a prolonged period of belt-tightening. For some states, however, especially the Latin ones, the deadline implied much more. Italy is the most dramatic example. Until the early 1990s, Italy had been governed throughout the postwar period by Christian Democracy (DC). A bitterly divided country in class, territorial and, above all, ideological terms, Christian Democracy had maintained consent by excessively generous use of the public finances. The state sector was overstaffed and unproductive; too many industries were the fiefs of the political parties and stuffed with political placemen;

pensions had been distributed so liberally that the country was facing unsustainable levels of public debt; infrastructure spending had too often been driven by the need to satisfy powerful political clients than by the objective requirements of the economy.[20] In the 1980s, increased political competition from the DC's "partner" in government, the Socialist Party (PSI), led to an intensification of these practices as both parties tried to buy votes. Italy's public debt expanded at an unsustainable speed (the public borrowing requirement was 10 percent of GDP per year or more throughout most of the 1980s), and investors increasingly demanded high rates of interest on the vast quantities of new government bonds being unloaded on the market every year.[21]

In 1992–1993, the political system collapsed as a result of judicial inquiries into the corruption of the political élite, leaving the new political movements that emerged in the wake of this crisis with the unenviable task of getting Italy into shape for the Euro. The center-left Ulivo ("Olive Tree") government that won the general elections of April 1996 made qualifying for the Euro its central priority. As Michele Salvati, a prominent Italian economist and politician, has argued, for Italy, meeting the Maastricht criteria represented a "Copernican revolution" in the organization of her economy.[22] The Ulivo government could no longer tolerate structural inefficiencies that boosted inflation and imposed costs on business since after the implementation of the Euro Italy could no longer rely on maintaining its competitiveness by devaluation. The government began an intense program of privatizations, pension reforms, labor market deregulation and local government reforms to this end. Public spending was frozen, tax collection rates improved and income taxes were raised, notably by a one-off "Euro tax" levied in fiscal year 1996–1997.

Austerity measures on this scale squeezed inflation and allowed the rate of interest paid on government bonds to come down. By the beginning of 1998, Italy was running the tightest economic ship of any major industrialized country in the world. Excluding repayments on the country's accumulated debt, Italy could boast a budget surplus of about 3 percent of GDP. There was nothing inevitable about this turnaround, which was the result of political will driven by the power of the European ideal for the Italian élites and among public opinion and, one should add, fear of the economic consequences of failure. As Alberta Sbragia has written: "Many assumed Italy would be simply unable to mobilize the political capital necessary for such a major restructuring . . . [Italy's success] . . . was a remarkable sustained effort supported by successive governments and the president of the Republic."[23]

Italy was the country that had to make the greatest sacrifices in order to get up to the Euro starting line. But the general belt-tightening had worked to good effect. When the Commission assessed the state of the EU's economies in March 1998, it found that there was a "very high degree of sustainable convergence." Inflation had been driven down to less than 2 percent throughout the Community; only Greece had failed to reduce its annual deficit to below 3 percent; yields on government bonds had converged everywhere. Admittedly, only four EU countries (Britain, Luxembourg, France and Finland) had a national debt of less than 60 percent of GDP, but national debt was falling relative to GDP everywhere except Germany (which, in any case, was only marginally above the 60 percent figure). In light of these results, the Commission promoted eleven countries to the Euro-zone and expressed reservations about two (Greece and Sweden). Britain and Denmark exercised their option not to participate.[24] At the beginning of May 1998, the heads of state and government, meeting in Brussels, accepted the Commission's recommendations. The occasion was marred, however, by wrangling over the nomination of the first governor of the ECB. French president Jacques Chirac tried to place a French central banker, Jean-Claude Trichet, in the job. The other states preferred the Dutch candidate, Wim Duisenberg. The majority eventually prevailed but only after France had obtained the concession that Duisenberg would not serve his full eight-year term of office. This decision was regarded as a breach of the "spirit, if not the letter" of the Maastricht treaty.[25]

In the face of the collapse of the EMS and the lakes of red ink in Europe's public accounts in the mid-1990s, the fact that eleven member states had succeeded in qualifying for the single currency was a remarkable demonstration of collective political will. The decision was ultimately political, not economic. Had the Maastricht tests been applied rigorously, EMU would not have happened in 1998. But that would have set the goal of greater economic and political integration back permanently. The experience of the 1990s had also underlined the Euro's advantages. Europe's nations had learned the hard way that in the absence of a single currency, ultimate sovereignty over monetary policy lay in the hands of the Bundesbank—or the anarchy of the currency markets.

In the run-up to the introduction of the Euro, economists advanced many other reasons for a single currency. The Euro promised significant immediate gains in price transparency (would-be buyers of a Volkswagen could tell at a glance whether the car of their choice was cheaper in Germany than across the border in Austria or Belgium), lower inflation (more expensive sellers of Volkswagens would have to reduce their prices) and transaction costs (the customer buying the car would no longer have to pay a bank to change his money). Investment and trade decisions would also obviously be facilitated by the removal of exchange rate fluctuations and so, less obviously, would labor market and administrative reforms. In the Euro-zone, the only way that member states will be able to maintain or gain competitiveness in the coming decades is to raise productivity and keep down costs. National governments will therefore be forced to embark on a root-and-branch search for structural reforms to the welfare state to reduce costs for business (or else lose economic ground to more efficient competitors). The massive efforts that Italy has had to make just to get up to the starting line are indicative, in the views of many economists, of a competitive pressure that will become generalized and permanent for all the Euro-zone's members.[26]

These powerful arguments adduced in the Euro's favor were not universally regarded as overwhelming, however. Critics suggested that the institutions of monetary governance established at Maastricht were inadequate to manage the Euro-zone. The critics worried that a one-size-fits-all approach to interest rates might lead to monetary policy being too lax in some countries and too high in others: this was not a theoretical concern in a continent where the growth rate of the Italian and German economies was languishing at 1 to 2 percent, while Ireland's was racing ahead as fast as the tiger economies of East Asia.

Losing the ability to devalue one's currency, or to reduce interest rates, also will weaken the power of the member states to respond to "asymmetrical shocks" (economic downturns or events affecting some states more than others). In the United States, the impact of a regional economic crisis can be absorbed by either (or both) federal financial transfers (subsidies or tax breaks) or labor market mobility. In Europe, the EU has a budget of just over 1 percent of the total economic activity produced within the Union, fiscal policy remains a matter for the member states and workers plainly face far greater linguistic, cultural and administrative difficulties preventing them from shifting from one member state to another in search of work. Migrating from Michigan to North Carolina or Arizona is not easy, but it is within the realms of possibility. Migrating from Greece to Denmark or from Sicily to Stuttgart is, even today, a once-in-a-lifetime decision.[27]

Probably the most important reason for adopting the Euro, however, was strategic. Adoption of the Euro held out the promise of insulating Europe's economy from the volatility of the dollar. Since 1971, the United States, with its huge domestic market, has not been as susceptible as Europe to economic shocks caused by exchange rate fluctuations. The dollar has charted a giddy series of highs and lows, but the U.S. consumer, the occasional spike in the cost of gasoline aside, has not noticed the effect since trade only represents a small part of GNP. With the adoption of the single currency, the Euro-zone too constitutes an internal market comparable in size to that of the United States.[28] Europeans now need worry less about the external value of their currency, although since much of world trade, especially of energy, is carried on in dollars, a permanently weak Euro might generate strong inflationary pressures. By and large, however, the Euro will probably "reduce the costs of transatlantic monetary conflict for Europe and . . . thereby shield European policy-makers from American pressure."[29]

This is a major consideration in new currency's favor. As we have seen already in this book, the knock-on effects of fluctuations in the dollar's value have caused deep problems for the European economy on several occasions in the past thirty years. The Euro has in fact already proved its worth in this regard. Since its introduction in January 1999, the Euro has mostly suffered by comparison with the dollar. It originally rose to almost \$1.20 before sinking in October 2000, in the wake of the dot.com boom, to as low as 85 cents. It has since gradually climbed back to parity as the American economy has weakened in the aftermath of 9/11 and the popping of the stock market bubble. Supporters of the Euro can truthfully claim that these substantial variations in the value of the dollar would have wrought havoc with EU exchange rates (and hence intra-European trade) in the Euro's absence.

The creation of the Euro, indeed, may even put the boot of exchange rate power on the other foot in the long run. If world demand for the Euro increased, either because the European economy was growing faster than its American counterpart or because investors lost confidence in the American financial system, it would quickly become more difficult for the United States to finance its substantial current account deficit (at present 4.5 percent of GNP, some \$430 billion) and hence to maintain its standard of living.

The prospect of the Euro rendering the EU more economically independent of the United States and transforming her at any rate potentially into a challenger to the U.S. hegemony in the world economy has ruffled a few feathers. Writing at the end of 1997, the Harvard economist Martin Feldstein published a much-discussed article entitled "EMU and International Conflict" in *Foreign Affairs*. Feldstein argued, in synthesis, that the introduction of the Euro could "lead to conflicts in Europe and confrontations with the United States." Within Europe, Feldstein predicted, the fact that membership of the Euro-zone was permanent might arouse anger when member states were hit by economic hardship; certainly, there were bound to be disagreements between the pro-growth French and the anti-inflation Germans. It would be foolish to think, he sustained, that these disagreements could not spill over into conflict.

But Feldstein was clearly more worried about the effect the Euro would have on international relations. A single currency was a "symbol of sovereignty." Europe was becoming a nation. Its next step would be to develop a separate foreign policy from the United States. The United States would not, at that point, be able to "count on Europe as an ally in all its relations with third countries." The Europeans, "guided by a combination of economic self-interest, historical traditions and national pride," might, Feldstein feared, "seek alliances and pursue policies that are contrary to the interests of the United States."[30]

In many ways, this article was alarmist and, to European eyes, somewhat naïve. As any citizen of the European Union knew, Europe was, in 1998, very far from becoming a federal nation-state with a coherent and ambitious foreign policy. But Feldstein was right to point out that monetary union did raise the issue of whether it should be one. The successful launch of the Euro has been a major reason for the rise of the question of the EU's *finalité*. What kind of organization does the EU want to be? Will it remain a confederal body preoccupied, mainly, with detailed economic questions? Or will it evolve into a federal state, with a central government with powers over tax policy, foreign policy, the spending of substantial sums of money? Or will some hybrid emerge? These questions have been discussed by Europe's intellectuals and politicians since the 1940s, but now that EMU is complete, they have become impossible to neglect.

ENLARGEMENT TO CENTRAL AND EASTERN EUROPE

The prospect of further enlargement to the new democracies of the former Soviet bloc has also put the issue of the EU's institutional future (as well as much else) on the agenda. The EU was able to conclude entrance negotiations with Austria, Finland and Sweden without too much difficulty in the early 1990s. All three countries were advanced industrial societies with small (though expensive) agricultural sectors that did not add greatly to the total population of the EU. The countries of central and eastern Europe (CEEC) presented an altogether different degree of difficulty. They were (and are) much poorer than the EU average, highly agricultural and possessed a relatively rudimentary legal framework. Yet there were important reasons for wanting to incorporate the new democracies into the EU as swiftly as possible. Entry into the EU, as for Greece, Spain and Portugal, would be an important act of democratic consolidation. Budapest, Prague and Warsaw are great bastions of European civilization; insofar as European unification has been driven by a belief in the continent's cultural identity—a theme that has been given relatively little weight in this narrative—it was impossible for the EU countries to turn their backs on their cousins east of the Elbe River. More practically, EU, especially German and Italian, direct investment immediately flooded into the more promising east European markets. The new democracies represented a pool of well-educated, skilled, relatively cheap labor that had the potential to develop as major new markets as their income levels rose. As a Commission report presented to the June 1992 Lisbon European Council stated: "Enlargement is a challenge which the Community cannot refuse."[31]

In the immediate aftermath of the downfall of the Communist regimes, the EU pumped aid into the new democracies via the Bank for European Reconstruction and Development (established at the Strasbourg European Council in December 1989) and the European Investment Bank and through its "Phare" program for technical and scientific assistance. Among many other grants, Phare committed over 1,000 million Euro for education, training and research between 1990 and 1998; nearly 1,200 million Euro for the restructuring of small businesses; and over 2,000 million in spending on infrastructure. Poland, with 2,000 million Euro in Phare funding, was the country that benefited most.[32] The EU also gradually negotiated so-called association agreements with the Eastern European states. These agreements provided for the gradual but asymmetric liberalization of trade between the individual new democracies and the EU, with the EU, naturally, opening its markets in everything except agriculture quicker and further. Once these agreements had come into force, the new democracies were free to join Turkey (which had applied in 1987), Malta (1990) and Cyprus (1990) in the queue to enter the Community.

Before the new democracies could apply, the EU's member states had had to rethink the fundamental principles underlying membership. They were determined to open negotiations with the new applicants, but not at the cost of destabilizing the status quo. As the Commission document presented at Lisbon in 1992 stated: "Widening must not be at the expense of deepening. Enlargement must not be a dilution of the Community's achievements."[33] All member states, it was decided, would have to accept the full Community *acquis*, which meant, in practice, harmonizing national law to EU law in every major policy field. This was a major obstacle. EU law is daunting even for member states. For countries emerging from the Communist system, lacking trained lawyers and an independent judiciary, the EU's decision was both a substantial technical obstacle and an erosion of their competitive position vis-à-vis the EU states. The costs of implementing and enforcing EU law on health and safety, or the environment, were bound to eat away some of the cost advantage that made building a plant near Pilsen instead of Pamplona worthwhile for foreign investors.

At the June 1993 Copenhagen European Council, the Twelve outlined three key principles (the "Copenhagen criteria") that all would-be entrants had to meet as a prerequisite for the opening of accession negotiations. First, candidate members had to possess stable democratic institutions that promoted respect for the rule of the law, human rights and ethnic minorities. Second, they had to possess a functioning market economy and be able to survive the competitive economic pressures of EU membership. Third, they had to be able, eventually, to "take on the obligations" of membership "including adherence to the aims of political, economic and monetary union."[34] These conditions, too, were a formidable obstacle. Indeed, in 1993, an uncharitable observer might have argued that the Copenhagen criteria ruled out Britain and Denmark (who were not enthusiasts for political union), Greece (whose economy was extremely weak in the early 1990s) and Italy (whose political system was in a state of collapse) from membership.

Despite the size of the hurdles placed in their path, the new democracies were ready to bid for membership by the mid-1990s. Hungary, whose association agreement came into force in February 1994, applied for EU membership on 31 March 1994. She was followed just a few days later by Poland. A second wave of applications was received in June–July 1995, when Romania, the Slovak Republic and Latvia all requested membership. Estonia, Lithuania, Bulgaria, the Czech Republic and Slovenia had all followed suit by June 1996. Without even counting Turkey, these applications implied an eventual expansion of one-third in the territorial area of the EU and of over 100 million new citizens. These new citizens, moreover, would be, even by the standards of the Mediterranean enlargement in the 1980s, much poorer than the existing member states. In 1998, the Commission found that only Cyprus, the Czech Republic and Slovenia had per capita incomes of over 60 percent of the EU average, measured at purchasing power parity (PPP). Hungary's figure was 49 percent; Poland, with its 40 million inhabitants, just 39 percent. Romania, Latvia and Bulgaria had incomes of only one-quarter of the EU average. In economic terms, to cite *The Economist*'s brilliant analogy, enlargement to the CEEC is "Europe's Mexico option." It is as if the United States had decided to accept a proposal for the incorporation of the various Mexican provinces as states of the Union and had committed itself to bringing these provinces to American standards of infrastructure and social provision.[35]

Rapid accession of all these countries plainly promised a future of mass migration from east to west, or else massive investment on a scale to dwarf the amounts invested by the EU in the Paquet Delors in 1988, to build up the entrants' economies. At the Madrid European Council in December 1995, the Commission was asked to "prepare a detailed analysis of [what] enlargement would mean for the EU" and to assess the readiness of the applicant countries to begin entry negotiations. The Commission responded with the document *Agenda 2000: For a Stronger and Wider Union* in July 1997. In this document, the Commission spelled out the costs of enlargement. The Commission asserted bluntly: "A first wave of accessions will affect the budgetary positions of all the present Member States, reducing the positive balances of net beneficiaries and increasing the negative ones of others."[36] The net beneficiaries, Spain, Belgium, Portugal, Greece and Ireland, were, when *Agenda 2000* came out, benefiting from a new and even larger wave of regional development spending (the so-called Delors II package agreed after Maastricht). In 1997, Spain was in the black to the tune of 5,500 million Ecu; Portugal, with a much smaller population, was taking home 2,700 million; now-rich Ireland, 2,800 million. These countries stood to lose their lucrative position as the poor cousins of the EU family. Although the amount transferred to any country cannot, under EU rules, exceed 4 percent of GDP, every one of the applicant members will qualify for assistance from the structural and regional funds. Since the EU also committed itself in the 1990s to keeping the EU's overall budget to under 1.27 percent of its economic output, this inevitably means that the Mediterranean bloc will have a less privileged future position in the EU's accounts.

The Commission nevertheless recommended that entry negotiations should begin with the Czech Republic, Estonia, Hungary, Poland, Slovenia and Cyprus. Negotiations with these countries duly began on 31 March 1998. The Commission subsequently approved beginning negotiations with Bulgaria, Latvia, Lithuania, Malta, Romania and the Slovak Republic, and these duly began in February 2000. The decision not to open negotiations with Turkey was seen as an affront in Ankara. Turkey's ambiguous human rights record, her far from stable democracy, her rigid treatment of the Kurdish minority, her occupation of part of Cyprus and her multiple economic problems (inflation was 85 percent in 1998 and the Turkish lira is one of the weakest currencies in the world) provide, however, a clear justification for the Commission's stance.

There is no need to go into excessive detail about the ongoing negotiations. In general, however, it may be said that the largest problems, predictably, have occurred in agriculture. Agriculture is the worst problem associated with enlargement, especially in Poland. About 5 percent of the EU's population is employed in farming, or farming-related activity. In Poland, the figure is over 20 percent. Farms in central and eastern Europe are smaller, less mechanized (some still make do without tractors) and less productive. They are also much less subsidized and bureaucratized and their produce is both cheaper and, in some ways, of better quality. Enlargement has thus posed the EU with an uncomfortable dilemma. Would it be wiser to extend the EU's subsidy regime to the farmers of any new members, thus causing the most substantial budget increase in the EC–EU's history, or would it be better to reduce levels of subsidy to individual farmers, but ensure that the new members' peasants get their fair share? The EU's farmers, many of whom are in genuine economic difficulty despite the transfers they receive from the CAP, would revolt against this latter option, and they have shown in the past, with their road blockades and motorway go-slows, that they have the power to disrupt the domestic politics of their respective nations.

The EU's solution, unveiled in February 2002, is to phase in subsidies to the newcomers, so that they enjoy equal treatment within ten years of entry. To start with, however, they will receive only a quarter of the cash lavished upon the farmers already in the system. EU production quotas will also be imposed and these will in many cases lower the amount the farmers are already producing. These conditions have aroused much disquiet among the candidate countries, who fear that that they may turn economic logic on its head by allowing subsidized agricultural produce from the rich west to gain market share in the east.[37] The absence of agriculture from the association agreements has already led to the new democracies' incurring a substantial trade deficit with the EU since 1994.[38] On the other hand, the applicant countries' preferred option—reduced subsidies and a market in agricultural products determined by producer costs—is a nonstarter. No major EU state supports outright laissez-faire in agriculture—and some even seem to think that the CAP is a productive way of distributing resources.

The entrance of the Central and Eastern European countries (CEEC), in short, has the potential to drag the EU back to the days of the early 1980s and to interminable squabbles about the budget contributions of the member states. In the long term, the rising prosperity of these new states will almost certainly give the EU an economic shot in the arm. In the short term, however, the costs will equally certainly be far larger than anybody wants to admit and will cause the demands upon the EU budget to balloon—with predictable and damaging consequences for the internal harmony of the Union. Short of dramatic rejections of EU membership by the electorates of the candidate countries, enlargement is nevertheless going to happen. On 12–13 December 2002, the Copenhagen European Council, after some feverish last-minute haggling over terms, decided that Poland, the Czech Republic, Hungary, Slovakia, Lithuania, Latvia, Slovenia, Estonia, Cyprus and Malta would be ready to join in 2004 and could sign their accession agreements in April 2003.

THE INSTITUTIONAL QUESTION

Enlargement has also kept the so-called institutional question on the boil throughout the 1990s. It has been apparent since the early 1990s that the entry of the CEEC means that the EU will have to undergo a fundamental rethink of its institutions. How many commissioners should there be? How many votes should the applicants get in the Council of Ministers? How many policy questions should be decided by unanimity in the Council of Ministers? Can a Union with well over twenty members decide *anything* unanimously? How large should the European Parliament become? What should the national division of seats in the Parliament be?

During the 1990s, there were two IGCs, which led to the treaties of Amsterdam (October 1997) and Nice (February 2001), that were supposed to address these problems. Neither of these treaties in fact did much more than add decoration to the three-pillar façade of the Maastricht treaty. Amsterdam, in particular, evaded the issue of EU governance. Two well-known scholars described the treaty as a "melting pot of disparate measures lacking a coherent vision of either substantive cooperation in a particular area or the future institutional structure of Europe."[39]

Mixed metaphors apart, it is hard to dissent. At Amsterdam, Britain's newly elected Labour government, represented by Tony Blair, agreed to end its opt-out from the "social chapter" of the Maastricht treaty. Liberty, democracy and respect for human rights were made a condition of membership, and member states could be suspended from membership if the other member states unanimously agreed that a "serious and persistent breach" of these principles had been recorded in a member state. The European Parliament gained the right formally to approve or reject the European Council's nominee as president of the Commission and obtained further powers of co-decision. After Amsterdam, only agriculture, foreign policy, justice and home affairs were not subject to the co-decision procedure. Richard Corbett has written that these new powers meant that the legislative process of the EU was "virtually a bicameral system."[40] The Schengen treaty was absorbed into the EU framework and a new "high representative" was to be in charge of strategic planning in the field of foreign policy and defense—together with the commissioner responsible for external affairs and the foreign minister presiding over the Council of Ministers. Triumvirates are an unstable form of leadership and the "new troika" decided upon at Amsterdam has proved no exception to this rule.

Last but not least, EU governments agreed, at French insistence, to include a new "title" on employment in the EU treaty. The EU governments pledged to "work towards developing a coordinated strategy for employment and particularly for promoting a skilled, trained and adaptable workforce and labor markets responsive to economic change." To this end, the Council of Ministers could set "guidelines" in these areas by QMV, but national governments merely had to take such guidelines "into account" when making policy in this area. The introduction of this title was motivated by French fears that the "Rhineland" model of a workforce legally protected from layoffs by a huge body of complex legislation might crumble under competitive pressure from Britain's loosely regulated labor market. Britain's lower corporate tax rates and flexible labor markets had, in fact, been persuading a number of French companies to relocate to Britain in the months before the June 1997 Amsterdam summit.

The Amsterdam treaty, while containing a number of innovations of interest to scholars of European integration, had thus "failed pathetically" to deal with the thorny institutional questions posed by enlargement.[41] Europe's leaders did, however, pledge that before even one new member had been admitted they would decide how votes would be reweighted in the Council of Ministers and on what basis the Commission would be constituted. They conceded, too, that a major reform of the EU's institutions would be needed before the new member states joined.[42] This commitment by the European Council provided the impetus for a second IGC on institutional affairs that led to the December 2000 summit of EU leaders in Nice and the Treaty of Nice.

Expressed in this way, it might appear as if the reforms decided at Nice had been the result of a carefully crafted process of negotiation. In fact, the chief provisions of the Treaty of Nice were decided at the last moment, in an atmosphere of near panic by the heads of state and government. As two policymakers who had been involved in the IGC have written: "IGC negotiations usually advance in three stages: preparation, negotiation and endgame . . . this time it seemed as if 18 months of preparation had been thrown out of the window and negotiations started from scratch."[43] The Nice European Council, which lasted four days, was the longest in EU history and was characterized by feverish negotiations as the member states tried to square the circle of amending the EU's institutions while retaining their powers of nomination and voting. It was, in fact, a dispiriting spectacle that only emphasized the fear that the EU's intergovernmental model was reaching its efficient limits.

In brief, the Nice summit made the following decisions. First, it welcomed a Charter of Fundamental Rights drawn up by a panel of jurists in the course of 2000 without, however, adding the charter to the treaty. The charter is essentially an updating of the 1950 Convention on Human Rights to take into account contemporary concerns with generational, environmental, gender and social rights. Among other articles, it outlawed the death penalty, guaranteed the "right of access" of every individual to education, ruled in affirmative action as a means of obtaining equality between men and women and insisted that a "high level of environmental protection" was a right that the EU should enshrine in law.[44]

Second, it decided to reform the Commission by reducing, from 1 January 2005, the number of commissioners to one per member state (Germany, France, Britain, Italy and Spain currently nominate two). When the twenty-seventh member state joins, the number of commissioners will be reduced to less than the number of member states and a system of rotation introduced. The president of the Commission will in the future be chosen by QMV, not unanimity, in the European Council. Every new Commission will have to be approved as a body by the European Parliament. The president is furthermore given, under article 217 of the revised treaty, the specific power to allocate portfolios and to demand an individual commissioner's resignation.

Third, also effective 1 January 2005, the summit agreed to change the procedure for QMV to a so-called triple majority system. This new procedure was thrashed out at Nice and "could not have been predicted by anybody in advance."[45] The new system requires that for a decision to be made there must be a specified number of votes (169 out of 237) in favor. The number of votes per country was increased at Nice and the weighting was changed to strengthen the weighting of the five most populous member states, which will have 60 percent of the votes compared with the current 55 percent. A decision shall not be made, however, unless there is also a numerical majority of member states in favor. Moreover, it will be possible for any member state to request verification that the qualified majority represents at least 62 percent of the Union's population. QMV was extended to some twenty-seven new provisions, most of them relatively minor.

Fourth, the summit decided to expand the Parliament to an elephantine 732 MEPs for the elections held in June 2004. It was anticipated that these elections would be contested by the fifteen current member states and some at least of the applicant countries. From 2009, the number of MEPs belonging to the fifteen current members will drop to 535, with only Germany and Luxembourg retaining their current number of deputies. The precise number of seats in the European Parliament and the precise number of votes to be allocated to new member states were to be established during the accession negotiations. The institutional decision of the Nice European Council, in short, was to amend the mechanisms of intergovernmental cooperation among the fifteen existing member states and to integrate all new members one by one into the same structure. There would, however, a protocol to the treaty added, be yet another IGC on institutional reform in 2004.[46]

This result had already been discounted by some of the more integration-minded member states, notably Germany. In May 2000, in a speech commemorating the fiftieth anniversary of the Schuman Plan, Joschka Fischer had already drawn an enticing picture of a more sweeping reform of the EU's institutions, for which the ongoing IGC was to be only a prelude.

Fischer's speech has rapidly entered into the canon of documents most cited by supporters of the European project since it essentially reprised the language and proposals of the early federalists. Fischer started from the premise that "introducing increased majority voting," while important, could only be a "first step towards reform." Enlargement to twenty-seven to thirty member states "will hopelessly overload" the EU's ability to deal with crises and major issues. Fischer asked: "How, with the system of institutions that exists today, are thirty states supposed to balance interests, take decisions and eventually act?" "How can one prevent the EU from becoming utterly intransparent . . . and the citizens' acceptance of the EU from eventually hitting rock bottom?" In his view, there was a "very simple answer": "the transition from a union of states to full parliamentarianization as a European Federation . . . this Federation will have to be based on a constituent treaty."[47]

Fischer at once faced the objection that this proposal would meet such resistance from the member states that it would be completely unworkable. He retorted that it would be "an irreparable mistake" to try to "complete political integration against the existing national institutions rather than by involving them." The completion of European integration, he argued, would have to be based on the principle of subsidiarity: upon a "division of sovereignty" between Europe's institutions and the member states. The "competences" of the Union and those of the member states had to be clearly enshrined in a constitution in such a way that every issue that was not explicitly stated to be a question for the federation was handled at the level of the member states.[48] The EU, Fischer clearly believes, has evolved into a transnational regulatory regime, in which law binding upon all Europe's citizens is made far from democratic scrutiny by technocrats and by interstate bargaining.

For Fischer, both ethical and practical considerations meant that this situation had to be reformed. His vision of the future institutional structure of the proposed federation was, however, flexible. The new federation's legislature, he suggested, would have to possess two chambers, one directly elected, one representing the member states. The second chamber, however, could be a senate, on the American model, with directly elected members, or it could be a "chamber of states," on the German model, with representatives from the various national governments. The executive of the federation could be the European Council, or else it could be a directly elected president of the Commission with "far-reaching executive powers." It was in fact clear from Fischer's text that he preferred this latter option since he explicitly worried that a thirty-member European Council might take "days, maybe even weeks" to reach decisions on any issue of importance.[49]

Most of the latter half of Fischer's speech was concerned with the issue of "enhanced cooperation." This is the possibility, written into the Amsterdam treaty, for a core group of states to press ahead with common policies in policy areas not currently covered by the treaties. Fischer, in his speech, interpreted the phrase as an invitation to proceed to the creation of a federation along with an avant-garde of equally federalist states. Such a group of states, Fischer visualized, "would establish a government which within the EU should speak with one voice on behalf of the members of the group" and would have its own parliament and directly elected president. It would also be open to "all member states and candidate countries," for "it would be historically absurd and utterly stupid if Europe . . . were to be divided once again." In the 1990s, influential members of the European establishment had advocated again and again this idea of an avant-garde, or nucleus, or inner core of member states pressing ahead towards full federation. Not every country in the EU is prepared any longer to hobble along towards political integration at the pace of the most unwilling members of the group. The Treaty of Nice did in fact loosen the rules on enhanced cooperation by reducing the minimum number of states required to undertake enhanced cooperation to eight (less than one-third of an enlarged EU) and by removing the other member states' right of veto of such initiatives. Such initiatives, however, will have to respect "the single institutional framework" of the Union and will have to satisfy a series of conditions to ensure that the EU's achievements (above all, the single market) remain unharmed.

Fischer's speech provoked a flurry of counterspeeches and position statements from Europe's great and good. There is little doubt that the chief reason that it attracted so much attention was that it proposed a remedy—albeit a controversial one—to a widespread feeling of malaise. What Fischer was saying, in essence, was that the EU's institutions were inefficient and suffered from what the flourishing literature on the subject among political scientists calls the "democratic deficit" in the EU. The charge is that the EU has robbed national parliaments of their traditional legislative role since 1986, but EU institutions are not accountable to voters in the way that national parliaments were and are.

Objectively, there is some truth in this accusation. Decisions over interest rates are now made by a committee of central bankers, not elected politicians accountable to public opinion. Major policy decisions are made by the European Council and then passed on for implementation by the Commission, the Council of Ministers and the Parliament. Citizens, especially the citizens of the small countries, inevitably feel excluded from this process, because short of working through a transnational lobbying group, they can only influence the national politicians of one country, not all fifteen. Back in 1992, in the wake of the Danish and French referendums, the Birmingham European Council, in the so-called Birmingham Declaration, asserted that "decisions must be taken as closely as possible to citizens" and affirmed that "national parliaments should be more closely involved in the Community's activities," but little has been done, at any rate in the eyes of public opinion, to live up to these pledges.[50] Most voters do not understand the process by which EU legislation is made, or even who is making legislation on their behalf. Knowledge of the European Parliament and its activities, for instance, despite the enhanced powers it acquired at Amsterdam, remains low. Europe's institutions appear remote to the EU's citizens. While the EU has multiplied what the German scholar Fritz Scharpf calls the *output* side of democratic politics (increased welfare and prosperity), it has undoubtedly weakened the *input* side (the possibility of democratic participation).[51]

The European Parliament has done its best to raise its profile with the European electorate. Along with the rest of the EU's institutions, it has embraced the Internet with vigor and strives to makes its debates and legislative procedures as transparent as possible. More important, perhaps, to a greater extent than ever before the Parliament attempted to act in the 1990s as a democratic check on the decisions of the European Council and to hold the Commission to account. In July 1994, the newly elected Parliament almost refused to endorse the member states' choice of replacement for Jacques Delors, the prime minister of Luxembourg, Jacques Santer. The original favorite to replace Delors had been the Belgian Christian Democrat Jean-Luc Dehaene. For Britain, the problem with Dehaene was that he was another figure in the same mold as Delors: a keen activist for extending the role of the EU's institutions. Prime Minister John Major accordingly vetoed his nomination. The Parliament struck back by confirming Santer only after a "nail-biting vote of approval."[52] Santer's nomination passed only by 260 votes to 238, with no fewer than 23 abstentions.

Santer's presidency was to be a fraught one. The president of the Commission proved unable to control his Commission, which included such big beasts of the Brussels jungle as Leon Brittan, the powerful trade commissioner, Neil Kinnock, a former leader of the British Labour Party, and Edith Cresson, a former prime minister of France. But what was more important was that his Commission became a byword for lax standards of public probity. Following an investigation by the Court of Auditors (the body that scrutinizes EU expenditure to prevent fraud), a number of commissioners were suspected of abusing public funds, mismanagement and nepotism at the beginning of 1999. Madame Cresson, for instance, was shown to have appointed—on a remarkably generous salary—a retired provincial dentist, who was also a close personal friend, to be a special political adviser. Cresson was also singled out for having failed to act to control waste and fraud in one of the biggest programs financed by her directorate. In January 1999, the European Parliament threatened to use the biggest weapon in its constitutional armory and censure the Commission. To avoid the humiliation of being the first president of the Commission to be sacked by the Parliament, Santer agreed to allow an independent inquiry into the management of the Commission to be carried out by a committee of independent experts and agreed to abide by its findings. This committee's report was damning. It highlighted a number of serious lapses in judgment by several commissioners, especially Cresson, and painted a general picture of cronyism, inefficiency and waste in the management of the EU. Most severely of all, it concluded that "it is difficult to find anyone who has even the slightest sense of responsibility" for the abuses the committee had uncovered.[53] This shattering phrase obliged the Commission to resign en masse once the report was published on 15 March 1999. Santer was replaced as president of the Commission by Romano Prodi, the Italian prime minister who deserved much of the credit for having successfully steered Italy into the single currency.

The Parliament's zealous pursuit of the Commission's bad management might have been expected to raise its profile with the EU electorate. However, the scandal merely seems to have confirmed the European electorate's increasingly gloomy perception of the Union's institutions. Shortly after Santer's enforced resignation, the EU's member states had to go to the polls for the June 1999 elections for the European Parliament. The elections revealed widespread dissatisfaction and apathy among Europe's voters. Britain recorded the lowest turnout in a nationwide election (24 percent) since democracy began. But Britain, while the worst offender, was far from being the only guilty party. In supposedly Europhile Germany, under half the electorate (45.2 percent) voted: this was a drop of 15 percent compared to the previous elections in 1989 and 1994. The Netherlands—another country whose enthusiasm for the European project has never been in doubt—rivaled Britain for the low turnout record: only 29.9 percent of the Dutch voted. In France, where 47.0 percent of the electorate voted, more than one million blank ballots were cast as a symbolic protest, although the protest was aimed as much at France's corrupt political élite as at the EU. Perhaps most damning of all, the elections failed to inspire much enthusiasm in the three most recent entrants to the Union. Only 30 percent of the Finns, 38 percent of the Swedes and 49 percent of the Austrians cast a ballot. Overall, turnout was a meager 49 percent.

There were exceptions to this tendency towards lower participation: 90 percent of the Belgians voted; more of the Spanish (64.3 percent) voted than ever before; Greece's turnout, while down, was still over 70 percent. The Irish and the Portuguese also voted in increased numbers. It is, however, instructive to compare this list of the virtuous with the list of net beneficiaries from the Union budget.

The poor turnout at the European elections was doubtless one of the factors that persuaded Fischer to speak out. But Fischer, as his speech made clear, was also concerned with the issue of subsidiarity. The popular perception that European integration was encroaching on national prerogatives was shown to be widespread in the 1990s by a series of referendum defeats for the EU's core projects. Just as in Italy in the late 1980s and early 1990s, when voters alienated by a detached and venal political class enforced change on the political system by direct democracy, so, since Maastricht, Europe's voters have consistently rebelled against the treaties negotiated by their leaders. We have already seen in this chapter how the Danes and the French almost sank the Maastricht treaty in 1992. The Danes voted against the Euro again in a separate vote in September 1999.

In the summer of 2000, the chancellor of Austria, Wolfgang Schüssel, threatened to hold a national referendum over the sanctions imposed by the rest of the EU after he formed a coalition government with the far-right Austrian Freedom Party (FPÖ) in February 2000. Many Austrians who were repulsed by the FPÖ's Nazi-apologist leader Jorg Haider nevertheless did not see why other European countries should use the Treaty of Amsterdam's insistence on member states' respecting democracy and human rights to justify their refusal to maintain normal diplomatic relations with Austria. The FPÖ had been democratically elected, and while its views on most subjects (immigration especially) were very right-wing, the party had not been implicated in acts of violence and had not disavowed democratic principles. Panicked at the thought of the referendum becoming a plebiscite on EU membership, the other member states backed off after the publication of a report by a group of "wise men" stating that human rights were not then at risk in Austria. It is hard to dispute Dinan's judgment that "the abiding memory" of what he calls the "Austrian imbroglio" is of "self-righteousness and political ineptitude" on the part of several member states.[54] Several EU governments, notably Belgium and Portugal, had used the machinery of the EU to attack a government they did not like and to interfere in the domestic politics of another member state.

Most recently, in June 2001, the Irish electorate voted against the Treaty of Nice by 54 to 46 percent, albeit on a low poll of just 35 percent.[55] This time, the main issues were the EU's decision (see the following) to create a Rapid Reaction Force—rapidly dubbed a "European Army"—and the facilitation by the Nice treaty of enhanced cooperation. As with the Danes in 1992, the Irish were quickly told that their "no" would not hold up ratification elsewhere and that they would have to put the treaty to the voters again. In October 2002, they ratified the treaty by a large majority on a much higher turnout.

It is important not to exaggerate the extent of either the "democratic deficit" or the occasional voter rebellions against EU policy via referendums. Problems of low political participation and alienation from politics are common in other continent-wide democracies, too. American voters, for instance, are notoriously uninterested in national politics. Moreover, the treaties of Maastricht, Amsterdam and Nice have aroused little indignation in most of the EU's member states. Nevertheless, the period since Nice has been characterized by a growing recognition among European governments that an EU with a single currency, more member states and ever-increasing burden of regulatory responsibility cannot continue with its present decision-making mechanisms. Joschka Fischer may be judged wrong in thinking that a federal state is the best way forward for the EU of more than twenty countries that seems certain to arrive by 2004–2005. But the present institutional structure emerged when "Europe" had only nine members and was little more than a customs union with pretensions to higher things.

THE EU'S GROWING WORLD ROLE

This pressure for institutional change will grow even stronger if the EU continues to strengthen its responsibilities in foreign and defense policy. Historically, the EU's "external" role has mainly been confined to two areas: international trade and relations with the member states' former colonies in Africa, the Caribbean and the Pacific (the ACP countries).

In the 1990s, both of these areas were themselves the subject of important developments. In trade, the French government finally yielded in the Uruguay round talks and allowed the EU in December 1992 to make a deal that considerably liberalized world trade and which created the new World Trade Organization (WTO) to act as an independent arbiter of trade disputes.[56] The

WTO has since been the seat for a series of high-level trade disputes between the EU and the United States, which has objected strongly to the EU's banana import regime, its opposition to the import of hormone-treated meat and genetically modified wheat and subsidies of Airbus Industries, Boeing's successful chief rival in the production of commercial airliners. The Europeans, on their side, reacted angrily to the American imposition of tariffs on steel imports in March 2002. The EU's steel industries rationalized their productive capacity much earlier than U.S. producers, at some cost in unemployment, and they now produce high-quality steel more cheaply than U.S. producers can manage. In general, the creation of the WTO has sharply raised the EU's profile on the international stage.

Relations with the ACP countries—who now number over seventy—have been governed through the four Lomé Conventions (Lomé is the capital of the African republic of Togo) signed since 1975.[57] Like their predecessor, the Yaoundé agreement (see chapter 4), the conventions have provided a framework for the distribution of Community aid through the European Development Fund (EDF) and have offered signatories to the conventions privileged access to the European market. The failure of the African nations, in particular, to move towards greater democracy and higher levels of economic development, has however caused EU policymakers to rethink its aid program. The fifth Lomé Convention, signed in June 2000, proposed a free trade area with the EU by 2020 and allocated €13,500 million in aid for the period from 2000 to 2006. It insisted, however, that aid would be closely linked to constructive policies to build democratic institutions and improve human rights. As a sign that it means business, the EU has since imposed sanctions on Zimbabwe following the tyrannical behavior of President Robert Mugabe towards Zimbabwe's white farmers and towards the democratic opposition.[58]

These high-profile developments in the traditional areas of "external activity" have been matched by several new initiatives. Growing trade with Asia and China has led to the institution of annual EU–China summits.[59] The growing problem of migration from the countries of North Africa stimulated the EU to launch the so-called Euro-Mediterranean process with twelve Mediterranean and Middle Eastern states at Barcelona in November 1995.[60] The goal of the process is the creation of a free trade area by 2005. In the meantime, the EU is also contributing €1,000 million in annual aid to its partners. Romano Prodi has called the Euro-Mediterranean process "a historic opportunity with economic, political and moral dimensions that the European Union cannot let slip."[61] The EU has a clear interest in ensuring that the problems of demography and Islamic fundamentalism currently straining the political systems of these countries do not spill over into social breakdown and civil disruption.

Potentially the biggest innovation in the area of foreign and defense policy, however, was the decision made by the December 1999 Helsinki European Council to institute a "European Rapid Reaction Force" (ERRF) of approximately 60,000 troops supported by a fleet of 100 ships and 400 warplanes. This decision would never have been possible had British premier Tony Blair not "crossed a European rubicon" in 1998 by softening British policy towards the concept of independent European forces.[62] The St. Malo declaration (3 December 1998) by Blair and French president Jacques Chirac, which spoke of a European "capacity for autonomous action backed up by credible military forces," was the starting point for the ERRF.[63] During the war against Yugoslavia in the spring of 1999, which demonstrated that "though their defense expenditure amounted to two-thirds of that of the Americans, [the Europeans] were capable of delivering only one-tenth of the firepower," the EU realized that it did not have such forces.[64] The EU had to rely on the United States to fight the conflict for it, even though it was taking place on the EU's doorstep. Work is now proceeding on the ERRF, and the force is expected to become a reality in 2003.

If the EU is going to develop a credible military capacity, however, it will have to find answers to four related problems. First, it is going to have to spend more on defense and spend it better by raising the technological prowess of European troops. Second, it is going to have to convince a skeptical European public that its tax Euro ought to be spent on such armaments—no easy task in antimilitarist countries like Germany, Italy or the Netherlands. Third, if the first two tasks can be successfully accomplished, it is going to need to develop foreign policy decision-making procedures that will enable the new military capacity to be used swiftly and efficiently. Fourth, it is going to have to clarify its relationship with the United States, since NATO has been the fulcrum of European foreign and defense policy since 1949. Will the search for a common foreign and defense policy lead to a cooler relationship with the United States, or simply to greater parity between the two economic superpowers? While it is very important not to overestimate the degree of tension existing between Europe and the United States, it is clear that policymakers on both sides of the Atlantic are beginning to see the relationship as one of friendly rivalry.[65] The risk with this, of course, is that the rivalry may spill over into unfriendliness.

Nevertheless, foreign and defense policy is seen in Brussels as both a necessary and natural candidate for Europeanization. In May 2002, a Commission strategy document, *A Project for the European Union*, argued that from now on, the "European Union must exercise the responsibilities of a world power." With the accession of the CEEC, the Commission contended, the Union will be from 2004 the largest economy in the world and would need to "defend" its values and "model of society" against the pressures of globalization—a word that is very often a euphemism for the preferences of the United States. To this end, the Commission proposed combining the posts of commissioner for external affairs with that of the high representative for foreign affairs in order to create a new institutional figure very similar to an American secretary of state, possessing wide powers of "action and initiative." QMV would be used in the European Council or the Council of Foreign Ministers to back or overturn this figure's suggested initiatives.[66]

The road from Commission wish list to treaty implementation is, of course, a long one. The Commission's proposals are nevertheless indicative of current thinking about the EU's role in world politics and emphasize the centrality of foreign policy for the EU today.

A CONSTITUTIONAL CONVENTION

A Project for the European Union was submitted to the "Convention" on the EU's institutional and political future set up by the Laeken European Council in Belgium in December 2001. Chaired by Giscard d'Estaing, the Convention is composed of two vice chairmen, fifteen representatives nominated by the national governments, thirty members of national parliaments (two per state), sixteen members of the European Parliament and two representatives from the Commission. The applicant countries are each sending a government representative and two parliamentarians to participate in the Convention, but they are not be able "to prevent any consensus which may emerge among the member states."

The Convention held its inaugural meeting on 1 March 2002. It appointed an inner drafting committee, a "praesidium," to "lend impetus and provide an initial working basis." All the Convention's discussions are in the public domain and public opinion can influence the debate via a "forum" to which interested organizations, citizens, academics and business groups contribute ideas. The Convention's mandate runs until January 2003, when it will present the European Council with a final document, which may offer different options or outright recommendations. These recommendations will be the starting point for the discussions of the 2004 IGC, which will make "the ultimate decisions" about the future of an EU with twenty-five member states and may supersede the treaties with a written constitutional document.[67]

It remains to be seen whether the Convention will provide the EU with the "great constitutional debate" that an American political philosopher, Larry Siedentop, has insisted is needed in Europe today.[68] Giscard has no doubts. With characteristic humility, he has compared the Convention to the delegates who met at Philadelphia in September 1787. A better comparison might be with the Assembly of the ECSC in 1952. Then, as now, the drafters had to balance supranationalism with respect for the rights and sensitivities of the member states.

This comparison does not imply that Europe is on the verge of completing itself by transforming itself into a United States of Europe. National pride prevented the realization of a strong federal state in the 1950s and may do so again. Many influential scholars and thinkers, moreover, have suggested that the federal model is a superseded one. To give just one example from a vast literature, the British sociologist and philosopher Anthony Giddens, explicitly arguing against Joschka Fischer's May 2000 speech, has stated that "the federalist model" advanced in the 1940s and 1950s does not fit the requirements of contemporary European and post–Cold War politics. Giddens favors moving away from a hierarchical, state-centric model of governance to a more devolved, pluralist system of "cosmopolitan nations." Authority needs to be devolved away from the nation-state to the regions, from the regions to towns, from the member states to the EU (but also from the EU back to the member states), from the EU to global institutions of governance. The EU, by providing a means whereby the national government could pool national sovereignty to solve specific problems, has already been a pioneer in this postmodern approach to governance, and, in a sense, Giddens is saying that Europe needs to recognize the logic of what it has actually done, rather than revert (under the illusion of pressing ahead) to the creation of a strong, but essentially old-fashioned federal state.[69] Joseph Weiler was expressing the same worry when he said (of the Maastricht treaty) that "it would be more than ironic if a polity set up as a means to counter the excesses of statism ended up coming round full circle and transforming itself into a (super) state."[70] The eminent German political scientist Wolfgang Wessels has argued, however, that thinkers like Weiler need not disturb themselves. Wessels does not expect Europe's leaders to be able to agree to "a constitution with a clear *finalité politique*," as Fischer wanted, but to carry on as present towards inventing ever more complex forms of institutional cooperation in an increasing number of public policy areas.[71]

It may be, of course, that the national politicians themselves have not realized that the idea of strong federal institutions is a superseded one and that they are committed to a future of increasing complexity of governance. Fischer's vision for the future of Europe has been backed up by several authoritative figures, most notably Jacques Delors. In April 2001, Delors asserted that "we have reached a stage where the political agenda can no longer hide behind the economic one, and must assert itself in its own right" and added that democratic legitimacy and the need to make Europe's voice count in the world required the creation of a "federation of nation-states," with its own parliament and council of ministers, by an "open vanguard" of member states.[72]

Then again, there is the interesting paradox that the creation of a traditional federal state by such a vanguard group would only add to the complexity of European governance. Under such circumstances, one can imagine that the EU would evolve into the institutional mechanism whereby the legislative preferences of the vanguard group were negotiated and harmonized with the

wishes and interests of the member states who had chosen to stay out. It is perhaps for this reason that the Commission, in *A Project for the European Union*,
emphasized vehemently that "an *à la carte* Europe is not the right option for
the future of the Union" and, indeed, suggested that existing derogations such
as the ones enjoyed by Denmark and Britain should be phased out.[73] The
Commission, in addition to its recommendations on foreign policy, is arguing
for the abandonment of the three-pillar structure, the ubiquity of QMV in the
Council of Ministers and co-decision by the European Parliament for all EU
legislative acts. As this book went to press, the debate in the Convention was
divided between supporters of a "Union of States" and the views of outright
federalists such as Fischer. But it did seem likely that the Convention would approve a draft constitution that substantially enhanced the range of questions
decided at "federal" level and that strengthened the power of Brussels relative
to the national capitals.

Once a historian begins speculating on the future, it is probably time for
him to stop and look back over his narrative. The Convention, and the IGC
that will follow, is almost certainly the latest of a series of defining moments
in the EU's history. The Schuman Plan, together with Britain's diffidence towards Europe in the 1940s and early 1950s, was the first. It meant that Europe proceeded on its journey at the speed dictated by Germany and, above
all, France. The decision to reject the Fouchet plan was the second. It prevented de Gaulle from trying to turn Europe into a superpower and confirmed his rejection of the gradual supranationalism preferred by Monnet
and Hallstein. The consequence was that the EEC was reduced to being an
intergovernmental association of states until the 1980s. The conflux of factors that led to the signing of the Single European Act was the third turning
point in Europe's history. In retrospect, the SEA was the pivotal moment in
our story. Until 1986, the EC, for all its rhetoric, was an association of states
concerned mostly with agriculture. Thereafter, it had a project and an identity. Rightly or wrongly, many of the most representative statesmen of their
time (Jacques Delors, Helmut Kohl, François Mitterrand) believed that the
"space" cleared by Cockfield and Delors had to be filled with a single currency, common social policy standards, assistance for the less-developed parts
of Europe, high environmental standards and so on. Between 1986 and
1993, they bulldozed these things through.

But the gradual transfer of policy competences to the Union has only underlined the political implications of economic unification. In the 1990s,
these implications have dominated the Union's debate and would probably
have done so even had there not been the imminent arrival of a dozen new
members anxious to participate in the project. Fifty years on from Monnet's
announcement that "the United States of Europe have begun" to the Assembly of the ECSC, Europe's statesmen are still searching for a vision of
Europe's future that will satisfy public opinion and strengthen their ability to

respond to the challenges of a rapidly changing political and economic environment. In the meantime, they also face the headaches of a new decade of consolidation that is likely to dissipate their energies and to prove as rancorous as even the early 1980s. Like most families, the European family of nations is always at its worst when its members are talking about money.

But it would also be wrong to end this book on too pessimistic a note. Since 1945, Europe's leaders, especially the principal statesmen of France and Germany, have brought their peoples peace and prosperity on an unprecedented scale. Economic cooperation through the institutions of the EC has raised standards of living in some of the poorest parts of Western Europe (Spain, Portugal, Ireland) to levels unimaginable even twenty years ago. These achievements are ultimately due to the consistent willingness of Europe's postwar leaders to put the process of discovering common solutions ahead of the practice of imposing national ones. Europe's nation-states have superseded the traditional methods of realpolitik in the past fifty years, and Europe as a whole is a better, safer place for their restraint.

NOTES

1. David Marquand, *Parliament for Europe* (London: Cape, 1979), 102.

2. For the entry of Austria, Finland and Sweden, see Francesco Granelli, "The European Union's Enlargement Negotiations with Austria, Finland, Norway and Sweden," *Journal of Common Market Studies* 33, no. 1 (March 1995): 117–141.The September 1995 edition of the same journal contains specific articles on Austria, Finland and Norway by well-known experts.

3. Jolyon Howorth, "European Defense and the Changing Politics of the European Union: Hanging Together or Hanging Separately," *Journal of Common Market Studies* 39, no. 4 (November 2001): 767.

4. Jacques Delors, *La France par l'Europe* (Paris: Grasset, 1988), 60. The original French reads as follows: "Faire l'Europe, dans le rapport actuel des forces mondiales, cela revient à se réapproprier une capacité de décision autonome. Faire l'Europe, c'est retrouver un degré de liberté nécessaire à une 'certaine idée de la France.'"

5. See David Marsh, *Germany and Europe: The Crisis of Unity* (London: Mandarin, 1995), 63–99. The quotation from John Major in this paragraph is from *John Major: The Autobiography* (London: HarperCollins, 2000), 313.

6. Bernard Connolly, *The Rotten Heart of Europe* (London: Faber and Faber, 1995), 122.

7. Connolly, *Rotten Heart of Europe*, 137.

8. Desmond Dinan, *An Ever Closer Union* (London: Macmillan, 1994), 186.

9. Quoted Marsh, *Germany and Europe*, 149.

10. See Connolly, *Rotten Heart of Europe*, 144–47, for an account of this explosive meeting.

11. *The Economist*, 26 September 1992, 15.

12. For blow-by-blow accounts of the events on Black Wednesday and the days

immediately before and after, see *The Birth of the Euro*, ed. Dan Bilefsky and Ben Hall (London: Penguin, 1998), 63–74. John Major's direct personal account in *John Major: The Autobiography*, 330–41, is fascinating reading. Major went to bed on 16 September "half-convinced my days as prime minister were drawing to a close."

13. *The Economist*, 29 August 1992, 19; 19 September 1992, 1.

14. *The Economist*, 26 September 1992, 15.

15. Sir Leon Brittan, *Europe: The Europe We Need* (London: Hamish Hamilton, 1994), 46.

16. *The Economist*, 23 December 1995–January 1996, 45.

17. *Bull. EC*, no. 12/95, 25.

18. Background to Germany's economic diplomacy in the mid-1990s can be found in S. Bulmer, C. Jeffrey and W. Paterson, *Germany's European Diplomacy: Shaping the Regional Milieu* (Manchester, U.K.: Manchester University Press, 2000), 92–103.

19. The draft of the "Stability and Growth Pact" is in the *Bull. EC*, no. 12/96, 20–30.

20. Sergio Fabbrini and Mark Gilbert, "When Cartels Fail: The Role of the Political Class in the Italian Transition," *Government and Opposition* 35, no. 1 (Winter 2000): 27–48.

21. See Mark Gilbert, *The Italian Revolution: The End of Politics, Italian Style?* (Boulder, Colo.: Westview, 1995), ch.1 *passim*.

22. Michele Salvati, "Moneta unica, rivoluzione copernicana," *Il Mulino*, January 1997, 5–23.

23. Alberta Sbragia, "Italy Pays for Europe: Political Leadership, Political Choice and Institutional Adaption," in *Transforming Europe*, ed. Maria Green Cowles, James Caporaso and Thomas Risse (Ithaca, N.Y.: Cornell University Press, 2000), 95.

24. For the Commission's recommendations, see *Bull. EC*, no. 3/98.

25. *The Economist*, 9 May 1998, 22.

26. There are some who hold the contrary position and argue that the economic costs of maintaining Europe's welfare state will be so great as Europe's population ages that some of the Euro-zone's member states will exert pressure on the ECB to follow a lax monetary policy that will inflate away their debts. The political tensions that arise from this pressure may cause the Euro to fold like the Latin Monetary Union in the nineteenth century. See Niall Ferguson and Lawrence Kotlikoff, "Can the Euro Survive?" *Foreign Affairs* 79, no. 2 (2000): 110–21.

27. This skim through the pros and cons of the Euro is indebted to John Peet, "An Awfully Big Adventure," survey, *The Economist*, 11 April 1998; Bilefsky and Hall, eds., *The Birth of the Euro*, 94–158; and an excellent short book by a Euro-insider, Lorenzo Bini Smaghi, *L'euro* (Bologna, Italy: Il Mulino, 1998).

28. The eleven countries constituting the Euro-zone had a joint product of $6,300 billion in 1998. The U.S. figure was $8,100 billion. Vicky Bakshi, "Watch Out Dollar," in *The Birth of the Euro*, ed. Dan Bilefsky and Ben Hall (London: Penguin, 1998), 254–57.

29. C. Randall Henning, "Europe's Monetary Union and the United States," *Foreign Policy*, no. 102 (1996): 83–100 at 94.

30. Martin Feldstein, "EMU and International Conflict," *Foreign Affairs* 77, no. 4 (November/December 1997): 66–73 for quotes.

31. See Anna Michalski and Helen Wallace, *The European Community: The Challenge of Enlargement* (London: Royal Institute of International Affairs, 1992), 152–67.

32. The statistics on the Phare program are taken from European Commission, *European Union Enlargement. A Historic Opportunity* (Luxembourg: European Union, 2001), 44–45.

33. Quoted Michalski and Wallace, *European Community*, 158.

34. The Copenhagen Criteria are discussed in European Commission, *European Union Enlargement*, 9.

35. "Europe's Mexico Option," *The Economist*, 5 October 2002, 36.

36. European Commission, *Agenda 2000: For a Stronger and Wider Union* (Luxembourg: European Union, July 1997), 67. See also Michael Baun, *A Wider Europe: The Process and Politics of European Union Enlargement* (Lanham, Md.: Rowman & Littlefield, 2000).

37. *The Economist*, 9 February 2002, 33–34.

38. For trade statistics, see European Commission, *European Union Enlargement*, 40–41.

39. Andrew Moravcsik and Kalypso Nicolaidis, "Federal Ideals and Constitutional Realities in the Treaty of Amsterdam," *Journal of Common Market Studies* 36 (annual review of 1997): 14.

40. Richard Corbett, "Governance and Institutions," *Journal of Common Market Studies* 36 (annual review of 1997): 39.

41. *The Economist*, 21 June 1997, 15.

42. Corbett, "Governance and Institutions," 43.

43. Mark Gray and Alexander Stubb, "The Treaty of Nice: Negotiating a Poisoned Chalice," *Journal of Common Market Studies* 39 (annual review of 2000): 13.

44. The Charter of Fundamental Rights was published in the *Bull. EC*, no. 12/2000, app. 2.2.1.

45. Gray and Stubb, "Negotiating a Poisoned Chalice," 15.

46. In addition to the text of the treaty itself, this account of the "constitutional" changes introduced by the Treaty of Nice was based upon an 18 January 2001 "Memorandum to the Members of the Commission," document reference SEC (2001), 99, from David O'Sullivan, a member of Romano Prodi's cabinet.

47. Joschka Fischer, "From Confederacy to Federation—Some Thoughts on the Finality of European Integration," speech at the Humboldt University in Berlin, 12 May 2000, 5. The version I have used is the official English translation of the advance copy of the speech to be found on the website of the University of Leiden at www.let.leidenuniv.nl/history/rtg/res1/fischer.htm.

48. Fischer, "From Confederacy to Federation," 5.

49. Fischer, "From Confederacy to Federation," 6.

50. "Birmingham Declaration," *Bull. EC*, no. 10/92.

51. See Fritz Scharpf, "Community and Autonomy: Multi-Level Policy-Making in the European Union," *Journal of European Public Policy* 1 (1994): 219–42.

52. *The Economist*, 23 July 1994, 35.

53. The report of the "Independent Experts" is printed in full in *Bull. EC*, no. 3/99, 139–44.

54. Desmond Dinan, "Governance and Institutions 2000: Edging Towards Enlargement," *Journal of Common Market Studies* 39 (annual report of 2000): 41.

55. For a succinct account of the Irish referendum, see Desmond Dinan, "Ireland Says No," *EUSA Review* 14, no. 3 (Summer 2001): 7.

56. In addition to establishing the WTO, the agreement cut industrial tariffs by 40 percent, liberalized trade in textiles and services and opened public procurement to international bidding. The estimated direct economic gain of the deal was $200,000 to $300,000 million in increased economic activity by 2002.

57. For an overview of the Lomé process in the 1990s, see David Lowe, "The Developmental Policy of the European Union and the Mid-Term Review of the Lomé Partnership," *Journal of Common Market Studies* 34 (annual review, August 1996): 15–28.

58. The EU Council of Foreign Ministers suspended EU aid programs and froze the assets held within the EU of several important members of the Mugabe regime in February 2002. *Bull. EC,* no. 1-2/2002, point 1.6.157.

59. The first of these was held in London on 2 April 1998.

60. The twelve states were Algeria, Cyprus, Egypt, Israel, Jordan, Lebanon, Malta, Morocco, the Palestinian authority, Syria, Tunisia and Turkey.

61. Romano Prodi, *Europe As I See It* (Cambridge: Polity, 2001), 70.

62. Howorth, "European Defense," 767.

63. Quoted Howorth, "European Defense," 772. For detailed background on the St. Malo Declaration, see the same author's *European Integration and Defence: The Ultimate Challenge?* Chaillot Paper no. 43 (Paris: WEU-ISS, 2000).

64. Pinder, *European Union: A Very Short Introduction* (Oxford: Oxford University Press, 2001), 121.

65. See William Wallace, "Europe, the Necessary Partner," and Anthony J. Blinken, "The False Crisis over the Atlantic," both in *Foreign Affairs* 80, no. 3: 16–48, for two insightful discussions of the present state of EU-U.S. relations. A much more pessimistic analysis is to be found in Robert Kagan, "Power and Weakness," *Policy Review,* no. 113 (June/July 2002), available at www.policyreview.org/. This article, with its arresting opening sentence "It is time to stop pretending that Europeans and Americans share a common view of the world, or even that they occupy the same world," has been intensely debated by policymakers on both sides of the Atlantic.

66. European Commission, *Project for the European Union,* 14–21. Convention document 229/02. All Convention documents can be accessed through the EU's website *Europa,* www.europa.eu.int/.

67. The Declaration of Laeken is published in *Bull. EC* 12/2001, point I.27

68. Larry Siedentop, *Democracy in Europe* (London: Penguin, 2001), 1.

69. Anthony Giddens, "A Third Way for Europe," in *The Pro-European Reader,* ed. Dick Leonard and Mark Leonard (London: Palgrave, 2002), 164–70.

70. J. H. H. Weiler, *The Constitution of Europe* (Cambridge: Cambridge University Press, 1999), 250.

71. Wolfgang Wessels, "Nice Results: The Millennium IGC in the EU's Evolution," *Journal of Common Market Studies* 39, no. 2 (June 2001): 215.

72. Jacques Delors, "Where Is the European Union Heading?" speech given on a lecture tour of the United States, 26 March–4 April 2001. Text available at eurunion.org.

73. European Commission, *Project for the European Union,* 23.

Bibliographical Essay

Rather than give a full list of books and articles that I have read while writing this book, since many of them are already cited in the endnotes to each chapter, I thought it would be more constructive to give a guide to some of the key published sources in English that, for example, a liberal arts college teacher preparing an undergraduate course in post-1945 European history or a graduate student preparing her "comps" might wish to read and use as the basis for a syllabus.

HISTORIES AND REFLECTIONS

The most detailed, though very theoretical, history of the interstate "bargains" that have punctuated European unification is Andrew Moravcsik's *The Choice for Europe: Social Purpose and State Power from Messina to Maastricht* (Cornell University Press, 1998). I have in several places disagreed with the conclusions of this book, but it is an indisputable achievement that those interested in European integration need to treat as a cornerstone of their reading. More general histories do exist, although one of my main reasons for writing this book was that they are not nearly so common as one might expect. The first chapters of Desmond Dinan's outstanding *Ever Closer Union?* (Macmillan, 1994) and Richard McAllister's *From EC to EU* (Routledge, 1997) are useful historical surveys, while *The Dynamics of European Union*, ed. Roy Pryce (Routledge, 1989) is a first-class collection of essays on significant moments in the EC's history. J. H. H. Weiler's *The Constitution of Europe* (Cambridge University Press, 1999) and Stanley Hoffmann's *The European Sisyphus* (Westview, 1991) are very important collections of analytical essays by two eminent scholars in the field. Weiler's "Do the New Clothes Have an Emperor?" which is included in *The Constitution of Europe,* was probably the most thought-provoking article I read while preparing this book.

MEMOIR AND BIOGRAPHY

The main protagonists of European unification have left a good stock of memoirs and have themselves been extensively studied by biographers. There is no need to mention all the possible biographical sources here. I found Robert Marjolin's *Architect of European Unity* (Weidenfeld and Nicholson, 1989) to be the single most useful autobiography. Like Roy Jenkins's *A Life at the Centre* (Macmillan, 1994), it is a transparently honest book that gives a real insight into the mind of the European political élite of his time. The chapters on European matters in Margaret Thatcher's *Downing Street Years* (HarperCollins, 1995) contain, unsurprisingly, very blunt judgments on what she regarded, by the time she wrote her memoirs, as the Community "Babel Express." Among biographies, Hans-Peter Schwarz's monumental *Konrad Adenauer: German Politician and Statesman in a Period of War, Revolution and Reconstruction* (Berghahn, 1995 vol. 1, and 1997 vol. 2) is a very lucid, informative and well-structured account of the German states-man's life. Its only weakness is that it takes a fortnight to read! François Duchêne's life of Jean Monnet, *The First Statesman of Interdependence* (Norton, 1994) and Charles Grant's splendidly readable *Delors: The House that Jacques Built* (Brealey, 1994) are both extremely valuable books. We lack, however, biographical accounts in English of the main Italian protagonists: the absence of a life, times and policy of Alcide de Gasperi, or at least a well-documented account of his European policy, is a glaring gap in the literature. It is a gap I hope myself to fill in the not-too-distant future.

EARLY YEARS

The early years of European integration are the subject of Alan Milward's *The European Rescue of the Nation State* (Routledge, 1992, 2d edition), which, by giving eighty pages to the travails of the Belgian coal industry and just over twenty to the "lives and teachings of the European saints," makes its methodological priorities almost excessively explicit. Milward's *The Reconstruction of Europe 1945–1951* (Routledge, 1992), however, is a classic of contemporary history: its breadth of archival research and clarity of exposition are almost intimidating. The European movement is chronicled in detail by Walter Lipgens, Alan Milward and Wilfried Loth's *A History of Euro-*

pean Integration 1945–1947 (Clarendon Press, 1987), while U.S. policy to Europe is the main subject of Michael Hogan, *The Marshall Plan: America, Britain and the Reconstruction of Western Europe* (Cambridge University Press, 1987), Mark Trachtenberg, *A Constructed Peace: The Making of the European Settlement 1945–63* (Princeton University Press, 1999) and Pascaline Winand, *Eisenhower, Kennedy and the United States of Europe* (St. Martin's, 1993). Robert Lieshout, *The Struggle for the Organization of Europe* (Edward Elgar, 1999) is very good on the negotiation of the Treaties of Rome.

DE GAULLE AND THE 1960s

Works on de Gaulle and Gaullism are legion. The standard biography of de Gaulle in French is Jean Lacouture's three-volume work; the latter two volumes are available in English as *De Gaulle the Ruler 1945–1970* (Harvill, 1991). On the question of British entry into the EEC, Miriam Camps, *Britain and the European Community 1955–1963* (Princeton University Press, 1964) is still essential reading, as is Lois Pattison de Ménil, *Who Speaks for Europe? The Vision of Charles de Gaulle* (Weidenfeld and Nicholson, 1977). Otto Bange's *The EEC Crisis of 1963* (Macmillan, 2000), while a little fragmented in narrative structure, is very convincingly argued. *Britain's Failure to Enter the European Community 1961–63*, ed. George Wilkes (Cass, 1997) brings together a collection of essays by leading European scholars: the contributions of Gustav Schmidt and Maurice Vaisse are particularly important. John Newhouse's *Collision in Brussels* (Faber, 1967) remains a very readable account of the "Empty Chair" crisis.

THE BRITISH QUESTION

So much of the EC's history since the death of de Gaulle has been dominated by two issues: Britain's troubled membership and the question of monetary policy. The former of these subjects is surveyed in Stephen George, *The Awkward Partner: Britain and European Cooperation* (Oxford University Press, 2001, 3d edition). Hugo Young's *This Blessed Plot* (Macmillan, 1998) covers the same ground very elegantly. The debate between Eurosceptics and Europhiles in Britain has produced two anthologies compiled almost entirely from British sources, *The Pro-European Reader*, ed. Dick Leonard and Mark Leonard (Palgrave, 2002) and *The Eurosceptical Reader*, ed. Martin Holmes (Macmillan, 1996). It also adds spice to *John Major: The Autobiography* (HarperCollins, 2000), which gives a very illuminating picture of the civil war over Europe within the British government after Maastricht. The best general account of the relationship of the Thatcher and Major governments with the accelerating pace of European integration in the 1980s and early 1990s is Philip Stephen, *Politicians and the Pound* (Papermac, 1996), which is also a useful starting point for anybody interested in monetary union.

ECONOMIC AND MONETARY UNION

On this latter topic, Kenneth Dyson and Kevin Featherstone's *The Road to Maastricht: Negotiating Economic and Monetary Union* (Oxford University Press, 1999) is a superdocumented and intricate history of monetary policy within the EC since the Werner Report; this book's only failing is the jargon with which its (nevertheless important) theoretical chapters are filled. Tommaso Padoa-Schioppa's *The Road to Monetary Union in Europe* (Clarendon Press, 1994) is technical in places but very stimulating. Peter Ludlow's *The Making of the European Monetary System* (Butterworths, 1982) is a vital source on the early years of the EMU project and the creation of the EMS. All three of these books are broadly (in the case of Padoa-Schioppa, passionately) sympathetic to EMU. Bernard Connolly's *The Rotten Heart of Europe* (Faber and Faber, 1995), while it becomes splenetic at times, is an engagingly savage account of the same subject that casts a good deal of doubt on the purity of the Bundesbank's motives and on the general utility of monetary union. Last, but not least, Dennis Swann's *The Economics of the Common Market: Integration in the European Union*, eighth edition (Penguin, 1995), has an outstanding chapter on monetary policy. Swann's book is a central text for all students and scholars of European integration.

AFTER THE SINGLE EUROPEAN ACT

On developments within the EC between the SEA and Maastricht, Richard Corbett, *The Treaty of Maastricht: From Conception to Ratification* (Longman, 1993) is a good starting point. R. Keohane and S. Hoffmann, *The New European Community* (Westview, 1991) and *Euro-politics*, ed. Alberta Sbragia (Brookings Institution, 1993) are outstanding collections of essays by leading EU scholars. George Ross, *Jacques Delors and European Integration* (Polity Press, 1995) is very (too?) kind to its subject, but gives a compelling picture of what working for the upper reaches of the Commission during Delor's presidency was like. David Marsh, *Germany and Europe: The Crisis of Unity* (Mandarin, 1995) and Timothy Garton Ash, *In Europe's Name* (Vintage, 1994) are helpful for understanding the economic and diplomatic significance of German reunification. Michael Baun, *A Wider Europe: The Process and Politics of European Union Enlargement* (Rowman & Littlefield,

2000) is the best secondary source on the thorny issue of enlargement, though here the EU's own documentation is both clear and accessible.

EUROPE IN THE 1990s

Anybody claiming to have read all of the literature on the EU in the 1990s should be treated with some suspicion. The years since Maastricht have seen a quantum leap in the number of EU studies as experts, many of them American, have dissected the strange new polity emerging in Europe. The most important of these, probably, are *Policy Making in the European Union*, ed. H. Wallace and W. Wallace (Oxford University Press, 1996); *Supranational Governance: The Institutionalization of the European Union*, ed. A. Sandholtz and A. Stone Sweet (Oxford University Press, 1998); *Transforming Europe*, ed. Maria Green Cowles, James Caporaso and Thomas Risse (Cornell University Press, 2001). All these books, while of high scholarly quality, are written by political scientists and policy scientists for (or against) other political scientists and policy scientists, and they require a definite prior familiarity with a large body of complex theoretical literature.

The reader who simply wishes to know what the main developments were within the EU between 1992 and 2002 would probably do better to rely on the very accessible and highly informative annual reports on the EU published as a supplement to the *Journal of Common Market Studies*. These reports each contain a keynote article on a major development within the Union during the year in question and empirical, well-researched articles on the EU's institutions, its internal and external policy, legal affairs, major developments within the member states, and the economic situation of the Union and its members, as well as a useful chronology of the year's main events. The EU's website, *Europa* (www.europa.eu.int), and the *Bulletin of the European Community* are essential sources for published documents.

Index

Acheson, Dean, 39, 40
ACP (Africa, Caribbean, Pacific) countries, 249, 250
Action Committee, 64–65, 70, 108
Action Party (Italy), 27, 28
Adenauer, Konrad, 16, 29, 39, 41, 51, 57, 66, 68, 87, 94, 102–3, 104, 199
Adonnino, Giuseppe, 169
Agenda 2000: For a Stronger and Wider Union, 239
agriculture: EU enlargement and, 240; subsidies for, 2; trade liberalization in, 71–72. *See also* CAP (common agricultural policy)
Allied Control Commission, 36, 37
Amato, Giuliano, 10–11
"ambush in Rome", 201
Amministrazione delle Finanze dello Stato v. Simmenthal (case 106/77), 147
Amsterdam summit (1997). *See* Treaty of Amsterdam (1997)
Andreotti, Giulio, 174, 179, 220
Andriessen, Frans, 179
Armand, Louis, 65, 70
Assembly of EEC: composition of, 148; political party representation in 1979, 150; role of, 108, 109, 148. *See also* European Parliament
Assembly of the Council of Europe, 35, 53–54
association agreements, 238, 240–41
Athens summit (1983), 168

Atlantic Charter, 133–34
Attlee, Clement, 42, 43
Austria, 237, 248
Austrian Freedom Party (FPÖ), 248

Bad Godesberg summit meeting (1961), 91
Badinter, Robert, 211
Ball, George W., 45
Balladur, Edouard, 229
Banca d'Italia, 230
Bange, Oliver, 102, 104
Barber, Anthony, 131
Barre, Raymond, 140, 157
Basic Law (German constitution), and promotion of European Union, 221
Berlin airlift, 33, 37
Berlin Wall: construction of, 93; fall of, 198, 221
Bermuda conference of Western leaders (1953), 60
Bevin, Ernest, 23, 28, 31, 32, 34, 41, 42
Beyen, Jan Willem, 64
Bidault, Georges, 29, 35, 38, 40
Birmingham Declaration, 246
Black Wednesday, 230
Blair, Tony, 241, 251
Blum, Leon, 29, 31
border controls, 171, 195–96
Bosnia-Herzegovina, 211
Boult, Sir Adrian, 29
Boyer, Robert, 157

Brailsford, H. N., 26, 27
Brandt, Willi, 126, 132, 205
Bretherton, Russell, 67
Brezhnev, Leonid, 140
Briand, Aristide, 25
Bridges, Sir Edward, 42
Brioni Agreement, 209
British Trade Unions Congress, 193
Brittan, Leon, 247
Bruges speech of Margaret Thatcher, 193–96
Brussels Pact (Treaty on Western Union) (1948), 31, 32, 33, 62, 207
Brussels summit (1984), 169
Buchan, David, 205
Bulgaria, 239, 240
Bull, Hedley, 92
Bundesbank, 128, 131, 144, 191–92, 220, 228, 229, 230, 231
Bush (George W.) administration, 187
Butterfield, Herbert, 8, 9

Callaghan, James, 144, 149
CAP (common agricultural policy): Britain and, 98, 100; and development of common market, 71–72; and "Empty Chair" crisis, 105, 107, 111; and enlargement, 225–26, 240, 241; negotiation of, 88–90; percentage of budget for, 161; reform of (early 1980s), 163–64
Carr, E. H., 26
Carr, Jonathon, 139
Carrington, Lord Peter, 209
Carter, Jimmy, 139, 140
Cassis de Dijon case (no. 120/78), 156, 170–71
Catholic political parties, 19
CEEC. *See* Committee on European Economic Cooperation
central banks of national governments, 190, 214
Central Europe: assistance to, 237–38; EU enlargement and, 1, 221, 225, 237–41
Charter of Fundamental Rights, 243
Cheysson, Claude, 170
Chicago School, 156
China, 32, 250
Chirac, Jacques, 140, 149, 234, 251
Christian Democracy party (DC) (Italy), 232–33
Christian Democrats, 3, 19, 29
Churchill, Winston, 28–29, 31, 60

citizens: attitude toward EU of, 247; and citizenship, 212; political participation in EU by, 212, 226, 245, 246, 247–49
Clayton, Will, 21
Cockfield, Lord Arthur, 170, 171–72, 175, 254
co-decision, 217
Cold War, 19, 37
Cole, G. D. H., 26, 27
Cologne, 16
Colombo, Emilio, 159, 160
Colorni, Eugenio, 27
Commission of EEC: dispute over role of (1965), 106–8; power of, 72–73; role of, 72
Commission of Human Rights, 35
Committee of Ministers: and ECSC High Authority, 53, 54; and intergovernmentalism, 12; role in EEC of, 72; role of, 2
Committee of Permanent Representatives (COREPER), 106
Committee on European Economic Cooperation (CEEC), 22, 23
common agricultural policy. *See* CAP
common market: and agriculture, 71–72; Delors and, 189; establishment of, 50; proposal for, 64. *See also* European Monetary System; European Monetary Union; monetary union
Commonwealth, and EEC entry considerations, 98–99
Communism: American fear of, 17, 23–24; collapse of, 198; postwar attitudes toward, 19–20
Communist political parties: and boycott of Congress of Europe, 29; strength in postwar Western Europe of, 20
Community Charter of Basic Social Rights for Workers, 196–97
Community law: areas of, 2; court rulings on primacy of, 146–47, 156, 170–71; new members and, 238; relation to national law of, 3–4
Conference on Security and Cooperation in Europe, 127
Congress of Europe (1948), 4, 29–31, 33, 137
Connolly, Bernard, 158
Connolly, John, 129
Conservative Party (Great Britain), 18, 99, 149, 202–3, 214

constitutional convention, 252–55
Convention for the Protection of Human
    Rights and Fundamental Freedoms
    (1950), 35, 243
convergence criteria for EMU, 213–14, 216,
    231, 233–34
convertibility of U.S. dollar, 129
cooperation. *See* economic cooperation;
    intergovernmental cooperation;
    supranational cooperation
Copenhagen criteria, 238
Copenhagen report, 123
Copenhagen summits: 1978, 143; 1993,
    238; 2002, 241
Coppé, Albert, 52
Corbett, Richard, 242
Cossiga, Francesco, 162
Costa v. Enel (case 6/64), 146
Council of Europe (1949), 34
Council of Foreign Ministers (CFM), 32,
    36–37
Court of Auditors, 247
Court of Human Rights, 35
Court of Justice. *See* European Court of
    Justice (ECJ)
Couve de Murville, Maurice, 104, 109, 110
Craxi, Bettino, 156, 174
Cresson, Edith, 247
Cripps, Sir Stafford, 32, 42
Croatia, 208–11
Crotty, Raymond, 179
cultural issues, Congress of Europe and, 30
currency: and crisis of 1992–1993, 230;
    revaluation of, 130. *See also* Euro;
    European Currency Unit; monetary
    crises; monetary union
Curry, W. B., 27
customs posts, 171
customs union. *See* common market
Cyprus, 238, 239, 240, 241
Czech Republic, 239, 240, 241
Czechoslovakia, 29, 198

Daily Express (newspaper), 43
De Gasperi, Alcide, 29, 31
de Gaulle, Charles: and Adenauer, 103; and
    agricultural concerns, 100–101; on
    American influence in EEC, 101–2; and
    criticism of EEC (1965), 109–10; and
    EDC, 61; and EEC, 69, 85–115; and
    Free Trade Agreement, 86–87; and
    Nassau defense agreement, 99–100, 102;

and 1965 election, 110; and opposition
    to supranationalism, 109–11, 112; and
    political unification in EEC, 90–96; and
    promotion of France, 90, 112–13; role in
    European integration of, 8, 9, 80, 254;
    and veto of British EEC entry, 99–104,
    111–12
defense, military, 251
Defrenne v. Sabena (case 43/75), 147
Dehaene, Jean-Luc, 246
Dell, Edmund, 43
Delors, Jacques, 155, 158, 170, 172, 175,
    199, 201, 204, 218, 227, 228, 254; and
    EC foreign policy, 205, 206–8; and
    monetary union, 190–93, 220; and
    regional development, 189–90; vision for
    EC of, 183, 189, 193, 221, 253, 254
Delors Commission, 189–93
democracy, and European integration, 16.
    See also citizens: political participation in
    EU by
Denman, Sir Roy, 123, 125
Denmark: Copenhagen criteria and, 238;
    entry into EEC, 126; and national
    sovereignty issue, 4; rejection of
    Maastricht Treaty, 228
Deutsche Mark (DM), 37
dictatorships, popular support in 1930s for,
    26
Dien Bien Phu, Battle of (1954), 60
Dillon round of trade talks, 87
Dinan, Desmond, 248–49
Dixon, Joly, 191
Dooge, James, 169
Dooge committee, 172, 173–74
Dublin summits: 1979, 162; 1990, 200;
    1996, 232
Duisenberg, Wim, 234
Dulles, John Foster: and EDC treaty
    ratification, 60, 61; and European
    unification, 59, 68, 81n14; and Schuman
    Plan, 40
Dyson, Kenneth, 220

East Germany, 198, 199
Eastern Europe: assistance to, 198, 237–38;
    EU enlargement and, 1, 221, 225–26,
    237–41; France and inclusion of, 199
EBRD. *See* European Bank of
    Reconstruction and Development
ECA. *See* Economic Cooperation Agency
ECB. *See* European Central Bank

Ecofin (Council of Economics and Finance Ministers), 215
economic cooperation, as purpose of EU, 1–2
Economic Cooperation Agency (ECA), 24
Economic League for European Cooperation, 29
economic liberalism, ECSC and, 52
economic reconstruction, postwar, 16–17, 20
Economist, The (newspaper), 44, 71, 142, 230, 239
economy: Congress of Europe and, 30; postwar, 21, 23; Single European Act and projections for, 188–89; as stimulus to integration, 1–2, 40, 50, 113–15. *See also* trade; trade liberalization
ECSC. *See* European Coal and Steel Community
Ecu. *See* European Currency Unit
EDC. *See* European Defense Community
Eden, Anthony, 29, 43, 57, 62, 68
Egypt, 134
Eisenhower, Dwight, 57, 59, 90
Empty Chair crisis, 104–9
EMS. *See* European Monetary System
EMU. *See* European Monetary Union
enhanced cooperation, 182, 245, 249
enlargement: and agriculture, 240–41; Central and Eastern Europe, 225–26, 237–41; and Copenhagen criteria for new members, 238; and EU institutional structure, 241; Mediterranean countries, 165–66, 168; philosophy of, 238; projected effects of, 241
environmental policy, Single European Act and, 178
EPU. *See* European Payments Union
Erasmus program, 30
Erhard, Ludwig, 66, 69, 86, 103, 104, 113
ERM. *See* exchange rate mechanism
ERP. *See* European Recovery Program
ESCB. *See* European System of Central Banks
Estonia, 239, 240, 241
Etzel, Franz, 52
Euratom (Atomic Energy Community), 12, 65, 66; demise of, 106; treaty establishing, 68, 69–70
Euro: and 1998 establishment of Euro-zone, 234; advantages of, 234, 235–36; criticisms of, 235; and currency volatility, 235–36; and EU institutional structure, 237; introduction of, 1, 225; naming of, 232
Euro-Mediterranean process, 250

European Act (draft), 159
European Bank of Reconstruction and Development (EBRD), 198, 237
European Central Bank (ECB), 1, 191–92, 213, 214–16, 219, 229, 234
European Coal and Steel Community (ECSC), 51–56: actions of, 55; beginning of, 49; demise of, 106; and European integration, 51; and federalism, 54–55; and "New League" of nations plan, 26; purposes of, 52; Schuman Plan and, 39–45; Treaty of (1951), 49, 51
European Commission: and CAP reform of 1980s, 163; extension of powers through Single European Act, 177; restructuring of, in Nice Treaty, 243; role of, 2; scandal in (1999), 247; and supranationalism, 12
European Community (EC): and enlargement, 165–66, 168; Franco-German rapprochement and, 18; overview of 1970s, 119–20; and U.S. relations in 1973, 134, 135–36. *See also* European Economic Community; European integration; European Union
European Council: agenda-setting in, 2; Amsterdam (1997) (*see* Treaty of Amsterdam [1997]); Athens (1983), 168; Brussels (1984), 169; Copenhagen (1978), 143; Copenhagen (1993), 238; Copenhagen (2002), 241; creation of, 119, 136; Dublin (1979), 162; Dublin (1990), 200; Dublin (1996), 232; Fontainebleau (1984), 168, 169, 219; Helsinki (1999), 250–51; integration into EU decision-making of, 217; and intergovernmentalism, 12; Laeken (2001), 227, 252; Lisbon (1992), 228, 237, 238; Luxembourg (1980), 162; Madrid (1995), 232, 239; Nice (2001) (*see* Treaty of Nice [2001]); role of, 2; Rome (1990), 201, 205; and social policy, 137–38
European Court of Justice (ECJ), 156; and ECSC High Authority, 54; Maastricht Treaty and, 217; and precedence of Community law, 146–48, 156, 170–71; role in EEC of, 73–74; role of, 3; and supranationalism, 12, 74–75
European Currency Unit (Ecu): Britain's hard Ecu proposal, 200–201; creation of, 144
European Customs Union, 31
European Defense Community (EDC), 56–62: establishment of, 49; and NATO,

57–58; proposal for, 57; and
supranationalism, 50; and treaty
ratification, 59–61
European Development Fund (EDF), 250
European Economic Community (EEC):
Commission of, 17; common agricultural
policy (CAP) of (*see* CAP); de Gaulle's
proposal for political unification, 90–96;
de Gaulle's vision for, 86; economic and
monetary policies of early 1970s,
120–21; "Empty Chair" crisis and
Luxembourg compromise, 104–11;
establishment of, 4; first four years of,
86–90; funding of, 120; increased
integration in, 105–6; treaty amendments
by Maastricht Treaty, 213; treaty
establishing, 50, 68, 70–71. *See also*
European Community; European
integration; European Union
European Elections Act, 148–49
European Free Trade Agreement (EFTA),
69, 87, 96, 98
European identity: and EU enlargement to
Central and Eastern Europe, 237;
Thatcher's view of, 194
European integration: achievements by 1958
in, 75; Communism's collapse and, 198;
Congress of Europe and, 30; and Dooge
committee, 173–74; economic approach
to, 1–2, 40, 50, 113–15; EEC treaty and,
70–71; effect of British opposition to,
18–19, 31–32, 44; European leaders and,
10, 11; explanations of, 9; functionalist
interpretation of, 50–51; 1948 study
group for, 33–34; obstacles to in 1980s,
181–82; political integration, 198–200,
225, 244 (*see also* Intergovernmental
Conference on political union); positive
and negative, 113–15; Schuman Plan
and, 40; Single European Act and, 179;
and strengthening of nation-states, 79,
227; Tindemans Report and tactics of,
137; and Treaty on European Union
draft (1984), 173; vision of, 15–16,
25–31, 76–78, 220. *See also* European
Community; European Economic
Community; European Union
European Investment Bank, 71, 237
European Monetary Cooperation Fund, 127
European Monetary Fund, 143
European Monetary Institute (EMI), 213
European Monetary System (EMS), 138–45;
creation of, 138; demise of (1992–1993),

227–31; and European integration, 146;
significance of, 119; and trade
liberalization, 156
European Monetary Union (EMU): EMS
demise and threat to, 228–29;
establishment of, as political decision,
234; postponement of third stage of
(1995), 232; three stages of achieving,
213–16. *See also* Intergovernmental
Conference on EMU; monetary union
European Movement (1948), 31, 35
European Parliament: and co-decision, 217;
elections to, 3, 138, 148; and European
Act draft, 160; extension of powers in early
1970s, 122, 138, 148; extension of powers
through Maastricht Treaty, 216–17;
extension of powers through Single
European Act, 176; proposals in 1980s for
increased powers, 173–74; and proposed
bicameral structure, 226; and push for
more powers in 1990, 198; role of, 2–3;
size of, 168, 244; and supranationalism,
12. *See also* Assembly of EEC
European Parliamentary Union, 29
European Payments Union (EPU), 50, 63
European Political Community (EPC),
58–59
European Rapid Reaction Force (ERRF),
249, 251
European Recovery Program (ERP), 23–24
European Regional Development Fund
(ERDF), 161, 166
European Round Table, 170
European Social Fund, 71
European System of Central Banks (ESCB),
214–16
European Union (EU): characteristics of, 1;
China and EU–China summits, 250;
citizens of (*see* citizens); compared to
federal state, 2; and constitutional
convention, 252–55; and defense, 251;
and EC compared, 219–20; and
enlargement to Central and Eastern
European countries, 225–26, 237–41;
exploratory commissions for (1984), 169;
historical interpretations of, 9; institutional
structure of, 219, 225–27, 237, 241–45,
252–55; law of (*see* Community law);
mismanagement in (1999), 247;
Tindemans Report and, 136–38; world
role of, 249–52. *See also* European
Community; European Economic
Community; European integration

European Unit of Account, 143–44
exchange rate mechanism (ERM), 144, 158, 192, 193, 201, 231
exchange rates: bilateral grid of, 145; monetary union and, 192; and policy-setting, 215

Fanfani, Amintore, 94
fascism, and economic nationalism, 26
Featherstone, Keith, 220
Federal Union movement, 27
federalism: and 1979 Assembly election, 149; Action Committee and, 64–65; American advocacy of, 17; and constitutional convention, 252–54; and EPC, 58–59; European Community in 1970s and, 150; failure of postwar movement for, 35; Fischer and, 244–46; Haas and, 78; and IGC on political union, 204; and opposition to Fouchet plan, 95–96; postwar European, 25–31; and Single European Act, 179–80; and Tindemans Report, 138; and "two-speed" Europe, 226
Feldstein, Martin, 236–37
Finland, 237
Fischer, Joschka, 244–46, 248, 249, 253
Florin, 232
Fontainebleau summit (1984), 168, 169, 219
food consumption, postwar, 16
Foreign Affairs (journal), 236
foreign policy: cooperation in early 1970s, 122; failures in 1970s, 133–36; Maastricht Treaty and, 210; and Middle East in 1973, 134–35; new troika and, 242; Persian Gulf crisis, 205–8; recent issues and, 226–27, 250–51; Single European Act and, 178–79; Yugoslavian crisis, 208–12, 223n52, 251
Forster, Anthony, 214
Fouchet, Christian, 91, 94
Fouchet plan, 91–96, 102, 254
France: African colonies and Treaty of Association, 87–88; and agriculture, 88–90 (*see also* CAP); anti-Americanism and EC foreign policy (1990–1991), 207–8; approval of Maastrict Treaty, 229–30; and Council of Foreign Ministers, 32; de Gaulle and economic crisis, 85–86; economic troubles in early 1980s, 157–58; and EDC, 56–57, 59–61; and employment title in

Amsterdam Treaty, 242; and EMS, 140–41; and European Defense Community, 49; European Elections Act and national sovereignty, 149; and federalism, 27; and founding of EC, 18; and German support in opposing British EEC entry, 102–4; and nuclear weapons, 66, 68, 90, 93; and opposition to American energy proposals (1974), 136; and Persian Gulf Crisis, 205, 206; and postwar Germany, 18, 37–38, 39; and Schuman Plan, 39–45; and social benefits, 157; and trade liberalization, 66–68, 157–58. *See also* de Gaulle, Charles; Delors, Jacques; Monnet, Jean
Franco-German Treaty of Friendship (1963), 103–4
free trade. *See* trade liberalization
Free Trade Agreement (FTA), 86–87
French Council for a United Europe, 29
functionalist interpretation of European integration, 50, 75–78, 79–80, 112–13, 181

Gaitskell, Hugh, 99
General Agreement on Trade and Tariffs (GATT), 105
Genscher, Hans-Dietrich, 159, 160, 190
Genscher-Colombo initiative, 159
German question, 36–45
German unification: concerns raised by, 199; French response to, 198–99; influence on European integration of, 187–88, 199–200, 220
Germany: Berlin Wall, 93, 198; economic policy after reunification and EMS, 227–28, 230; encouragement of supranationalism in 1990s by, 187; and monetary unification, 190–91, 215–16; and Persian Gulf Crisis, 205, 206; postwar economic miracle, 38; postwar reintegration of, 18, 36–45, 49; postwar relations with France, 39; and Schuman Plan, 39–45; and strengthening of European Union, 221; and support for French veto of British EEC entry, 102–4; unification of (*see* German unification); and Yugoslavian crisis, 210–12. *See also* East Germany; German question; German unification; West Germany
Giddens, Anthony, 253

Giscard D'Estaing, Valery, 157, 162, 227, 252; and EMS, 139–41, 143–45
globalization, 251
Gonzales, Felipe, 167–68
Gorbachev, Mikhail, 199
Grant, Charles, 221
Great Britain: budget questions and EC, 160–64; and Congress of Europe, 29; contentious issues at Strasbourg summit (1989), 197; Copenhagen criteria and, 238; and Council of Foreign Ministers, 32; domestic politics over EC entry, 125–26; versus EC over monetary union (1990), 201–2; economic troubles in 1950s, 96; economic troubles in 1960s, 123; and EDC, 57; and EMU, 214; and EU social policy, 241–42; and European Economic Community, 43; European Elections Act and national sovereignty, 149; and Free Trade Agreement, 86–87; geopolitical troubles in 1950s, 97; and intergovernmental cooperation, 31–36; and Maastricht Treaty, 218; and national sovereignty issue, 4, 18; and 1950s trade liberalization, 67, 68–69; 1961 EEC entry attempt, 96–104; 1967 EEC entry attempt, 111–12; 1970 EEC entry attempt, 123–24; and nuclear weapons, 99–100; and opposition to European integration, 18–19, 31–32, 44; postwar economy of, 20; and postwar Germany, 36–37; and referendum on EC membership, 141; and Schuman Plan, 41–45; and Single European Act, 174–76, 181; and U.S. relations in 1949, 33; and vision of European integration, 25–27, 32–33. *See also* Thatcher, Margaret
"great man" history, 11
Greece, 155, 164–68, 211, 238
Greek temple approach to political union treaty, 204–5
Group of Ten, 130
Guidance and Guarantee Fund, 89, 105

Haas, Ernst, 50, 51, 75–80, 105, 111, 181
Haider, Jorg, 248
Hall-Patch, Sir Edmund, 24
Hallstein, Walter, 60, 73, 106–7, 111, 138, 254
Hanover summit of the Twelve (1988), 190
Harriman, W. Averell, 24

Harrod, Roy, 29
Haughey, Charles, 199
Healey, Dennis, 64
health policy, Single European Act and, 177–78
Heath, Edward, 43, 97–98, 99, 123, 124, 125, 127, 131, 133
Helsinki Declaration on Human Rights, 127
Helsinki summit (1999), 250–51
Herriot, Edouard, 33, 61
Heseltine, Michael, 202–3
High Authority, of ECSC, 39, 40, 41, 42, 51; checks on powers of, 53–54; composition of, 52; powers of, 52–53
High Commission for Germany, 56
historical method, 8–9, 11
Hoffman, Paul, 24–25
Hoffmann, Stanley, 92, 100, 112–13, 114–15
Hogan, Michael, 22, 23, 25, 32
Howe, Geoffrey, 193, 202
human rights, 30, 35
Hungary, 239, 240, 241
Hurd, Douglas, 202
Hussein, Saddam, 205

IGC. *See* Intergovernmental Conference on EMU; Intergovernmental Conference on political union; Treaty of Amsterdam (1997); Treaty of Nice (2001)
Independent on Sunday (newspaper), 200
Independents, 3
Indochina, 60
inflation, 132, 156
institutionalist interpretation of European integration, 9
integration. *See* European integration
interest rates, 215, 228, 230
Intergovernmental Conference on EMU, 203
Intergovernmental Conference on political union: fall of Berlin Wall and, 221; and form of treaty, 204; opposing viewpoints of, 203–4
Intergovernmental Conferences on institutional affairs. *See* Treaty of Amsterdam (1997); Treaty of Nice (2001)
intergovernmental cooperation: British postwar European vision and, 31–36; Council of Europe and, 34; and "Greek temple" approach to political union, 204; Maastricht Treaty and JHA, 218–19;

versus supranationalism in 1970s and 1980s, 181
intergovernmentalism, definition of, 12
International Energy Agency, 136
International Institute for Strategic Studies (IISS), 206–7
International Monetary Fund, 133
Internationale Handelgesellschaft v. Einfuhr und Vorratsstelle Getreide (case 11/70), 146–47
Interpol, 219
Iraq, 205–6
Ireland, 126, 190, 249
Irish Republican Army, 196
iron curtain, and British interest in European integration, 29
Islamic fundamentalism, 250
Israel, 134, 135
Italian Socialist Party, 156
Italy: and Brussels Pact, 62; Copenhagen criteria and, 238; EMU criteria and domestic politics, 232–33; end to diplomatic isolation of, 34; and federalism, 27; and Persian Gulf Crisis, 206
Izetbegović, Alija, 211

Jenkins, Roy, 119, 125, 160; and EMS, 139–45
Jennings, Ivor, 27
Jobert, Michel, 134, 136
Justice and Home Affairs (JHA), 218–19

Kaiser, Karl, 199
Kant, Immanuel, 25
Keep Left group, 28
Kennedy, John, 93, 94, 99–100, 103
Kennedy round trade talks, 105
Khrushchev, Nikita, 93
Kinnock, Neil, 247
Kissinger, Henry, 133–34, 135, 136
Kohl, Helmut, 156, 168, 190, 198–99, 216, 227; and European integration, 199–200, 201, 220–21, 254
Korean War, 49, 56–57
Kunz, Diane, 45, 129. *See also* Union of Soviet Socialist Republics
Kuwait, 205

labor: Amsterdam Treaty and policy on, 242; Delors' vision of EC and, 193; and migration because of economic crisis,

235; mobility of, 1; Single European Act and, 175; social rights for, 196–97
Labour Party (Great Britain), 18, 28, 29, 31, 32, 44, 99, 141, 149, 241–42
Lacanuet, Jean, 110
Lacouture, Jean, 102
Laeken summit (2001), 227, 252
Lamont, Norman, 229
Laniel, Joseph, 60
Laski, Harold, 26, 27
Latvia, 239, 240, 241
law. *See* Community law
Lawson, Nigel, 193
Le Monde (newspaper), 229
League of Nations, 25, 26
Lee, Sir Frank, 96
legislation: European Commission and, 2; qualified majority voting and, 3; legulations and directives, 13n2
Leigh-Pemberton, Robin, 192
liberalism. *See* economic liberalism
Lisbon summit (1992), 228, 237, 238
Lithuania, 239, 240, 241
Locarno Pact (1925), 25
Lomé Conventions, 250
Ludlow, Peter, 132
L'unità europea (journal), 27
Luxembourg, 51
Luxembourg compromise (1966), 110–11
Luxembourg summit (1980), 162

Maastricht Treaty (1992), 4, 212–21: assessment of, 219–21; as compromise, 187; and economic and monetary union, 213–16; and European Council, 217; and European Parliament, 216–17; and Justice and Home Affairs, 218–19; and social policy, 218; and Yugoslavian crisis, 210
Macedonia, 211
Macmillan, Harold, 29, 67, 68, 90, 97, 99, 100, 104
Madariaga, Salvador de, 30
Madrid summit (1995), 232, 239
Major, John, 202, 203, 214, 218, 228, 229, 246
Makins, Roger, 42
Malfatti, Franco Maria, 138
Malta, 238, 240, 241
Manifesto di Ventotene (1941), 27
Mansholt, Sicco, 73, 107, 138
Marjolin, Robert, 17, 24, 44, 63, 64, 66, 67, 68, 72, 73, 87, 107, 108, 111

market liberalization. *See* trade liberalization
Markovic, Ante, 208
Marquand, David, 148, 225
Marshall, George, 21, 22
Marshall Plan, 17, 32, 37, 39
Martin, David, 198
Martin I report, 198
Martin II report, 198
Masefield, John, 29
Mauroy, Pierre, 157
Maxwell-Fyfe, Sir David, 29
Mendès-France, Pierre, 60–61
mercantilism, EEC and, 73
Merger Treaty (1965), 92, 106
Messina summit meeting (1955), 64
Meyer, René, 55, 60
military, 251
Military Assistance Act (1949), 39
Milosevic, Slobodan, 208
Milward, Alan, 21, 22, 51, 78–80
Mitterand, François, 110, 157, 158, 167,
    168, 169, 183, 229; and political
    integration, 198–99, 199–200, 220, 221,
    254
Mollet, Guy, 68
monetary crises, 128–33
monetary union: "ambush in Rome", 201–2;
    Britain's hard Ecu proposal and,
    200–201; Delors Committee and,
    190–93; dispute over (1980s), 175–76;
    economist approach to, 130–31, 142;
    Maastricht Treaty and, 213; monetarist
    approach to, 131, 142; national self-
    interest and, 220. *See also* Euro;
    European Monetary Union
Monnet, Jean, 78, 110, 180, 254; and
    economic supranationalism, 35, 39–42;
    and ECSC, 26, 51, 52, 55; and EDC,
    57, 61; and European integration, 64; as
    founding father of EC, 18; and nuclear
    energy, 65; postwar modernization plan
    of, 20, 37; and WEU, 62
Morán, Fernando, 168
Moravcsik, Andrew, 9, 90, 100–102, 140,
    150, 169, 220
Morrison, Herbert, 42
Mounier, Emmanuel, 189
Mouvement Républican Populaire (MRP),
    60
Movimento federalista europeo (MFE), 27
Mugabe, Robert, 250
Mussolini, Benito, 27

Nassau defense agreement, 99–100, 102
Nasser, Gamel Abdel, 68
Natali, Lorenzo, 170
nation-states. *See* national sovereignty
national sovereignty: and constitutional
    convention, 252–54; and de Gaulle's
    attitude toward EEC, 86, 112–13;
    diminishment of, 3–4; and EDC, 58, 61,
    62; and European Elections Act, 149;
    and political versus economic issues, 50;
    and postwar strengthening of nation-
    states, 78–80; QMV and, 155; tied to
    EU political integration, 227; and "two-
    speed" Europe, 226; and veto rights,
    174, 175
NATO, 50; and EDC, 57–58, 60; and
    postwar defense, 56–57; U.S. on NATO
    and EC/EU defense, 207, 251. *See also*
    North Atlantic Treaty (1949)
Netherlands, 95–96, 206
New Statesman and Nation (journal), 28
Nice summit (2001). *See* Treaty of Nice
    (2001)
Nine, 1972 declaration, 126–27
Nixon, Richard, 129, 133
North Atlantic Treaty (1949), 33, 210
Nouvelles Equipes Internationales, 29
nuclear energy, and European integration,
    65. *See also* Euratom
nuclear weapons: France and, 66, 68, 90, 93;
    Great Britain and, 99–100; postwar
    period, 56; Soviet-American agreement
    on (1973), 134; United States and, 93
Nuttall, Simon, 211

oil, imports of Middle Eastern, 70, 134–35
oil shock of 1973, 132
Olivi, Bino, 8, 59, 135, 180
OPEC, 134, 139
Organization for European Economic
    Cooperation (OEEC), 17, 31;
    composition of, 24; and Free Trade
    Agreement, 86; and Marshall Plan aid,
    24; Monnet's disregard for, 52; and trade
    liberalization, 63–64
Ortoli, Francois-Xavier, 138, 142
Orwell, George, 28

Padoa-Schioppa, Tommaso, 189, 190
Palestinians, 135
Paquet Delors, 189–90
Partito d'Azione. See Action Party

passports, 137, 175, 218
Permanent Commission of the Western
    Union, 31
Persian Gulf crisis, 205–8
Phare program, 238
Pinay, Antoine, 60
Pinder, John, 113–15, 181
Pleven, René, 49, 57
Pleven Plan, 57
Pöhl, Karl-Otto, 191, 192
Poland, 239, 240
policy, European Council and, 2
political community, Haas's definition of,
    76–77
political integration. *See* European
    integration: political integration;
    Intergovernmental Conference on
    political union
political parties: representation in 1979
    Assembly, 150; representation in EU, 3
Pompidou, Georges, 120, 124, 126
Poos, Jacques, 209
Portugal, 137, 155, 164–68, 190
postmodern approach to governance, 253
Potsdam conference (1945), 19, 36
Powell, Enoch, 125
Prodi, Romano, 250
product standards, 156, 171
Project for the European Union, A, 251, 252,
    254
protectionism, ECSC and, 55
Pubblico ministero v. Ratti (case 148/78),
    147

qualified majority voting (QMV), 3, 54, 155,
    166, 174, 175, 243

Ramadier, Paul, 30
Reagan, Ronald, 155
realist interpretation of European
    integration, 10, 50–51, 78–80, 158
reconstruction. *See* economic reconstruction
regional development: Delors II and, 239;
    and enlargement to Central and Eastern
    European countries, 225–26; and
    monetary union (1973), 127; Paquet
    Delors and, 189–90; percentage of
    budget, 2. *See also* European Regional
    Development Fund
regulations, 13n2
revaluations of currency, 130
Rey, Jean, 111, 138
Reynaud, Paul, 29

Ridley, Nicholas, 200
Robbins, Lionel, 27
Romania, 239, 240
Rome summit (1990), 201, 205
Rome treaties (1957), 69–75, 146
Ross, George, 189, 208
Rossi, Ernesto, 27
Ruhr (Germany) coalfield, 38
Russell, Bertrand, 29

Saarland, 62
safety policy, Single European Act and,
    177–78
Salvati, Michael, 233
Santer, Jacques, 208, 246–47
Sbragia, Alberta, 219, 233
Scharpf, Fritz, 246
Schengen agreement, 195
Schengen Treaty, 218
Schiller, Karl, 130
Schlesinger, Helmut, 229, 230
Schmidt, Helmut, 135, 136, 156, 162; and
    EMS, 139–41, 143–45
Schroeder, Gerhard, 103
Schuman, Robert, 18, 39–45
Schuman Plan, 39–45, 220, 254
Schüssel, Wolfgang, 248
Schwarz, Hans Peter, 103
Séguin, Philippe, 229
September 11, 2001 terrorist attacks, 219
Serbia, 208–11
Sforza, Carlo, 34
Siedentop, Larry, 252
Single European Act (SEA), 174–83, 254;
    and American economic model, 156;
    circumstances influencing, 182–83;
    contrasting perspectives on, 177; and
    vision of European integration in, 179
single market. *See* common market
Six: de Gaulle on new members, 101; and
    EEC treaty, 70–71; and European
    integration, 64, 75, 78; meeting at the
    Hague (1969), 120; and trade
    liberalization, 64
Six-Day War, 134, 135
Slovak Republic, 239, 240, 241
Slovenia, 208, 239, 240, 241
Snake, the, 130–31, 132, 137, 138, 143,
    144
Soares, Mario, 164
Social Democrats, 19
social policy: Delors' vision of EC and, 193;
    European Commission and (1989),

196–97; Maastricht Treaty and, 218;
Schengen group and, 195; Single
European Act and, 177–178; Thatcher in
Bruges speech on, 196
socialism: and European integration, 27, 28;
in France in 1980s, 157–58
Socialist Party (PSF) (France), 158
Socialist Party (PSI) (Italy), 233
Socrates program, 30
Solemn Declaration on European unification,
158, 160
Solomon, Robert, 132
Soviet Union. *See* Union of Soviet Socialist
Republics
Spaak, Paul-Henri, 31, 34, 60, 64; Spaak
report, 65, 66, 67
Spain, 155, 164–68, 190, 206
Spanish Socialist Party (PSOE), 164
Spectator (magazine), 200
Spiegel affair, 103
spillover effects in functionalist theory, 77,
105
Spinelli, Altiero, 27, 28, 173, 179
St. Malo declaration (1998), 251
Stability and Growth Pact, 232
Strang, Sir William, 42
Strasbourg summit (1989), 197–98
Strauss, Franz-Josef, 103
Stresemann, Gustav, 25
subsidiarity, 212, 244
Suez Canal crisis, 67–68
Sun (newspaper), 201–2
supranational cooperation, five factors in,
15–19
supranationalism: definition of, 11–12;
European Act draft and, 159; and
Maastricht Treaty, 212–13; the Twelve
and increase of, 220–21
Sweden, 237
Syria, 134

taxes, 1–2, 172
Taylor, Paul, 181–82
Thatcher, Margaret, 124, 149, 155, 160,
161–62, 168, 169, 172, 174; Bruges
speech and vision of EC, 193–96; and
free market values, 194, 195; and
German unification, 200; and monetary
union, 192–93, 200–202; resignation of,
202–3; role in European integration of,
8; and Single European Act, 175,
177–81, 183; and supranationalism, 195
The Hague, 4

Third Force, 28, 90
Thorn, Gaston, 163, 170
Thorn Commission, 171
Tindemans, Leo, 120, 136
Tindemans Report, 136–38, 159
trade, postwar, 21, 63. *See also* trade
liberalization; World Trade Organization
Trade Expansion Bill, 94
trade liberalization, 50, 62–69, 249–50;
blocking of FTA and, 87; EEC treaty
and, 70–71; embrace of, in 1980s,
155–56; France in 1950s and, 66–68; of
internal market, 170–72; political
obstacles in 1980s to, 156
travel, freedom of, 1, 137, 218
Treaty of Accession (1972), 125
Treaty of Amsterdam (1997), 182, 218,
241–42, 246, 248
Treaty of Association, 87–88
Treaty of Brussels. *See* Brussels Pact (Treaty
on Western Union)
Treaty of Nice (2001), 182, 241, 242–44,
249
Treaty of Rome (1957), 69–75, 146
Treaty of St. James Palace (1949), 34
Treaty on European Union (1992). *See*
Maastricht Treaty (1992)
Treaty on European Union draft (1983), 173
Treaty on Western Union. *See* Brussels Pact
tree approach to political union treaty, 204
Tribune (journal), 28
Trichet, Jean-Claude, 234
triple majority voting system, 243
Truman doctrine, 20
Truman, Harry, 39, 40
"tunnel" (currency), 130–31
Turkey, 238, 240
2+4 talks, 199, 200
"two-speed" Europe, 226, 230

U.K. Boundaries Commission, 149
Ulivo party (Italy), 233
unilateralism: significance of, 10; U.S. use of,
14n13
Union Européenne des fédéralistes (UEF),
27–28, 29
Union of Soviet Socialist Republics (USSR):
and Council of Foreign Ministers, 32;
and Czechoslovakia takeover (1948), 29;
disappearance of, 226; European defense
needs against, 17; European integration
and, 26, 28, 29; and nuclear weapons,
56; and postwar Germany, 36–37

Union of States, 91–96
United Europe Movement (UEM), 29
United Nations, 210, 211
United States: and Atlantic Charter, 133–34;
    and British relations in 1949, 33; and
    Council of Foreign Ministers, 32; and EC
    foreign policy, 207–8; as economic model
    to postwar Europe, 17, 25, 156; and
    EDC, 58; and EU institutional structures
    compared, 219; and EU military, 251;
    and Euro, 235–36; and European
    integration, 17, 19–25; and European
    postwar economy, 21–22; and fear of
    Communism, 17, 23–24; Kennedy
    administration and EEC, 94; monetary
    policy in early 1970s, 129; monetary
    problems in Carter administration,
    139–40; national debt in early 1970s,
    128–29; and postwar aid, 22–23, 37, 39;
    and postwar Germany, 36–37, 49, 57;
    and postwar isolationism, 24; as sole
    military superpower, 226; and trade
    disputes with EU, 250; Washington
    conference with EC about oil (1974),
    135–36; and Yugoslavian crisis, 210, 211
Uri, Pierre, 65
Uruguay round of trade talks, 195, 207, 249
USSR. *See* Union of Soviet Socialist
    Republics

van den Broek, Hans, 179
*Van Gend en Loos v Nederlandse
    Administratie der Berlastingen* (no.
    26/1962), 74, 146

Van Zeeland, Paul, 29, 30, 51
Vandenberg, Arthur H., 24
Vedel, Georges, 122
Versailles Treaty (1919), 25
von der Groeben, Hans, 85, 106
voters. *See* citizens

Weiler, J. H. H., 10, 148, 253
Werner, Pierre, 120–21
Werner Report, 120–21, 145
Wessels, Wolfgang, 253
West Germany: and abolishment of
    Occupation Statute, 57–58; and Brussels
    Pact, 62; and EMS, 139–40;
    establishment of, 38; militarization of,
    58; and postwar defense, 56–57; and
    price stability, 128–29
Western European Union (WEU), 62,
    206–7, 209, 210
"Whig history", 8
Wilson, Harold, 111–12, 125, 133, 141
Wilson, Woodrow, 25
Wirtschaftswunder (economic miracle,
    German), 38
Wolfers, Arnold, 11
Wootton, Barbara, 27
World Trade Organization (WTO), 249–50

Yaoundé Convention, 88, 250
Young, Hugo, 42, 179, 181, 183
Yugoslavian crisis, 205, 208–12, 223n52,
    251

Zimbabwe, 250

About the Author

Mark Gilbert was born in Chesterfield (Great Britain) in September 1961. Since June 2002, he has been associate professor of contemporary history at the University of Trento in northern Italy. He previously taught in the department of political science of Dickinson College and at the University of Bath, where he was lecturer in Italian history and politics. His books include *The Italian Revolution: The End of Politics, Italian Style?* (1995) and, with Anna Cento Bull, *The Lega Nord and the Northern Question in Italian Politics* (2001).